Plunder for Profit

Exploring over a century of Zimbabwe's colonial and postcolonial history, Elijah Doro investigates the murky and noxious history of that powerful crop: tobacco. In a compelling narrative that debunks previous histories glorifying tobacco farming, Doro reveals the indelible marks that tobacco left on landscapes, communities and people. Demonstrating that the history of tobacco farming is inseparable from that of colonial encounter, Doro outlines how tobacco became an institutionalised culture of production, which was linked to state power and natural ecosystems and driven by a pernicious heritage of unbridled plunder. With the destruction of landscapes, the negative impacts of the export trade and the growing tobacco epidemic in Zimbabwe, tobacco farming has a long and varied legacy in southern Africa and across the world. Connecting the local to the global, and the environmental to the social, this book illuminates our understandings of environmental history, colonialism and sustainability.

ELIJAH DORO is a research fellow at the University of Agder and an environmental historian with an interest in southern Africa. His research on agrarian and environmental histories is inspired by his personal experiences growing up in Zimbabwe's tobacco-farming countryside and participating in the tobacco production economy.

African Studies Series

The African Studies series, founded in 1968, is a prestigious series of monographs, general surveys, and textbooks on Africa covering history, political science, anthropology, economics, and ecological and environmental issues. The series seeks to publish work by senior scholars as well as the best new research.

Other titles in the series are listed at the back of the book.

Plunder for Profit

A Socio-environmental History of Tobacco Farming in Southern Rhodesia and Zimbabwe

ELIJAH DORO
University of Stellenbosch

CAMBRIDGE
UNIVERSITY PRESS

CAMBRIDGE
UNIVERSITY PRESS

Shaftesbury Road, Cambridge CB2 8EA, United Kingdom

One Liberty Plaza, 20th Floor, New York, NY 10006, USA

477 Williamstown Road, Port Melbourne, VIC 3207, Australia

314–321, 3rd Floor, Plot 3, Splendor Forum, Jasola District Centre, New Delhi – 110025, India

103 Penang Road, #05–06/07, Visioncrest Commercial, Singapore 238467

Cambridge University Press is part of Cambridge University Press & Assessment, a department of the University of Cambridge.

We share the University's mission to contribute to society through the pursuit of education, learning and research at the highest international levels of excellence.

www.cambridge.org
Information on this title: www.cambridge.org/9781009096256

DOI: 10.1017/9781009093071

First published 2023
First paperback edition 2025

A catalogue record for this publication is available from the British Library

Library of Congress Cataloging-in-Publication data
Names: Doro, Elijah, author.
Title: Plunder for profit : a socio-environmental history of tobacco farming in Southern Rhodesia and Zimbabwe / Elijah Doro, University of Stellenbosch, South Africa.
Description: New York, NY : Cambridge University Press, [2023] | Series: ASS African studies | Includes bibliographical references and index.
Identifiers: LCCN 2022040985 (print) | LCCN 2022040986 (ebook) | ISBN 9781009098397 (hardback) | ISBN 9781009096256 (paperback) | ISBN 9781009093071 (epub)
Subjects: LCSH: Tobacco industry–Zimbabwe. | Tobacco farms–Zimbabwe.
Classification: LCC HD9147.Z552 D67 2023 (print) | LCC HD9147.Z552 (ebook) | DDC 338.1/7371096891–dc23/eng/20221221
LC record available at https://lccn.loc.gov/2022040985
LC ebook record available at https://lccn.loc.gov/2022040986

ISBN 978-1-009-09839-7 Hardback
ISBN 978-1-009-09625-6 Paperback

To the memory of my late father, Keniard Doro, a tobacco farmer from rural Muzarabani who taught me how to dream, and to my mother, Dorothy Simbi, who gave me hope when it rained on me while working in the tobacco fields.

Tobacco is without doubt one of the most destructive plants on the planet even before it hits the lungs.

Standard Schaeffer, *Counterpunch Magazine*, 2007

Contents

Figures

Tables

Acknowledgements

Growing up in rural Muzarabani and Mount Darwin within the white commercial farming areas of Mutwa Estates and in the communal lands of Chawarura and later in Mukwengure resettlement areas in Zimbabwe nothing shaped our entire lives more significantly than the tobacco crop and tobacco farming. Our existence revolved around the routines of tobacco farming and the many rituals of tobacco culture from the nursery to the auction floors. The crop defined us and had such an overwhelmingly preponderant stranglehold on our consciousness, identity, material being, perceptions and worldviews. Tobacco was the source of life, the giver of meaning, the supplier of a living, the source of sustenance, the gateway to the good life and luxuries. It was more than a crop, but a whole social, cultural system around which our lives orbited. In more than one way, we were all inextricably connected to the tobacco crop and the tobacco production cult so much so that it can be said tobacco produced us. The crop had its own agency that enmeshed with our own lives changing not only our bodies and communities but also our physical landscapes: rivers, forests, birds and other species. This book is distilled from these experiences and the imperative to frame co-constituted histories about crops and their agency in changing landscapes, humans and political economy.

I would want to thank my academic mentor Professor Sandra Swart under whose guidance and mentorship I was able to bring together the ideas in this book. I would also want to appreciate the emotional support I received from my mother Dorothy Simbi, the retired tobacco farmer; my wife Alima; my son Farai; and the rest of the family. Special mention also goes to my friends – Tapiwa Madimu, for exhorting me to continue this path, Godfrey Hove, Wesley Mwatwara, Ushehwedu Kufakurinani and Together Kaseke; to my History Friday Morning colleagues – Innocent Dande, Bryan Kauma, Lloyd Maphosa, Yustina Komba, Mia Uys, Lyle Lennox, Este Kotze, Tinashe Takuva and the late and the dearly missed Muhammad Maakato, who passed away while finishing his own research; and to my social network of friends who lifted my spirits when the going got tough – Trevor Chikowore, Admire Phiri, Tafadzwa Chiyangwa and Levi Bumhira. Many thanks to the individuals who agreed to be interviewed and participated in this research in Mazowe, Mount Darwin and Muzarabani districts. I must also express gratitude to Sibanengi Ncube for showing me around and driving me during research and fieldwork. The staff at the National Archives of Zimbabwe gave me the best assistance as did the staff at the Tobacco Research Board. Special thanks also to the Parliament of Zimbabwe and my peers there, particularly Ruvimbo Matinhari, Betty Munowenyu, Angela Gutu and Martin Mugova.

Abbreviations

AAA	Agricultural Adjustment Act
ACS	American Cancer Society
Agritex	Agricultural Extension
BAT	British American Tobacco
BBC	British Broadcasting Corporation
CFU	Commercial Farmers Union
Conex	Department of Conservation and Extension
DDT	dichlorodiphenyltrichloroethane
EPA	Environmental Protection Agency
FCTC	Framework Convention for Tobacco Control
FDT	Farmers Development Trust
HRW	Human Rights Watch
ICA	Intensive Conservation Area
ILO	International Labour Organization
ITGA	International Tobacco Growers Association
NAZ	National Archives of Zimbabwe
NLHA	Native Land Husbandry Act
NPA	Native Purchase Areas
NRB	Natural Resources Board
RF	Rhodesian Front
RNFU	Rhodesia National Farmers Union
ROTA	Rhodesian Oriental Tobacco Association
RTA	Rhodesia Tobacco Association
STP	Sustainable Tobacco Program
TIMB	Tobacco Industries and Marketing Board
TIRC	Tobacco Industries Research Council
TMB	Tobacco Marketing Board
TRB	Tobacco Research Board
TTL	Tribal Trust Lands

TTLDCOR	Tribal Trust Lands Development Cooperation
UDI	Unilateral Declaration of Independence
WHO	World Health Organization
ZANU PF	Zimbabwe African National Union Patriotic Front
ZTA	Zimbabwe Tobacco Association

Note on Currency, Units and Weight

For the measurement of weight, the imperial system is used in much of the book as this was the common method during the colonial period. The unit for measuring weight used is lbs, and 1 lb is the equivalent of 0.454 kilograms in the metric system. For currency, £, s, d represents Rhodesian pounds, shillings and pennies, respectively. R$ represents Rhodesian dollars, which is the currency that came into use in March 1970 based on the 1967 Decimilisation Act. It was used until 1980 when the Zimbabwean dollar was introduced.

Introduction

The critical importance of tobacco to the Zimbabwean economy is reflected by the profoundly flattering epithets deployed over the years to describe the crop: 'leaf of gold', 'most promising weed', 'crucible', 'life-blood', 'golden lining'. Tobacco is situated at the nerve centre of the body politic, central to the country's political economy. Zimbabwe is the largest producer of tobacco in Africa, and the fifth largest producer of flue-cured tobacco in the world after China, Brazil, India and the United States.[1] The crop is the country's second largest foreign currency earner after gold and contributed 15 per cent to total national export receipts in 2020.[2] During the 2017/2018 season, Zimbabwe produced what was then a record-breaking flue-cured tobacco crop of 252 million kilograms.[3] This surpassed the previous record crop of 236 million kilograms harvested in 2000 at the height of the occupation of white-owned commercial farms by landless black peasants during the Fast Track Land Reform Programme (FTLRP).[4] The 2017/2018 tobacco season was

[1] BDO Zimbabwe Chartered Accountants, 'Tobacco Industry and Marketing Board Study into Cost of Tobacco Production in Zimbabwe', 2015, 1. Also see, 'Zimbabwe major producer of tobacco in Africa', *The Herald*, 10 November 2015.

[2] Historically, tobacco was Zimbabwe's top foreign currency until production went down after the land reform programme in 2000 and it was overtaken by gold. In 2020, out of a total close to US$5 billion national export revenue tobacco contributed US$741 million and gold US$982 million. See Ministry of Finance and Economic Development, 'The 2022 National Budget Statement Presented to the Parliament of Zimbabwe by Hon. Prof Mthuli Ncube', 21.

[3] A. Matibiri, 'Tobacco Production and Marketing Trends in Zimbabwe in the Last Two Decades', Coresta conference paper, Victoria Falls, 2 April 2019.

[4] In 2000, a series of land invasions started by war veterans led to the occupation of white- owned commercial farms and the Fast Track Land Resettlement Programme (FTLRP). The land reform programme transferred over 10 million hectares of land to 146,000 black smallholder farmers. Its impact on tobacco production was profoundly felt as, up until then, about 2,000 white commercial farms had dominated tobacco production. See, S. Moyo, 'Three Decades of Agrarian Reform in Zimbabwe', *The Journal of Peasant Studies*, 38, 3 (2011), 493–531; I. Scoones

celebrated by the government and the tobacco industry in the country as a milestone and epic achievement crowning the success of the Land Reform Programme and black economic empowerment. It created an ephemeral effervesce of euphoria over the prospects of the crop to improve the economy and boost smallholder agriculture within the new agrarian dispensation. However, in the same year, the international humanitarian watchdog Human Rights Watch (HRW) cast a dark and ominous shadow on this glorious moment by releasing a damning report that chronicled a litany of human rights abuses and infractions within the tobacco farms in Zimbabwe and exposed the sinister side of the tobacco 'success story' narrative.[5] These included the prevalence of child labour, the hazardous chemicalised tobacco work environments, nicotine poisoning, exposure of workers to toxic pesticides and abuse of small-scale farmers by tobacco contracting companies.[6] This report was dismissed by the Zimbabwean government as 'not factual' and not 'independently confirmed'.[7] However, labour exploitation in the tobacco farms and the widespread use of child labour is widely documented and confirmed not only in Zimbabwe but in other tobacco producing countries in the world.[8]

et al., 'Tobacco, Contract Farming, and Agrarian Change in Zimbabwe', *Journal of Agrarian Change*, 28 (2018), 22–42.

5 See Human Rights Watch, 'A Bitter Harvest: Child Labour and Human Rights Abuses on Tobacco Farms in Zimbabwe', (April 2018).

6 Ibid., 28–73.

7 S. Mhofu, 'Zimbabwe Government Dismisses HRW report on Child Labour', available on www.voanews.com/africa/zimbabwes-government-dismisses-hrw-report-child-labor, accessed on 24 July 2019.

8 The International Labour Organization (ILO) in its 2009 report on commercial agriculture and child labour notes that the existence of child labour in tobacco production is rampant particularly amongst children from poor and vulnerable backgrounds. These children work under poor conditions such as long working hours, extreme heat, and exposure to pesticides and risks from injuries. The prevalence of child labour in tobacco farming is largely because the crop is labour intensive, and children are a cheap source of labour. See 'Child Labour, Commercial Agriculture and the Role of Tobacco', International Labour Organisation, Geneva, (2009). In 2014 a Human Rights Watch report, based on 141 interviews with children between the ages of 7 and 17 working on tobacco farms in the United States between 2012 and 2013, documented that there was extensive exploitation of children on the farms who worked long hours, were paid poorly and were exposed to harmful tobacco pesticides. See Human Rights Watch, 'Tobacco's Hidden Children: Hazardous Child Labour in United States Tobacco Farming', Washington, (2013). Another report by Human Rights Watch in 2010 documents similar labour exploitation practices in tobacco farms in Kazakhstan. See, 'Hellish

The negative impact of tobacco farming in Zimbabwe has also been felt outside the social and individual human body – on the natural environment. Tobacco farming has caused significant deforestation, land degradation, and both air and water pollution. The country's forestry conservation body, the Forestry Commission of Zimbabwe (FCZ) estimates that between 1998 and 2013 15 per cent of tree cover was lost to tobacco farming.[9] It further confirmed in 2016 that 50,000 hectares (ha) of forestry cover were being lost annually to tobacco farming and the crop contributed 20 per cent to total national deforestation.[10] Tobacco farmers in Zimbabwe rely almost exclusively on indigenous forestry resources to cure flue-cured tobacco and this has affected forests and woodlands in tobacco farming areas further threatening biodiversity, animal habitats and waters supplies. Environmental experts reckon that 5.3 million trees are hewed every year by tobacco farmers.[11] In 2013, for instance, an estimated 46,000 ha of forest (1.38 million cubic metres of wood) were cleared to cure 127 million kilograms of tobacco.[12] Consequently, environmental experts project that with the current rate of wood consumption in the tobacco sector the country will experience devastating desertification by 2048.[13] Ultimately, the biggest challenge faced by tobacco farmers in Zimbabwe has been the development of measures and strategies to 'maximise use of natural resources while minimising the effect of resource degradation'.[14]

Work Exploitation of Migrant Tobacco Workers in Kazakhstan', www.hrw.org/report/2010/07/14/hellish-work/exploitation-migrant-tobacco-workers-kazakhstan, accessed 25 July 2019.

9 'The Impact of Tobacco Farming on Deforestation', Forestry Commission of Zimbabwe, Harare, 2013, 6.

10 'Forests suffer amid Tobacco Record Breaking Euphoria', *The Herald*, 30 July 2018.

11 'Tobacco Farmers Must Stop Deforestation', Available at www.herald.co.zw/tobacco-farmers-must-stop-deforestation/, accessed on 4 July 2021.

12 R. V. Chivheya, 'Indigenous Forest Level of Deforestation, Forest Dependency and Factors Deserving Willingness to Participate in Indigenous Forestry Conservation: Evidence from Resettled Farmers in Shamva' (Unpublished PhD thesis, University of Fort Hare, 2016), 5.

13 'Tobacco Farmers Fuel Deforestation', *The Zimbabwe Independent*, 28 March 2014, available at www.theindependent.co.zw/2014/03/28/small-scale-tobacco-farmers-fuel-massive-deforestation/, accessed on 25 July 2019.

14 C. Chivuraise, 'Economics of Smallholder Tobacco Production and Implications of Tobacco Growing on Deforestation in Hurungwe District of Zimbabwe' (Unpublished Master of Science thesis, University of Zimbabwe, 2011), 4.

On a global scale, the socio-environmental panorama presented by tobacco production is no less apocalyptic. In 2004, the World Health Organization (WHO) released a report that revealed the causal link between tobacco farming and poverty in low-income countries.[15] The report noted that, while the profits of the big tobacco companies soar, the burden of tobacco farming on national economies in the form of the cost to public health facilities, the human toll due to pesticide exposure, the circle of debt by farmers owed to tobacco companies and the pernicious effects on the natural environment creates a 'vicious cycle of poverty'.[16] The 'Bellagio Statement on Tobacco and Sustainable Development' also concluded that in the developing world, 'tobacco poses a major challenge not just to health, but environmental sustainability'.[17] Approximate data from the mid-1980s confirmed that tobacco farming depletes between 1 million and 2.5 million hectares of woodlands annually .[18] An authoritative study by Fraser in the mid-1980s drew similar results on the negative ecological effects of

[15] See, 'Tobacco and Poverty: A Vicious Cycle', World Health Organization, Geneva, 2004.

[16] This report critiques the narrative often promoted by tobacco companies to farmers in low-income countries that tobacco farming brings prosperity. It points out that in 2002 the Chief Executive of the largest tobacco company Philip Morris earned US$ 3.2 million in salaries and bonuses. The reports note that it would take six years for an average Brazilian farmer to earn what the Executive earns in a day and 2140 years to earn his annual salary. Also, in 2002 the net revenue of the three top tobacco companies in the world Philip Morris, Japan Tobacco and British American Tobacco was US$ 121 billion, which was more than the combined GDP of Zimbabwe, Zambia, Cameroon, Botswana, Albania, Bahrain, Belize, Bolivia, Cambodia, Estonia, Georgia, Ghana, Honduras, Jamaica, Jordan, Macedonia, Malawi, Malta, Moldova, Mongolia, Namibia, Nepal, Paraguay, Senegal, Tajikistan, Togo and Uganda. The report also pointed out that in high income countries the cost of health care attributed to tobacco stood at between 6 per cent and 15 per cent of the total national health care bill. Finally, according to the report in southern Africa, 1400 km^2 of indigenous woodland are destroyed annually because of tobacco farming, which accounts for 12 per cent of overall annual deforestation.

[17] Representatives of twenty-two scientific organisations from across the world had a meeting in Bellagio, Italy in 1995 to examine the global impact of tobacco production and consumption. The meeting reached consensus that tobacco cultivation posed a major threat to sustainable development in low-income countries. For the full report see, 'Bellagio Statement on Tobacco and Sustainable Development', *Canadian Medical Association Journal*, 153, 8 (1995), 1109–1110.

[18] H. J. Geist, 'Global Assessment of Deforestation Related to Tobacco Farming', *Tobacco Control*, 8, 1 (1999), 18–28.

tobacco production.[19] Tobacco farming contributes to siltation of rivers, water reservoirs and the extinction of species due to habitat overexploitation.[20] Relative to other crops, tobacco facilitates accelerated soil erosion and imposes excessive demands on soil nutrients. Tobacco depletes more than ten times as much nitrogen, twenty-four times as much potassium and thirty times as much phosphorous as cassava, for example.[21] Farmers growing tobacco also use a lot of fertilisers, chemicals and insecticides. Run-off from these fertilisers and pesticides usually contaminate water bodies.[22] Thus, the exceptionality of tobacco farming relative to other crops is that it depletes soils, causes extensive deforestation, requires a lot of (frequently coerced) labour and uses a lot of agrochemicals and pesticides that contaminate both human and natural environments. The consumption of tobacco is also harmful to human health and is responsible for diseases such as lung cancer which has caused millions of deaths.[23]

In 2005, WHO came up with a Framework Convention on Tobacco Control (FCTC) to restrict 'the globalisation of the tobacco epidemic' by limiting tobacco demand and supply through multi-lateral cooperation in reducing consumption and counteracting the tobacco

[19] Alastair Fraser, in his 1986 study, revealed that tobacco growing areas are in parts of the developing world that are identified by FAO as being wood deficient. He also argued that most forests in Asia and Africa are now below the levels of meeting the current and future wood fuel needs on a sustainable basis. See, A. Fraser, *The Use of Wood by the Tobacco Industry and the Ecological Implications* (Edinburgh: International Forest Science Consultancy, 1986).

[20] N. Lecours et al., 'Environmental Health Impacts of Tobacco Farming: A Review of the Literature', *Tobacco Control*, 21, 2 (2012), 191–196. A recent report published in 2018 confirmed that tobacco farming contributes to climate change through acidification, high fossil energy consumption and soil and water depletion. The report noted that the global production of 32.4 million megatons of green tobacco contributed 82 megatons of carbon emissions which was 0.2 per cent of global emissions in 2014. See M. Zafereidou, N. Hopkinson and N. Voulvoulis, 'Cigarette Smoking: An Assessment of Tobacco's Global Environmental Footprint Across Its Entire Supply Chain', *Environmental Science and Technology*, 52, 15 (2018), 8087–8094.

[21] R. J. A. Goodland, C. Watson and G. Ledee, *Environmental Management in Tropical Africa* (Boulder, 1984), 78.

[22] R. J. Tobin and W. I. Knausenberger, 'Dilemmas of Development: Burley Tobacco, the Environment and Economic Growth in Malawi', *Journal of Southern African Studies*, 24, 2 (1998), 405–424.

[23] Tobacco has been dubbed by WHO the single largest cause of death during the last century estimated to have claimed more than a hundred million casualties through sickness.

industry's lobbying and advertising activities.[24] The convention also recommends the development of sustainable models that ameliorate tobacco production's social and environmental costs.[25] However, current global tobacco-control intervention regimes have not been very effective.[26] The Zimbabwean government has been an outspoken and harsh critic of this convention and of several tobacco-control measures. In 2000, during the WHO public hearings on a global tobacco-control regime in Geneva, the Zimbabwe Tobacco Association (ZTA) criticised the work of the FCTC as arrogant and iniquitous, 'representing an attack on Zimbabwe's national sovereignty'.[27] The country also refused to ratify the Tobacco Control Convention when it entered into force in 2005, declaring that the convention would harm its tobacco industry.[28] Although Zimbabwe eventually ratified the treaty in December 2014, it has remained highly critical of global tobacco-control initiatives and aloof from much of the efforts to reduce tobacco consumption such as curtailing marketing of tobacco products, illicit trade of cigarettes, limiting tobacco production and searching for alternative crops. This policy negligence raises critical questions about the long-term social and environmental sustainability of tobacco farming in Zimbabwe and the economic prospects for smallholder tobacco farmers within the context of changing global and local pressures such as public health advocacy, falling consumption trends, stochastic market dynamics and socio-ecological factors.

[24] J. Chung-Hall et al., 'Impact of the WHO FCTC Over the First Decade: A Global Evidence Review Prepared for the Impact Assessment Expert Group', *Tobacco Control*, 28 (2018), 119–128.

[25] This is contained in Article 18 of the convention.

[26] Tobacco companies (specifically BAT and Philip Morris) created supply chains in the 1990s to improve production and access to markets. These supply chains were used in the 2000s to legitimate the portrayal of tobacco as socially and environmentally friendly instead of taking meaningful steps to eliminate child labour and deforestation, with the result that the companies benefited to the tune of US$ 64 million annually in money that would have been used to avoid tobacco related deforestation in the top 12 global tobacco-producing countries, including Zimbabwe. See, M. Ortenez and S. Glantz, 'Social Responsibility in Tobacco Production? Tobacco Companies Use of Green Supply Chains to Obscure the New Costs of Tobacco Farming', *Tobacco Control*, 20, 6 (2011), 403–411.

[27] A. Lown et al., 'Tobacco Is Our Industry and We Will Support It: Exploring the Potential Implications of Zimbabwe's Accession to the Framework Convention on Tobacco Control', *Globalisation and Health*, 12, 2 (2016), 1–11.

[28] Ibid., 1–11.

The FTLRP changed the tobacco farming landscape in Zimbabwe as the whole infrastructure of white commercial production that had sustained tobacco production since the colonial days collapsed and black smallholder farmers took over.[29] Smallholder production has grown exponentially over the years with the number of black smallholder flue-cured tobacco farmers rising from 8,537 in 2000 to 140,895 in 2018.[30] The production dynamics have also radically shifted in terms of net contribution of smallholder farmers to national output as they have outperformed the commercial sector.[31] While production figures have been impressive and show a growth trajectory, accelerated production of tobacco has generated anxieties amongst environmental experts over the long-term sustainability of tobacco farming based on the current common property resource use models in the resettlement farming areas and the limits imposed by the availability of such resources in the future.[32] Although palliative measures such as afforestation, using fast-growing exotic trees, has been espoused by the tobacco industry as an alternative, implementation of that policy has been weak. A forest control law was introduced through a statutory instrument in 2012.[33] Subsequently, an afforestation levy was imposed on tobacco farmers by the state in 2015.[34] However, these regulations are yet to be institutionalised. In July 2016, tobacco farmers confronted the government over the allocation of the funds generated under the

[29] By July 2001 half the approximately 2,000 white owned tobacco farms had been designated for resettlement purposes. See D. Cole and J. Cole, 'Tobacco Research and Development', in M. Rukuni et al. (eds.), *Zimbabwe's Agricultural Revolution Revisited* (Harare, 2006), 405.

[30] Tobacco Industries Marketing Board Annual Report, 2018, 26.

[31] Statistics from the Tobacco Industries and Marketing Board show that small-scale farmers produce well over 90 per cent of total national output of flue-cured tobacco. In 2018, small-scale production contributed 91 per cent to national output. See, Tobacco Industries and Marketing Board (TIMB) Annual Report 2017.

[32] The Zimbabwe Forestry Commission has constantly pointed out the long-term unsustainability of current tobacco production models on forestry resources. In 2018, a Forestry Commission official noted that 20 per cent of national forestry cover lost was a result of tobacco farming. She added that during the year tobacco farmers had destroyed 60,000 hectares of forests wood to cure tobacco. See 'Forests suffer amid tobacco record breaking euphoria', The Herald, 30 July 2018.

[33] This was passed under the Control of Timber and Forests Produce Regulations.

[34] This was effected by the Tobacco Afforestation Levy.

afforestation levy.[35] The state had collected US$12 million but had not channelled anything towards supporting afforestation in tobacco-growing areas.[36] During the presentation of the 2019 budget statement the Minister of Finance ordered the fund to be shared between the Forestry Commission and the Tobacco Industries and Marketing Board (TIMB) and to be invested in afforestation within tobacco farming areas.[37] Also, more worryingly for tobacco farmers, other alternative energy sources for tobacco curing such as coal and fast-growing *Eucalyptus* trees have also come under new global environmental scrutiny.[38]

Moreover, the social costs of tobacco to the country are ominous. In 2019, the prevalence of tobacco use in Zimbabwe was estimated to be between 19 per cent and 35 per cent of the population.[39] A study by WHO in 2016 worryingly revealed that 20 per cent of young people between the ages of 13–15 in Zimbabwe were smokers and 12.5 per cent of children started smoking at the early age of seven.[40] There is

35 'Farmers Cry Foul over Levy', *The Zimbabwe Independent*, 29 July 2016.

36 Ibid.

37 The 2019 National Budget Statement by Hon. Prof. Mthuli Ncube Minister of Finance and Economic Development, 22 November 2018, 63.

38 Scientific studies have established that *Eucalyptus*, which is the ideal afforestation tree for the tobacco industry, rapidly depletes the water table and threatens water security. See J. M. Albaugh, P. J. Dye and J. S. King, 'Eucalyptus and Water Use in South Africa', *International Journal of Forestry Research*,(2013), doi.10.1155/2013/852540; 'Mounting Pressure Against Eucalyptus in Kenya Described as a Water Guzzler', World Rainforest Movement, Bulletin 147, October 2009, available at https://wrm.org.uy/articles-from-the-wrm-bulletin/section2/mounting-pressure-against-eucalyptus-in-kenya-described-as-the-water-guzzler/, accessed on 22 August 2019; V. Engel et al., 'Hydrological Consequences of Eucalyptus Afforestation in the Argentine Pampas', *Water Resources Research*, 41 (2005), 1–14. Another alternative source coal has high carbon emissions and greenhouse gas effects. As a result of these concerns major global cigarette manufacturers such as Philip Morris have resolved to eliminate the use of coal in tobacco curing processes by 2020 under the sustainable tobacco programme by not purchasing tobacco cured with fossil fuels. This is a serious threat to Zimbabwe's tobacco industry and prompts more proactive and cost-effective renewable energy sources for tobacco curing. This becomes even much more imperative considering that the country has struggled with a huge energy deficit since 2000 and relies on electricity imports from its neighbours particularly South Africa, Mozambique and Democratic Republic of Congo (DRC).

39 S. Hayson, 'The Illicit Tobacco Trade in Zimbabwe and South Africa', Working paper, Scowcroft Centre for Strategy and Security, (March 2019), 4.

40 'Waking Up to Teenage Smoking in Zimbabwe', www.dw.com/en/waking-up-to-teenage-smoking-in-zimbabwe/a-19026965, accessed 24 November 2019.

also laxity in regulations to reduce demand for tobacco products as well as limited central government investment in tobacco-control agencies and public awareness on the dangers of smoking. The global health body pointed out that existing laws designed to curb smoking amongst school children were not being implemented.[41] The long-term public health burden that the escalating use of tobacco might impose on the country's health sector will be substantial. The financial gains from tobacco farming will not be able to cover these social costs. Even more, farm incomes from tobacco have declined year-on-year, to the point that 'tobacco success story narratives' have become contested. The country's economic decline over the past twenty years or so has also affected tobacco farmers whose earning has significantly dwindled with the result that many are not growing the crop profitably.[42] Between 2000 and 2010, the country experienced an unprecedented inflation rate of 231,000,000 per cent and an unemployment rate of over 90 per cent.[43] Although the economy significantly improved between 2010 and 2020, the country is still burdened by high inflation rate, cash shortages, arbitrage in forex exchange regulations and high cost of goods and services. Despite selling their crops in United States Dollars, tobacco farmers get part of their incomes in local currency at official exchange rates which are usually undervalued. This has snuffed out the prospects for capital investments in afforestation, agricultural innovation and diversification. In the end, tobacco-growing communities have been caught in the vicious cycle of indebtedness to tobacco contracting companies, while failing to sustain themselves.[44]

[41] Ibid.

[42] These are perennial concerns that haunt every tobacco marketing season. See 'Zimbabwe Tobacco Sector Booming but Farmers Growing It Are Not', Voice of America, 30 May 2017, available at www.voanews.com/africa/zimbabwe-tobacco-booming-farmers-growing-it-are-not, accessed on 22 August 2019; 'Tobacco Farmers Cry Foul over Forex Payments', *The Herald*, 23 April 2019; 'Farmers Cry Foul over Pricing of Golden Leaf', www.zbc.co.zw/farmers-cry-foul-over-pricing-of-golden-leaf/, accessed on 22 August 2019; 'Tobacco Farmers Cry Foul over Cash Withdrawal Limits', accessed on 22 August 2018; 'Tobacco Prices Go up in Smoke', available at www.businesslive.co.za/fm/features/africa/2019-06-13-tobacco-prices-go-up-in-smoke-in-zimbabwe/, accessed 22 August 2019.

[43] C. Munangagwa, 'The Economic Decline of Zimbabwe', *The Gettysburg Economic Review*, 3, 9 (2009), 110–129.

[44] R. Chingosho, C. Dare and C. Van Walbeek, 'Tobacco Farming and Current Debt Status among Smallholder Farmers in Manicaland Province in Zimbabwe', *Tobacco Control*, 30, 6 (2021), 610–615.

However, despite these apparent negative socio-environmental effects the expansion of the country's tobacco sector continues to be framed largely in terms of livelihoods and rural incomes for small-scale tobacco producers.[45] These triumphalist discourses permeate much of the discussions on tobacco production in Zimbabwe where tobacco is a political crop inextricably tied to the successes of the political status quo. These dominant and hegemonic narratives gained traction and momentum after the Land Reform Programme when the state conscripted tobacco farming within the script of national survival, black empowerment, and national sovereignty.[46] Within this political landscape responsible environmental policy interventions in tobacco farming have been neither effectively nor robustly articulated.

[45] Literature on contemporary tobacco farming in Zimbabwe after the year 2000 generally falls into two categories. The rural livelihoods and accumulation approach examine the changing patterns of production from dominance by white commercial farmers to the rise of black smallholder producers (which intensified after the land invasions in 2000) within the context of increased incomes and new patterns of rural accumulation. See, I. Scoones et al., 'Tobacco, Contract Farming, and Agrarian Change', 22–42; J. Masvongo, J. Mutambara and A. Zvinavashe, 'Viability in Tobacco Production Under the Smallholder Farming Sector in Mount Darwin District', *Journal of Development and Agriculture Economics*, 5, 8 (2013), 295–301; D. Magadlela, 'A Smoky Affair: Challenges Facing Some Smallholder Burley Tobacco Producers in Zimbabwe', *Zambezia*, XXIV.I, (1997), 13–30. The environmental scholarship emphasises the ecological disruptions instigated by the surge in the number of tobacco producers on the limited land and natural resources. See P. Nyambara and M. Nyandoro, 'Tobacco Thrives, but the Environment Cries: The Sustainability of Livelihoods from Small-Scale Tobacco Growing in Zimbabwe, 2000–2017', *Global Environment*, 12, 2 (2019), 304–320; T. G. Nhapi, 'Natural Resource Degradation through Tobacco Farming in Zimbabwe: CSR Implications and the Role of the Government', *South African Journal for Communication Theory and Research*, (2019), 1–15.

[46] On 27 October 2017, *The Patriot* newspaper, which is a mouthpiece for the ruling party ZANU PF, published an article in which it attacks WHO for policies against tobacco farming. The article eulogises (then) President Robert Mugabe for his stance in defending the black-dominated tobacco farming industry and protecting the interests of his nation and people. The article points out that tobacco is key to the economy as it brings in billions in foreign currency and capital investments, supports 1.2 million people directly and another 4.8 million who are dependent on the crop. It adds that tobacco production 'testifies to the success story of the Land Reform and Resettlement Programme which empowered 400,000 indigenous families from the previous 4,000 commercial white farmers'. See, 'WHO can't change Mugabe standing', *The Patriot*, 27 October to 2 November 2017.

This book integrates the contemporary narratives on tobacco farming in Zimbabwe into socio-environmental history research as a way towards understanding not only how the present crisis is linked to bigger historical patterns in cultures of predatory agricultural production but also to illuminate on the context and potential of tobacco-control policy within the country. A long durée approach to environmental history is important during the age of the Anthropocene, to connect the past, present and future in understanding the outstanding issues that must shape economic choices and policies in agricultural production during a time of volatile climate, ecological and social uncertainty.[47] It is important to write stories that locate environmental change in historical time and show how contemporary environments and environmental systems have been shaped across history and how these have also shaped humans and human culture. Contemporary environmental crises in Africa and the rest of the world are connected to past human activities and policies that continue to shape the present – with future implications.[48] This study connects with contemporary narratives and historicises the environment, society and commercial tobacco farming in Zimbabwe (Southern Rhodesia).[49] It

[47] The term 'Anthropocene' was introduced by J. P. Cruitzen and E. F. Stoermer in 2000 to designate a new geological age distinct from the Holocene era. They argue that the Anthropocene is the 'age of humans' and is defined by rapid climate change, expansion of human and livestock populations, rapid urbanisation, increased consumption of fresh water, extinction of animal species, landscape and waterway modification, and the decline of natural resources. They designate this era as beginning between 1750 and 1800. The debate has been taken up and although there are disagreements on when exactly the age began there is unanimity that human activity has altered the planet more significantly during this era. See, J. P. Cruitzen and E. F. Stoermer, 'The Anthropocene', *Global Change Newsletter*, 41 (2000), 17–18. For debates on the age of the Anthropocene see N. Möllers, 'Cur(at)ing the Planet – How to Exhibit the Anthropocene and Why?', *RCC Perspectives*, 3 (2013), 57–66; T. J. Braje, 'Earth Systems, Human Agency, and the Anthropocene: Planet Earth in the Human Age', *Journal of Archaeological Research*, 23, 4 (2015), 369–396; M. P. Diogo, I. Louro and D. Scarso, 'Uncanny Nature: Why the Concept of Anthropocene is Relevant for Historians of Technology', *Icon* , 23 (2017), 25–35.

[48] A. Isaacman, 'Historical Amnesia or the Logic of Capital Accumulation: Cotton Production in Colonial and Post-Colonial Mozambique', *Environment and Planning: Society and Space*, 15 (1997), 757–790; M. Tiffen et al., *More People, Less Erosion: Environmental Recovery in Kenya* (London, 1994).

[49] Present-day Zimbabwe was known as Southern Rhodesia from 1890 to1964. In 1964 when Northern Rhodesia (present day Zambia) got its independence the

focuses on the interaction between tobacco farmers and the environment from 1893 onwards and how that relationship shaped socio-economic and political landscapes, physical environments, agrarian ecosystems, and even impacted on the human body.

While scientific approaches to the tobacco-control debate concentrate on contemporary practices in tobacco production systems and the tobacco value chain, this book broadens this understanding by critically historicising tobacco culture and the attendant production institutions and regimes. These were forged over a hundred years from the pioneer settler tobacco farms to the contemporary small-scale producer in the resettlement areas. Tobacco production in Southern Rhodesia and Zimbabwe always defined the political economy and constructed agricultural landscapes and social relations since the early colonial days. But while farmers grew the crop and made decisions on how to grow it that in turn affected the environment, the tobacco crop itself also exerted a significant amount of subtle agency. Richard Foltz argues that crops and nature also carry agency so much that historians who have focused exclusively on humans have missed the complexity that all human actions take place in an ecosystem that involve other non-human agents.[50] Emily Gorman and Andrea Gaynor emphasised the imperative for historians to tell 'more than human histories' and embrace other species to give primacy to the dynamic relations of entities, organisms and multiple voices to uncover novel methodological and theoretical approaches.[51] Thus, while humans developed the social, economic, political and cultural milieu that dictated how the tobacco crop was to be grown, the crop itself has biological features that determined its requirements for growth and lifespan that in turn influence human choices and the concomitant socio-economic institutions for its production. This book also discusses how crops carry hegemonic symbols of power through their cultivation and production, which reified certain

country changed its name to Rhodesia until 1980 when it got majority rule and independence. The term 'colonial Zimbabwe' is used to refer to the colonial state (1890 to 1980). The name shall be used interchangeably with Southern Rhodesia and Rhodesia to reflect the period before and after 1964 respectively.

50 R. C. Foltz, 'Does Nature Have Agency? World History, Environmental History, and How Historians Can Help Save the Planet', *The History Teacher*, 37, 1 (2003), 9–28.

51 E. O'Gorman and A. Gaynor, 'More-than-Human Histories', *Environmental History*, 25 (2020), 711–735.

racial ideologies, identities and stereotypes within and beyond the colonial state.

This book illuminates not only on the effects of tobacco farming on the environment, but how the tobacco environment affects the human body. This dimension is important because the interaction between humans and nature is not unidirectional, but a dialectical process, a dialogue in which human and natural systems shape and influence each other.[52] In studying environmental change therefore, it is necessary to understand that human activities have environmental consequences, and change in natural ecosystems, whether induced by humans or not, inevitably affects humans, and the human body.[53] To this end, farming landscapes must not be viewed as 'just' physical spaces of production but also as socio-environmental sites of struggle on which humans and nature interact to produce not only new ecosystems and environmental change but also new relations of society. The dialectical nature of human and landscape interaction is central to historical change and natural landscapes are not neutral external backdrops to human activities.[54] Tim Ingold emphasises the temporality of physical landscapes as they are neither 'built nor unbuilt but are perpetually under construction'.[55]

This book explores how tobacco farming systems, shifts in politics and cultural practices by white settler farmers and African farmers

[52] In essence this can be distilled as the most basic definition of 'socio-environmental history', that is narratives that explain the human past using the lens of how humans and nature have interacted, influencing each other in the process and creating new social institutions, economic systems, physical landscapes, ecologies and ecosystems.

[53] W. Cronon, 'The Uses of Environmental History', *Environmental History Review*, 17, 3 (1993), 1–22.

[54] See, T. Ingold, 'The Temporality of Landscapes', *World Archaeology*, 25, 2 (1993), 152–174.

[55] Ibid.. Ingold further explains that humans do not act upon the landscape to 'do things to it' but rather move along with it and are integral to the transformation of the landscape. Also see, W. Cronon, *Changes in the Land: Indians, Colonists, and the Ecology of New England* (New York, 2003). Cronon presents nature and landscapes as being more than stages for human activity but also actors. For an engaged reading on the construction of landscapes in Zimbabwe see, J. Fontein, *Remaking the Mutirikwi: Landscape, Water and Belonging in Southern Zimbabwe* (Suffolk, 2015). Fontein examines the construction of landscapes around Lake Mutirikwi in Zimbabwe during both the colonial and post-colonial periods and shows that this process is both 'imaginative and material'. Also see, D. M. Hughes, 'Hydrology of Hope: Farm Dams, Conservation, and Whiteness in Zimbabwe', *American Ethnologist*, 33, 2 (2006), 269–287.

changed landscapes, environments and social relations over time in Southern Rhodesia and Zimbabwe. The book shows that this process was complex and shaped by factors outside the domain of the environment such as global economic and political conditions like the Great Depression, the two World Wars and the 'Dust Bowl' environmental disasters in the USA and accompanying conservation discourses. The book uses the broader historiographical theories on the rise of conservation ideologies within white settler agriculture in southern Africa and global discourses on modern environmentalism to interrogate how tobacco farming practices contributed to environmental degradation, contamination or improvement.

The political ecology of tobacco farming also involved power relations constructed along lines on race. Africans suffered both as labourers in the white settler tobacco farms and then as tobacco farmers themselves. As labourers, Africans were exploited and exposed to dangerous tobacco chemicals, and as farmers they were marginalised and deprived of access to land and natural resources, capital and markets. But indeed, Africans were not just passive victims under the colonial tobacco economy. Between 1900 and the early 1930s they seized the market opportunities offered by the establishment of mining settlements and towns to produce their 'indigenous' tobacco and sell it to earn enough money to pay their taxes and buy goods.[56] During the 1950s, 1960s and 1970s – at the height of state promotion of Turkish and Burley production in African areas – a few African farmers were also able to benefit and invest some of their tobacco capital in soil and water conservation.

Tobacco in Southern Rhodesian Environmental History

In 1935 the Rhodesia Tobacco Association (RTA) sent out circulars to white settler tobacco growers plaintively imploring them to reduce acreages. This appeal ruefully noted that overproduction by itinerant, peripatetic and speculative tobacco farmers was creating desolate and derelict farming landscapes within the Rhodesian countryside:

[56] B. Kosmin, 'The Inyoka Tobacco Industry of the Shangwe People: The Displacement of a Pre-colonial Economy in Southern Rhodesia; 1898–1938', in R. Palmer and N. Parsons (eds.), *The Roots of Rural Poverty in Africa in Central and Southern Africa* (London, 1977), 268–287.

One sees a number of farms which are entirely useless for tobacco production, and will be for many years to come, with not one piece of timber worthy of that name left; with soil erosion tremendously hastened because of its barrenness and with the soil palpably exhausted, so that a reduction of acreage is not all loss for it extends the life of the farm.[57]

The 1937 circular reiterated – in apocalyptical imagery – that 'miserable derelict farms reminiscent of the Sahara desert' were now a familiar sight within the tobacco belt in Southern Rhodesia.[58] In 1939, the Natural Resources Commission of Enquiry that had been set up by the state to investigate the destruction of the resources of the colony attributed a plethora of environmental infractions to the 'careless and indifferent' tobacco farmers.[59] Three years later, the Veterinary Branch raised the alarm on the high mortality of livestock and wildlife due to poisoning caused by tobacco fertilisers and field sprays.[60] During the 1960s medical studies in Southern Rhodesia established a causal relationship between *Carcinoma of the Bronchus* and smoking and showed that 87.5 per cent of African males with lung cancer were cigarette smokers.[61] During the 1970s and 1980s, several incidences of mortality amongst African labourers due to chemical poisoning were reported in the tobacco farms.[62] The Natural Resources Board (NRB) also noted a widespread depletion of fauna on most tobacco farms due to chemical sprays.[63] These incidences extensively documented in Southern Rhodesia's agricultural archives shine a critical spotlight on a dimension that is not only shockingly unexplored up until now, but rings a familiar and doleful note to

[57] National Archives of Zimbabwe (NAZ), Harare (Salisbury), S1827/1245/3, Tobacco cultural practices; 1931–1941, RTA circular to growers, February 1935: Regulation of production.

[58] NAZ, S1827/1245/3, Tobacco cultural practices; 1931–1941, RTA circular to growers, February 1935: Regulation of production.

[59] See, NAZ, S2496/1080/1/5, Report of the Commission of Enquiry into the Conservation of the Colony's Natural Resources, 1939.

[60] P. D. Huston, 'Veterinary Notes: A Note on the Poisoning of Stock by Nitrate of Soda', *Rhodesia Agricultural Journal*, 39, 2, (March–April 1942), 88–89.

[61] M. Gelfand, A. Graham and E. Lightman, 'Carcinoma of the Bronchus and the Smoking Habits of Rhodesian Africans', *British Medical Journal*, 3, 5616 (1968), 468–469.

[62] See, for instance 'Poisonings Caused by Careless Handling', *Rhodesia Sunday Mail*, 18 December 1979; 'Farm Workers Exposed to Killer Sprays, Says Survey', *Sunday Mail*, 15 April 1983.

[63] Natural Resource Board, 'The Pesticide Dilemma', *Newsletter*, 8 (September 1981).

contemporary observers of Zimbabwe's tobacco industry – that is how tobacco farming plunders natural ecosystems, physical landscapes and human bodies for profit.

There are two distinct scholarly traditions within the historiography of the Southern Rhodesian tobacco industry: the first one – 'the virgin land' scholarship valorises and glorifies white settler pioneer tobacco farmers for their entrepreneurship and pioneering endeavour in opening vast 'untamed bushes' and establishing thriving tobacco settlements that transformed the 'wilderness'. This brand of scholarship is more accurately represented by Frank Clements and Edward Harben's (themselves tobacco farmers) pioneering literature sponsored by the RTA in 1962 as an official history of the industry.[64] The second historiographic school belongs to a more critical tradition that looked past the romanticised façade of individual white male settler tobacco growers' resilience – to interrogating the role of the state in the growth of the industry and the exploitation of African labour. The latter school offered critical insights into the role of the colonial state's coercive power in the development of the Rhodesian tobacco industry through the creation of an infrastructure that buttressed the interests of white tobacco growers.[65] Victor Machingaidze trail-blazed this critical tradition by showing how the white settler tobacco farmer (far from being an independent entrepreneur) benefited from the racial infrastructure of the colonial state.[66] Steven Rubert joined the critical tradition with a rich social history of colonial labour narratives that weaves the odyssey of the Rhodesian tobacco industry through the lives of Africans whose bodies became raw

[64] See F. Clements and E. Harben, *Leaf of Gold: The Story of Rhodesian Tobacco* (London, 1962). Both Frank Clements and Edward Harben were themselves tobacco farmers which make their accounts even much more liable to subjective 'insider' views. Other works from the first-generation literature include H. R. Roberts, 'The Development of the Southern Rhodesian Tobacco Industry', *South African Journal of Economics*, 19, 2 (1951), 177–188; W. E. Haviland, 'Tobacco Farm Organisation, Cost and Land Use in Southern Rhodesia', *The South African Journal of Economics*, (1953), 367–380; W. E. Haviland, 'The Use and Efficiency of African Labour in Tobacco Farming in Southern Rhodesia', *The Canadian Journal of Economics and Political Science*, 20, 1 (1954),100–106.

[65] For the systematic disruption of African tobacco producers by the state in colonial Zimbabwe see Kosmin, 'The Inyoka Tobacco Industry of the Shangwe People', 268–287.

[66] V. E. M. Machingaidze, 'The Development of Settler Capitalist Agriculture in Southern Rhodesia with particular Reference to the Role of the State, 1908–1939' (Unpublished PhD thesis, University of London, 1980).

materials in producing the 'golden leaf'.[67] His research exposes the grisly world of child labour in dingy tobacco barns, gangs of labourers toiling in the settler tobacco fields and the festering farm compounds. A more recent addition to this school has been Sibangeni Ncube's works on the politics of colonial tobacco industry from the watershed 1945 tobacco boom, through the stormy years of isolation and the tobacco embargo when Rhodesian tobacco was placed under international sanctions until independence in 1980.[68] Ncube focuses on the nexus between local and international politics in the development of the Rhodesian tobacco industry and closes a hitherto yawning gap in post–World War II Southern Rhodesian tobacco grower-state relations that had only been addressed by David Rowe's 2001 publication on state-grower relations during the Unilateral Declaration of Independence (UDI).[69]

However, despite their profundity as texts on the political economy of Rhodesian tobacco, this new critical historiography on colonial tobacco history neglects the fundamental dialectical interaction between political economy, materialities, landscapes and human bodies. The silence of existing tobacco literature in Southern Rhodesia on how physical landscapes were shaped and transformed by agrarian encounters and how the transformation of landscapes in turn affected the political economy of production is very conspicuous and deafening. Much so when juxtaposed within a milieu of historical writing that has come to examine how imperial power and capital restructured indigenous landscapes.[70] Streams of historical literature have sprung up and

[67] S. Rubert, *A Most Promising Weed: A History of Tobacco Farming and Labour in Colonial Zimbabwe, 1890–1945* (Athens, 1998).

[68] See S. Ncube, 'Colonial Zimbabwe Tobacco Industry: Global, Regional and Local Relations, 1949–1979' (Unpublished PhD thesis, University of the Free State, 2018); S. Ncube, 'We Must Adapt to Survive: International Sanctions, Settler Politics, and White Tobacco Farmers' Struggles for Economic Survival in Rhodesia, 1966–1979', *African Economic History*, 48, 2 (2020), 67–91; S. Ncube, 'Beyond the State? Organised Settler Tobacco Interests and the Consolidation of Southern Rhodesia's Tobacco Industry in the Early Post–Second World War Years', *Journal of Southern African Studies*, DOI: 10.1080/03057070.2022.2049492.

[69] D. M. Rowe, *Manipulating the Market; Understanding Economic Sanctions, Institutional Change and the Political Unity of White Rhodesia* (Ann Arbor, 2001).

[70] Much scholarship from the 1970s has looked at how colonial agrarian encounters changed indigenous environments. More recently the work of Hannah Hollerman focused on how the spread of white settler colonialism at the

reconstructed landscapes of the past to tell stories of environment and society.[71] That said, Ian Phimister perhaps in a sense pioneered an environmental history of tobacco farming in Southern Rhodesia over three decades ago in his 1986 article on conservation.[72] He pointed to the deteriorating soil conditions in tobacco farms that were conspicuous during the inter-war years as a result of speculative farming and limited state conservation intervention. He argued that this pattern continued in the post-war boom years as prices improved and tobacco farms took much-needed capital and resources from other crops, resulting in unbalanced agricultural development and a concomitantly delayed impeded pace of conservationism. This book draws on Phimister's seminal research but nevertheless diverges from it in two key respects. First, the corpus of tobacco environmental history contained in his article is too thin to constitute a comprehensive environmental history of tobacco farming as it covers a short period, 1938 to 1950. Second, even in that narrow coverage of time, his article neglects the fundamental transitions in the tobacco farm environment and landscapes that were generated by

end of the nineteenth century brought with it the cultivation of new areas and the development of new systems of coercive labour. Imperial capitalism led to land dispossession, displacement of indigenous people and the establishment of plantation agriculture and intensive cultivation that precipitated widespread environmental degradation in most colonial states. See, H. Hollerman, *Dust Bowls of Empire: Imperialism, Environmental Politics, and the Injustice of 'Green' Capitalism* (New Haven, 2018) Also see, D. Worster, *Rivers of Empire; Water Aridity and the Growth of the American West* (New York, 1985); D. Worster, *Under the American Skies: Nature and History in the American West* (New York, 1992); Henry Nash Smith, *Virgin Land: The American West as Symbol and Myth* (Cambridge: Harvard University Press, 1970); Cronon, *Changes in the Land.*

71 See, for instance, O. M. Wapulumuka, *Conservation Song: A History of Peasant State Relations and the Environment in Malawi, 1860–2000* (Cambridge, 2010).

72 I. Phimister, 'Discourse and the Discipline of Historical Context: Conservatism and Ideas about Development in Southern Rhodesia, 1930–1950', *Journal of Southern African Studies*, 12, 2 (1986), 263275. This article was also later reproduced in Phimister's ground-breaking 1988 book publication. See, I. Phimister, *An Economic and Social History of Zimbabwe, 1890–1948: Capital Accumulation and Class Struggle* (London, 1988), 228–234. Phimister was responding to William Beinart's 1984 article that argued colonial governments in southern Africa were preoccupied with the conservation of natural resources and soil erosion from the 1930s to the 1950s. See, W. Beinart, 'Soil Erosion, Conservationism and Ideas about Development: A Southern African Exploration, 1900–1960', *Journal of Southern African Studies*, 15, 1 (1984), 52–83. The debate is more comprehensively covered in Chapter 4 of this book.

the post–World War II tobacco boom and indeed private capital. Thus, an unintentionally uniform reading of environmental change between 1938 and 1950 was constructed, while this book argues that the tobacco farms were not static, but a fluid set of landscapes being structured and restructured by a plethora of factors.

In contributing to the environmental history of Southern Rhodesia, this book integrates the conservation historiography of southern Africa to show how ideas about the environment and conservation ideologies proliferated into Southern Rhodesia and influenced tobacco farmers and state policy from around the late 1920s.[73] It further draws from American environmental historiography that locates the origins of environmental degradation within wasteful and predatory capitalist agricultural systems. This book critiques romanticised narratives of pioneer colonial agricultural settlements based on the agrarian myth of progressive tobacco farming. American environmental historians such as Donald Worster, Henry Nash Smith, Richard Hofstadter, Leslie Hewes and Douglas Hurt have all pointed out the severe impacts

[73] While there is also scant focus on the environment from the tobacco history literature, other agrarian history works have looked at conservation within the white settler agrarian sector in the region and in Southern Rhodesia. Regional studies have focused on the development of conservationism in Southern Africa from the seventeenth century and the proliferation of these ideas into colonial doctrines and their application in white and African agriculture. See, R. Grove, *Green Imperialism: Colonial Expansion, Tropical Island Edens and the Origins of Environmentalism, 1600–1860* (Cambridge, 1996) and also R. Grove, 'Scottish Missionaries, Evangelical Discourses and the Origins of Conservation Thinking in Southern Africa, 1820–1900', *Journal of Southern African Studies*, 15, 2 (1989), 163–184; W. Beinart, *The Rise of Conservation in South Africa: Settlers, Livestock, and the Environment, 1770–1950* (Oxford, 2003); William Beinart, 'The Politics of Colonial Conservation', *Journal of Southern African Studies*, 15, 2 (1989), 143–162; W. Beinart, 'Soil Erosion, Conservationism and Ideas about Development: A Southern African Exploration, 1900–1960', *Journal of Southern African Studies*, 15, 1 (1984), 52–83; K. Showers, 'Soil Erosion in the Kingdom of Lesotho: Origins and Colonial Responses, 1830s–1950s', *Journal of Southern African Studies*, 15, 2 (1989), 143–162; K. Showers, *Imperial Gullies: Soil Erosion and Conservation in Lesotho* (Athens, 2005); J. McGregor, 'Woodland Resources: Ecology, Policy and Ideology: An Historical Case Study of Woodlands Use in Shurugwi Communal Area, Zimbabwe' (Unpublished PhD thesis, Loughborough University of Technology, 1991); J. A. Tropp, *Natures of Colonial Change: Environmental Relations in the Making of the Transkei* (Athens, 2006); I. Phimister, 'Discourse and the Discipline of Historical Context', 263–275.

of colonial farming systems on labour exploitation, class conflict and the environment.[74]

Much of the pioneering work on soil conservation in the settler agrarian sector in colonial Zimbabwe offers a rich analysis and an entry point into the debates framed around conservationism in the colonial state and the history of soil conservation in the white settler farms. However, their focus is broad and general extending to a myriad of sectors in agriculture presenting white farmers as a homogenous block.[75] Indeed, Paul Mosley in his study of the Rhodesian and Kenyan settler economies stressed the importance of zooming in on 'the settler economics of fault lines' between economic sectors.[76] He emphasised that the category of white capital must not be seen as one sector, but several if policy is to be understood. This book thus extends Mosley's contention to include not only differences between economic sectors but the fault lines within an economic sector – the intra sectoral dynamics within the agrarian economy. To this end therefore, merely homogenising state policy on settler agriculture without unpacking the internal heterogeneities that differed from one sector to the other, and from one crop to the other, leads to unfortunate historical generalisations about conservation in white farms. Angus Selby criticises such historical constructions that perceive white farmers as a homogenous rural bourgeoisie since it shrouds their differences when viewed

[74] See, D. Worster, *Dust Bowl: The Southern Plains in the 1930s* (Oxford, 1979); D. Worster, *Rivers of Empire; Water Aridity and the Growth of the American West* (New York, 1985); D. Worster, *Nature's Economy: The Roots of Ecology* (San Francisco, 1972); D. Worster, 'The Dirty Thirties: A Study in Agricultural Capitalism', *Great Plains Quarterly*, 6, 2 (1986),107–116; H. N. Smith, *Virgin Land: The American West as Symbol and Myth* (Cambridge, 1970); R. Hofstadter, *The Progressive Historians: Turner, Beard and Parrington* (New York, 1968) and L. Hewes, *The Suitcase Farming Frontier: A Study in the Historical Geography of the Central Great Plains* (Lincoln, 1973).

[75] See, S. Maravanyika, 'Soil Conservation and the White Agrarian Environment in Colonial Zimbabwe, 1908–1980' (Unpublished PhD thesis, University of Pretoria, 2013); M. Musemwa, 'Contestation Over Resources: The Farmer-Miner Dispute in Colonial Zimbabwe, 1903–1939', *Environment and History*, 15, 1 (2009), 79–109. Also, see, T. Madimu, 'Farmers, Miners and the State in Colonial Zimbabwe, c.1895–1961' (Unpublished PhD thesis, University of Stellenbosch, 2017); V. Kwashirai, 'Dilemmas in Conservationism in Colonial Zimbabwe, 1890–1930', *Conservation and Society*, 4, 4 (2006), 541–561.

[76] P. Mosley, *The Settler Economies: Studies in the Economic History of Kenya and Southern Rhodesia, 1900–1963* (Cambridge, 1983), 45.

through lenses of land and race.[77] White farmers as an interest group and an economic sector were enduringly divided by their backgrounds, geography, land uses and crop types as Selby Angus and Rory Pilossof have shown.[78] Also, the cultural practices and the production systems of tobacco differed very much from other crops, as this book argues. To this end a general conservation history of the white agrarian environment does not suffice to explore the nuanced socio-environmental attributes of tobacco and its production context, which differed markedly from those of maize and other crops.

Besides being general agrarian conservation historical narratives, most pioneering works on agrarian environmental histories of Southern Rhodesia focused on conservation-based discourses that were fashionable before the rise of modern environmentalism in the 1960s. These discourses looked at the environment through the prism of preservation of the wilderness and conservation of resources such as timber and soil enforced through legislations and regulations on the consumption of nature. Frank Uekotter designates this conservation dispensation as having been born in traditions of nature protection, the establishment of national parks and western conservation efforts that became more discernible from 1900.[79] The rationale for these conservation efforts was to protect space, govern access to ownership of natural resources and limit conflict in a way that conferred power and legitimacy to the state. Charles Maier further adds that these 'space-based' conservation efforts were a result of the age of 'territoriality' when nation states had to enforce rules in peripheral regions.[80] Thus, in this regard conservation regulations in colonial systems can be seen as one of the ways used to control peripheral spaces, an important tool of colonial intervention into control of people and scarce resources.[81] Indeed, as this

77 A. Selby, 'Commercial Farmers and the State: Internal Group Politics and Land Reform in Zimbabwe' (Unpublished PhD thesis, University of Oxford, 2006), 10.

78 Selby, 'Commercial Farmers and the State', 10. Also see, R. Pilossof, 'The Unbearable Whiteness of Being: White Farming Voices in Zimbabwe and their Narration of the Recent Past, c.1970–2004' (Unpublished PhD thesis, Sheffield University, 2010), 4. Rory Pilossof argues that 'a singular and cohesive white rural identity does not exist'.

79 F. Uekotter, 'Consigning Environmentalism to History? Remarks on the Place of the Environmental Movement in Modern History', *Rachel Carson Center [RCC] Perspectives*, 7 (2011), 1–36.

80 C. Maier, 'Consigning the Twentieth Century to History? Alternative Narratives for the Modern Era', *American Historical Review*, 105 (2000), 807–831.

81 Wapulumuka, *Conservation Song*, 3.

book argues, conservation laws such as the Land Apportionment Act (1930) and the Native Land Husbandry Act of 1951 became subtle strategies used by colonial officials in Southern Rhodesia to control Africans and contain them in geographic spaces amenable for effective coercive administration.

From the end of the Second World War, with the expansion on the use of agrochemicals, the discourse of environmentalism began to change in fundamental ways to become global, and to emphasise more on environmental degradation and its relationship to human health as problems of pollution and industrial waste became endemic. Post-war environmental activism emphasised global ecological interconnectedness and was given great impetus by the publication of Rachel Carson's epoch-defining book *Silent Spring* in 1962.[82] The book birthed modern environmentalism and made the environment a subject for government policy and global governance.[83] This book draws on, but also challenges and extends, the pioneering agrarian environmental histories of Southern Rhodesia in that it goes beyond conservation discourses to engage with these new insights on the environment generated in the 1960s and to show how the global environmental seismic wave generated by Carson on pesticides use played out in Southern Rhodesia. In engaging with Carson, the book uses Rob Nixon's twin concepts of 'slow violence' and 'the environmentalism of the poor', which reflect on how disempowered social groups disproportionally suffer the effects of environmental violence, and how this violence happens

[82] P. Warde, L. Robin and S. Sörlin, *The Environment: A History of the Idea* (Baltimore, 2018), 6–18. Also see, A. Rome, 'Give Earth a Chance: The Environmental Movement and the Sixties', *The Journal of American History*, 90, 2 (2003), 525–554. Prior to the publication of Carson's work that ignited a global environmental avalanche other writers had begun advocating for planetary environmental histories showing how ecological disruptions in local settings had global ramifications and consequences. See, W. Vogt, *Road to Survival* (New York, 1948), 283–288.

[83] See, R. Carson, *Silent Spring* (London, 1963). For discussions on how the book changed discourses on environmentalism see M. H. Lytle, *The Gentle Subversive: Rachel Carson, The Silent Spring and the Rise of the Environmental Movement* (New York, 2007); L. J. Lear, 'Rachel Carson's Silent Spring', *Environmental History Review* 17, 2 (1993), 23–48; R. H. Lutt, 'Chemical Fallout: Rachel Carson's Silent Spring, Radioactive Fallout and the Environmental Movement', *Environmental History Review* 9, 3 (1985), 210–225; L. Culver, 'Reading *Silent Spring* as a Challenge for Contemporary Environmentalism', *RCC Perspectives*, 7 (2012), 31–34.

slowly and invisibly over time.[84] The concept is used to reflect on the impact of tobacco farming on the human body by pointing to the violence tobacco farming wrought on African labour through rigid labour control, mechanisms, exposure to tobacco chemicals and other unsafe working conditions within which they became victims of 'slow death'.

The International Tobacco Context

This book similarly engages the global history of tobacco to understand the overarching political, economic, social and environmental forces that shaped the production dynamics in the past and continue to determine contemporary production processes. These global narratives are important because they contextualise the study in broader historiographies to show interconnectedness, historical continuities and change and the construction of farming traditions and socio-environmental change on a global scale. During much of the eighteenth century, tobacco cultivation was attached to colonialism and the establishment of European settlements. Its expansion in the twentieth century as a commercial agricultural commodity to most parts of the world including Asia and Africa was principally a result of the association between European settlement and tobacco culture. The crop went through various transitions in production systems from the planter slave economy during the seventeenth and eighteenth centuries into the globalised cultures of production in the nineteenth century which saw the rise of dependent producers and huge powerful global tobacco co-operations. Therefore, tobacco is best understood in historical terms, as there is a complex process of cultural accretion associated with changes in its cultivation, production and marketing, and only by such a historical understanding can its amelioration – maybe even eradication – as a harmful socio-environmental product be successful.[85]

Peter Benson's anthropological and ethnographic study looks at tobacco farming through the lens of the globalisation of tobacco capitalism and the changing models of production in tobacco farms,

[84] R. Nixon, *Slow Violence and the Environmentalism of the Poor* (Cambridge, 2011), 2.

[85] J. Goodman, *Tobacco in History: The Cultures of Dependence* (New York, 1993), 245.

the global tobacco economy and the accompanying social changes.[86] His work explores the evolution of labour regimes in production from the jungle tobacco plantation farms in the Americas to modern mechanised tobacco farm systems that still thrive on conditions of structural violence, endemic poverty, racism, stigma and economic exploitation. He delves into the role of big cigarette manufacturers like Philip Morris in obfuscating the debates on public health and smoking as well as the global tobacco-control initiative in the new millennium and the prospects for the future of tobacco-control. Benson makes the poignant observation that although many people feel they have no relationship with tobacco, the crop has shaped society in so many determinate ways that they do have a relationship – just not of their own choosing.[87]

The globalisation of the tobacco epidemic is part of the historical structural changes of the tobacco industry from national to multinational and changes in tobacco consumerism to the cigarette whose revolutionary power transformed the political economy of smoking.[88] The cigarette century revealed the drama of historical change: 'before the cigarette, there was tobacco', but the rise of the cigarette technology in the twentieth century popularised Virginia tobacco and flue-curing technology.[89] The cigarette also led to changes in the harvesting techniques from those used before the twentieth century that constructed newer labour regimes and made tobacco farming more labour intensive.[90] Sarah Milov identifies the political dynamic to the cigarette and how its history was significantly shaped by political institutions during the twentieth century.[91] The history of the cigarette is the history of the government complex machinery and its levers of power through 'associational state-making'.[92] Thus, the growth of cigarette technology in the twentieth century resulted in a lot of significant changes in tobacco cultivation and culture – that in turn affected social relations, the environment and the human body.

86 See, P. Benson, *Tobacco Capitalism: Growers, Migrant Workers, and the Changing Face of a Global Industry* (Princeton, 2012).
87 Ibid., 269.
88 See, A. M. Brandt, *The Cigarette Century: The Rise, Fall, and Deadly Persistence of the Product that Defined America* (New York, 2007), 12; S. Milov, *The Cigarette: A Political History* (Massachusetts, 2019).
89 Brandt, *The Cigarette Century*, 30.
90 N. M. Tilley, *The Bright Tobacco Industry* (Chapel Hill, 1948) 57–58.
91 Milov, *The Cigarette*. 92 Ibid, 79–85.

The 'cigarette century' made tobacco the single largest cause of preventable death in the world: killing one hundred million people in the twentieth century, and projected to kill one billion in this century.[93] WHO estimates that the majority of tobacco deaths will occur in the developing world where the tobacco industry has popularised smoking and is subtly recruiting youths through its commercial and public relations machinery.[94] The popularisation of the cigarette has globalised tobacco consumption and production into the developing world and multinational tobacco companies have gained significant foothold and secured political leverage and government support.[95] The globalisation of tobacco poses significant challenges to developing countries which unlike their peers in the western world are less capable of effectively regulating tobacco companies. In the developing world, illicit cigarettes trade, smuggling of tobacco products and tobacco tax evasion has created a criminal underworld involving government officials and state institutions in corrupt scams benefiting tobacco multinationals. In 2015, British American Tobacco (BAT) was accused of bribing civil servants in east Africa to undermine anti-smoking measures.[96] Recent studies have revealed how tobacco companies besmirch law enforcement officials in southern Africa leading to the capture of state institutions and the corruption of politicians, businessmen and ordinary citizens.[97] Independent estimates suggest that South Africa alone loses five billion Rand (approximately US$322,272,000) annu-

93 Benson, *Tobacco Capitalism*, 37.

94 'Report on the Global Tobacco Epidemic', WHO, Geneva, 2008, 4.

95 The shrinking market space in the developed world because of tobacco control regulations has been a cause for concern for most cigarette companies. Between 1975 and 1994 cigarette sales in the USA declined by 20 per cent, while production rose by 11 per cent prompting cigarette manufacturers like Philip Morris to look for other markets. The globalisation of free trade and world commerce has helped this initiative so much that new frontier markets have been found in the developing world where demographic and population explosion create conducive conditions. In addition to opening of frontier markets another feature of the globalisation of the tobacco industry has been the proliferation of international companies such as BAT in the developing world where tobacco contract farming is now prevalent. See, Brandt, *The Cigarette Century*, 449–458.

96 'The Secret Bribes of Big Tobacco', www.bbc.com/news/business-34964603, accessed 10 July 2021.

97 J. Van Loggerenberg, *Tobacco Wars: Inside the Spy games and Dirty Tricks of Southern Africa's Cigarette Trade* (Cape Town, 2019).

ally to this illicit tobacco trade.[98] Big tobacco companies like BAT have stimulated intensive contract production of flue-cured tobacco in the third world resulting in a breakdown of ecologies and social relations. In Honduras, flue-cured tobacco production at the behest of BAT between 1952 and 1995 reinforced social inequality and environmental degradation such that when the tobacco industry collapsed it left behind 'a mess of mud, fallen trees and a crisis in the agricultural economy'.[99] In Kenya, tobacco contract farming disrupted the existing pastoral economies and resulted in ecological disruption, deforestation and a disruptive reordering of social relations.[100]

The tobacco industry's responses to its withering criticism on the harmful impact of their product has always been flexible and creative. These range from sponsoring and funding parallel scientific studies to advancing protectionist arguments and whitewashing the industry's complicity in socio-environmental violence through its public relations machinery.[101] Furthermore, the tobacco companies have used political donations to lobby favourable legislative and policy decisions from governments to eschew regulative scrutiny.[102] The last chapter of the book

98 G. Hosken, 'Smoking out the Conspirators', *Sunday Times*, 28 July 2019.

99 W. Loker, 'The Rise and Fall of Flue-Cured Tobacco in the Copan Valley and Its Environmental and Social Consequences', *Human Ecology*, 33, 3 (2005), 299–327.

100 B. K. Chacha, 'From Pastoralist to Tobacco Peasants: The BAT and Socio-ecological Change in Kuria District Kenya, 1969–1999', (Unpublished paper), available on www.academia.edu/4153302/From_Pastoralists_to_Tobacco_Peasants_The_British_American_Tobacco_B.A.T_and_Socio-ecological_Change_in_Kuria_District_Kenya_1969-1999, accessed on 26 July 2019; S. Heald, 'Tobacco, Time and the Household Economy in Two Kenyan Societies: The Teso and the Kuria', *Comparative Studies in Society and History*, 33, 1 (1991), 130–157; S. Heald, 'Agricultural Intensification and the Decline of Pastoralism: A Case Study from Kenya', *Journal of the International African Institute*, 69, 2 (1999), 213–237.

101 Benson, *Tobacco Capitalism*, 43–62. For a wider discussion on how the tobacco industry has sponsored parallel research to scuttle evidence linking its product to cancer and other diseases see, N. Oreskes and E. M. Conway, *Merchants of Doubt: How a Handful of Scientists Obscured the Truth on Issues from Tobacco Smoke to Global Warming* (New York, 2010), 136–165.

102 WHO estimates that between 1995 and 2000 tobacco companies in the USA alone spent over US$ 32 million in donations to political candidates and federal officials, See www.who.int/tobacco/en/atlas24.pdf?ua=1, accessed 6 August 2019. Also, *The Guardian* reporter Jessica Glenza reported in 2017 that the tobacco industry had a strangle-hold on top White house officials and the industry had a 'pervasive' influence upon Capitol Hill. She added that tobacco industry representatives held frequent meetings with administration officials on

engages with how the tobacco industry in Southern Rhodesia and Zimbabwe created a mutual relationship with the state bureaucratic institutions to entrench the tobacco export economy and how this defended it from the global public health scrutiny that arose from the 1950s. The power of 'big tobacco' is still visible in Zimbabwe as tobacco corporations influence tobacco-control politics through political donations.[103] In September 2021, BAT was implicated by the British Broadcasting Corporation (BBC) in a huge financial racket that involved funding the controversial election campaign of Zimbabwe's ruling party ZANU PF to the tune of between US$300,000 and US$500,000 in 2013.[104]

Structure and Layout of the Book

This book is divided into eight chapters. Chapter 1 begins from 1893 (which is roughly the year tobacco production by white settler farmers in Southern Rhodesia began) and ends in 1945. The chapter explores the early history of settler pioneer tobacco settlements and their interaction with land and natural resources in their production systems. The chapter integrates the tobacco cultural practices of the pioneer farmers in Southern Rhodesia within the global historical narratives of pioneer

regulation of e-cigarettes, tobacco packaging and advertisement. America's biggest tobacco companies Reynolds and Altria are rumoured to have donated US$ 1,5 million for the inauguration of President Donald Trump. During the first quarter of 2017, tobacco companies spent $US 4.7 million on political lobbies resulting in politicians with deep ties to the industry heading the health department, the attorney offices and the Senate. In 2001, later USA Vice-President, but then member of the House of Representatives Mike Pence argued that 'smoking doesn't kill'. See J. Glenza, 'Tobacco Companies Tighten Hold on Washington under Trump', available on www.theguardian.com/world/2017/jul/13/tobacco-industry-trump-administration-ties, accessed on 6 August 2019.

103 In 2015, BAT signed a Memorandum of Understanding with the government of Zimbabwe towards the creation of the Zimbabwe Tobacco Empowerment Trust – a funding facility for youths to have access to credit for tobacco farming. The funding was worth US$ 527,000. See 'Government, BAT sign MoU', available at www.herald.co.zw/govt-bat-sign-mou/, accessed on 6 August 2019. This funding violates Article 5.3 of the FCTC that emphasises states to protect public health from the vested commercial interests of the tobacco industry and not have conflict of interests.

104 'British American Tobacco Negotiated Bribe for Mugabe, New Evidence Suggests', available on www.bbc.com/news/world-58517339, accessed on 10 July 2021.

agricultural settlements to give a dense context and broader perspectives on the construction of new landscapes and ecologies. The chapter also examines the impact of global forces such as the Great Depression and the Dust Bowl disaster in the USA on farming landscapes in the colonies and the writ of colonial conservation and production intervention. The chapter argues that tobacco opened new farming frontiers in Southern Rhodesia that led to deforestation and the degradation of soils in the sand veld. The chapter further examines the exploitation of African labour and the various systems of labour recruitment, control and discipline that were used by white settler tobacco farmers. The chapter reflects on how the construction of labour regimes in tobacco farming that accentuates social violence and rigidifies racial and class hierarchies are part of the historical heritage of the crop.

Chapter 2 looks at the post-war tobacco boom and the concomitant changes to tobacco farming environments brought by the huge flow of capital as tobacco overtook gold as the colony's chief export commodity. Simultaneously, the chapter engages the key historiographical debates on the evolution of colonial conservation in southern Africa and the roots of conservation thinking in Southern Rhodesia.[105] The debates are situated within the chapter as a theoretical fulcrum to trace the genesis and development of colonial environmental policy and the distinctive characteristics of state-led conservation initiatives. The chapter examines how the post-war tobacco boom and flow of capital changed the landscape of tobacco farms in Southern Rhodesia. The chapter concludes that the impact of the tobacco boom to farming landscapes was more nuanced and transcended degradation narratives. The dynamic of tobacco capital and high production costs was changing farming systems and bringing in

105 The debate is linked to the beginning of conservation thinking in Southern Rhodesia. William Beinart views the colonial state as a significant agent in conservationist intervention before the twentieth century. Beinart, further argues that these ideas had become established at the Cape around the 1860s where future capitalist agrarian development came to be viewed as dependent on rational planning, the application of technology, and the unbridled freedom to exploit natural resources for private gain was condemned. Ian Phimister vehemently rejected the importance attached to conservationism in shaping the pattern of state intervention in Southern Rhodesia. He maintains that the roots of the conservation movement were shallow in Southern Rhodesia, and these were applied only assiduously in relation to African peasants, and not settler farmers. See Beinart, 'Soil Erosion, Conservationism and Ideas about Development', 52–83; Phimister, 'Discourse and the Discipline of Historical Context', 263–275.

biological conservation that integrated cropping systems with dairying and beef production.

Chapter 3 offers an insight into the use of pesticides in tobacco production from 1945 when there was a huge global revolution in pest control technology. The chapter traces the evolution of pest and disease control in Southern Rhodesia's tobacco farms from 1945 and the attendant socio-environmental challenges. This chapter engages with the global debates on environmentalism that emerged in the global north in the 1960s with the publication of Rachel Carson's book *Silent Spring* in 1962. It critiques the application of these ideas in the global south by reflecting on how the Rhodesian tobacco industry appropriated the banning of certain pesticides and their controlled use. The chapter shows how the use of pesticides in tobacco farming claimed casualties in the human and natural environment.

Chapter 4 discusses African peasant tobacco producers in Southern Rhodesia from 1900 to 1980. It analyses shifting state policy towards African tobacco producers, the concomitant impact on peasant economies, accumulation patterns and the rural physical landscape and peasant responses. It focuses on the changing agricultural commodity value chains, cash crop asymmetries and global market forces to explain colonial responses to peasant production and peasant agency. The chapter discusses the various colonial tools that were employed to curtail the rise of independent African tobacco producers until the 1950s when state policy under the new post-war modernisation thrust changed to begin to actively encourage Africans' cultivation of Turkish and Burley tobacco in the Native Purchase Areas and Tribal Trust Lands. The chapter concludes that the nature of colonial policy on African tobacco producers was premised on the need to limit African participation in the colonial tobacco economy where their role was supposed to be that of labourers and consumers of European produced tobacco.

Chapter 5 engages with the politics of the UDI from 1965 to 1980, the tobacco embargo and international sanctions and its impact on tobacco farming landscapes in Southern Rhodesia. Unlike previous histories that examined the impact of the UDI in strictly political and economic categories, this chapter extends the historical projection to the impact of economic sanctions on conservation farming and agricultural ecologies. It looks at the impact of resultant agricultural diversification into cotton and other crops on tobacco sand veld ecosystems and how financial constraints compelled tobacco farmers to abandon progressive conservation practices such as 'contour farming' that led to massive land degradation. The chapter also examines the environmental impact of the War of Liberation (1972–1980) on tobacco farms, as most of them were abandoned during the worst of the civil conflict.

Chapter 6 focuses on the debates on smoking and public health and the evolution of tobacco-control narratives and how these were articulated in Southern Rhodesia and the post-colonial Zimbabwean state from the 1950s to 2000s. It also looks at the changing dynamics of tobacco farming in post-colonial Zimbabwe from 1980 to the present with the increasing participation of black growers and growth of smallholder production. The chapter discusses the nature of the tobacco lobby in Southern Rhodesia and its activities in protecting tobacco vested interests at the height of the non-smokers' movement during the 1960s and 1970s. It discusses the transition of this lobby into the post-colonial period and the role of the state in obfuscating the social costs of tobacco and the public health implications in contemporary Zimbabwe. The conclusion sums up the central arguments of the book and discusses the implications of tobacco's socio-environmental historical legacy on contemporary landscapes and the tobacco-control narrative. It engages current conversations on the globalisation of the tobacco epidemic and offers historicised policy recommendations.

Sources for Reconstructing Socio-environmental Change in the Tobacco Farms

While change in physical landscapes, environmental ecosystems and social conditions is discernible qualitatively, evaluating socio-environmental change in quantitative scientific terms can be difficult. The major methodological challenge in the study, however, was in quantifying the impact, and levels of socio-environmental degradation caused by tobacco farming during the colonial period in quantitative environmental science and epidemiological categories. This study acknowledges and confronts the challenges in coming up with objective scientific data to measure the extent over time. The colonial state concealed certain information for the purposes of constructing flattering narratives, as well as because they lacked more technologically sound means during the period of measuring environmental impact assessments. This problem is aptly captured by Kate Showers who, in her study of colonial Lesotho and the problem of soil erosion noted that the colonial state lacked technical expertise in landscape evaluation and surveys: so much that the records on early development of soil erosion and soil conservation is primarily a collection of incomplete anecdotal observations and perceptions by missionaries and colonial administrators who were untrained in landscape evaluations.[106] To remedy a similar shortfall, this study relied on qualitative testimonies, reports and evaluations on socio-environmental impacts that captures the historical magnitude of the problem. Moreover, statistical figures on land conservation, contour farming and land use patterns in the tobacco farms are provided in the book to demonstrate environmental and landscape change over time.

Most of the sources are primary archival sources from the National Archives of Zimbabwe, official documents, correspondences, reports, statistical data, minutes of meetings, newspapers, agricultural magazines, and journals. These were important in understanding the attitudes of all the major players in the tobacco industry towards the environment, the factors that shaped those attitudes and how these changed over time. Also, the archive offered an official vantage point from which to glean the nature of state intervention in tobacco production and how environmental policy and legislation was crafted and enforced upon tobacco farmers.

The Tobacco Research Board (TRB) in Harare also houses collections of tobacco journals such as the *Rhodesian Tobacco Journal* (which was a publication of the Rhodesian Tobacco Association (RTA) and launched in 1949), *Tobacco Today*, *The Rhodesian Tobacco Grower and Food Producer*, *The Tobacco Forum of Rhodesia* and *Nyasaland*, which later changed its name to *The Tobacco Forum of Rhodesia* when the Federation ended in 1963. The tobacco journals contain a huge collection of material on the technical issues on tobacco cultural practices from as early as 1903. The journals provide crucial primary material on production changes and policy shifts across time and the impact on the land and environment. The technical articles contained in the journals shed light on how the tobacco farming shaped the environment through tobacco cultural practices such as the control of eel worm in tobacco, rotation practices, tobacco curing systems, the evolution of mechanisation models on tobacco farms, farm planning and chemical control of pests, diseases and weeds.

Although the archive is a useful source of colonial tobacco history, it does not tell a very objective story of about the experiences of African tobacco producers and African tobacco farm workers. The archive

106 Showers, 'Soil Erosion in the Kingdom of Lesotho', 143–162.

constructs the colonial state and the European tobacco farmer as a benevolent patron dispensing a lot of technical and financial assistance towards African tobacco farmers to develop their areas through promoting cash crop production. These sources ignore the challenges African farmers had to face to compete with white farmers who had the benefit of access to the colonial state's socio-environmental infrastructure conducive for production such as land, water resources, labour and capital. The archive also ignores the plight of farm workers who were exploited and poisoned in the European tobacco farms. To fill in this gap, I have had to complement archival sources with a range of oral interviews with African tobacco farmers and farm workers to understand their experiences and challenges. Indeed, as Brian Williams and Mark Riley argue, oral sources are important for environmental history research to avoid the pitfalls of the top down biases contained in colonial archival sources.[107] Unfortunately, but understandably, given the huge lapse of time and geographic displacement of people that has happened across the years within these areas, I could only get a limited number of participants (seven), but their oral testimonies were valuable in understanding the plight of African tobacco producers and farm workers and the levels of socio-environmental challenges they faced. I tried to interview white commercial farmers to get their perspectives, but unfortunately the attempt to approach them through the Commercial Farmers Union (CFU) was a failure. However, this was not much of a methodological inconvenience as the voices of the white tobacco farmers are contained in the sources at the archives and the various tobacco journals previously mentioned. Interviews were conducted with smallholder farmers in Muzarabani district most of whom are beneficiaries of the FTLRP and their views helped to construct narratives on post-land-reform tobacco farming.

Embedded ethnography and personal experiences were also used to reflect on the socio-environmental experiences of tobacco farming landscapes. I have had personal lived experiences in a tobacco farming area from the late 1980s. I grew up on a commercial white tobacco farm, lived in a black

[107] B. Williams and M. Riley, 'The Challenge of Oral History to Environmental History', *Environment and History*, 26, 2 (2020), 207–231. For methodology on environmental history research Donald Worster also pointed out that the primary object of environmental history must be to discover how a whole culture perceived nature and not only fragments of it. See, D. Worster, 'Doing Environmental History', in D. Worster (ed.), *The Ends of the Earth: Perspectives on Modern Environmental History* (Cambridge, 1988), 303.

Figure I.1 The author standing in his tobacco field during harvesting in 2016

resettlement where my father grew tobacco on a small-scale basis, and I myself have grown tobacco, when I needed to. The image in Figure I.1 is the author during his time as a tobacco farmer. From 2011–2016, I grew 2–3 hectares of flue-cured tobacco each season in Centenary district northern Zimbabwe, Mashonaland central province. The 12-acre farm is part of land the government parcelled out to African peasant farmers at Jutland farm under Land Resettlement Programme during 1990–1991. My family still grow tobacco on this farm, albeit on a smaller scale. These experiences compose a large body of personal knowledge on conditions of tobacco farm labour and labour practices, cultural practices, relations of production, exploitation of natural resources in tobacco farms and general changes in landscapes and farm environments observable across time. These experiences form a latent body of knowledge that also inspired me to write this history and some of them are contained in this book.[108]

[108] From 2011–2016, I grew 2–3 hectares of flue-cured Virginia tobacco each season in Muzarabani district northern Zimbabwe, Mashonaland central province. The 12-acre farm is part of land the government parcelled out to African peasant farmers at Jutland farm in Mukwengure ward under Land Resettlement Programme during 1990–1991.

1 Global Perspectives and Local Narratives

A Socio-environmental History of Pioneer Tobacco Farming in Southern Rhodesia, 1893–1945

Virginia growers are heirs – not always literally, of course – to an unbroken history of tobacco cultivation that links them to the origins of the plantation and chattel slavery in North America and, by extension, to the larger consequences of both for world history.

Evan P. Bennett, 2012

An Amerindian crop – transplanted to Europe, transplanted back to America, grown by an English-Algonquian couple, and transplanted to Africa – miraculously justifies whites' position in Zimbabwe. With such aptitude for meanings and materials, surely whites could make their home in both Virginias[1] or anywhere in Africa.

David McDermott Hughes, 2006

The Agrarian Myth and Tobacco Culture in Colonial History

The colony of Southern Rhodesia was founded in 1890 by a private commercial concern, the British South Africa Company (BSAC). The basis for colonial occupation was the hope of finding the second Rand and the belief in the existence of an African *Eldorado*. In 1892, after visiting the country, Lord Randolph Churchill judged the environment hostile to farming and concluded that agriculture on a large scale, except for the feeding of a large mining population, would be a

[1] 'Virginia' is used with reference to two geographic places. The Virginia state in the USA famous in history as the place where Virginia flue-cured tobacco culture originated. The second is the name of a farming area in the district of Marondera in Zimbabwe so-named because the area had a lot of white-owned commercial farms on which Virginia flue-cured tobacco was grown before the advent of the Fast Track Land Resettlement Programme in 2000.

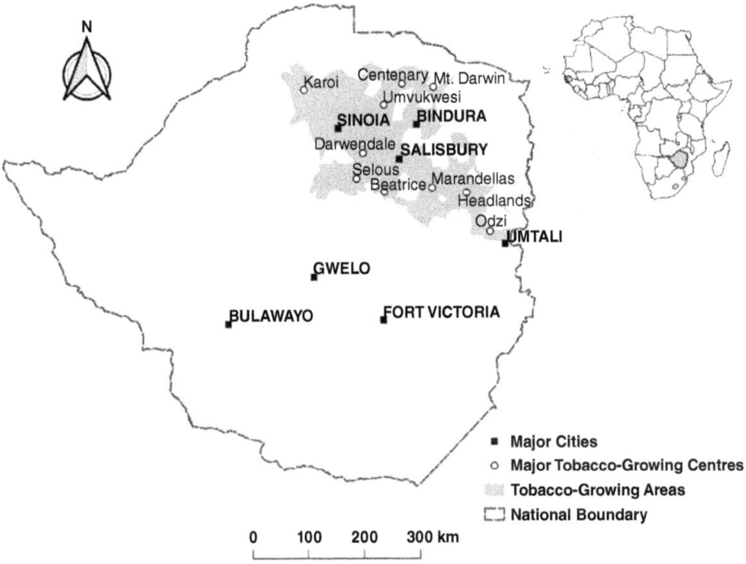

Figure 1.1 Map of Southern Rhodesia showing the tobacco belt
Source: Map by Dr. Gerald Chikowore.

'ruinous enterprise'.[2] However, many of the mineral prospectors who sought the elusive motherlode were frustrated – searching in vain for the vein of bright metal. When gold disappointed them, several turned their hands to cultivating the soils surrounding the reefs. Here they found a different kind of gold: the potential to grow the rich golden leaf of tobacco.

These pioneer white settler farmers carved out farms in the sand veld virgin lands in the northern and north-eastern parts of the colony (see map on Figure 1.1) – an area that was later to assume the appellation 'tobacco belt'.[3] Between 1894 and 1945, tobacco growing expanded exponentially to become a key pillar of the colonial economy contributing a third to export earnings and becoming the colony's major export. However, the development and expansion of the settler colonial tobacco economy in Southern Rhodesia was not a simple, triumphalist,

[2] M. G. B. Rooney, 'European Agriculture in the History of Rhodesia, 1890–1907' (Unpublished MA Thesis, University of South Africa, 1968), 35.

[3] P. Scott, 'The Tobacco Industry of Southern Rhodesia', *Economic Geography*, 28, 3 (July 1952), 189–206.

whiggish story of success. It came at the cost of an environmental onslaught and social struggles whose import must be contextualised within the broader global narratives. Tobacco cultivation constructed new social relations, produced and reproduced new environments and ecological landscapes in Southern Rhodesia. To reconstruct a more nuanced and multi-directional narrative on the interaction between the tobacco crop, the colonial pioneer farmers and the environment this chapter draws on a global historiography and explores comparative trajectories of tobacco's early colonial history in the New World where the crop first became a global commercial commodity. The chapter engages with global histories, especially North American environmental history scholarship on early agricultural settlements, pioneer tobacco planters and the African environmental history historiography on the 1930s stimulated by the Dust Bowl storms and the Great Depression to locate Southern Rhodesia in a broader global history of tobacco farming ecosystems and global conservation discourses.[4]

In explaining the rise of tobacco cultivation in Southern Rhodesia and the tobacco economy, most local historians have looked at it as a neutral and even benign interaction of 'man' and 'nature' out of which white settler communities pioneered new productive patterns that promoted expansion, development and growth.[5] Indeed, the historiographic traditions of the earlier works on Rhodesian tobacco centred

[4] The focus on American scholarship is based on several similar historical reference points between America and Southern Rhodesia. The first being the parallel significance of pioneer tobacco settlements to colonial economic development and the expansion of the agrarian frontier. Second, American settlers achieved demographic, economic and political dominance establishing what Alfred Crosby calls a 'neo-Europe'. See, A. Crosby, *Ecological Imperialism: The Biological Expansion of Europe, 900–1900* (Cambridge, 1986), 2. Southern Rhodesia was also established based on the same model, but the whites failed to achieve demographic superiority – becoming what David McDermott Hughes called a 'failed neo-Europe'. See, D. M. Hughes, 'Hydrology of Hope: Farm Dams, Conservation, and Whiteness in Zimbabwe', *American Ethnologist*, 33, 2 (May 2006), 269–287. Third, both countries have been dominant global tobacco producers throughout history.

[5] For historical works on early tobacco farming in Southern Rhodesia that offer lionising accounts of the enterprising spirit of the white pioneer farmers who, with private capital, hewed out the Rhodesian bushes, planted the seeds of tobacco growth as a commercial crop and established the industry with their own sweat and savvy. See, F. Clements and E. Harben, *Leaf of Gold: The Story of Rhodesian Tobacco* (London, 1962); T. Mbanga, *Tobacco: A Century of Gold* (Harare, 1991); Scott, 'The Tobacco Industry of Southern Rhodesia', 189–206.

more on a glorified and romanticised 'virgin lands' tradition of the role of private capital and the enterprise and ingenuity of individual (white, male) farmers captured in the glow of public relations and promotional literature.[6] This literature ignored the exploitation of huge pieces of 'virgin lands' on a larger scale than before, the despoliation of fragile ecologies in the sand veld areas of the country, the extraction of forestry resources of the colony, and the linked social violence meted on African labour in the tobacco farms.

The study of pioneer settler colonial agricultural communities is extensive, conceptually challenging and controversial.[7] The early literature from the 1920s pioneered by Frederick Jackson Turner followed an upbeat, cheerful model that glorified pioneer agricultural communities and entrenched the 'mythical' vision of settler farmers devoted to ploughing virgin lands, putting in crops and transforming vast untamed colonial lands into Edenic gardens.[8] This historiography was challenged

[6] S. Ncube, 'Colonial Zimbabwe Tobacco Industry: Global, Regional and Local Relations, 1949–1979', PhD Thesis, University of the Free State, 2018, 6.

[7] Much scholarship on settler colonial societies concurs in conflating settlers and colonial forms of settler colonisation by pointing out to the collective spirit to build and plant new communities far away from home and extending the frontiers of those communities through private capital and initiative, exploiting indigenous resources and populations. See, L. Hartz (ed.), *The Founding of New Societies: Studies in the History of the United States, Latin America, South Africa, Canada, and Australia* (San Diego, 1964); K. Good, 'Colonialism and Settler Colonialism: A Comparison', *Australian Outlook*, 33, 3 (1979), 339–351; R. Horwitz, 'Whites Settlement in Africa', *African Studies*, 5,1 (1946), 63–66; A. G. Price, *White Settlers and Native Peoples* (Melbourne: Cambridge, 1950); A. G Price, *White Settlers, in the Tropics* (New York, 1978). However, Lorenzo Veracini accuses much earlier historiography of conflating settler and colonial forms of settler colonisation and makes a critical distinction that settler colonialism only emerged as a category of analytical enquiry within the 1960s and 1970s within the context of the protracted anti-colonial struggles involving settler minorities particularly in Africa. Prior to that, Veracini argues, settlers and colonialism are entirely unrelated as the two do not occupy the same analytical field. See, L. Veracini 'Settler Colonialism: Career of a Concept', *The Journal of Imperial and Commonwealth History*, 41, 2 (2013), 313–333. Southern Rhodesia was, however, a settler colony because of the nature of its occupation, settlement and administration in which its relationship to the imperial government was looser than in most African colonies. It was administered for the first three decades by a commercial company the BSAC. In 1923, when company administration ended, the settlers were granted self-government.

[8] See, F. J. Turner, *The Frontier in American History* (New York, 1921). Other works after Turner that glorified the frontier and pioneers include I. Bowman, 'The Pioneer Fringe', *Foreign Affairs*, (27 October 1927) and W. P. Webb, *The Great Frontier* (Cambridge, 1951). Bowman anthropomorphised the pioneer as a youthful spirit intent upon winning from taming the wilderness with strong hands and building

by revisionist historians in the 1950s who criticised the frontier hypothesis as an 'agrarian myth'.[9] During the 1970s, this critical scholarly tradition gained greater traction and Turner was attacked by new environmental histories for not acknowledging the sinister side of the westward expansion.[10] Richard Hofstadter and others criticised Turner's romantic western history for ignoring the shameful side of westward expansion, particularly the land speculations, the arrogance of American expansionism and the stories of the conquered indigenous populations.[11]

Within these debates about the nature of pioneer agrarian frontiers, the expansion of tobacco farming settlements in the Americas from the end of the seventeenth century attracted plenty of scrutiny from environmental historians. Tobacco had been cultivated by the 'native' Americans long before the so-called discovery of the Americas by European explorers.[12] Indeed, the genus *Nicotiana*[13] is believed to have its roots in South America where it grew naturally and was cultivated by 'native' Indians who used it for religious, spiritual and pharmaceutical purposes.[14] The European settlers displaced indigenous groups in the growing of the crop, commercialised it and transformed it from an

homes for posterity. Prescott Webb argued that the American frontier had not only shaped American institutions but was indeed a universal frontier. Also See, G. C. Fite, 'The Pioneer Farmer: A View Over Three Centuries', *Agricultural History*, 50, 1 (1976), 275–289.

9 H. N. Smith, *Virgin Land: The American West as Symbol and Myth* (Cambridge, 1970) 251.

10 These revisionist historians include R. G. Athearn, *The Mythic West in 20th Century America* (Kansas, 1986) and R. Hofstadter, *The Progressive Historians: Turner, Beard and Parrington* (New York, 1968). Also see, D. Worster, *Under the Western Skies: Nature, History and the American West* (Oxford, 1982), 3–18.

11 Hofstadter, *The Progressive Historians*, 103–104.

12 A. M. Brandt, *The Cigarette Century: The Rise, Fall, and Deadly Persistence of the Product that Defined America* (New York, 2007), 19.

13 There are dozens of species of *Nicotiana* but the two most important are *Nicotiana Tabacum L.* which is largely grown for commercial industrial purposes and *Nicotiana Rustica L.* which is produced for household consumption and small-scale industrial purposes. Both species contain nicotine which has pharmacological properties that increase mental focus and reduce anxiety. *Nicotiana Rustica* though has a higher nicotine content than *tabacum*.

14 For the history of the tobacco plant see, B. Laws, *Fifty Plants That Changed the Course of History* (New York, 2010), 136–139; S. L. Gilman and Z. Xun, *Smoke: A Global History of Smoking* (London, 2004); Brandt, *The Cigarette Century*, 19–25; J. Goodman, *Tobacco in History: The Cultures of Dependence* (New York, 1993), 19–36.

Amerindian into a new 'European commodity'.[15] From the Americas, the crop spread to and proliferated in other parts of the world – finding its way to Africa, India, the Mediterranean and becoming grafted into supposedly 'indigenous agrarian ecologies'.[16] From the 1600s, tobacco had become an important crop for European merchants and political elites following the establishment of tobacco settlements in the American colonies.[17]

Tobacco became more than a crop. It acculturated itself into an integral part of the colonial culture defining a range of values, labour systems and cultural practices including the calendar itself.[18] In the tobacco states life was organised around idiosyncratic rituals of making the crop from the nursery, to the lands, harvesting and curing.[19] Tobacco dominated and regulated colonial life more than any other agricultural activity.[20] The plant not only affected perceptions of time, but also other dimensions of the colonial culture, as both human and material geography were affected by the crop as it determined settlements and social relations through its cultivation[21] The growing of tobacco controlled the frontier environment as farmers moved into new virgin lands as soon as their soils showed exhaustion, clearing forest and extending the boundaries of the colony.[22] Most colonial historians have been critical of the agricultural practices of the tobacco farmers, the plantation economy, slavery and row crop cultivation.[23] In Chesapeake, where colonial land was opened by tobacco

[15] Goodman, *Tobacco in History*, 167. [16] Ibid., 51–55.

[17] The standard type of tobacco that was grown in the earliest settlements was dark-fired tobacco which was cultivated within the fertile lands of Virginia and Maryland. By 1800, there was a quest for a tobacco of a lighter and milder quality that witnessed the migration of tobacco culture from the traditional areas of Virginia and North Carolina into the Piedmont region. After 1812, traders began to demand a milder, light coloured and more aromatic tobacco resulting in the rise of flue-cured bright tobacco and flue-curing technology. Bright tobacco popularity witnessed the extension of cultivation into the lighter thin sterile soils of Ohio and Kentucky by 1850. For an early history of bright tobacco culture see, N. M. Tilley, *The Bright Tobacco Industry, 1860–1929* (Chapel Hill, 1948), 3–36.

[18] Brandt, *The Cigarette Century*, 22.

[19] R. Isaac, *The Transformation of Virginia, 1740–1790* (Chapel Hill, 1982), 41.

[20] J. Brooks, *The Mighty Leaf: Tobacco through the Centuries* (Boston, 1952), 92.

[21] Goodman, *Tobacco in History*, 174. [22] Brooks, *The Mighty Leaf*, 97.

[23] See, H. Bennett, *Soil Conservation* (New York, 1939); L. C. Gray, *History of Agriculture in the Southern States to 1860* (Gloucester, 1958); S. P. Hays, *Conservation and the Gospel of Efficiency: The Progressive Conservation*

farmers between 1780 and 1840, erosion of tobacco fields as a result of soil exhaustion led to the sedimentation and clogging of streams.[24]

Although it is not clear at what point tobacco was introduced to Africa, it is generally accepted that by the end of the seventeenth century the crop had penetrated much of the continent as a result of Portuguese, French, English and Arabic trade networks.[25] The Dutch settlers at the Cape in what later became South Africa planted tobacco in 1652 and the crop became popular amongst the Khoisan who traded it in exchange with their labour, cattle and land.[26] The Yao of Malawi and Mozambique accumulated wealth by supplying coastal traders with tobacco during the 1600s, and traders in the Niger delta disposed of tobacco at higher prices during the nineteenth century.[27] By 1800, with the establishment of colonial settlements in Africa, tobacco became a key crop for white settler colonial agricultural development in eastern and southern Africa. Therefore, the history of tobacco production is a global narrative that cuts across different cultures and epochs. The heritage of the crop across history has etched itself on the environment, human relations and the human physical body in ways that evoke the need to write stories that reflect the transnationality of the crop across time. Indeed, Richard Foltz challenged historians to expand their gaze and write transcontinental environmental histories.[28] To this extent, the early story of tobacco in Southern Rhodesia must be linked with the global history of the crop and its role in the construction of new social relations and environmental landscapes.

Movement 1890–1920 (Cambridge, 1959); A. Craven, *Soil Exhaustion as a Factor in the Agricultural History of Virginia and Maryland, 1606–1860* (Urbana, 1925).

24 L. C. Gottschalk, 'Effects of Erosion and Navigation in Upper Chesapeake Bay', *Geographic Review*, 35 (1945), 219–238.

25 See, J. E. Philips, 'African Smoking and Pipes', *Journal of African History*, 24 (1983), 303–319; C. S. Duvall, 'Cannabis and Tobacco in Precolonial Africa', Oxford Research Encyclopaedia of African *History*, (2017), doi.org/10.1093/acrefore/9780190277734.013.44.

26 Ibid. 27 Ibid.

28 R. C. Foltz, 'Does Nature Have Historical Agency? World History, Environmental History, and How Historians Can Help Save the Planet', *The History Teacher*, 37, 1 (2003), 9–28.

Early Settler Tobacco Farmers, Land Settlement and the Environment in Southern Rhodesia, 1893–1928

Tobacco production in Southern Rhodesia began long before the settlement of Europeans in the country where it is believed to have been brought by the Portuguese traders in the fifteenth century.[29] Early accounts point out that in most parts of Mashonaland and Matabeleland Africans cultivated patches of tobacco in their gardens for their own consumption, trade and the payment of tribute.[30] The most popular of these pre-colonial tobacco producers were the Shangwe people who had a thriving tobacco industry that the colonialists found and later undermined.[31] The exact date for the beginning of white cultivation is unclear, but what is evident is that by 1893, a few settler farmers had begun experimenting with commercial production on very small plots.[32] The BSAC Reports from 1889 to 1892 note that tobacco cultivation had promising prospects in the colony.[33]

These earliest white settler tobacco farmers were experimenting with the 'indigenous' tobacco varieties largely of the genus *Nicotiana Rustica*.[34] However, in 1898 the settler government distributed to white farmers, fifteen varieties of *Nicotiana Tabacum* seed bought from America. The following year the Secretary Department of Agriculture reported that the excellent samples of tobacco harvested

[29] H. Weinmann, *Agricultural Research and Development in Southern Rhodesia, 1890–1923* (Harare: University of Rhodesia, 1972), 12.

[30] See, Joseph Garbett Wood, *Through Matabeleland: The Record of a Ten Months' Trip in an Ox Wagon through Mashonaland and Matebeleland*, Reprint of 1893 edition (Bulawayo, 1974), 42; T. M. Thomas, *Eleven Years in Central South Africa* (Cardiff, 1873), 180–181; G. H. W. Knight-Bruce, *Memories of Mashonaland* (London, 1895), 100.

[31] The Shangwe people had a thriving tobacco industry prior to the coming of Europeans which is well documented by Barry Kosmin's book chapter, 'The Inyoka Tobacco Industry of the Shangwe People: The Displacement of a pre-colonial economy in Southern Rhodesia', in R. Palmer and N. Parsons (eds.), *The Roots of Rural Poverty in Central and Southern Africa* (London, 1977). This will be more comprehensively covered in Chapter six, which solely focuses on African tobacco production from 1900–1980.

[32] BSAC reports from 1892–1894 refer to these few tobacco farmers during the pioneer days. They mention a certain Father Boos, Jesuit priest who grew an experimental crop at Chishawasha mission in 1893.

[33] Weinmann, *Agricultural Research and Development in Southern Rhodesia*, 12.

[34] For the botanical, chemical and industrial differences between species of *nicotiana* see, footnote 24.

proved the suitability of the climate and soils for tobacco farming.[35] By 1902, the crop was being cultivated in most parts of the colony by Europeans, with the newly established Department of Agriculture reporting that 11, 000 lbs were exported to Kimberley in South Africa.[36] The 1903 Customs Agreement between the Union of South Africa and Southern Rhodesia under which animal products and crops were guaranteed duty free exchange provided a ready market for Rhodesian tobacco.[37] However, during much of these early days not much farming was done, and land was rather held for speculative purposes as the hunger for gold drew many of the farmers away from their farms as they sought quick fortunes in gold mining.[38]

In 1903, the tobacco-growing industry was slowly getting established with about 100 white settler farmers cultivating the crop.[39] Earl Grey, the director of the BSAC, was so enthusiastic about this development that he hired George Odlum, an agriculturalist from Canada as the government tobacco expert and sent him to the United States of America (USA) for a year to study tobacco culture.[40] Upon his return, the BSAC endeavoured to stimulate production and company shareholders began to actively support the cultivation of tobacco for export to build and sustain a stable white agricultural community.[41] In 1904, 147,355 lbs of tobacco were harvested.[42] In 1905, the figure increased to 500,000 lbs.[43] The growth of tobacco as an export crop had significant ramifications for the land settlement plans of the BSAC. The sand veld that consisted of some of the poorest soils in the colony suddenly found a unique appeal. The company took advantage of this opportunity and hyperbolically pointed to its shareholders that the entire colony of Southern Rhodesia was favourable to the cultivation of tobacco.[44] In 1904, Odlum emphasised

35 Weinmann, *Agricultural Research and Development in Southern Rhodesia*, 13.

36 Report of the Department of Agriculture, 1903.

37 V. E. M. Machingaidze, 'The Development of Settler Capitalist Agriculture in Southern Rhodesia with particular Reference to the Role of the State, 1908–1939', (Unpublished PhD Thesis, University of London, 1980), 23.

38 P. F. Hone, *Southern Rhodesia* (London, 1909), 195. Also see I. Phimister, *An Economic and Social History of Zimbabwe* (London, 1988), 58.

39 Clements and Harben, *Leaf of Gold*, 68.

40 S. Rubert, *A Most Promising Weed: A History of Tobacco Farming and Labour in Colonial Zimbabwe, 1890–1945* (Athens, 1998), 28.

41 V. Kwashirai, 'Dilemmas in Conservationism in Colonial Zimbabwe, 1890–1930', *Conservation and Society*, 4, 4 (2006), 541–561.

42 Weinmann, *Agricultural Research and Development in Southern Rhodesia*, 46.

43 Clements and Harben, *Leaf of Gold*, 57.

44 BSAC Company Reports, 1903.

that tobacco was a crop that was peculiarly adapted for a new country such as Southern Rhodesia because of an abundance of cheap virgin soils and a plentiful supply of labour.[45] In 1905, the BSAC tobacco expert retorted: 'land is cheap in Rhodesia; if you want more tobacco, plant a bigger acreage'.[46] As a result of this propaganda, flue-cured tobacco barns sprang up all over the countryside and good crops were grown and prices of 1.s to 1.s.6d per lb were obtainable.[47]

The cultivation of tobacco on a more extensive scale as an export crop was yoked in tandem with the colony's general agricultural outlook that began to improve from around 1907 following the visit of the company's directors. That year, the directors declared that the outlook for agriculture in the colony was auspicious.[48] In 1908, the 'White Agricultural Policy' was launched.[49] For much of these early years from the launch of the White Agricultural Policy the BSAC pursued a policy of encouraging the introduction of large capital to open up the farms as these were envisaged as possessing the capacity to more rapidly develop the resources of the colony than the smaller individual enterprises.[50] Thus much of the earliest tobacco farming was done by big companies such as Holt and Holt Limited which was granted 30,000 acres of land in 1905 for tobacco production.[51] Another company formed for the purposes of growing tobacco the Hunyani Estates had a capital of £100,000 and 30,000 acres of land but only managed to produce 4,000 lbs in 1905.[52]

The first tobacco sales in Southern Rhodesia were conducted by private treaty and growers received lucrative prices such that profits

[45] G. M. Odlum, 'Tobacco Notes', *Rhodesia Agricultural Journal*, 2, 1 (September 1904), 19–22.

[46] G. M. Odlum, 'The Culture of Tobacco', BSAC, Department of Agriculture, 1905, 15.

[47] E. Plewman de Kock, *Various Outspans* (Bloemfontein, 1948), 83.

[48] BSAC Co. Directors Reports, 1907.

[49] Agrarian historians of Southern Rhodesia have generally agreed that the year 1908 marks a key shift in the Company administration's perception of settler agriculture as the Company became more amenable to the economic prospects of agriculture and began supporting settler farmers. See R. Palmer, *Land and Racial Domination in Southern Rhodesia* (London, 1977), 80.

[50] Hone, *Southern Rhodesia*, 197.

[51] NAZ, L2/1/108, Tobacco Culture, Application for a grant of land by F.E. Mann to the Assistant Secretary BSAC, 31 July 1908.

[52] NAZ, A11/2/2/13 Tobacco 1904–November 1909, J. A. Stevens to Administrator BSAC, 27 0ctober 1906. (American settlers for tobacco growing).

per acre were as high as £25.[53] The main buyers were the United Tobacco Company (UTC) in South Africa. In 1910, the first sale by auction was conducted in Salisbury coinciding with the organisation of the growers into the Tobacco Planters Association. This later became the Rhodesia Tobacco Planter's Co-operative Society in 1913 whose objective was to find new markets outside of the traditional Union market. In 1914, however, the UTC could not buy much stock of Rhodesian tobacco because of overproduction and a glut which the South African market could not absorb. The result was the 1914 tobacco crash that bankrupted many tobacco growers who abandoned their farms.[54] More significantly, the tobacco crash eliminated the dominance of big companies in tobacco production and paved the way for the rise of small tobacco farmers.[55]

So, after the 1914 crash most tobacco companies were bankrupted and the BSAC came to view the small farmer as the pillar upon which the future foundation of the tobacco industry depended.[56] Clements and Harben argue that it was these small farmers after the 1914 crash who permanently settled on the land and changed the face of the landscape as the frontier of tobacco settlements spread further and advanced into new areas.[57] Clements and Harben glorify these settler tobacco farmers as they 'tamed the land so today, unlike the bulk of Rhodesia, it reflects in its landscape more often the work of man than the savage exuberance or dull monotony which characterise Central Africa'.[58] Commenting on the early development of tobacco farming in Southern Rhodesia the Tobacco Industry Council also exhorted the passion shown by the early pioneers:

> The distinguishing feature of the early tobacco pioneer was his boundless enthusiasm and energy; with no experience to draw on, little by the way of capital, new growers and their labourers hacked lands out of the Rhodesian bush, and with a simple faith put all they had into tobacco crops.[59]

[53] Clements and Harben, *Leaf of Gold*, 64.
[54] See, Machingaidze, 'The Development of Settler Capitalist Agriculture in Southern Rhodesia', 23; Clements and Harben, *Leaf of Gold*, 76–77.
[55] R. Hodder-Williams, *White Farmers in Rhodesia: A History of the Marandellas District, 1890–1965* (London, 1983), 56.
[56] Ibid., 56. [57] Clements and Harben, *Leaf of Gold*, 78–80. [58] Ibid., 68.
[59] The Tobacco Industry Council, 'The History of Tobacco in Rhodesia', 1975, 2.

These pioneering whiggish 'virgin land' narratives were constructed around what J. M. Coetzee called 'dream topographies' – fantasies of viewing colonised land as empty and unoccupied spaces.[60] This reinforced the notion of the conquered territory as a pristine wilderness in which native subjects and environmental resources were raw materials for the expansion of settler agricultural communities. These 'dream topologies' and virgin land fantasies constituted a Jeffersonian ideology of progressive white yeomanry turning a 'howling wilderness' into a garden of settler nationhood in which white settlers and the land become unified and the 'native' is rendered invisible.[61] Thus, attracted by cheap land and the lure of the golden tobacco crop, immigrants from Britain, Europe and South Africa had flocked to the colony and bought huge chunks of land. But to cultivate the most fertile soils, these pioneers had to do heavy stumping and clearing of indigenous trees.[62] In time, the countryside began to change as the new immigrants altered the very landscape. Native woodlands and grass veld suffered. Veld fires to burn new areas of the sand veld became common, and at the meeting of the directors in 1907 the issue was brought up.[63] An editorial of the *Rhodesian Agricultural Journal* in 1908 complained that maize and tobacco farmers were burning grass to clear their land and, in the process, many forests were lost. The editorial mused: 'what farmer would think of planting mealies or tobacco in soils devoid of humus, yet every year we take away by fire the only means our grasslands have of gaining any'.[64]

In the American colonies the expansion of tobacco farming during pioneer days had created severe ecological problems. Tobacco being a soil nutrients' draining crop lowered the yielding capacity of the soil, and with scarce capital for fertilisers all the burden was thrown on the soils immediately available.[65] As a result tobacco farming as practised during the early colonial days in America was an itinerant business. Newcomers to the colony would always petition to move from public

60 J. M. Coetzee, *White Writing: On the Culture of Letters in South Africa* (New Haven, Cape Town, 1988), 7.
61 Hughes, 'Hydrology of Hope', 269–287
62 L. H. Gann, *A History of Southern Rhodesia: Early days to 1934* (London, 1965), 71.
63 Ibid.
64 'Editorial', *Rhodesia Agricultural Journal*, 3 (February 1908), 153–159.
65 Brooks, *The Mighty Leaf*, 97.

lands to which they had been assigned on the plea that their farms were depleted for further tobacco crops.[66] In the Madison County of North Carolina the boom in flue-cured tobacco during the 1870s and 1880s witnessed huge waves of tobacco cultivation that encroached on forested mountain tops and ridges.[67] The timbered sandy land was stumped and cropped with tobacco for a few years until the virgin fertility was exhausted by crop removal, cultivation and erosion.[68] Farmers cleared new lands on the precipitous steep slopes, and the cutting of fuelwood caused deforestation. The countryside was heavily gullied as a result.[69] The practice of burning the ground for seed bed preparation to kill insects and their larvae was also so common that during late winter the tobacco belt presented 'a hazy appearance from the great number of glowing fires' that consumed so much firewood and was so wasteful that there was a scarcity of wood fuel.[70]

Similar problems abounded in Southern Rhodesia because of the activities of the pioneer tobacco farmers. In 1910, the company government of Southern Rhodesia had hired the services of Mr. J. Simms, a forest officer of experience from South Africa to visit Rhodesia and assess the condition of its natural forests. His report pointed out the haphazard and wasteful ways in which forestry resources were being exploited by farmers and miners.[71] He noted that most of Rhodesia's forests were poorly stocked and many of the trees damaged by fires caused by farmers burning early grass and not controlling the fire, with disastrous effects on the soil and the deterioration of forests.[72] He added:

> The legitimate cutting of timber for fuel, and the clearing of lands suitable for agriculture is necessary and desirable, but the felling of trees as practised in this country is so wasteful and indiscriminate that it can only be classified as destructive.[73]

[66] Ibid.
[67] K. Algeo, 'The Rise of Tobacco as a Southern Appalachian Staple: Madison County, North Carolina', *South-eastern Geographer*, 37, 1 (May 1997), 46–60.
[68] F. A. Stinson, 'Research and Sound Farming', *The Rhodesian Tobacco Quarterly*, 1 (June 1953), 4.
[69] F. A. Sondley. *A History of Buncombe County North Carolina* (Spartanburg, SC, 1977), 733.
[70] Tilley, *The Bright Tobacco Industry*, 43.
[71] 'Extract from J. Simms Report on Forestry in Southern Rhodesia', *Rhodesia Agricultural Journal*, 1, 3 (February 1911), 197–222.
[72] Ibid. [73] Ibid.

Figure 1.2 Clearing of virgin land on a tobacco farm in Marandellas in 1912
Source: A Handbook of Tobacco Culture in Southern Rhodesia, 16.

Producers of flue-cured tobacco in particular required wood for curing tobacco, and constructing tobacco barns, as well as large tracts of virgin bushes to clear every year to put up new crops.[74] Figure 1.2 shows the practice of clearing virgin bushes for tobacco farming. Seed bed preparation also required a lot of firewood to burn the ground for the control of insect pests and weeds.[75] When European settlers established farms in the virgin bush, deforestation and soil erosion became

[74] Hodder-Williams, *White Farmers in Rhodesia*, 53.

[75] This was the common practice before the advent of herbicides and nematicides in the 1940s. Also, insect pests and diseases of tobacco were not prevalent until the 1920s and 1930s when tobacco acreages expanded exponentially causing overproduction. The main pest problems during the early days were grasshoppers, cutworms and caterpillars. Chemical control was very limited during those days but in 1906 Odlum recommended Paris Green (Sodium Arsenate) for the control of grasshoppers and other leaf eaters. See, G. M. Odlum, 'Tobacco Notes', *Rhodesia Agricultural Journal*, 4, 1 (October 1906), 268–270. However, the most common means of pest control were cultural including clean cultivation and hand-picking. In 1913 farmers were recommended to use flocks of turkeys and fowl to follow behind ploughing implements and pick up caterpillars and grasshoppers. See, *A Handbook on Tobacco Culture for Planters in Southern Rhodesia* (Department of Agriculture, Southern Rhodesia, 1913), 14, 17. Also see, E. Doro, 'An Environmental History of Tobacco Pests and Diseases in Southern Rhodesia, 1893–1940', Environment & Society Portal, *Arcadia*, 31 (Summer 2019), Rachel Carson Center for Environment and Society, www.environmentandsociety.org/node/8766.

the major challenges and environmental hazards.[76] This was more accentuated in the tobacco farms as the crop typically depletes the soil more than any other crop since it has a voracious appetite for nutrients such as potassium, calcium and nitrogen.[77]

The depletion of the soil was particularly deleterious in the sand veld because the soils were so light and of poor fertility that fertilisers were first used for tobacco ahead of any other crop.[78] A writer in 1898 noted of the poor nature of the sand veld soils in Southern Rhodesia that 'they do not remain fertile unless manured' adding that 'at present manuring is not possible as there are no cattle'.[79] He also pointed out that another trouble caused by the sandy nature of the soil was that it was so loose a heavy shower of rain always washed it away.[80] However, in the later days of tobacco cultivation farm manure and green manure were recommended as well as wood ash supplemented with commercial fertilisers.[81] In 1906, the net worth of fertilisers used was only £114, but jumped to £15, 222 in 1913, an increase of 113 fold as a result of the expansion of tobacco acreages.[82] *The Handbook for Tobacco Planters in Southern Rhodesia* emphasised that in order to produce a profitable leaf per acre in the granitic soils large quantities of fertilisers had to be used.[83] In Nyasaland, where production of flue-cured had begun in the southern provinces in 1904, soil exhaustion was also becoming a serious problem because of the increasing pressure on the land from around 1910.[84] As migrants pushed into the southern province 'less and less acreage was available', and when planters could not find virgin land, they had to import chemical fertilisers to revive their fields.[85]

In 1912, the Southern Rhodesia chief tobacco officer Mr Rice warned growers that tobacco could not be grown in the same lands

[76] Kwashirai, 'Dilemmas in Conservationism', 541–561.
[77] B. C. Akehurst, *Tobacco* (London, 1981), 138.
[78] 'The Fertilisers Farm Foods, Seeds and Pest Remedies Ordinance', *Rhodesia Agricultural Journal*, 11, 5 (June 1914), 746.
[79] Thomson, *Rhodesia and Its Government*, 68. [80] Ibid., 69.
[81] G. M. Odlum, 'Tobacco Notes', *Rhodesia Agricultural Journal*, 1 (1903–1904), 185–187.
[82] 'The Fertilisers Farm Foods, Seeds and Pest Remedies Ordinance', 746.
[83] *Handbook of Tobacco Culture for Planters in Southern Rhodesia*, 92.
[84] T. Woods, 'Why Not Persuade Them to Grow Tobacco: Planters, Tenants and the Political Economy of Central Malawi, 1920–1940', *African Economic History*, 21 (1993), 131–150.
[85] Ibid.

for more than two years, and it would be advantageous in the third year to put in a leguminous crop such as cow peas and 'kaffir beans' to restore the fertility of the soil to a considerable extent.[86] This practice, however, was received with little enthusiasm by tobacco growers who preferred to use new lands each year thus extending opened-up lands and making them in succession very susceptible to degradation.[87] Cognisant of these emerging environmental challenges, in 1913 the irrigation officer had written an article 'The Dangers and Prevention of Soil Erosion' in the *Rhodesian Agricultural Journal*.[88] In the article he insisted that erosion was beginning to show its effects in the territory of Southern Rhodesia, and several farms in Mashonaland had suffered significantly with siltation of rivers along most of the occupied farms.[89] In October 1914, Mr. Lionel Cripps, one of the pioneer tobacco farmers moved a motion in the Southern Rhodesia Legislative Assembly exhorting the government to take steps to combat soil erosion in Southern Rhodesia, since in his words 'a stich in time saves nine'.[90] He correctly observed that the erosion problem was being most felt in the sand veld tobacco farms that composed of light soils more liable to be washed away.[91] This view was supported by another legislator Mr Cleveland who observed in 1919 of tobacco farmers that they had been growing an article which they could export or sell very profitably resulting in large areas cultivated year after year with the fertility of the soil significantly extracted with nothing being put back.[92]

The environmental problems nascently manifesting themselves in the tobacco farms were compounded by the tobacco boom occasioned by the war. The First World War accelerated the rise of the cigarette consumer culture as patterns of use amongst servicemen increased its consumption.[93] The tobacco economy became more allied with the state and in the USA the Federal government recognised the tobacco industry as an 'essential' industry resulting in a huge boom in cigarette manufacturing and consumption.[94] This positive upward trend in the

[86] 'Editorial', *Rhodesia Agricultural Journal*, 9, 4 (April 1912), 510. [87] Ibid.

[88] W. M. Watt, 'The Dangers and Preservation of Soil Erosion', *Rhodesia Agricultural Journal*, 10, 5 (June 1913), 667–673.

[89] Ibid. [90] Southern Rhodesia Legislative Council Debates, 9 October 1914.

[91] Ibid. [92] Southern Rhodesia Legislative Assembly Debates, 2 May 1919.

[93] Brandt, *The Cigarette Century*, 54.

[94] S. Milov, *The Cigarette: A Political History* (Cambridge, 2019), 26.

global export market for Southern Rhodesian tobacco was given another jolt in 1919 by the granting of an imperial preference of 1/6 duty free by the United Kingdom government on tobacco grown anywhere in the empire and marketed in the United Kingdom (UK).[95] The result was an expansion in tobacco acreages such that in 1920 tobacco which had hitherto taken up less land than beans became the second most important crop after maize.[96] The imperial preference offered a great export opportunity for Rhodesian and colonial tobacco to access the UK market without facing competition from old and established tobacco-growing countries such as the USA, Turkey and Greece.[97] In 1925, the British government increased the existing imperial preference from 1/6 to 1/4. The Wembley exhibition that was held during the same year in London supplied a platform to showcase Rhodesian tobacco to UK and European buyers. Consequently, from 1925 the Southern Rhodesian tobacco industry had shifted its interests from the United Tobacco Company and South African market towards the Imperial Tobacco Company (ITC) and the UK market.[98] The demand for Rhodesian tobacco on the UK market created a tobacco rush between 1925 and 1928 as well as an influx of new settlers from Britain willing to cash in on the bubble brought in by the imperial preference.[99] The policy of the Responsible government that had come to power in 1923 was to encourage many white settlers immigrating to Southern Rhodesia to grow tobacco.[100]

Consequently, from 1925, tobacco barns sprang up all over the colony, and tobacco farming spread further into the bush in areas such as Banket and Umvukwesi.[101] The number of white settler tobacco growers increased from 189 in 1925 to 336 in 1926, once again increasing to 763 in 1927.[102] The influx of new settlers caused by the tobacco rush created a host of conditions for land settlement particularly visible in the planting of larger acreages, agricultural speculation

95 Report of the Proceedings at the 24th Annual Congress of the Rhodesian Agricultural Union held on 14–18 September 1926.

96 Report of the Department of Agriculture, 1920.

97 Machingaidze, 'The Development of Settler Capitalist Agriculture in Southern Rhodesia', 177.

98 Clements and Harben, *Leaf of Gold*, 90.

99 Ibid., 91.

100 Machingaidze, 'The Development of Settler Capitalist Agriculture in Southern Rhodesia', 193.

101 Clements and Harben, *Leaf of Gold*, 91.

102 Ibid.,98.

and the growing of low-quality tobacco.[103] Because of high prices paid for tobacco, a lot of farmers left cotton and maize to grow tobacco between 1925 and 1927 resulting in a 'startling' expansion of the tobacco industry.[104] In addition to planting large acreages the pioneer tobacco farmers also rarely practised crop rotations. During the 1926/1927 season 30,164 acres were devoted to tobacco, a total increase of 16,249, from the 1925/1926 season acreage.[105] The report for summer crop returns for 1926/1927 revealed that the expansion in acreages had resulted in single-crop systems and the neglect of crop rotations. The report noted:

It will be observed that 448 farms only grow a single crop (tobacco) and are therefore not practising crop rotation at all. The land planted to tobacco is not regularly used in rotation. It is evident therefore that this important side of agricultural practice is not given the attention it deserves.[106]

In August 1927, the British Secretary for Dominion Affairs Lord Amery visited Southern Rhodesia during the Salisbury Agricultural Show and proclaimed that the country was producing very little tobacco as the UK market could absorb as much as ten times the amount of tobacco being produced up to 200 million lbs.[107] Lord Amery's statement prompted a huge increase in tobacco acreages during the 1927/1928 season. Area planted to tobacco went up from 30,164 to 46,622 acres.[108] Resultantly, production multiplied more than fourfold from 5,660,000 lbs during the 1926/1927 season to 24,889,000 lbs in1927/1928.[109] There was a crisis of overproduction as there was no ready market to absorb the surplus leaf. Table 1.1 shows the importance of the UK and Union markets for Southern Rhodesia's tobacco industry. Between 1925 and 1929 the UK and Union of South Africa imported 49,000,000 lbs of flue-cured tobacco from Southern Rhodesia against 845,000 lbs for all the other importing destinations.

103 Report of the director of Agriculture, 1927.
104 Clements and Harben, *Leaf of Gold*, 97. Also see, Phimister, *An Economic and Social History of Zimbabwe*, 136.
105 NAZ, S7878, Reports on the summer crop returns, 1926–1927.
106 Ibid.
107 Clements and Harben, *Leaf of Gold*, 100.
108 NAZ, S7878, Reports on the summer crop returns, 1927–1928.
109 Scott, 'The Tobacco Industry of Southern Rhodesia', 189–206.

Table 1.1 *Southern Rhodesia tobacco exports, 1925–1929*

Year	Union of South Africa	United Kingdom	Other Countries	Total Lbs
1925	2,015,507	360,502	59,498	2,435,507
1926	2,629,269	1,417,349	241,216	4,287,833
1927	7,439,103	8,160,761	157,118	15,756,802
1928	4,836,138	9,504,356	204,687	14,545,181
1929	8,355,230	3,380,819	182,005	11,918,054
Totals	25,275,246	22,823,787	844,524	48,943,377

Source: Machingaidze, 'The Development of Settler Capitalist Agriculture', 199.

The ITC relied on American leaf and could not readily take larger amounts of Rhodesian tobacco into their popular brands. The report of the Select Committee on the Position of the Tobacco Industry noted this reality and admitted that British manufacturers held a big interest in American tobacco and would be disinclined to do anything to affect those interests by pushing for brands made entirely from Rhodesian tobacco.[110] The disaster of 1928 caused a tobacco crash that had far-reaching consequences for the industry. The implications of this disaster for tobacco farming will be discussed in a later section.

Cultivating Class, Race and Social Violence: Tobacco Farming and Labour in Southern Rhodesia, 1900–1945

The history of African labour in Southern Rhodesia's economic growth has received a great deal of scholarly attention.[111] The history of labour in tobacco farming, however, has received no other detailed attention outside the seminal work of Steven Rubert who documented various labour regimes in the settler tobacco farms and a rigorous African labour discipline and control system described as 'benevolent paternal

[110] Southern Rhodesia Legislative Assembly Debates, 13 June 1929.

[111] See, C. Van Onselen, *Chibharo, African Mine Labour in Southern Rhodesia, 1900–1933* (London, 1976); D. Johnson, 'Settler Farmers and Coerced African Labour in Southern Rhodesia', *Journal of African History*, 33,1 (1992), 111–128; G. Arrighi, 'Labour Supplies in Historical Perspective: A Study of the Proletarianisation of the African Peasantry in Rhodesia', *Journal of Development Studies*, vi (1970), 198–233.

autocracy'.[112] While Rubert's tobacco labour history is an authoritative account, it did not integrate itself in a broader and more nuanced global frame linking labour practices in tobacco production within world-wide theories of the history of labour and tobacco production. The problems associated with tobacco production and labour exploitation have all come to be viewed in global terms through the appropriation of a global language and a global framework.[113] Thus, Rubert did not connect to the broader global studies on tobacco production and labour regimes but wrote a localised history of tobacco labour practices and regimes in Southern Rhodesia that missed how these practices connect to the globalised social disruptive heritage of the crop. Tobacco farming is an 'intensive, tedious, year-round occupation' involving a series of operations carried out manually.[114] Tobacco requires much more labour than any other crop. Tobacco requires more scrupulous management per acre than cotton, rice, or sugar.[115] Throughout the nineteenth and twentieth centuries, while the production of other agricultural products was becoming more mechanised tobacco continued to demand an even greater degree of meticulous hand labour. Consequently, the cultivation of tobacco through its huge labour demands reified cultural meanings of belonging, identity, race, class and gender within the social landscape.[116]

The demand for labour in tobacco production imposed hierarchised social order that transitioned across the centuries as the locus of production shifted from plantations to the independent yeomanry. The plantation tobacco economy in the Americas initially relied on the labour of indentured white servants, but by the late 1600s tobacco planters turned to black slave labour and this shift was accompanied by new forms of labour control and management and a racialised reordering of the social hierarchy within the tobacco estates.[117]Tobacco cultivation absorbs about half a year of working

[112] Rubert, *A Most Promising Weed*, 89.

[113] Issues of tobacco production and labour have come to command global attention where various international labour organisations, human rights organisations and inter-governmental organisations have developed transnational frameworks and partnerships. In that regard when historicising labour in tobacco production, there is need to adopt a holistic global historical narrative.

[114] Brooks, *The Mighty Leaf*, 284.

[115] Benson, *Tobacco Capitalism*, 67.

[116] Ibid., 66.

[117] See, Goodman, *Tobacco in History*, 176; Brandt, *The Cigarette Century*, 23.

time and it is often merciless with labour.[118] Labour peak tasks[119] include transplanting, weeding, suckering, topping, harvesting, curing and grading.[120] Tobacco cultivation was closely tied to the use of gangs of labourers who worked under rigorous and aggressive managerial strategies to maximise the quality of the leaf.[121] When slavery ended, there was a renegotiation of labour relations on tobacco farms. During the twentieth century, the locus of production shifted to the household where male farmers exploited the unpaid labour of women and children.[122] Production became centred on smaller areas of about three acres on which two thirds of women and children's labour was devoted.[123] The conditions for family labour in American tobacco farms were so grim that one writer observed that women and children slept in bedrooms crowded with tobacco and the children were 'gummy and dirty from contact with the tobacco stalks, their youthful faces tired'.[124] Studies of contemporary tobacco-production systems have also been able to confirm the continuation of social violence as part of the historical heritage of tobacco cultivation labour regimes.[125]

118 The tobacco production cycle from the seedbed to grading of the leaf for sale to the auction floors usually takes at least six months.

119 Tobacco tasks include suckering, topping, harvesting, curing and grading. Topping is the removal of the flower head or the terminal bud to concentrate nutrients on the leaves. It is a tedious process as it must be administered to every plant. After topping, the shoots that develop must be removed periodically to maintain the supply of nutrients to the leaves in a process called suckering. The harvesting process is done in various stages by 'priming' which is the picking of ripe leaves from the tobacco stalk individually. Harvesting usually takes two months. The harvested leaves are hung in the barns for curing. After curing each leaf is meticulously graded according to colour and texture and subdivided according to quality and colour. The graded leaves are then tied into small bundles called 'hands' consisting of fifteen to twenty leaves. The hands are then packaged for marketing in bales. For a description of the tobacco labour process see Brooks, *The Mighty Leaf*, 279–293; *A Handbook of Tobacco Culture for Planters in Southern Rhodesia*, 20–25.

120 Goodman, *Tobacco in History*, 173. 121 Benson, *Tobacco Capitalism*, 65.

122 P. Daniel, *Breaking the Land: The Transformation of Cotton, Tobacco, and Rice Cultures since 1880* (Urbana, 1985), 23–31.

123 Tilley, *The Bright Tobacco Industry*, 102.

124 Tilley quotes a writer in *Progressive Farmer* F. H. Jeter writing on 23 October 1928. See Tilley, *The Bright Tobacco Industry*, 102.

125 See, 'A State of Fear: Human Rights Abuses in North Carolina's Tobacco Industry', Oxfam Report (2011); B. Gamlin, 'My Eyes are Red from Looking and Looking: Mexican Working Children: Perspectives on How Tobacco Affects Their Bodies', *Vulnerable Children and Youth Studies*, 6.4 (December 2011), 339–345; M. G. Otañez, M. E. Muggli, R. D. Hurt and S. A. Glantz,

From the earliest pioneer days, the major problem that confronted settler tobacco farmers in Southern Rhodesia was perennial shortages of African labour. In 1906 at its Annual General Meeting the Mashonaland Farmers Association pointed out that the lucrative potential for tobacco production was going to waste as a result of the unwillingness of 'natives' to be engaged as labourers in the farms.[126] The position of most tobacco farmers with respect to labour was reported in the *Rhodesia Herald* as being so bad that many growers were obliged to suspend operations until the necessary labour had been procured.[127] In 1911, the 'native' labour question was described as the 'most acute crisis' in Southern Rhodesia, and in several districts the lack of labour had been so great that tobacco farmers were without 'boys' (meaning African adult men in the demeaning nomenclature of the time) for reaping their crops.[128] The labour crisis was endemic and was particularly caused by the unwillingness of Africans to work for wages in European farms because they could grow their own crops and sell surplus to earn enough for subsistence and pay their taxes.[129] The report

'Eliminating Child Labour in Malawi: a British American Tobacco Corporate Responsibility Project to Sidestep Tobacco Labour Exploitation', *Tobacco Control*, 15, 3 (June 2006), 224–230; A. K. Ramos, 'Child Labour in Global Tobacco Production: A Human Rights Approach to an Enduring Dilemma', *Health and Human Rights Journal*, 20, 2 (December 2018), 235–248. Also, in May 2019, *The Guardian* reported that there was rampant exploitation of African immigrants in the tobacco farms of Campania in Italy. These immigrants included children and adults who were forced to work up to 12 hours a day without contracts and enough health and safety equipment. They were also under-paid and most of them complained of body pains and lack of proper rest. See www.theguardian.com/global-development/2019/may/31/i-had-pain-all-over-my-body-italys-tainted-tobacco-industry, accessed 5 July 2019.

126 'The Labour Problem', *Rhodesia Herald*, 11 May 1906.

127 J. S. Loosley, Secretary of the Rhodesian Agricultural Union in a letter to the Editor, *Rhodesia Herald*, 27 November 1908.

128 'Editorial', *Rhodesia Agricultural Journal*, 9, 1 (October 1911), 3.

129 The African peasant economy in Southern Rhodesia expanded between 1900 and 1908 because of the market opportunities afforded by the colonial economy. For a discussion of African peasantries and the colonial economy in Southern Rhodesia see, I. Phimister, 'Peasant Production and Underdevelopment in Southern Rhodesia, 1890–1914', *African Affairs*, 73, 291 (April 1974), 217–228; G. Arrighi, 'Labour Supplies in Historical Perspective: A Study of the Proletarianisation of the African Peasantry in Rhodesia', *Journal of Development Studies*, 6 (1970), 197–234; T. Ranger, *Peasant Consciousness and the Guerrilla War in Zimbabwe* (London, 1985); R. Palmer, 'The Agricultural History of Rhodesia', in R. Palmer and N. Parsons

of the Native Labour Committee (1927–1928) acknowledged this inconvenience with regret:

Considerable inconvenience and in some cases, loss is suffered yearly by many farmers during the months of November to January owing to a large percentage of indigenous labourers going to their homes for the purpose of ploughing and planting at the very time when farmers require additional labour.[130]

The few Africans willing to be employed for wages preferred working in mines where they were paid higher wages.[131] The importance of African labour as a raw material for tobacco cultivation was captured by one colonial official:

Natives resemble tobacco in as much as they love veld where tropical and sub-tropical conditions make the struggle for a livelihood comparatively easy, and consequently they avoid the watersheds and are found in their numbers on the low veld, and a good supply of native labour is essential to the tobacco planter.[132]

Between 1910 and 1914, the average labour required for cotton in Southern Rhodesia was 60–100 man-hours per acre, for maize 37–100 man-hours per acre and for tobacco of all kinds 356 man-hours per acre.[133] Before the advent of extensive mechanisation in the post–World War II era, seventy acres of tobacco needed a labour requirement of about 150 'native' boys.[134] Consequently, African labour expended a lot of capital resources as an expenditure item on the tobacco farm. The cost of African labour fluctuated across the years but by the post– World War II years as a single item, it accounted for 27 per cent of total costs on the farm while expenses for European labour gobbled up 18 per cent of total costs.[135] The Select Committee appointed in 1949 to investigate the reasons for labour shortages in

(eds.), *The Roots of Rural Poverty in Central and Southern Africa* (London, 1977), 221–245.

130 Report of the Native Labour Committee, 1927–1928.

131 Hone, *Southern Rhodesia*, 75.

132 *Handbook of Tobacco Culture for Planters in Southern Rhodesia*, 92.

133 NAZ, 982/T/2F- Rhodesia Tobacco Association General, 1 July 1954– 13 March 1955, Labour cost for tobacco.

134 Captain I. H. Morten, 'Rhodesia Flue Cured Tobacco', *Empire Journal, XLI*, 6 (1950), 6.

135 See W. E. Haviland, 'The Use and Efficiency of African Labour in Tobacco Farming in Southern Rhodesia', *The Canadian Journal of Economics and Political Science*, 20, 1 (1954), 100–106.

Table 1.2 ***Labour requirements in agriculture in Southern Rhodesia, 1940–1949***

Crop or Stock	Unit	Unitary Labour Requirement
Tobacco	Per acre	10.0
Grain	"	1.3
Groundnuts	"	5.0
Potatoes	"	5.0
Cotton	"	3.0
Other Crops	"	1.0
Dairy Cows	Per head	1.5
Other Cattle	"	0.3
Pigs	"	0.5
Sheep and Goats	"	0.2

Source: Native Labour in Agriculture, 246.

agriculture and its maldistribution noted the huge disparities in labour requirements between tobacco and other agricultural commodities and enterprises.[136] It pointed out that tobacco absorbed more work units per acre than other crops as shown by Table 1.2.[137]

The mechanisation of agriculture between 1900 and 1945 did not have a significant impact in changing the labour demands in tobacco production as most of the later stages in the production process of tobacco such as priming, topping, suckering, reaping and grading could not be successfully mechanised. Therefore, despite headway in mechanisation that had been made particularly in securing traction, the average man-hours per acre for tobacco production in Southern Rhodesia was estimated to be as high as 1600 hours.[138]

The perennial labour crisis within the colony led to the creation of the Rhodesian Native Labour Bureau (RNLB) in 1903 mostly to supply mine labour, but it became a very useful conduit for the supply of *chibaro* labourers to tobacco farmers.[139] During periods of critical

[136] V. M. Wadsworth, 'Native Labour in Agriculture', *Rhodesia Agricultural Journal*, XLVII,3 (May–June 1950), 234–253.

[137] A work unit represent the work performed by one African labourer in one day under average conditions.

[138] NAZ, 982/T/2F- Rhodesia Tobacco Association General, 1 July 1954– 13 March 1955, Labour cost for tobacco.

[139] Van Onselen, *Chibharo: African Mine Labour in Southern Rhodesia*, 116. Also see, J. M. MacKenzie, 'Colonial Labour Policy and Rhodesia', *Rhodesia Journal*

labour shortages some white settler tobacco farmers would coerce the company administration to use more effective methods of procuring labourers faster than the RNLB.[140] As the demand for tobacco farm labour rose, the bureau (RNLB) recruited labourers from Nyasaland, Northern Rhodesia and Mozambique and distributed them to tobacco farmers at prescribed rates and fees. A transport service system called *Ulere* was established for smooth transportation of labour from Nyasaland and Northern Rhodesia.[141] The cost of procuring each labourer for twelve months service including cost of return journey was £1.10s.[142] The labour crisis compelled tobacco farmers to adopt nefarious labour recruitment methods that included kidnappings and coercion. Tobacco farmers set up offices in various parts of the country and used all forms of shrewd means to snatch up labourers from maize and cattle farmers.[143] In one of the cases of recruitment by coercion, two African labourers were hoodwinked by a white tobacco farmer to travel from Bulawayo to Salisbury (a distance of 430 kilometres) upon being promised work in a Salisbury factory only to find out that they had been forcibly recruited as tobacco labourers for a farm in Umvukwesi:

I was contracted by Mr Morrison in Bulawayo, he offered us £2/ month if we agreed to work in Salisbury, we agreed to his terms and 8 natives came to Salisbury with him. We were taken before the Native Commissioner Salisbury and we were told we would be required to work in his tobacco farms in the Umvukwesi for £1/month for 12 months. We refused the

of Economics, 8 (1974), 12–13. The word *chibaro* was used in Southern Rhodesia to refer to the colonial system of forced and contract labour enforced by the Rhodesia Native Labour Bureau from 1903–1933. The word was used differently in various regional colonial contexts to refer to systems of coercive labour recruitment. In South Africa, the term was deployed as *Isibalo* to refer to forced labour in Natal during the late nineteenth century. During the mid-1920s the word *shibaru* in Mozambique was used to mean forced labour, and in Nyasaland *cibalo* was used to refer to contract labour.

140 Machingaidze, 'The Development of Settler Capitalist Agriculture in Southern Rhodesia', 39.

141 Rubert, *A Most Promising Weed*, 38–55.

142 'Farm Labour', *Rhodesia Agricultural Journal*, VII,1 (October 1909), 831–833.

143 In 1925, The Victoria Cattle and Maize Farmers Association wrote a letter to the Minister of Lands and Agriculture complaining that tobacco farmers (whom they described as parasites) were coming into their districts using touts and luring their employed 'natives' away. See NAZ, S138/40, Labour recruitment, 1924–1928, Victoria Farmers to Minister of Agriculture, 4 August 1925.

offer ... Mr Morrison then said, alright you can walk back to Bulawayo where you will be arrested. We had neither money nor food, so we had to accept.[144]

Another nefarious recruitment practice popular in the tobacco farms in Southern Rhodesia was the employment of children. In 1928, The Southern Rhodesian Legislative Assembly passed the Native Juvenile Employment Act to regulate the employment of 'native' juveniles particularly in the European farms.[145] The Act was simply an attempt to codify and legislate for something which was already a fact in many farms and economic sectors of Southern Rhodesia.[146] During the debate on the bill, one legislator Sir Ernest Montagu pointed out that on many tobacco and cotton farms women had arrived with very young and small children who had been rather useful in picking cotton and reaping tobacco.[147] The President of the Makoni section of the Rhodesian National Farmers Union (RNFU), however, noted that, the seriousness of the bill was clearly demonstrated by the fact that the League of Nations had laid it down that forced labour for private gain was slavery.[148] Sir Lionel Cripps described the bill in his correspondence with the Governor of Southern Rhodesia as representing a 'peculiarly

144 NAZ, S138/40, Labour recruitment, 1924–1928, Extracts of a letter from Mr. R.K. Robinson, Forced recruitments: Tome and Pembi farms, 3 February 1928.

145 The Act came at the instigation of the Rhodesian Agricultural Union's recommendation at its 1924 annual conference on the need to indenture native juveniles. The argument for the proposed Act was that most native juveniles were loafing around unemployed and could be a source of crime and trouble if not occupied with work. For a general discussion on child labour in colonial Southern Rhodesia see B. Grier, 'Invisible Hands: The Political Economy of Child Labour in Colonial Zimbabwe, 1890–1930', *Journal of Southern African Studies*, 20, 1 (1994), 27–52.

146 Charles van Onselen points out that child labour was used in mines since the days of the Rhodesian Native Labour Bureau (RNLB) when young boys in the rural areas were recruited forcibly for mine labour. This practice had become pervasive by as early as 1905 and the 'native' juveniles so recruited conducted such tasks as sweeping and cooking. On Asbestos mines, child labour was used to separate mineral fibre from the rock. In the mica mines half the labour force composed of children aged from ten to fifteen years. These children cut, split and sorted the mica. See Van Onselen, *Chibaro: African Mine Labour in Southern Rhodesia*, 124–125. Van Onselen though does not discuss the nature and prevalence of child labour on the farms.

147 Southern Rhodesia Legislative Council Debates, 2 November 1928.

148 NAZ, S138/255, The Native Juveniles Employment Act, 1926–1928, A. C. Parkinson to the Chairman Peace Committee of the Society of Friends, 13 May 1927.

odious form of child slavery'.[149] In the House of Commons in Britain the bill received a lot of scrutiny and attacks from British law-makers. One speaker who spoke in opposition to the bill pointed out that the law was being enabled and given succour by the profits being realised by Rhodesian tobacco farmers because of the imperial preference on empire-grown tobacco.[150] The imperial preference was now spurring Rhodesian growers to produce much tobacco at low labour costs and exploit African children.

On 29 December 1927, the Chief Native Commissioner noted that there was a growing entry of small children into the tobacco industry, and children were being employed on a larger scale.[151] He admitted that child employment was already a common practice and during the past thirty years children had been 'regularly employed' on tobacco farms.[152] A concerned missionary pointed out in a private letter to the Chief Native Commissioner that in his view the tobacco industry was factory work, calling for factory work precautions with respect to children.[153] Children were employed in the tobacco farms because their labour was cheaper amounting to three or four pence a day and five shillings for a month.[154] Children were considered better suited than adults for such tasks as grading and stringing of tobacco as they were considered 'nimble-fingered' and 'sensitive to touch'.[155] The report of the Native Labour Committee vindicated the use of child labour on the tobacco farms and noted that the light nature of several branches of work in the tobacco industry provided very suitable conditions for the employment of the 'native' youth and would 'undoubtedly attract more and more in the near future'.[156] In 1949, the report on native labour admitted that children of about eight years upwards were employed on both casual and permanent basis on tobacco farms for lighter seasonal work.[157] By the late 1940s, juveniles constituted a significant proportion of labour on most tobacco

149 NAZ, S138/255, The Native Juveniles Employment Act, 1926–1928, Sir Lionel Cripps to Governor Southern Rhodesia: Objections to the proposed bill, 29 August 1926.

150 NAZ, S138/255, The Native Juveniles Employment Act, 1926–1928, Extracts from the House of Commons official report of 5 December 1927.

151 NAZ, S138/255, The Native Juveniles Employment Act, 1926–1928, CNC to the Secretary to the Premier, 29 December 1927.

152 Ibid. 153 Ibid. 154 Rubert, *A Most Promising Weed*, 164.

155 Ibid., 64.

156 NAZ, S235/473, Report of the Native Labour Committee, 1927–1928.

157 'Native Labour in Agriculture', 234–253.

farms in Southern Rhodesia varying from between 15–25 per cent of the total labour force.[158]

Conditions of Tobacco Farm Labourers in Southern Rhodesia, 1900–1945

Eurocentric social histories of tobacco farm labour in Southern Rhodesia framed the white settler tobacco farmer as a benevolent patron presiding over 'primitive' but happy and contented 'native' labourers.[159] The African tobacco farm labourer is cast as distinctively better off than his companion in African townships and urban centres who was overcrowded and restricted.[160] However, Rubert's work illuminated on the grim conditions of African labour that extended from the tobacco fields to their social lives on the farm compounds. Tobacco farming activities in Southern Rhodesia took much of the year and revolved around three production phases. The low-level labour period ranging from May to August and September to November was for grading and nursery respectively; the high level (peak) period from February to April involved harvesting and curing; the middle level period from December to January was the phase for planting and field culture.[161] The work hours on a tobacco farm varied depending on the nature of the work and tasks but on average male employees worked for 265–285 days in a year with a typical workday varying between six and eighteen hours and labourers working from dawn to dusk.[162] Labour organisation and efficiency on tobacco farms was based on the notion that Africans responded to a rigid form of

[158] W. E. Haviland, 'The Use and Efficiency of African Labour in Tobacco Farming in Southern Rhodesia', *The Canadian Journal of Economics and Political Science*, 20, 1 (1954), 100–106.

[159] See, Haviland, 'The Use and Efficiency of African Labour', 100–106 and Clements and Harben, *Leaf of Gold*, 186–197. Clements and Harben narrative of African tobacco labourers is distinctly upsetting as they view Africans as primitive. These views of the African as raw, primitive and childish were part of how Europeans imagined Africans and it became entrenched within the native policy of Southern Rhodesia in the 1920s. See D. Jeater, 'Imagining Africans: Scholarship, Fantasy, and Science in Colonial Administration, 1920s Southern Rhodesia', *The International Journal of African Historical Studies*, 38, 1 (2005), 1–26.

[160] See, Clements and Harben, *Leaf of Gold*, 186–197.

[161] See, Haviland, 'The Use and Efficiency of African Labour', 100–106.

[162] Ibid. Also see, Rubert, *A Most Promising Weed*, 109.

discipline and that 'natives' understood force and coercion.[163] There was the use of physical violence sometimes to instil discipline through caning, whipping and clouting.[164] There were two forms of labour organisation on tobacco farms in Southern Rhodesia – task work and gang labour. Contract or task work involved the allocation of daily work to each employee. Contract work was more commonly used for the annual stumping of virgin lands, collection of wood fuel, weeding, untying cured tobacco and grading.[165] Gang labour was used for tasks that required intensive use of labour such as planting, suckering and reaping.

Tobacco farm labour in Southern Rhodesia was very gendered. Most of the work was done by adult males and women were not seen as 'actual workers'.[166] Globally, the history of labour in tobacco production reveals that gender roles were distinct, and much of the labour-intensive work on the farm was the domain of men while women played at most complementary roles. In America for instance the role for women labourers in tobacco farms during much of the nineteenth century was to prepare food and cook meals for gangs of male labourers.[167] In Southern Rhodesia women and girls were usually only hired during the busy and peak periods of farm work. They were employed as casual labourers during the period February or March to June and July usually only when male labour shortages were acute.[168] Even then, female labourers would receive less wages (usually two thirds of what males were getting) than their male counterparts and were not allocated rations. Women's tasks involved weeding, suckering, untying tobacco and grading.[169] The average wages for African labour varied across the years but they were generally below the cost of living as testified by the 1927/1928 Native Labour Committee.[170] In 1913, the average wage

[163] A. S. R. Richardson, 'Farm Labour in Rhodesia', *Rhodesia Agricultural Journal*, III,5 (June 1906), 537–541.

[164] Rubert, *A Most Promising Weed*, 90, 95. [165] Ibid., 90. [166] Ibid., 148.

[167] R. Beausaert, 'From Kitchen to Kiln: Women's Culinary Labour on Ontario Tobacco Farms, 1950s–1970s', Available at https://niche-canada.org/2020/08/04/from-kitchen-to-kiln-womens-culinary-labour-on-ontario-tobacco-farms-1950s-1970s/?fbclid=IwAR0VZTEf6rlV_xAmhO9b_HfYleY75iXyuOoYU74VdksNUoCovgLtI4zqwmo, accessed 14 September 20202.

[168] Haviland, 'The Use and Efficiency of African Labour', 100–106.

[169] 'Native Labour in Agriculture', 234–253.

[170] NAZ, S235/473, Report of the Native Labour Committee, 1927–1928.

was 20s, in 1923/1924 17s.5d, then 19s.16d for 1925/1926 and 21s.4d during the 1926/1927 season.[171] There was a discernible and conspicuous social and wage hierarchy on tobacco farms. In 1947, European managers were being paid between £20–£40 per month plus a percentage of net profits varying from 10 to 25 per cent.[172] Keep and accommodation were also provided in addition to the average gross wages. Boss boys (task supervisors) were at the top of the social hierarchy on a tobacco farm and earned £3.2s.6d/month by 1945, and tractor boys earned an average wage of £3.[173] The rates for general labourers fluctuated even on the same farm between £1.5s and £2.5s in 1945. Young children were paid anything between 2s.6d and £1 with an average rate running at 14s. To justify the poor salaries, white farmers and colonial officials often argued that the wage incentive was weaker with African labourers as they had fewer wants and needs which could be satisfied by other non-monetary incentives.[174] Rations – weekly supplies of food items were the most popular incentives used by tobacco farmers to keep African labour on the farms. Although the quantities and variety of rations differed from farm to farm the standard weekly ration on a tobacco farm usually consisted of 14–16 lbs mealie meal, 2 lbs of beans or monkey nuts, 1–3 lbs meat or 1 lb dried fish and 4 oz of salt.[175] Sometimes tobacco and soap would be added to the rations.[176] The supplies of rations were inadequate for subsistence and farm labourers had to supplement with growing their own food in small pieces of land, hunting game and brewing and selling beer.[177]

The compound was the centre of farm social life on a tobacco farm. The compound as the living space for working Africans has been explored in labour history of southern Africa as not only physical space but denoting a system for labour control and discipline.[178] The

[171] Report of the Native Labour Committee, 1927–1928.
[172] 'Native Labour in Agriculture', 234–253.
[173] 'Native Labour in Agriculture', 234–255.
[174] See Clements and Harben, *Leaf of Gold*, 190; Haviland, 'The Use and Efficiency of African Labour', 100–106.
[175] Haviland, 'The Use and Efficiency of African Labour', 100–106.
[176] 'Native Labour in Agriculture', 234–255.
[177] Rubert, *A Most Promising Weed*, 106.
[178] See Van Onselen, *Chibharo*, 128–136; R. Turrell, 'Kimberly: Labour and compounds, 1871–1888', in S. Marks and R. Rathbone (eds.), *Industrialisation and Social Change in South Africa: African Class Formation, Culture, and Consciousness, 1870–1930* (Essex, 1982), 45–76; S. Moroney, 'The

compounds on tobacco farms were much adopted to conform to the tribal aspects of African life so that the 'native' would have access to the conveniences of his 'primitive' lifestyle. The compounds resembled African villages and composed of mud and straw huts. The farm compound was constructed around colonial prejudices about Africans being happier and contented living in conditions akin to their kraal life.[179] These prejudices became an alibi for not constructing proper housing facilities in the compounds as 'brick-built cottages' were not always to the liking of Africans who 'preferred a snuggery without windows'.[180] The houses for tobacco labourers were poor. The report of the Native Labour Committee in 1927 observed that most of the conditions in the farming compounds were deplorable. There was lack of proper sanitary accommodation on almost all farms and most compounds had 'grass shelters and leaky hovels' detrimental to the health of the employees.[181] The Report on labour shortages echoed this and noted that housing provided on most tobacco farms was of poor quality and made from pole and dagga.[182] The farm compounds also lacked the basic sanitary infrastructure and tobacco farmers were reluctant to spend money on lavatories for their workers such that they had to defecate in the bushes around their living areas.[183] However, from the 1940s as a result of the tobacco boom which is explored in the next chapter some tobacco farmers had started to offer some more social amenities on their farms. A survey of eighty tobacco farms in 1949 revealed that twenty employed a native schoolteacher and one farmer provided a private clinic, school hall and recreational hall for a staff of 100 boys.[184] Three farms had laid aside football pitches and organised teams for leisure.

Development of the Compound as a Mechanism of Worker Control 1900–1912', *South African Labour Bulletin* 4, 3 (May 1978), 29–49.

179 See, Rubert, *Most Promising Weed*, 126. Rubert cites two tobacco farmers E. D. Palmer and Michael Howell who observed that Africans were contented living in their villages and loosely supervised compounds.

180 Clements and Harben, *Leaf of Gold*, 190. Some farmers argued that brick houses made their African labourers sick while grass huts reduced the danger of diseases amongst their African workers. See Rubert, *Most Promising Weed*, 130.

181 Report of the Native Labour Committee, 1927–1928.

182 'Native Labour in Agriculture', 234–255.

183 Rubert, *A Most Promising Weed*, 131.

184 'Native Labour in Agriculture', 234–255.

The Global Depression and the Tobacco Crisis in Southern Rhodesia, 1930–1934

The 1930s witnessed two momentous global developments that markedly impacted the patterns of settler agriculture in colonial Africa – the Great Depression and the Dust Bowl disaster.[185] The Great Depression riled settler and African agricultural economies as export markets collapsed and farmers went bankrupt. The Dust Bowl disaster chastened colonial officials over the ecological crisis that could ensue from unbridled agricultural expansion and instigated concerns about environmental stewardship at a time when overproduction of cash crops was causing land degradation and soil erosion.[186] To this end, there is a consensus amongst historians that state intervention in agricultural economies in colonial Africa during the 1930s was influenced by the financial pressures of the Depression and the ecological apprehensions evoked by the dust storms in the USA. The Dust Bowl amplified ecological concern and thrust soil conservation within the precincts of colonial intervention resulting in several ambitious conservation programmes prioritising the construction of contour banks and

[185] From 1930 to 1936 droughts accompanied by heat waves, locust outbreaks and dust storms and land degradation precipitated low farm commodity prices and great distress in most parts of the USA southern plains. The drought resulted in the loss of 4,500 human lives, US$25 million in farm losses per day such that the financial cost amounted to one-half the money America put into World War I. American environmental history scholarship points to an analytic link between the Dust Bowl and the Great Depression as both revealed the fundamental weaknesses of American consumption and production culture in ecological and economic terms respectively. The literature argues that the Dust Bowl came about because of the expansionary energy of agricultural capitalism encountering a 'volatile marginal land, destroying the delicate ecological balance'. See, D. Worster, *Dust Bowl: The Southern Plains in the 1930s* (Oxford, 1979); R. Douglas Hurt, *Dust Bowl* (Chicago, 1981); L. Hewes, *The Suitcase Farming Frontier: A study in the Historical Geography of the Central Great Plains* (Lincoln, 1973); R. Lowitt, *The New Deal and the West* (Bloomington, 1984); D. Worster, 'The Dirty Thirties: A Study in Agricultural Capitalism', *Great Plains Quarterly*, 6, 2 (Spring 1986), 107–116.

[186] See, D. Anderson, 'Depression, Dust Bowl, Demography, and Drought: The Colonial State and Soil Conservation in East Africa during the 1930s', *African Affairs*, 83, 332 (1984), 321–343; O. M. Wapulumuka, *Conservation Song: A History of Peasant State Relations and the Environment in Malawi, 1860–2000* (Cambridge, 2010); H. Hollerman, *Dust Bowls of Empire: Imperialism, Environmental Politics, and the Injustice of 'Green' Capitalism* (New Haven, 2018).

protection of arable land with storm drains. This became much pronounced as the twin conditions of overpopulation in African areas and overproduction in white settler areas were contributing to land degradation.[187] Intensive cash cropping in both the settler areas and African reserves had resulted in overproduction and a deep crisis in the colonial agricultural economies. However, although white settler farmers and African peasants were both equally to blame for land degradation and soil erosion due to overproduction and monocropping, Africans' wasteful agriculture was always used as a convenient scapegoat to marginalise African rural producers during the 1930s.[188]

[187] There is plenty of literature on colonial conservation in Africa that concurs on the influence of the Dust Bowl disaster in shaping patterns of state intervention in settler and African agriculture from the 1930s. See, D. Anderson, 'Depression, Dust Bowl, Demography, and Drought: The Colonial State and Soil Conservation in East Africa during the 1930s', *African Affairs*, 83, 332 (1984), 321–343; J. McGregor, 'Conservation, Control and Ecological Change: The Politics and Ecology of Colonial Conservation in Shurugwi, Zimbabwe', *Environment and History*, 1 (1995), 257–279; K. Showers, 'Soil Erosion in the Kingdom of Lesotho: Origins and Colonial Responses, 1830s–1950s', *Journal of Southern African Studies*, 15, 2 (1989), 143–162; K. Showers, *Imperial Gullies: Soil Erosion and Conservation in Lesotho* (Athens, 2005); S. Maravanyika, 'Soil Conservation and the White Agrarian Environment in Colonial Zimbabwe, 1908–1980' (Unpublished Ph.D. Thesis, University of Pretoria, 2013); W. Beinart, *The Rise of Conservation in South Africa: Settlers, Livestock, and the Environment, 1770–1950* (Oxford, 2003); W. Beinart, 'Soil Erosion, Conservation and Ideas about Development: A Southern African Exploration, 1900–1960', *Journal of Southern African Studies*, 11, 1 (1984), 52–83. In 2003, Beinart, however, revised the importance he had attached to the USA experiences as a model for intervention in South Africa. He, however, still maintained that South African environmental consciousness had grown from the eighteenth century within the international and imperial context. He points to American influences such as dry farming and soil conservation committees.

[188] The banner and sceptre of conservation and land degradation and protecting the environment was often invoked by the colonial state in its interventionist agenda to pursue land centralisation in African areas. See, D. Anderson and D. Throup, 'Africans and Agricultural Production in Colonial Kenya: The Myth of the War as a Watershed', *The Journal of African History*, 26, 4, World War II and Africa (1985), 327–345; W. Beinart, 'The Politics of Colonial Conservation', *Journal of Southern African Studies*, 15, 2 (1989), 143–162; J. A. Elliot, 'Soil Erosion and Conservation in Zimbabwe: Political Economy and Environment' (Unpublished PhD Thesis, Loughborough University of Technology, 1989); J. A. Tropp, *Natures of Colonial Change: Environmental Relations in the Making of the Transkei* (Athens, 2006); D. Anderson and R. Grove, *Conservation in Africa: People, Politics and Practice* (Cambridge, 1987).

The global agricultural recession that intruded agricultural economies in colonial Africa during the 1930s and drew the attention of the state was a result of overproduction that had created a glut.[189] New areas had been opened for agricultural expansion spurred by a rise in global agricultural commodity prices during the 1920s. The cash crop boom witnessed much intensive exploitation of grasslands and marginal areas that culminated in soil erosion and land degradation in many countries.[190] In 1931, the International Economic Conference of the League of Nations pointed out that low agricultural prices in comparison with production expenditure were a result of overproduction stimulated by improved technical methods and the cultivation of new areas.[191] In the USA, the agricultural crisis hit the tobacco sector so severely that prices fell dramatically between 1928 and 1931 precipitating an acute crisis in most tobacco-producing states and resulting in conditions of poverty, homelessness and unemployment.[192]

When the Great Depression arrived in Southern Rhodesia; it found a tobacco sector that was already struggling – facing overproduction, insufficient markets and a concomitant dramatic fall in prices. While tobacco exports had contributed 46.4 per cent and 42.7 per cent of all agricultural exports in 1927 and 1928 respectively, the figure had dropped precipitously to 17.1 per cent and 17.4 per cent in 1929 and 1930 respectively ruining most of the commercial farmers, who were forced to close shop.[193] The disaster of the 1928 and 1929 crop claimed the scalp of three quarters of the total producers and saw production falling sharply to 5,500,000 lbs in 1930 from a record high

[189] The global dynamics in agricultural production in the late 1920s reflected an acute drop in profit margins because of falling commodity prices, exacerbated by the Great Depression of 1929 to 1930. Prices for agricultural commodities had been maintained in the post–World War I years until the spring of 1921 but had begun to drop in 1922 by a margin of approximately 30 per cent. See *The Report on the Economic Position of the Agricultural Industry in Southern Rhodesia*, 1934. The report discusses the background to the global agricultural crisis of the 1930s and gives interesting perspectives.

[190] See, D. Worster, 'The Dirty Thirties: A Study in Agricultural Capitalism', *Great Plains Quarterly*, 6, 2 (Spring 1986), 107–116; A. Magnan, *When Wheat was King: The Rise and Fall of the Canada-UK Grain Trade* (Vancouver, 2016), 45.

[191] *The Report on the Economic Position of the Agricultural Industry in Southern Rhodesia*, 1934.

[192] A. J. Badger, *Prosperity Road: The New Deal, Tobacco and North Carolina* (Chapel Hill, 1980), 21; P. Benson, *Tobacco Capitalism: Growers, Migrant Workers and the Changing Face of a Global Industry* (Princeton, 2012), 77.

[193] Machingaidze, 'The Development of Settler Capitalist Agriculture', 183.

of 24,943,044 lbs during the 1927/1928 season.[194] One tobacco grower in the Umvukwesi area Mr H. J. Quinton tragically portrayed this gloomy scenario, noting wistfully that 'in 1928, you couldn't sell tobacco, in 1929, you couldn't sell tobacco, and in 1930, you couldn't sell tobacco'.[195] The depression obliterated all the progress that had been made in the sector during the previous ten years and many farmers abandoned tobacco and joined the ranks of the penniless unemployed.[196] The dissolution of the Customs Union between Southern Rhodesia and South Africa in 1930 further restricted the market for Rhodesian tobacco and exacerbated the crisis within the tobacco economy.[197]

The crisis within the agricultural economy compelled the state to begin to take an active role on an unprecedented level (mirroring developments in North America and Europe) in white settler agriculture from 1930.[198] Chief among these interventions was the creation of commodity control boards to regulate the production and marketing of maize, cotton, beef, and dairy products – as the state stopped its reliance on unregulated activities of private farmers.[199] In 1934, the

194 Clements and Harben, *Leaf of Gold*, 114.

195 NAZ, ORAL/QU2, Interview with H. J. Quinton, May 1977–May 1978. Also see Hodder-Williams, *White Farmers in Rhodesia*, 130.

196 Clements and Harben, *Leaf of Gold*, 115.

197 During the 1928 season, South Africa experienced its own surplus of tobacco production by 19 million lbs prompting the South African planters to pass a resolution demanding control of production and marketing of tobacco, and they urged the government to restrict imports from Southern Rhodesia. The Customs Union had afforded Southern Rhodesian tobacco duty free access to the South African market and disposed of 7 million lbs of tobacco annually. Thus, its collapse further compounded the marketing woes during a financial depression.

198 See, D. J. Murray, *The Governmental System in Southern Rhodesia* (Oxford, 1970), 83. Also, globally, state intervention particularly through marketing boards was fashionable during the depression years to stabilise prices and salvage farmers from inevitable economic ruin. The main purpose for the control schemes were restriction of production for the purposes of balancing supply with the needs of the market and to ensure orderly marketing. In Canada, after the disastrous collapse of wheat prices in 1929 which extended into 1931, the state had to assume control of the Central Selling Agency until 1935. See, Magnan, *When Wheat was King*, 50. In France, the tobacco industry was so regulated by the state that no one was allowed to grow, import or manufacture tobacco without official authorisation and cultivation of tobacco was only permitted in areas where the soils were suitable.

199 See, M. Rukuni, 'The Evolution of Agricultural Policy, 1890–1990', in M. Rukuni and C. K. Eicher (eds.), *Zimbabwe's Agricultural Revolution* (Harare, 1993), 23.

state, wary of the precarity of the agricultural industry instituted a Commission of Enquiry into the Economic Position of the Agricultural Industry in Southern Rhodesia under the Chairmanship of Mr Max Danziger, then Minister of Finance to review the farming position of the colony in general and suggest measures which could be taken to enable farming to be conducted more profitably.

The position of the growing side of the tobacco industry was described as 'parlous and insolvent' and the prospects of meeting a successful tobacco farmer as strenuous as those of finding 'a top hat in a nudist camp'.[200] Most of the farmers correctly blamed the tobacco crisis on the speculative spirit that had been rampant in Southern Rhodesian agriculture where during the boom years a deluge of speculative farmers joined the industry, produced a glut, and abandoned it leaving the bona fide farmers to face the stormy years of depression.[201] The farmers contended that the land settlement policies of the Responsible Government under the Rhodesian Party, which had come into power in 1923, were much to blame for the speculative spirit destroying Rhodesian farming.[202] The inefficient farmer had come to try his luck on every agricultural enterprise, rolling fortune's dice on every crop and making farming a mere game of luck.

The speculative tendencies rampant in white settler agriculture ruined more than the economy – they ruined the environment. In the tobacco farms monocultural over-cropping and soil erosion resulted in localised land degradation. Consequently, there were calls for the government to discourage settlement on virgin land.[203] This was thought necessary because most of the tobacco speculators would abandon the land during times of low prices after a few years cropping.[204] The Southern Rhodesian tobacco farmer's carefree attitude to

[200] NAZ, S1246/5/30 (C), Evidence of farmers on the farming Enquiry, Evidence given by Daniel Edward, 19 December 1933.

[201] See, NAZ, S1246/530(E), Statements forwarded by those unable to give evidence to the farming enquiry, Memorandum by E. C. Holmes, 14 June 1934; NAZ, S1246/530(E), Statements forwarded by those unable to give evidence to the farming enquiry, Memorandum by H. B. Cummings, 16 June 1934.

[202] NAZ, S1246/530(E), Statements forwarded by those unable to give evidence to the farming enquiry, Memorandum handed by Mr. H. Kneiser of Sinoa, 9 January 1934.

[203] NAZ, S1246/5/30 (C), Evidence of farmers on the farming enquiry, Evidence of Albert William Vincent Crawley (Macheke farmer).

[204] Ibid.

land and the environment was similar to that of his American counterpart who was described as a 'thriftless parasite who did no permanent work, destroyed firewood and took no thought of tomorrow'.[205] The itinerant monocropping of tobacco was one of the major problems in Southern Rhodesia. In Hartley district for instance, not more than 10 per cent of the tobacco farmers on the land obtained a living from it, with most of the land on the farms developed with barns and houses but now deserted, yet six years before such land had been occupied.[206] Both the long-term farmers and speculative farmers were single cropping tobacco and growing very little (if any) maize, and when they grew maize it was largely for their own domestic consumption.[207] These single-crop farmers were a liability to the farming industry as monoculture compounded the erosivity of the soil.[208]

The report of the *Commission of Enquiry into the Economic Position of Agriculture in Southern Rhodesia* declared that Southern Rhodesian forests had long been abused by tobacco farmers with the result that the colony was now confronted with falling timber supplies. The report observed that the colony of Southern Rhodesia was eating voraciously into its forestry capital and exhorted tobacco farmers to protect indigenous timber by less wasteful felling, fire protection, systematic re-afforestation and the employment of heat efficient furnaces.[209] The report also referred to the problem of soil erosion as a national question that if ignored would turn the country into a desert and exhorted famers to adopt contour ridges.[210] The report acknowledged the slow pace of tobacco research and the need for a more proactive government sponsored programme.[211]

205 Tilley, *The Bright Tobacco Industry*, 103.

206 NAZ, S1246/5/30(C), Evidence of farmers on the farming enquiry, Evidence of Arnold Pearson, 21 December 1933.

207 NAZ, S1246/5/30(C), Evidence of farmers on the farming enquiry, Evidence of Daniel Thomas De Kock, Tobacco grower, Inyazura, 19 December 1933.

208 NAZ, S1246/5/30(C), Evidence of farmers on the farming enquiry, Evidence of Mr Riley Bindura farmer, 20 December 1933.

209 The Report on the Economic Position of the Agricultural Industry in Southern Rhodesia, 1934.

210 Ibid.

211 *The Report on the Economic Position of the Agricultural Industry in Southern Rhodesia, 1934*. The first tobacco research station had been opened in 1924, the Hillside experimental station in Salisbury. The station focused much attention on tobacco rotations, green manuring, use of fertilisers, variety trials and methods of planting and cropping. However, because of the government

Tobacco Culture and the Environment in Southern Rhodesia, 1930–1945

The Danziger report had established that speculative production and gambling lay at the core of the tobacco crisis that lingered from 1928. Much of the environmental problems within the tobacco farms were a result of the cultural practices in tobacco production (mentioned before) from the nursery to the curing barn that involved veld burning, stumping and clearing of virgin lands. Tobacco farmers required wood for curing tobacco, and constructing tobacco barns, as well as large tracts of virgin bushes to clear every year to put up new crops.[212] Virgin lands were touted in official discourse as the most suitable areas for an ideal tobacco crop. Stumping virgin lands was an important routine and practice in the tobacco-production cycle and oft took much labour on the farm. Trees were felled with hand saws and axes, thick brush had to be cleared, logs were sliced for wood fuel, appropriate timber reserved for material for building tobacco barns while the rest of the brush was consumed with fire.[213] Stumping virgin land for tobacco production was so significant that as a cost in the mid-1920s it averaged between £1 to £1.15s an acre.[214] With vast areas of forested lands, cheap land prices, large farms measuring over 3,000 hectares the practice of stumping virgin land every year came with very low costs to the farmer.[215]

The cultural practice of stumping virgin lands every year for a new crop became more prevalent because of the eel worm and nematode problem.[216] The nematodes problem was so pervasive that in 1920,

fiscal stringency during the Depression the station was closed in 1931. In 1935, because of the recommendations of the Danziger report the Tobacco Research Act was passed to propel research in tobacco. This research infrastructure, however, remained basic throughout much of the 1930s and 1940s because of poor funding and thus it failed to become a significant pillar of conservation in the tobacco farms until the late 1940s.

212 Hodder-Williams, *White Farmers in Rhodesia*, 53. Also for a comprehensive reading on tobacco cultural practices in Southern Rhodesia see, *A Handbook of Tobacco Culture for Planters in Southern Rhodesia (*Department of Agriculture, Southern Rhodesia, 1913) 20–25.

213 Rubert, *Most Promising Weed*, 68. 214 Ibid., 69.

215 W. E. Haviland. 'Tobacco Farm Organisation, Costs and Land-Use in Southern Rhodesia', *South African Journal of Economics*, 21 (1953), 368.

216 Nematodes is a tobacco parasitic disease caused by eel worms. The disease attacks roots and makes them develop cysts. It is usually caused by continuous planting of tobacco in the same land and by general poor soil management. The disease

entomologist R. W. Jack had advised growers to totally abandon lands that showed heavy infestations.[217] In 1935, the problem was described by the Tobacco Research Board (TRB) as 'the gravest danger to the tobacco-growing industry in Southern Rhodesia'.[218] In 1938, a survey by the branch of entomology revealed that nematodes were ubiquitous on all soils except newly opened virgin lands.[219] As a result of this heavy infestation, large areas of land were opened up and cleared every year in the tobacco districts such that there were hundreds of abandoned farms and derelict lands, a situation which compounded the soil erosion problem of the colony.[220] Ironically, this peripatetic practice in settler tobacco cultivation was happening at a time when colonial officials were overtly critical and abhorrent over an almost similar practice of 'shifting cultivation' amongst African farmers which they reckoned 'primitive' and wasteful to the environment.[221] In 1934, Southern Rhodesian forester Edward Kelly pointed out that shifting cultivation was damaging to the environment, inhibited regeneration of the veld and depleted soils.[222] Consequently, the state in Southern Rhodesia had begun to enforce strict conservation principles and land centralisation in the African reserves from as early as 1925 to combat the wasteful practices of 'kaffir farming' that exhausted soils and destroyed grazing lands.[223] Indeed, much scholarship on colonial conservation historiography has affirmed that while the state zealously enforced conservation on Africans during the 1930s, its hand on settler farmers was very lax and noncommittal.[224] In colonial

depletes the soil to a point where cultivation of any other crop on affected lands might be costly without rehabilitation of the soil fertility.

217 W. R. Jack 'Tobacco Pests of Southern Rhodesia', *Rhodesia Agricultural Journal*, 17, 1 (1920), 28–33.

218 Report of the Tobacco Research Board, 1936.

219 J. C. Collins, 'Tobacco Eelworm', *Rhodesia Agricultural Journal*, 35, 4 (April 1938), 264–278.

220 I. Phimister, 'Discourse and the Discipline of Historical Context: Conservationism and Ideas about Development in Southern Rhodesia, 1930–1950', *Journal of Southern African Studies*, 12, 2 (1986), 263–275.

221 J. McGregor, 'Woodland Resources: Ecology, Policy and Ideology: An Historical Case Study of Woodlands Use in Shurugwi Communal Area, Zimbabwe' (Unpublished PhD Thesis, Loughborough University of Technology, 1991), 39.

222 Ibid., 40.

223 'Native Agriculture in Southern Rhodesia', *Rhodesian Agricultural Journal*, 27, 5 (May 1930), 466.

224 This is a point that Ian Phimister vigorously pontificates noting that the patterns of state intervention in conservation in Southern Rhodesia were more

Malawi for instance, while the state had imposed a harsh conservation campaign in the Native Trust Lands, its policy on environmental degradation taking place in the tobacco estate sector in the Shire highlands was one of 'benign neglect'.[225]

To make matters worse for the tobacco farmlands before the introduction of nematicides during the 1940s the only practicable and effective method of control for eelworm was exploitation of virgin lands. Although preliminary research from the 1930s pointed towards the use of grass in rotation with tobacco as a palliative, the scenario for most tobacco farmers was either virgin soil or abandoning production altogether since they did not have other crops or animal husbandry lines to integrate such rotations.[226] Although the ideal was for every tobacco farmer to be a mixed farmer, this did not work out well in practice during these days. The best tobacco was grown on the sand veld, and maize on the heavier soils. On the sand veld maize production was seldom a paying enterprise and when utilised as a rotation with tobacco it would deplete the soil so severely as to make the lands useless for future tobacco crops.[227] Thus, as a result, thousands of

assiduously pursued on African agriculture first and then settler farmers later. See, Phimister, 'Discipline of Historical Context', 263–275. Also see, E. Kramer, 'The Early Years: Extension Services in Peasant Agriculture in Colonial Zimbabwe, 1925–1929', *Zambezia*, XXIV, ii (1997), 159–179; McGregor, 'Conservation Control and Ecological Change', 257–279. This strand of thought though is at variance with discourses popularized by William Beinart and Richard Grove that locate origins of the application of conservation thinking within white settler agricultural ecosystem at the Cape. See, Richard Grove *Green Imperialism: Colonial Expansion, Tropical Island Edens and the Origins of Environmentalism, 1600–1860* (Cambridge, 1996); R. Grove, 'Scottish Missionaries, Evangelical Discourses and the Origins of Conservation Thinking in Southern Africa, 1820–1900', *Journal of Southern African Studies*, 15, 2 (1989), 163–184.

225 Wapulumuka, *Conservation Song*, 118.

226 Tobacco experimental trials at the Hillside station in Salisbury had revealed the fundamental value of incorporating grasses and legumes in tobacco rotations over a five-year rotation cycle. The first plantings had tobacco on virgin land and produced 366 lbs per acre yield. The second year the land was planted to Sudan grass for hay and reverted to tobacco in the third year resulting in an increased yield per acre of 418 lbs. The fourth-year green manuring with velvet beans was introduced before tobacco was planted in the fifth season and this resulted in increased yields to 545 lbs per acre. See E. A. K. Harvey, 'Tobacco Experimental Station, Salisbury; Report of General Crop Experiments', *Rhodesia Agricultural Journal*, 28, 9 (September 1931), 919–926.

227 African Explosives and Industries Limited, 'Rhodes Grass for the Rhodesian Tobacco Grower', *Rhodesia Agricultural Journal*, 32, 10 (October 1935), 700.

acres of land had to be abandoned after one-year cropping for want of a suitable rotation.

The crisis of overproduction and speculation also created other pest and disease problems in the tobacco farms particularly from the late 1920s as production spread into new areas. In 1932, *Leaf curl* the first insect borne disease in Southern Rhodesia was reported by entomologist H. H. Storey who identified the vector as white flies.[228] The culture of nomadic farming prevalent in tobacco farms meant that tobacco stalks and untidy fields were left unattended perpetually and as breeding points for vectors to spread. These unhygienic practices prompted the state to pass the Tobacco Pest Suppression Act in 1933 that made it mandatory for tobacco farmers to destroy their residual tobacco stalks by 1 August of each year.[229] However, unhygienic cultural practices continued leading to more disease outbreaks. In 1938, *Rosette* disease caused by aphids occurred in Umvukwesi.[230] The diseases caused 'bushy top' – the dwarfing and stunting of growth of tobacco plants.[231] The result was severe losses to most tobacco farmers. From 1937 to 1944 there was a huge outbreak of *Alternaria* (or brown spot disease, a fungal infection affecting the lower and mature tobacco leaves) in most tobacco-producing areas of Southern Rhodesia.[232] From 1937 to 1940 heavy losses had followed in all parts of the colony amounting to 3.5 million lbs of tobacco.[233] As a result of the prevalence of these tobacco diseases field-spraying experiments were conducted on a larger scale and the amount of fungicides and arsenic pesticides such as lead arsenate used annually for seed bed and field spraying steadily increased from around 1939.[234] Arsenic contaminates the environment, poisons the soil, and causes sickness and death to animals and humans.[235] The chemical contamination of the environment as a result

228 H. H. Storey, 'Leaf Curl of Tobacco in Southern Rhodesia', *Rhodesia Agricultural Journal*, 29, 3 (March 1932), 186–192.

229 Clements and Harben, *Leaf of Gold*, 118.

230 G. M. Wickens, 'A New and Serious Disease of Tobacco in Southern Rhodesia', *Rhodesia Agricultural Journal*, 35, 3 (March 1938), 181–182.

231 Ibid. 232 NAZ, S1828/PP/20A, Tobacco Alternaria, 1937–1944.

233 Ibid.

234 NAZ, S25101/1, TRB Tobacco pest spraying scheme, J. C. F. Hopkins, 'Field Spraying and the Control of Leaf Diseases on Tobacco: Review Report'.

235 See, R. Carson, *Silent Spring*, (London, 1963), 15; H. S. Satterlee, 'The Problems of Arsenic in American Cigarette Tobacco', *New England Journal of Medicine*, 254, (1956), 1149–1154. For a further discussion on tobacco production and chemical contamination of the environment see E. Doro,

of tobacco field sprays is more comprehensively covered later in Chapter 3 of this book. However, various veterinary reports and reports from the branch of chemistry between 1932 and 1938 record livestock and wildlife mortality due to arsenic poisoning.[236]

The other environmental problem that arose with tobacco farming during the 1930s was soil erosion. Soil conservation had also become a concern for the colonial state in Southern Rhodesia during the 1930s.[237] There is consensus that before 1930 soil erosion and conservation were not key priorities of the colonial state, and 'rapacious settler farming' dominated the agricultural landscape.[238] However, the institutionalisation of these ideas is subject to much critical scholarly debate. Beinart locates the South African Drought Investigation Committee Report of 1921 as a key influence in shaping the development of soil-conservation ideas not only in Southern Rhodesia, but in the whole of the subregion.[239] Ian Phimister, on the other hand, is

'An Environmental History of Tobacco Pests and Diseases in Southern Rhodesia, 1893–1940'; E. Doro and S. Swart, 'A Silenced Spring? Exploring Africa's "Rachel Carson Moment": A Socio-environmental History of the Pesticides in Tobacco Production in Southern Rhodesia, 1945–80', *International Review of Environmental History*, 5, 2 (2019), 5–39.

236 See, Annual Report, Branch of Chemistry 1932, 1934; 'Poisoning by Arsenic: Warning to Stock Owners', *Rhodesia Agricultural Journal*, 31,1, (January 1934), 11–13; A. D Husband and J. F, Duguid, 'The Toxicity to Grazing Animals of Grass Sprayed with a Solution of Sodium Arsenite', *Rhodesia Agricultural Journal*, 31, 1 (January 1934), 25–39.

237 Maravanyika's Ph.D. thesis offers a rigorous discussion on the evolution of the soil erosion and conservation ideology in Southern Rhodesia's agrarian sector from the 1930s and links it with developments in other parts of the world particularly the United States. The Dust Bowl Storms had ruined much of the agricultural lands in the 1930s and prompted several state-aided conservation programmes during the Depression era. While Maravanyika provides a whole survey of the problem on the settler farms generally, this chapter focuses on the tobacco farm environments where a unique set of production circumstances prevailed such as the huge profit margins in tobacco farming which stultified a speculative element unseen in all the other crops, and the practice of stumping virgin lands every year for wood fuel and new lands to grow tobacco.

238 Elliot, 'Soil Erosion and Conservation in Zimbabwe', 54; Beinart, 'The Politics of Colonial Conservation', 143–162.

239 Beinart, 'The Politics of Colonial Conservation', 143–162. Beinart argues that in the late 1930s significant progress in construction of contour ridges had taken place such that a quarter of all settler land was contour ridged, a figure he reckons higher than had been achieved in South Africa during the same time. The length of land terraces constructed annually rose from 76 miles in 1929 to 1,742 miles in 1938. At the same time the area of land protected by terraces increased from 2,280 acres annually to 43,550 acres over the same period.

highly critical of Beinart's modest appreciation of state conservation efforts in settler farming in the 1930s and posits that significant progress only happened from 1938 when the pressures of the depression had ceded.[240] While Beinart points to the significant progress in conservation works in Southern Rhodesia, there were several production factors that militated against the effectiveness of this practice and its institutionalisation on the tobacco farms. First, tobacco was cultivated in the flimsy sandy loamy granitic soils that were very susceptible to sheet erosion. Even with contour ridges, the traditional vertical ridge ploughing for tobacco would always catalyse the erosion problem. The straight and vertical tobacco rows which were generally adopted by farmers departed from the curve of the contour with the ridge not having the necessary ability to hold and pass on water. This resulted in a concentration of silt laden run-off into the contour ridges, choking and breaking them. The conservation officer from the Irrigation Department, noted of this practice in 1945:

> Recently I visited a farm where this was causing a fantastic amount of erosion, though the land was contour ridged. To have flattened the slope of the tobacco rows to a safe gradient would have been impossible, owing to the irregularity of the ground caused by old erosion and in despair I remarked to the farmer, 'if you don't get rid of your ridging ploughs, you will get rid of your farm...'[241]

Most tobacco lands were badly ploughed down by ridging ploughs which left behind deep furrows that made most fields vulnerable to an extended amount of gully erosion.[242] But, even then the practice of building conservation works was generally uncommon amongst

Cumulatively, by 1938, 4,355 miles of terracing had been constructed – protecting 114,190 acres of land. See Report of the Natural Resources Commission of Enquiry, 1938.

240 Phimister, 'Discourse and the Discipline of Historical Context', 263–275.

241 NAZ, S1828/PP60, Conservation officer to irrigation department, ridging ploughs for erosion, 19 March 1945.

242 In the USA, beginning from the early 1930s the department of Soil Conservation Service had replaced straight contour rows with contoured crop rows in what was termed 'crazy quilt farming' or 'contour farming'. This slowed water run-off and decreased both the severity of washing away topsoil and gullying. Contour farming was later popularised in Southern Rhodesia from1953 by a technical bulletin on erosion called 'Conservation Farming for the Tobacco Grower' that advised against constructing ridges parallel to the contours.

tobacco farmers and this was pointed out by various agricultural conservation officials and reports from the late 1930s. Between 1931 and 1937, the colonial state had erected a rudimentary national soil erosion bureaucracy that included district conservation boards, conservation advisory councils and a soil erosion propaganda subcommittee.

Members of the Soil Erosion Propaganda Subcommittee pointed out in 1937 that the soil erosion problem was heavily linked to the rapacious farming practices of the settler tobacco growers. In their quest to maximise profits, they had adopted continuous and irresponsible cropping which was impoverishing the soil. They warned:

> In Mashonaland the areas of rich virgin lands which have been opened up since the days of the early settlers have been mined and the soil impoverished by continuous cropping and erosion until many of the lands have been abandoned as useless ... in other cases farmers have continued to flog the dead horse by trying to extract a living from an impoverished soil owing to the reduced yield, the acreage is extended in order to obtain a larger crop, and this process continues whether prices are low or high.[243]

In Nyasaland, white settler tobacco farmers were equally irresponsible and reckless with the control of erosion in their farms. When Southern Rhodesian irrigation engineer W. E. Haviland toured Nyasaland in 1930, he was baffled to see many tobacco farms in a state of disrepair as the estate owners did not use any methods to control erosion.[244] The lack of a robust thrust in state conservation intervention within the tobacco farming sector in both Southern Rhodesia and Nyasaland stands in contrast with the USA during the same time where the state had to assuage the financial turbulence and the crisis of overproduction with a coterie of measures that integrated production control, price support and soil conservation.[245] In 1938, the report of the Natural

243 D. Aylen and R. H. Roberts, 'Soil Erosion Technical Bulletin', *Rhodesia Agricultural Journal*, (February 1937), 64.

244 Wapulumuka, *Conservation songs*, 123.

245 The New Deal through the Agricultural Adjustment Act (AAA) introduced tobacco production controls through the Voluntary Domestic Allotment Plan that established a quota system in which farmers could only cultivate tobacco on a portion of their lands, plant soil-building crops and practice soil conservation in exchange for guaranteed prices. The soil conservation programmes under the New Deal created new and improved agricultural landscapes in the tobacco farming areas in the USA. See Goodman, *Tobacco in History*, 197. A. J. Badger, *Prosperity Road: The New Deal, Tobacco, and North Carolina* (Chapel Hill, 1980); Milov, *The Cigarette*, 62.

Resources Commission of Enquiry confirmed the importance of tobacco to the colony as an export crop whose receipts for the 1936/1937 season amounted close to £1 million, creating employment for many people and making possible the utilisation of large areas of the sand veld unsuitable for maize farming.[246] However, the report deplored the restrained pace of conservation amongst tobacco growers, amongst whom anti-erosion works had made the least progress because of the prevalence of eel worm infestations in old tobacco lands:

> A certain amount of indifference as to what happens in the meantime might result in the case of a careless farmer or in one attempting to plant an excessive area, but a doubt as to the effects of contour ridging on the eelworm menace possibly accounts for a hesitation on the part of many to spend on a project which might after all be found to be disadvantageous in another direction.[247]

The report further highlighted that through bad management over-cutting of indigenous timber had taken place in the tobacco farms to such an extent that with the rate of cutting that existed native timber supplies would be exhausted and there would be a break in the tobacco industry for probably fifteen to twenty years.[248] This situation had reached a climax in the Umvukwesi area where 30 per cent of the tobacco growers had been compelled to acquire new farms abandoning old ones as a result of depletion of timber resources.[249] In fact, in 1930, an editorial in the *Rhodesia Agricultural Journal* pointed out the imperative for re-afforestation within the district to make good the wastage caused by the cutting of timber by tobacco farmers as there was a distinctive danger of 'a timber famine' if remedial measures were not taken.[250] A worried conservator of forests buttressed the need for

[246] NAZ, S2496/1080/1/5, Report of the Commission of Enquiry into the Conservation of the Colony's Natural Resources, 1939. The Natural Resources Commission was set up in 1938 under the Chairmanship of Water Court Judge Robert McIlwaine. The objective of the committee was to investigate how the resources of the colony were being destroyed by soil erosion, destruction of trees, grasses, other vegetation in the course of mining and improper and undesirable methods of farming and land use. The Commission gathered evidence across a wide spectrum of settler farmers and other entrepreneurs on the land, and compiled a report.

[247] Ibid. [248] Ibid. [249] Ibid.

[250] 'The Umvukwesi Farmers and Tobacco Growers Association', *Rhodesian Agricultural Journal*, 27, 8 (1930), 793.

tobacco growers to adopt afforestation programmes with exotic *Eucalyptus* trees:

We are continuously getting at the tobacco farmer to look upon the product of fuel as a necessary part of ordinary tobacco operations. After all, if he has not got the fuel, he cannot cure his tobacco, and if he has not got the sufficient indigenous timber to give him his annual requirements, then afforestation with fast growing trees is needed. The situation for the tobacco grower is much simpler . . . because it is a fact that the tobacco-growing areas can grow trees.[251]

By 1942, the state was facing an acute food deficit resulting from shortages of fertilisers and labour caused by overproduction of tobacco. Food production committees had to be set up to allocate resources towards food production.[252] In 1942, the Natural Resources Board (NRB)[253] instituted an enquiry into the conditions of agriculture in the colony that were creating food shortages.[254] The speculative tendency amongst tobacco growers was pointed out as contributing a great deal to land degradation. Captain A. D. Collins of Tsungwesi Farm in Waterfalls revealed this predatory brand of rapacious farming where land was treated with high-handed and peremptory carelessness, exploiting it for private aggrandisement by mercenary tobacco farmers:

At Inyazura you will see an outstanding example of what I call 'the get rich quick tobacco grower'. You will see it from the Claires Estate to the Inyazura river. Every one of these farmers have acquired more land and the same thing is happening there. There is no doubt whatsoever that it has to be stopped otherwise this country has only another five or six years of tobacco life in front of it . . . the whole of the Claire Estates has been taken up now.[255]

In the Odzi district a similar pattern was also developing where tobacco farmers were fast encroaching into bigger areas with the majority of

[251] Report of the Commission of Enquiry into the Conservation of the Colony's Natural Resources.

[252] See, Phimister, 'Discourse and the Discipline of Historical Context', 263–275. Also, NAZ, S482/20/42, Food Production Committees, FPC Meeting, 23 March 1942.

[253] The Natural Resources Board (NRB) was set up in 1941 by the Natural Resources Act to exercise general supervision over the colony's natural resources.

[254] The Enquiry was known as the Natural Resources Board Farming Enquiry.

[255] NAZ, S987/1, Oral evidence; Farming Enquiry, Evidence by Captain A. D. Collins, 25 July 1942.

them 'merely exploiting the land', and if they had two or three good years of growing tobacco, they had no further use for that land.[256] In the Umvukwesi district, mass production of tobacco and the wastage of land had created farmers in the area who denuded the land, timber and then just left the ground to be washed out.[257] The appalling situation for the tobacco farmlands was summarised by one farmer Jacobus Petrus De Kock:

> Speaking not from the tobacco market point of view, but from the tobacco soil point of view ... I am afraid tobacco growers are mining their land. I have been in the district for 23 years and I have seen what happened here. I would prevent any tobacco grower if I had the power from planting unless the soil was contour ridged ... We grow tobacco mostly on the ridges, the crop is reaped, and the tobacco stalks are pulled out, but land is left unploughed for years afterwards and that encourages erosion. I have preached that to tobacco growers for many years, but it does not carry much weight with them. They just want to make as much money as possible with no eye to the future.[258]

State Intervention in Tobacco Production and Control, 1935–1945

The problem of tobacco overproduction had reared its ugly head again in 1934 when production totalled 26,792,092 lbs – provoking *déjà vu* in farmers, reminding them of the disastrous record crop of 1928.[259] Their fears of another slump drove the state's imperative for production control during the 1935–1936 season. The RTA observed that the main cause of the depression enveloping the industry and amounting almost to actual insolvency was the fact that growers were producing more tobacco than the market could handle.[260] The Association maintained that the aim was to place the industry on a sound economic

256 NAZ, S987/1, Oral evidence; Farming Enquiry, Evidence by J. T. Mungle, 24 July 1942.

257 NAZ, S987/1, Oral evidence; Farming Enquiry, Evidence of Mr George Grey, 26 June 1942.

258 NAZ, S987/1, Oral evidence; Farming Enquiry, Evidence by Jacobus Petrus De Kock, 16 July 1942.

259 Clements and Harben, *Leaf of Gold*, 115.

260 NAZ, S1194/1217, Tobacco: Restriction of output, 1934–1935, Consideration for the production and disposal of the 1934/1935 tobacco crop, Department of the Prime Minister, 19 May 1934.

basis, eliminate the fear of general insolvency on the one hand and the gambling element on the other hand:[261]

> The only person who would wish or could afford to take the gamble of producing more than his share would be the speculator, the chancer or the man of big money, and what might be a big gamble to him would be a very definite harm to the bona fide settled tobacco grower, and it is the economic stability of this type of producer which it is our very special business to safeguard.[262]

The RTA considered it necessary to reconstruct the industry and proposed for legislation dealing with production control, which would entail holding from the market all increases of production by growers over their 1933/1934 crops. It also proposed the establishment of an Appeal's Board where hardships would clearly be sustained by individuals by taking as a measure their production during the 1933/1934 season.[263] The Tobacco Quota Commission of Enquiry into applications from tobacco growers for increased production during the 1934/1935 season was appointed by the Ministry of Agriculture under the Chairmanship of Mr William Brown.[264] The RTA placed before the committee principles to be adopted regarding the quota. The Quota Commission received applications from growers, allocated quotas to every grower and made recommendations to the Ministry of Agriculture of the viable national quota capable of meeting facilities and market requirements.[265]

The principle of production control that the state and the RTA were pushing through had been adopted in the USA to control overproduction and had been effective in allaying some of the production and marketing fears brought forth by the Great Depression. In 1930, Governor of the tobacco-growing state of North Carolina, Max Gardiner had launched a 'Live at Home' propaganda campaign to exhort tobacco and cotton farmers to diversify into food crops and utilise agricultural resources more efficiently through cash crop

[261] Ibid. [262] Ibid.

[263] NAZ, S1194/1217, Tobacco: Restriction of output, 1934–1935, RTA control of production, 1934/1935.

[264] 'The Tobacco Quota Commission of Enquiry', *Rhodesian Agricultural Journal*, 32, 2 (1935), 78.

[265] Ibid.

acreage reductions.[266] In 1932, the New Deal looked at the problems of tobacco cultivators such as overproduction and marketing so that farmers would not suffer from price depressions that accompanied the Great Depression. The Agricultural Adjustment Act (AAA) was passed on 12 May 1933 and set up the requisite institutions and machinery to provide farmers and tobacco growers a route out of their economic misery.[267] There were production controls through the Voluntary Domestic Allotment Plan that established a quota system in which farmers could only cultivate tobacco on a portion of their lands.[268] In return for acreage and output reductions tobacco growers were offered guaranteed prices, as well as benefit support which resulted in improved prices.[269] Those who did not sign up and produced more than their allowance had their crops taxed at between 25 to 33.3 per cent, and a sum of $28 million was offered growers for reduced acreages.[270]

The acreages taken out of tobacco had to be left idle or cultivated with food crops.[271] The AAA became unconstitutional in 1936, but its key points were simply resurrected a month later under the Soil Conservation and Domestic Allotment Act which re-established the quota system under the regime of conservation.[272] The Soil Conservation and Domestic Allotment Act added to existing soil-conservation legislation incentives for farmers to plant soil-building crops and take soil-depleting crops out of production.[273] Tobacco was one such crop and production control was to be maintained through soil conservation. The New Deal encouraged better farming methods and attention to soil conservation. Tobacco cultivated lands were protected by strip cropping across with bands of grass, Lespedeza (a resilient legume that makes protein-rich hay), sorghum and other

[266] The 'Live at Home' Campaign was necessitated by North Carolina's heavy dependence on tobacco which was grown on more than a third of the state's 280,000 farms. There was thus a wasteful dependence on tobacco characterised by a relative absence of livestock and poultry in the state farms. The state had to rely heavily on other states for food and spent $250 million each year outside the state on foodstuffs. See Badger, *Prosperity Road*, 26.

[267] Algeo, 'The Rise of Tobacco', 46–60.

[268] Goodman, *Tobacco in History*, 197.

[269] Ibid.

[270] NAZ, S1827/1245/3, Tobacco production control: 1935, RTA circular to growers, February 1935: Regulation of production.

[271] Badger, *Prosperity Road*, 74.

[272] Goodman, *Tobacco in History*, 197.

[273] Badger, *Prosperity Road*, 123.

dense crops planted along the contours.[274] As a result of these measures, Lespedeza – an insignificant crop in 1929 – had the second largest acreage in the state by 1941.[275] Known as 'poor man's Lucerne' (now rebranded 'prosperity Lucerne') it was able to thrive on the worst soils and offered forage to livestock. The number of milk cows, beef cattle, sows and poultry increased significantly, and corn acreages expanded by 2 per cent over the decade.[276] Thus, the soil-conservation programmes under the New Deal and the AAA created new agricultural landscapes in which were planted the seeds of a reconfigured political geography that 'helped to tie the farming communities more closely to the Federal government'.[277]

Therefore, production control in the USA under the AAA and subsidiary legislations had the net effect of reshaping the agricultural countryside and etching more indelibly the state's imprint in shaping soil and land conservation programmes that were part of these policy interventions. To this extent, production control was an effective state tool used for conservation during much of the 1930s. Production control also led to significant improvement of farm incomes as in 1933, the average price paid to tobacco growers stood at 15.3 cents up one third from the previous year's price and double the 1931 figures.[278] In North Carolina, the 1933 crop brought in $112 million, compared to just over $56 million in 1932.[279] Intensive use of land was also greatly stimulated as a result of acreage allotments as the ideal of the small farm was upheld; the average tobacco farm size in North Carolina for instance fell from 5.8 acres to 4 acres between 1930 and 1950.[280]

However, unlike in the USA, this extended top-down conservation paradigm tying state-sponsored tobacco-production control and conservation programmes was weaker in Southern Rhodesia. The controls failed to institute ecological changes to the agricultural landscape between 1935 and 1945 as farm sizes remained large, acreages

[274] Extract of H. H. Bennet (Director USA Soil Erosion Service), 'The Relation of Grass Cover to Soil Erosion Control', *Journal of Agronomy*, (March 1935), cited in *Rhodesia Agricultural Journal*, 32, 6 (1935), 385–394.

[275] Badger, *Prosperity Road*, 207. [276] Ibid.

[277] N. Maher, 'Crazy Quilt Farming on Round Lands: The Great Plains: The Soil Conservation Scheme and the Politics of Landscape', *Western Historical Quarterly*, 31, 3 (2000), 319–339.

[278] Badger, *Prosperity, Road*, 65. [279] Ibid.

[280] G. P. Green, 'The Political Economy of Flue-cured Tobacco Production', *Rural Sociology*, 52, (1987), 221–241.

expanded, production increased sharply putting more pressure on the land and natural resources. The RTA had warned growers in 1935 that if their crop exceeded 80 per cent of the 1933/1934 crop, it would be far in excess of market requirements for the Union and the UK.[281] In spite of this warning, the 1934/1935 crop was in excess leaving a disposable surplus and forcing the state to pass the Tobacco Reserve Pool Act which took off 20 per cent of every growers' crop from the Union and British markets and placed it in a reserve pool to be disposed of elsewhere at cheaper prices.[282] On their part, the growers were virulently opposed to government control of production through legislative means. A Mr J. B. Parham of Romsley Estates pointed out that the agitation for control was being peddled by men who either did not grow tobacco at all or who did not produce the right article.[283] In his view, 'the expert tobacco grower does not ask for assistance, all he wants is to be left alone'. He added that there would not be any surplus of the leaf which the market wanted as the farmers could always sell a 'good thing'.[284] Farmers felt that it was fundamentally uneconomic to socialise production by legislation. They argued that the proposed legislation would not have any effect on the fluctuations of trade, and for a young country like Rhodesia it was important to take advantage of the improving global conditions.[285]

Despite this, in 1936, the Tobacco Market Stabilisation Act established the Tobacco Marketing Board to register growers, organise the compulsory sale of all tobacco through licensed auction floors and buyers, and to advise the government on the requisite production quotas.[286] The Act stipulated that should a grower grow an amount of tobacco in excess of what was allowed on his grower's certificate, the proceeds of the sale would be confiscated. The feeling was that gamblers and nomadic tobacco growers who had no strong attachment to Southern Rhodesia had been responsible for much of the reckless speculation, overproduction and land degradation, a point

281 NAZ, S1827/1245/3, RTA circular to growers, February 1935: RTA warning to growers September 1935.

282 Clements and Harben, *Leaf of Gold*, 115.

283 NAZ, S1194/1217, Tobacco: Restrictions of output legislation, 1934–1935, Papers submitted for perusal by Mr Vernall to the Department of Agriculture, 8 September 1934.

284 Ibid. 285 Ibid.

286 Murray, *The Governmental Systems in Southern Rhodesia*, 85.

that was stressed poignantly by Mr K. Killef in his letter to the Prime-minister Godfrey Huggins in 1936:

> If he (the grower) has had enough faith in Rhodesia to buy some of its land, he is obviously of greater value than a man who grows from lease to lease, taking what he can of the soil and using up the timber reserves. Such a man may be of value to himself, but his value to the industry or colony is very questionable and is not to be compared to the man who has planted his roots in this colony, who farms his land well and replaces his timber because the farm is his own.[287]

The RTA on its part encouraged 'progressive farmers' by reminding them that the quota system allowed them the opportunity to try a rotation of crops, and rest some of their tobacco lands for two years.[288] The encouragement was indeed relevant to conservation on the tobacco farms as crop rotations would go a long way in bringing to a halt the further exploitation of land and natural resources by limiting the amount of land under tobacco and restricting the encroachment of tobacco farms further into the land and forestry resources. Unfortunately, the war boom in tobacco prices beginning in 1939 spurred another wave of large-scale production so much that production control was drowned by the incentive of huge prices payable for tobacco.

By 1939, when World War II broke out, tobacco prices improved significantly to 10.11d. per lb as British buyers began looking at Southern Rhodesia as a reliable source of tobacco supplies.[289] Vast acres of unutilised tobacco virgin soils and abandoned tobacco barns from the boom of the 1920s created a conducive environment for new growers to enter the industry.[290] In 1940, a record crop of 34,500,000 lbs was produced in the colony with prices rising by 3d.[291] These somewhat improved conditions spurred the entry of many growers into the industry which created fertiliser shortages.[292] During the 1940/1941 season total sales of fertiliser amounted to 18,383 tonnes, of which 50 per cent were tobacco fertilisers.[293] The fertiliser crisis had grown

[287] NAZ, S482/114/39, Tobacco, 1936–1939, K. Killef to Prime Minister, 27 January 1936.
[288] NAZ, S482/114/39, Tobacco, 1936–1939, Production quotas: 1936.
[289] Clements and Harben, *Leaf of Gold*, 128. [290] Ibid. [291] Ibid.
[292] NAZ, S1215/1710/1, Fertilisers General, Chief Chemist to Controller of Supplies, 26 March 1941.
[293] Ibid.

so severely that the state was forced to intervene in 1940 through the proclamation of the Fertiliser Prices Order which controlled the fertiliser market, fixed prices and made allocations to growers on the basis of special permits obtainable from the Department of Agriculture.[294] Despite this, most tobacco farmers ordered more fertilisers than they could use creating several cases of hoarding and speculation.[295]

By 1942, the state was also facing an acute food deficit because of fertiliser and labour shortages caused by overproduction of tobacco. Food production committees were set up to allocate resources towards food production.[296] In its interim report for the period ending May 1942, the Food Production Committee noted the need for severe restrictions on artificial fertiliser use to be imposed on the tobacco crop during the 1942/1943 season.[297] The Secretary for Agriculture recommended that no tobacco grower should be supplied with more than 75 per cent or 80 per cent of fertiliser sold to that grower during 1941/1942.[298] This was to ensure that enough fertiliser could be available for food production as, in his words, 'tobacco farmers may not eat all the visible cake in one season'.[299]

The growing of tobacco on crown land[300] was prohibited in 1942, and all crown land leaseholders were compelled to produce food crops and livestock only to meet the growing demand for food during the war years.[301] The state also came in with several initiatives to curtail production of any tobacco grown at the expense of food production. Government Notice Number 207 of 1941 made agriculture a state-controlled industry and legislated that no person who had not grown

[294] NAZ, S1215/1710, Fertilisers General, Chief Chemist to Controller of Supplies, 26 March 1941.

[295] NAZ, S1215/1710, Fertilisers General, Cartwright to Secretary Department of Agriculture, 22 June 1940. Cartwright complained that there was one farmer who had bought 30 tonnes of fertiliser for 300 acres of tobacco but only grew 200 acres.

[296] NAZ, S482/20/42, Food Production Committees, FPC Meeting, 23 March 1942.

[297] NAZ, S955/22, Food production local committees, FPC interim Report for period ending 5 May 1942.

[298] NAZ, S482/32/42, Control of production, tobacco, 1942–1946, Secretary Department of Agriculture to the Parliamentary Secretary to the Prime Minister, 26 March 1942.

[299] Ibid.

[300] Crown lands were areas with unalienated land which could be leased to white settlers for farming. They were a product of the Land Apportionment Act of 1930.

[301] NAZ, S955/22, Food Production local committees, Crownlands: Use of unoccupied crown land for food production, 20 April 1942.

flue-cured tobacco during the 1939/1940 season could grow it after June 1943 without the consent of the Ministry of lands.[302] The legislation also stipulated that old growers were not supposed to increase their 1939/1940 acreages without seeking similar consent from the Tobacco Advisory Committee. During the latter part of 1941, three members of the Council of the RTA with the Secretary of the Department of Lands had acted as a consultative committee to which the control of industrial manpower would refer advice on the entry of new growers into the tobacco industry.[303] From 1942 to 1946, a number of measures were put in place to curtail production that included ensuring that increased production was only permissible if it did not conflict with the colony's need to recruit fighters or the production of food crops, and prohibiting the opening up of new farming areas for tobacco production without the consent of the consultative committee.[304]

Despite these measures, a huge tide of tobacco farmers joined the industry during the war prompting a Mr Geofrey Syfret of Inyazura district to complain to the Minister of Agriculture and Lands in May 1942 that he was alarmed by the number of 'Dutchmen' [Afrikaners] from South Africa who were entering the district and obtaining permits to grow tobacco.[305] War production of flue-cured Virginia tobacco soared significantly from 35,000,000 lbs in 1939 to 47,500,000 lbs in 1944.[306] Turkish tobacco production also grew significantly between 1943 and 1945. In 1943, there were 273 growers producing 250,000 libs, in 1945, the number increased to 1000 registered growers with a production of 5,000,000 libs.[307] Subsequently, the ecological pattern in the tobacco landscape remained largely unaltered. A vast number of speculators and gamblers were still on

[302] NAZ, S482/32/42, Control of production; tobacco, 1942–1946, Parliamentary Secretary to Secretary Department of Agriculture: Control of entry into the agricultural industry to new settlers and particularly persons desiring to enter flue-cured tobacco production, 5 March 1942.

[303] NAZ, S482/32/42, Control of production; tobacco, 1942–1946, Parliamentary Secretary to Secretary to the Prime Minister, 23 March 1942.

[304] Ibid.

[305] NAZ, S482/32/42, Control of tobacco production 1942–1946, Geoffrey Syfret to Minister of Lands and Agriculture, 8 May 1942.

[306] Rubert, *A Most Promising Weed*, 7.

[307] NAZ, S482/108/39, Turkish Tobacco 1944–1948, Minutes of the special meeting of the Turkish Tobacco Cooperative Company of Southern Rhodesia, 4 October 1945.

the land eliciting the view from one observer that, 'there are too many tobacco growers who boast openly that it is their intention to make a killing while prices are high and retire to Great Britain after the war when prices declined'.[308] In a letter to a farming and mining magazine in 1943, a Marandellas farmer complained about the exploitation of thousands of acres of heavily timbered veld by many tobacco farmers:

> I have the impression perhaps erroneously that because the tobacco industry has been prosperous for some years, the Natural Resources Board may not have examined the destruction of the country's natural resources by the tobacco industry as closely as by the general farmer. Yet the damage is appalling and a tour of some tobacco-producing areas will show large areas of played out sand veld, timber less, lacking any form of soil conservation and simply abandoned because the owner has moved to new ground.[309]

Conclusion

Thus, beyond the triumphalist and whiggish narratives of agrarian pioneer entrepreneurship, ingenuity and industriousness, the early history of tobacco farming in Southern Rhodesia was a story of exploitation of both the environment and human beings. This sinister episode in tobacco production has often been omitted from traditional 'virgin land' narratives that sought to write triumphal tobacco histories glorifying settler pioneer tobacco farmers. Indeed, later historians transcended this narrow historiography and included the role of the state in the pioneering endeavours of these early tobacco farmers and the social conditions of labour in the tobacco farms, but they still missed out on the environment. These historians also did not integrate their histories within a broader global perspective on tobacco to illuminate how local tobacco-production systems are in themselves not unique but part of a global historical heritage that makes the crop carry socio-environmental historical baggage. The role of the crop in history – in defining agrarian frontiers, creating new farming settlements, precipitating dramatic environmental change, producing new social hierarchies and rigidifying class and racial relations – must be understood as one of its enduring legacies. Through human history, post the great transition from hunter-gathering/transhumant

308 Letter to the Editor by Huntley Wilkinson (Marandellas farmer), *Vuka*, December 1943.
309 Ibid.

pastoralism, crops have possessed their own kind of agency that defined how humans constructed environmental and socio-political landscapes. Indeed, tobacco created Southern Rhodesia and in the words of Clements and Harben, 'it would be a foolish man who planned the future of Southern Rhodesia and who felt above all he could leave the European tobacco farmer'.[310] But it would be more foolish still to tell only the glorious story of the early pioneer Rhodesian tobacco industry and leave out the narratives of the plunder and despoliation of environment and the brutalisation of human bodies. It is all a part of one story.

[310] Clements and Harben, *Leaf of Gold*, 188.

2 *The Post-War Tobacco Boom and the Development of Conservationism in Southern Rhodesia, 1947–1960*

Almost equally marked for one who had no real opportunity of visiting tobacco districts for ten years was the healthy change in appearance of the farms. No longer did one see tobacco farms but general farming with fine herds, sheep, and poultry, many new dams, much contour ridging, schools, clinics, good farm roads, native churches and so on and all achieved through tobacco ... It has been my aim to discourage the word planter and insist on the fact that our tobacco producer is a farmer with herds and flocks.

Captain H. L. Morten, Southern Rhodesia Tobacco Representative to London in his Annual Report in 1949

Locating the Tobacco Boom in Colonial Conservation Historiography

The war boom in tobacco prices discussed in the previous chapter continued its swing into the post-war era on the back of two main factors – the dollar shortages in Europe and the 1947 London Agreement. Dollar shortages in war-torn Europe and the recessionary effects of the European Economic Recovery Programme forced most European countries to shift their tobacco import priorities from the traditional American suppliers to other major producers such as Southern Rhodesia. In 1947, the UK tobacco manufacturers and the Southern Rhodesian government signed an agreement that guaranteed the latter preferential and guaranteed access to the British market. These two factors produced a huge demand for Rhodesian leaf and prompted post-war production to soar until tobacco overtook gold as Southern Rhodesia's chief export in 1946.[1] The post-war tobacco boom culminated in several production dynamics. Many new entrants joined tobacco farming, and a lot of capital was invested by farmers into tobacco production. Subsequently, new patterns

[1] P. Scott, 'The Tobacco Industry of Southern Rhodesia', *Economic Geography*, 28, 3 (1952), 189–206.

of growth and accumulation also etched themselves on the agrarian landscape as this chapter will show. These new patterns were most conspicuous in the disproportionate share of national agricultural resources such as labour and capital that the tobacco sector exploited relative to other segments of Rhodesian agriculture, such as beef production and maize. This wave of agrarian developments precipitated by the tobacco boom has been subject to scrutiny within the conservation historiography of Southern Rhodesia. This scrutiny has focussed on the role of tobacco in agricultural growth, biological conservation, land husbandry and integrated farming in the European farms.

In 1989, the *Journal of Southern African Studies* published its special issue on the 'Politics of Conservation in Southern Africa'.[2] The special issue starred a cast of historians on colonial conservation ideologies in southern Africa such as Richard Grove, Jane Carruthers, Kate Showers, William Beinart and Terence Ranger.[3] The compilation offered a suite of essays on several themes on colonial conservationism: its intellectual roots, the development and evolution of the ideology in the subcontinent, the nature of state conservation policy in African and white settler areas, the development of national parks and game sanctuaries and the problem of soil erosion. This collection discussed the nature of colonial conservation ideologies, the texture of state intervention and the overall patterns of settler and African responses to the state conservation prescriptions.

The 1989 special issue came at the end of an ongoing historiographical debate between Ian Phimister and William Beinart. In 1984, William Beinart pointed out that the single most conspicuously ubiquitous strand in African colonial agricultural archives between the 1930s and 1950s was an immense preoccupation with soil erosion and the preservation of natural resources.[4] Beinart further asserts that the

[2] See the *Journal of Southern African Studies*, 15, 2 (1989).

[3] Contributions in the issue included J. Carruthers, 'Creating a National Park, 1910–1926', 188–216; T. Ranger, 'Whose Heritage? The Case of the Matobo National Park', 217–249; K. Showers, 'Soil Erosion in the Kingdom of Lesotho: Origins and Colonial Responses, 1830–1950s', 263–280; R. Grove, 'Scottish Missionaries, Evangelical Discourses and the Origins of Conservation Thinking in Southern Africa, 1820–1900', 163–184; W. Beinart, 'The Politics of Colonial Conservation', 143–162, *Journal of Southern Africa Studies*, 15, 2 (1989).

[4] W. Beinart, 'Soil Erosion, Conservationism and Ideas about Development: A Southern African Exploration, 1900–1960', *Journal of Southern African Studies*, 15, 1 (1984), 52–83.

ideology of conservation in southern Africa was not a progeny of the interaction between the colonial state and the African peasantry during agricultural centralisation projects. Rather, he argued, conservation ideologies arose at the Cape from concerns over the difficulties facing settler agriculture in the environs of rapidly expanding agricultural enterprise in fragile African ecologies.[5] Beinart further pointed out that these ideas had proliferated into the subregion, and in Southern Rhodesia, a number of conservation initiatives had been set up by the state beginning in the early 1930s such that by the late 1930s there had been significant progress in the construction of mechanical conservation works in white settler farms.[6]

In 1986, Ian Phimister challenged Beinart's argument for lacking context.[7] He issued a rejoinder, arguing in his rebuttal that conservation roots were shallower in Southern Rhodesia and conservation doctrines were first applied more assiduously to African peasants and then only later to white settler farmers during the first half of the twentieth century.[8] Phimister took the debate further to reveal the limited patterns of state conservation intervention in Southern Rhodesia by arguing that the post-war tobacco boom slackened the pace of conservation as it created unbalanced agricultural development between tobacco farmers and other agricultural practitioners, resulting in food deficits and inadequate African labour for the construction of conservation works. Phimister argued that while much progress had been done on the construction of mechanical conservation works, biological conservation integrating field husbandry and livestock

[5] Beinart's argument is in sync with Richard Grove who propounds that early conservation laws were directed towards the control of the ecological effects of settler agriculture. While Beinart begins his conservation ideology thread with developments in the Cape around the nineteenth century, Grove takes it back to the seventeenth century in the island colonies of Mauritius and St Helena where British and French colonial officials were probed by declining forestry resources to promote conservation. Grove points to how a series of droughts in southern Africa from 1821 to 1863 stimulated new ways in which colonial scientists began to interpret environmental change and human activity. See R. Grove, *Green Imperialism: Colonial Expansion, Tropical Island Edens and the Origins of Environmentalism, 1600–1860* (Cambridge, 1996).

[6] Beinart, 'The Politics of Colonial Conservation', 143–162.

[7] See I. Phimister, 'Discourse and the Discipline of Historical Context: Conservatism and Ideas about Development in Southern Rhodesia, 1930–50', *Journal of Southern African Studies*, 12, 2 (1986), 263–275.

[8] Ibid.

farming was still retarded in the white farms in Southern Rhodesia between 1930 and 1950.[9]

The Phimister–Beinart debate was perhaps a transient historiographical exchange, but it became significant in providing helpful insights into understanding the development of conservation ideologies in southern Africa. Phimister had sought to establish an empirical context to Beinart's general contention by pointing to a specific period in Southern Rhodesia's agrarian history (the post-war tobacco boom) and revealing the production dynamics in settler agriculture during the war and immediate post-war years.

Although the historiographic exchange between the two ended in the 1980s, the debate on conservationism lived on in many ways. In 2003, Beinart maintained his historiographical stance that progressive conservationism was an inherent attribute of European agrarian communities in colonial southern Africa.[10] He examined settler pastoral communities at the Cape from the late eighteenth century to mid-twentieth century and concluded that in spite of droughts, diseases and the threat of environmental degradation, these communities were progressive in harnessing environmental concerns and influencing state policy towards regulating the pastoral economy and encouraging more intensive use of natural resources. Therefore, from the 1830s when the ovine population increased and wool became the Cape's major export, conservation and scientific ideas about the state of the veld and its improvement were becoming established.[11] Between 1913 and 1952, the pastoral farmers progressively embraced intensive production and environmental management such that the arid and semi-arid farming regions switched to wildlife and viticulture with progressive ecological implications for biodiversity within the Cape whose heritage is still visible in contemporary landscapes.[12]

Beinart's 2003 publication sparked another debate – this time an abrasive, dramatic and apoplectic exchange between him and Lance Van Sittert in *The Journal of African History* that reopened the Phimister–Beinart debate. Beinart's progressive conservation ideology was scathingly reviewed by Van Sittert as an overblown and hyperbolic hagiography of the white farming communities at the Cape and

[9] Ibid.

[10] W. Beinart, *The Rise of Conservation in South Africa: Settlers, Livestock, and the Environment, 1770–1950* (Oxford, 2003).

[11] Ibid., 64. [12] Ibid., 386.

as an apologetic corrective project to redeem the white settler farmers from the charge of environmental degradation levelled against them by radical historians.[13] Furthermore, Van Sittert criticised Beinart for lacking context and for having conceded and recanted some of the earlier historiographical arguments he had made in 1984.[14]

This chapter joins this debate and counterbalances the 'environmental declensionist' narratives by showing how positive and progressive conservation attitudes were also spontaneously and simultaneously generated by the tobacco boom.[15] Environmental declension

[13] L. Van Sittert, 'The Nature of Power: Cape Environmental History, the History of Ideas and Neo-Liberal Historiography', *The Journal of African History*, 45 (2004), 305–313.

[14] Beinart himself modified three points he had previously argued in his 1984 article. He conceded that he had laid too much emphasis on the influence of the US conservation model in South Africa since much of the development of conservation concern was local and specific. Second, he revised the notion that conservation and environmental regulation was only coercively applied by the state to Africans. Beinart argued that, in certain instances, the state was coercive towards both Africans and Europeans. Third, he toned down his critique on ambitious scientific colonial interventions in African ecologies as authoritarian and argued that colonial scientific knowledge on African environments and ecologies constitutes invaluable knowledge towards understanding the history of conservation and ecology in colonial Africa. See Beinart, *The Rise of Conservation in South Africa*, 333–334.

[15] New environmental history scholarship has emerged in the 2000s challenging historical narratives that only tell stories of environmental decline and human degradation of the environment and ecosystems. These histories emphasise that stories of man's interactions with nature are more nuanced and complex than simple narratives framing humans as agents of destruction. The alternative to declensionist narratives is 'Georgic narratives' (named after classical Roman idyllic and pastoral poet Virgil's poetry collection, *The Georgics*, which glorified man and nature's symbiosis) that view humans and nature working together as counterparts to produce ecological value. See D. Richter, 'The Crisis of Environmental Narratives in the Anthropocene', in 'Whose Anthropocene? Revisiting Dipesh Chakrabarty's Four Theses', in R. Emmett and T. Lekan (eds.), *RCC Perspectives: Transformations in Environment and Society*, 2 (2016), 97–100; T. Steinberg, 'Down, Down, Down, No More: Environmental History Moves beyond Declension', *Journal of the Early Republic*, 24, 2 (2004), 260–266; T. Berry, *The Dream of the New Earth* (New York, 1990); M. McLaughlin, 'Counterbalancing Declensionist Narratives in Environmental History', Network in Canadian History and Environment, 3 February 2016, http://niche-canada.org/2016/02/03/counterbalancing-declensionist-narratives-in-environmental-history/, accessed 29 August 2019. Ted Stenberg critiques William Cronon's 2003 work which firmly concluded that capitalism and environmental degradation went hand in hand. See W. Cronon, *Changes in the Land: Indians, Colonists, and the Ecology of New England* (New York, 2003), 13.

narratives miss out an appreciation of the role of white tobacco farmers and private capital in conservation and embracing modern methods of farming during the second half of the twentieth century. At the same time, progressive conservation discourses are too embedded in optimism to understand that the spatial changes after the tobacco boom were not as rapid and linear as the Cape conservation *Georgic* narrative. Furthermore, Beinart's discursive context of the Cape and the pace of change in the institutionalisation of conservation ideas within that physical landscape presents a unique set of circumstances that cannot be directly extrapolated into Southern Rhodesia[16] Thus, while the fundamental conservationist logic posited by Beinart about the kinetic nature of environmental systems is a relevant conceptual beginning, his overall conclusions must not be superimposed on all settler colonial experiences and practices in southern Africa. Even then, Beinart himself was aware of the need for historiographic revisionism, and he pointed out in 2005 (referring to his 1984 article) that 'ten years on I have problems with this article, but it may yet form the basis of further regional history'.[17]

Phimister was certainly right about the restrained pace of biological conservation in Southern Rhodesia from the 1930s to 1950, but his pessimistic narrative of the tobacco boom perhaps throws the baby with the bath water as conservation was not static and several changes were taking place on the land as a result of the dynamics of tobacco capital, catalysed by the necessity to meet new production environments such as rising labour cost, cost of land as well as cost of production. Indeed, by 1960, significant changes *had* taken place in the integration of farm planning into conservation farming, research in effective tobacco rotational practices, biological conservation and livestock husbandry. Overall, tobacco farms had transited from planter agricultural schemes into integrated production systems based on more intensive land use and more efficient models of biological conservation.

[16] Van Sittert particularly points out that 'the tendency to disregard context has plagued Phimister's project from the start'. See Van Sittert, 'The Nature of Power: Cape Environmental History', 305–313.

[17] W. Beinart, 'Academic Amnesia and the Poverty of Polemics', *Journal of African History*, 46, 1 (2005), 127–137.

The London Agreement, the Tobacco Bonanza and the Land Boom, 1947–1950

The conditions created by the Second World War (1939–1945) set the tone for the prosperity of the Southern Rhodesian tobacco industry. During the war, cigarette consumption increased sharply, and between 1939 and 1945, tobacco prices more than doubled. The average price of Virginia tobacco rose from 10s.11d/lb during the 1939/1940 season to 21s.78d/lb during 1945/1946.[18] The post-war years opened a window of opportunity as countries in Europe (reeling from the effects of the European Recovery Programme) had to confine their dollar expenditures to a minimum and find substitute supplies of tobacco away from their traditional American market. During the post–Second World War era, tobacco came to have a bigger macroeconomic role of supplying much-needed revenue to European economies through taxation. The French, Italian and Austrian governments realised more than 30 per cent of total revenue from tobacco companies in 1946.[19] In the USA, the federal government built a huge network of state-supported tobacco export infrastructure through the Tobacco Associates that promoted the consumption of American leaf overseas.[20] The Marshal Aid plan provided dollars and aid to European countries for the purchase of America leaf, and tobacco came to represent the American post-war vision of 'capitalism and democracy'.[21] The post-war boom in tobacco demand created shortages for British manufacturers. During the 1947 season, British buyers found difficulty in obtaining desired quantities of leaf on the Rhodesian tobacco auction floors. To guarantee adequate supplies of Rhodesian leaf, the UK and Southern Rhodesia signed the London Agreement in 1947. This agreement reached between the Tobacco Advisory Committee to the Board of Trade in London (the body representative of British manufacturers and merchants) and the Tobacco Marketing Board (TMB) of Southern Rhodesia saw the UK guaranteeing to purchase two-thirds of Southern Rhodesia flue-cured crop (up to 70 million lbs) over a period of five years until 1953.[22] It was subject

[18] Annual Reports of the Tobacco Marketing Board, 1939/1940 and 1945/1946.

[19] S. Milov, *The Cigarette: A Political History* (Massachusetts, 2019), 87.

[20] Ibid., 79–85. [21] Ibid., 88.

[22] R. Hodder-Williams, *White Farmers in Rhodesia, 1890–1965; A History of the Marandellas District* (London, 1983), 190.

Figure 2.1 Tobacco production in Southern Rhodesia (lbs), 1942–1948
Source: Annual Report of the Tobacco Representative in London, 1948.

to renewal thereafter. Even if there was to be a fall in consumption, UK manufacturers guaranteed to take at least 40 million lbs annually from the Rhodesian market over five years.[23] To guarantee the supply to British buyers, a system of export control was introduced by the TMB so that exports to other markets would be restricted to 33.3 per cent of the crop.[24] The agreement prioritised the requirements of the UK market, South Africa, other preferential markets and the demands of local tobacco manufacturers respectively.[25] Subsequently, flue-cured tobacco production more than doubled from 34,000,000 lbs in 1945 to 80,000,000 lbs in 1948 as shown in Figure 2.1. In 1948, the UK manufacturers purchased 65.4 per cent of Rhodesian flue-cured leaf while South Africa and preferential markets procured 27.42 per cent and the local market only got 2.94 per cent (see Figure 2.2). The British American Tobacco (BAT), a major player at the Rhodesian tobacco auction floors, were also given preference to particularly cater to the Australian market. After signing the London Agreement, the Southern Rhodesian tobacco representative in London, Major L. H. Morten, wrote with a sense of optimism:

> There is no longer doubt or question, Southern Rhodesia flue-cured tobacco is firmly and permanently established in the British market, it is now

[23] Annual Report of the Tobacco Representative in London, 1948. [24] Ibid.
[25] F. Clements and E. Harben, *Leaf of Gold: The Story of Rhodesian Tobacco* (London, 1962), 143.

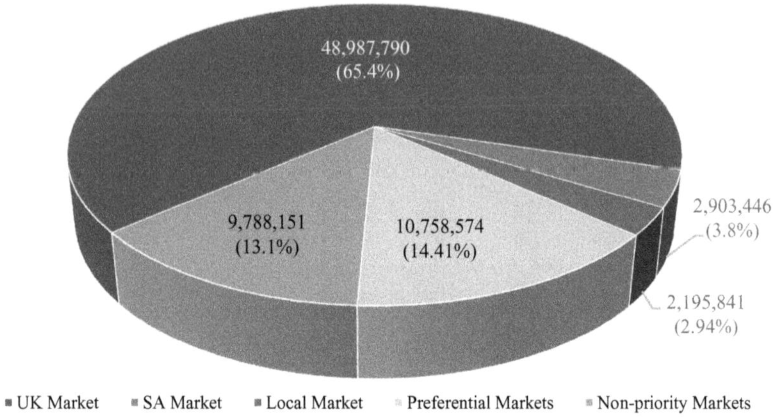

Figure 2.2 Southern Rhodesia tobacco destinations, 1948
Source: Annual Report of the Tobacco Representative in London, 1948.

penetrating into factories and brands which have never used it before and is smoked for the first time by many Britons, the continuation of this admirable trend depends so largely on the producer himself.[26]

The lucrative export incentives guaranteed by the London Agreement catalysed a tobacco boom that lured many new entrants into tobacco farming as well as new applications for land from European settlers wanting to settle in Southern Rhodesia.[27] Ex-servicemen and new immigrants joined the ranks of tobacco farmers. Tobacco production control measures and acreage quotas that had been put in place during the war to prioritise food production were removed to give impetus to the tobacco export market.[28] Privately owned property began changing hands for high figures on account of this huge demand for tobacco. Prices of land were determined by

26 Annual Report of the Tobacco Representative in London, 1948.

27 Many settlers who applied for land during this period wanted to cultivate tobacco. They were largely from South Africa and Britain. One of the applicants, Mr Wallace from the Transvaal, was thirty-three years of age and had served in the South African Air Force during the war and was employed in gold mining. He wrote to the Secretary of Agriculture on 14 January 1948 saying that he was keen to migrate to Southern Rhodesia and learn 'tobacco culture'. See, NAZ S2570, Tobacco: 1946–1950, Mr Wallace to Secretary of Agriculture, 14 January 1948.

28 Annual Report of the Chief Tobacco Officer, 1948.

proximity to rail or town, but the undeveloped farm land suitable for tobacco was fetching between 30 shillings– £5 an acre, while developed and semi-developed tobacco farms had prices ranging from £10,000 to £40,000 with an average farm being approximately 2,000 acres in extent.[29] The high prices paid for tobacco were responsible for the substantial increase in the value of farmland, which now ranged from between £4 to £8 an acre as compared to £2 in 1939.[30] Fully developed tobacco farms were being advertised at the rate of £10 to £12 an acre.[31] On an undeveloped tobacco farm the additional capital outlay required for buildings and equipment amounted to approximately £3,000 to £4,000.[32] Recurrent expenditure for African wages and food and general working expenses amounted to £2,000 a year.[33] The number of Virginia tobacco growers rose from 1,228 in 1947 to 1,893 in 1948, and the number of Turkish tobacco growers grew from 725 to 882 during the same period.[34] Consequently, the total number of black labourers employed on tobacco farms rose from 80,060 in 1947 to 92,640 in 1948 constituting more than half the total number of Africans employed in the agricultural industry.[35]

The dominance of tobacco farms within Southern Rhodesia's agricultural landscape was very much markedly intensive and extensive as shown in Figures 2.3 and 2.4. More than two fifth of the farms had tobacco as a principal crop by 1950.[36] The number of tobacco farms rose from 800 out of a total of 3,400 European farms in 1945 to 2,200 out of 5,000 farms in 1950.[37] At the same time, the proportion of tobacco farmers to the total number of farms within the tobacco belt increased from one quarter to three quarters.[38]

This flow of capital and agricultural resources into tobacco production unleashed and sustained a series of forces that placed tobacco at the core of settler farming in Southern Rhodesia. Tobacco became key within the ideas about conservationism and development. This generated debates about the role of the crop in promoting balanced

[29] NAZ, S2570, Tobacco: 1946–1950, chief tobacco officer to K. Balfour (Natal Farmer), 6 September 1948.

[30] NAZ, S2570, Tobacco: 1946–1950, chief tobacco officer to Major Lloyd (England), 10 June 1949.

[31] Ibid. [32] Ibid. [33] Ibid.

[34] NAZ, S2570 Tobacco: 1946–1950, chief tobacco officer to Secretary of Agriculture, 23 January 1949.

[35] Ibid. [36] Scott, 'The Tobacco Industry of Southern Rhodesia', 189–206.

[37] Ibid. [38] Ibid.

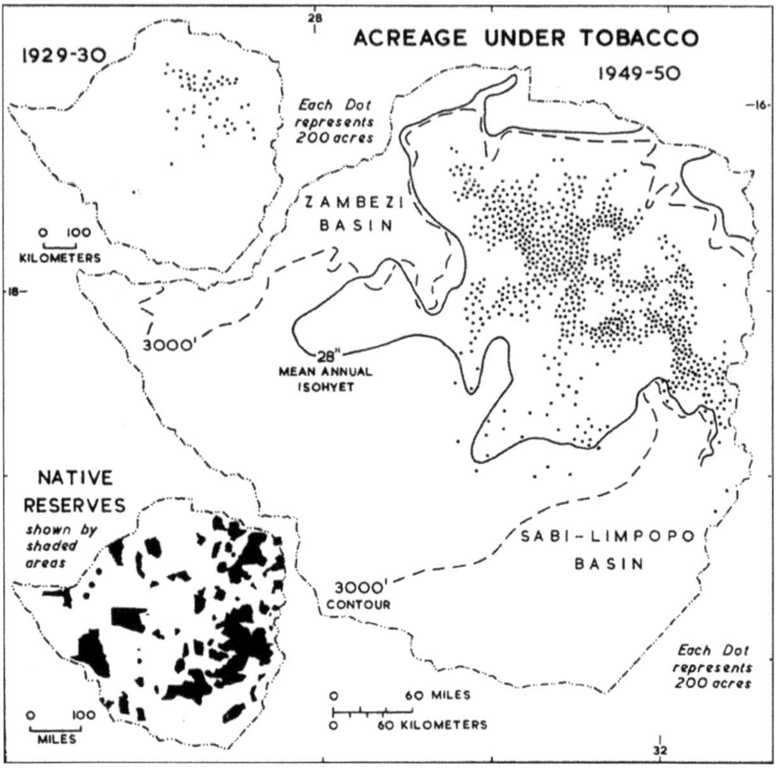

Figure 2.3 Map showing distribution of farms with tobacco as the principal crop in Southern Rhodesia, 1949–1950
Source: Scott, 'The Tobacco Industry of Southern Rhodesia', 192.

agricultural development and conservation of natural resources in the white-owned farms. These debates focussed on how the post-war tobacco complex could endanger the prospects of balanced agricultural development, resource conservation, and the actualisation of a diversified agricultural sector.

Phimister argues that the flow of capital and resources into tobacco production impacted negatively on developments in other agricultural sectors particularly beef and maize production.[39] Between 1945 and

[39] Phimister points out that during World War II and immediately after the war, the pace of domestic beef consumption was failing to catch up with supply resulting in deficits that had to be met by sacrificing export beef and slaughtering young cattle each year. At the same time maize output had declined in volume

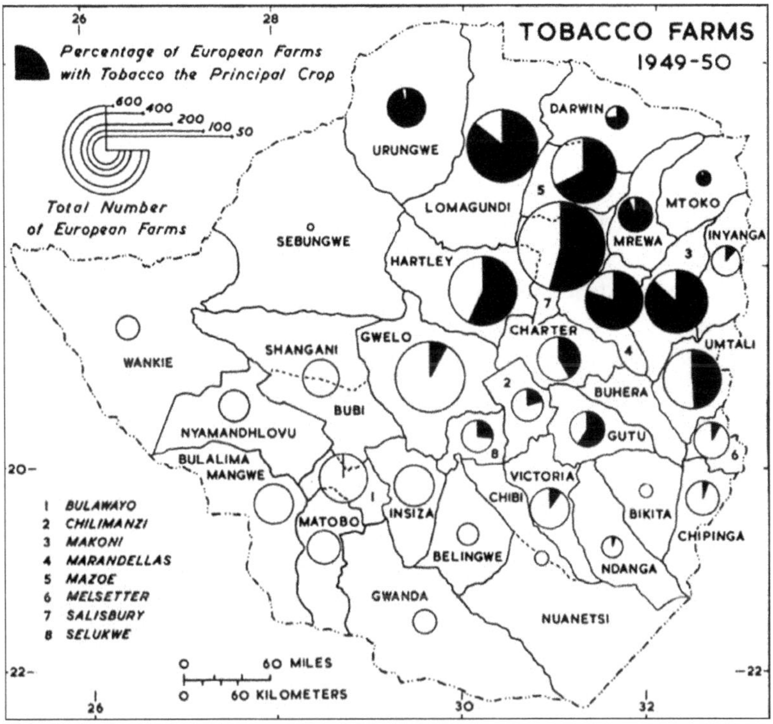

Figure 2.4 Map showing distribution and concentration of tobacco farms in Southern Rhodesia, 1949–1950
Source: Scott, 'The Tobacco Industry of Southern Rhodesia', 190.

1947, an estimated £7 million was invested by farmers into tobacco growing.[40] This expansion represented a shift of resources from other crops to tobacco production creating an imbalance. This imbalance not only created deficits in other agricultural products as more successful tobacco planters muscled out other farmers for the control of capital and labour but also resulted in a huge cutback in labour-intensive conservation and land husbandry practices.[41] Within this context, the role of state intervention in limiting the uneven flow of capital and agricultural resources into tobacco farms was highly

between 1945 and 1949 so that the colony was spending £750,000 per year on maize imports.

40 Phimister, 'Discourse and the Discipline of Historical Context', 263–275.

41 Ibid.

curtailed by the importance of tobacco to the colonial cash economy where it contributed over a third of export earnings.[42] Consequently, the state laid heavy emphasis on 'politically neutral' conservation projects such as the building of mechanical conservation works.[43] Thus, while between 1947 and 1950, 14,705 miles of contour ridges were constructed protecting 91per cent of total arable area on white commercial farms, the development of a more comprehensive state-led paradigm of biological conservation involving the integration of livestock farming, field husbandry, grazing control and 'correct farming in harmony with nature' lagged far behind.[44]

Indeed, this interpretation of the destabilising impact of the tobacco boom on agricultural development and conservation was acknowledged by various sectors of the colonial state. A report by the Division of Agriculture and Lands noted that tobacco production between 1939 and 1949 had doubled and claimed a larger part of resources such as capital, equipment and building material creating a vulnerable agricultural imbalance.[45] Moreover, as a result of the higher prices, tobacco was being grown on an increasing scale in marginal areas.[46] Farms which were only suitable for cattle ranching were now being offered as suitable for tobacco cultivation resulting in the growing of off-type tobacco.[47] In the Midlands districts of the country which was traditionally a cattle ranching area, farmers were switching in large numbers from growing food crops and cattle breeding to tobacco farming.[48] A writer in the *Rhodesia Herald* pointed out this imbalance when he noted that:

> I suggest that Southern Rhodesia far from having his fortunes founded on tobacco is rapidly being impoverished by it, and the disproportionate profits to be made from tobacco have forced the prices of farmlands far beyond the means of many who could augment the nation's internal supply and those who can find £ 10,000–£20,000 for a farm are forced to put a crippling charge on their produce to get anything like a reasonable return on their investments.[49]

In August 1947, J. C. Saseen, who identified himself as a tobacco farmer from Selukwe, wrote a letter to the Minister of Agriculture airing his concerns that tobacco farmers were limiting food crop

[42] Ibid. [43] Ibid. [44] Ibid. [45] *Rhodesia Herald*, 20 April 1951.
[46] Ibid. [47] Ibid. [48] *Rhodesia Herald*, 4 May 1951.
[49] *Rhodesia Herald*, 2 April 1951.

production and contributing to deforestation. He noted that the government's appeal for farmers to grow more food crops was only going to meet with partial success amongst the tobacco growers unless there were stringent regulations to force tobacco farmers to grow food crops and conserve their lands.[50] He reminded the government that:

> The remedy lies in your hands and success is 100 per cent guaranteed, not only for food production but the conservation of the land which is slowly being ruined of its forests in the mad rush of clearing plenty large tracts of land for tobacco. I have seen land in some areas which in a few years would be semi-desert.[51]

Saseen further expressed the general feeling that tobacco farmers were arrogant and most of them were simply plundering natural resources and profiteering rapaciously because of the boom while neglecting to play a bigger role in land conservation and food production. He noted that some farmers were simply putting assistants on their lands to grow tobacco for them on percentage basis and these assistants were not worried about foodstuff production and were simply planting the land to a 'desert jungle' with tobacco to enable themselves to earn better commissions.[52]

While this indeed was the case, it is important to contextualise some of the resentment towards tobacco farmers that was coming from other practitioners on the land who were struggling to keep up with the pace of tobacco growers in securing land, labour and capital, and who in the words of one tobacco farmer looked at the post-war success of tobacco farmers 'with a jaundiced eye of jealousy'.[53] Tobacco farmers had done so well after the war and this caused some resentment amongst the returning and immigrant soldiers. Even so the cattle ranchers and maize growers who had previously been chief producers of the colony and controllers of agricultural policy could not be expected to defend the case for the men who had usurped them.[54] In the words of one tobacco farmer:

> These focus their attention upon the four or five hundred old established growers, pioneers of the industry who have tasted the bitterness of hardship

[50] NAZ, S2570, Tobacco: 1946–1950, J. C. Saseen to Secretary Ministry of Agriculture and Lands, 9 August 1947.
[51] Ibid. [52] Ibid. [53] *Industry in Commerce of Rhodesia*, December 1949.
[54] Clements and Harben, *Leaf of Gold*, 157.

and sometimes even bankruptcy in the years when their tobacco was unwanted and unsold, but who today at long last are reaping the rich rewards of their courage and determination.[55]

Even on its part the government felt that the huge financial success of the tobacco grower in the post-war years had to pay for the colony's balance of payments. The United Party led by Godfrey Huggins, which was in power from 1933 to 1956, had farmers in its leadership, but these were not tobacco growers and were naturally disinclined towards them.[56] In 1949, the Finance Minister Edgar Whitehead tried to impose a 20 per cent tobacco tax without consulting the tobacco establishment. The government felt that the general rate of development had to be maintained and the best means of raising additional funds amounting to £1.5 million with the least injury to the country's economy was through an export duty on tobacco.[57] The growers through the RTA rejected the proposed tax. The state was forced to back down and accept a compromise levy as a five-year loan to the government.[58] But what the incident did reveal was the growing general envy and hostility towards the success of tobacco growers. Historians therefore need to be cautious when constructing narratives around the tobacco boom to avoid being swayed by sentiments of envy hyperbolising the negative effects of the tobacco boom on agricultural development and conservation. Equally, there is need to be cautious of overtly optimistic narratives from tobacco farmers' sources glorifying their conservation endeavours during the post-war boom.

While Phimister was right in suggesting that the tobacco boom brought about unequal agricultural growth and a slackened pace of conservation in Southern Rhodesia, that aspect was but one phase in a series of evolutionary changes that were happening on the farms because of the dynamic introduced by tobacco capital. This projects a monolithic conservation narrative in Southern Rhodesia which does not nuance the intricate and changing dynamics of capital accumulation caused by the tobacco boom and its impact on the physical

[55] *Industry and Commerce of Rhodesia*, December 1949.

[56] S. Angus, 'Commercial Farmers and the State: Internal Group Politics and Land Reform in Zimbabwe' (PhD Thesis, University of Oxford, 2006), 58.

[57] Clements and Harben, *Leaf of Gold*, 155.

[58] D. Rowe, *Manipulating the Market: Understanding Economic Sanctions, Institutional Change, and the Political Unity of White Rhodesia* (Ann Arbor, 2001), 69.

farming landscapes. The impression that for much of the 1930s to 1950 the only noteworthy conservation development within settler tobacco farms was the construction of contour ridges limits the ability to gaze at environmental change as a non-linear process. Indeed, Carville Earle's study of conservation practices amongst tobacco and cotton farmers in America's southern states attacks linear conceptions of history that entrench the hypothesis of unchanging human behaviour towards the environment.[59] In the end, Earle calls for 'a heuristic paradigm that accommodates a dynamic environmental history and the recurrence of agricultural innovation'.[60] New scholarly approaches have further challenged declensionist environmental narratives and established that the history of resource exploitations are more complex. Daniel Ritcher's study of the south Piedmont region of the USA which was once an epicentre of cotton production practices that degraded soils and natural landscapes shows how years later new landscapes and environmental narratives were created within the region.[61] Conevery Bolton Valenčius challenged declensionist historians to also emphasise the 'drama of the tumultuous ecological world', exhorting them to pay attention to story-telling and the drama associated with it.[62] Indeed, it is critical to transcend declension narratives and frame conservation ideas as shifting concepts that changed across historical time and with them environmental management and landscapes.[63] Environmental change cannot be described as a linear process of degradation and calling all change degradation has static value in understanding human-nature interactions.[64]

59 Carville Earle critiques the American conservation histories of the 1920s for their unrelenting polemics on agricultural practices in the southern states, particularly the tobacco and cotton soil farmers who were roundly scorned as mere 'soil miners'. While conceding that southern farmers were soil miners, Earle condemned these histories for failing to understand that the agronomic practices of tobacco and cotton growers in the south were not static but changed and adapted to the cyclic economic conditions resulting in agronomic practices that maintained soil fertility and minimised erosion losses. See, C. Earle, 'The Myth of the Southern Soil Miner: Macrohistory, Agricultural Innovation and Environmental Change', in D. Worster (ed), *The Ends of the Earth: Perspectives on Morden Environmental History* (Cambridge, 1988), 175–210.

60 Earle, 'The Myth of the Southern Soil Miner', 179.

61 Richter, 'The Crisis of Environmental Narratives in the Anthropocene', 97–100.

62 C. B. Valenčius, 'Mudslides Make Good History', *Journal of the Early Republic*, 24, 2 (2004), 252–259.

63 This is a central idea in Beinart's works on conservation histories at the Cape.

64 Beinart, *The Rise of Conservation in South Africa*, 390.

The dynamic of capital brought many changes into tobacco production systems as the cost of land, labour and inputs became high and it was no longer profitable to cultivate land extensively. The pace of the integration of these ideas might have been slower than anticipated, but the changes taking place in the Rhodesian countryside as a result of tobacco capital such as land development and conservation works were conspicuous in the post-war years and must not be disregarded. Indeed, the development of the conservation discourse amongst tobacco farmers from the late 1940s was a dynamic intricately linked to the changing production environments where exorbitant land prices and high costs of production were ensuring profitability only to those farmers who could utilise their land more intensively.

Extensive farming (the exploitation of vast acres of land on limited capital) was becoming unprofitable and unviable by the late 1940s because of high land prices. Where suitable land was available for tobacco production and climate allowed the regeneration of the veld, farmers planted tobacco in the same fields for two seasons before reverting the land for three to ten years under grass fallow.[65] The most common rotation, however, was two successive tobacco crops followed by maize, then green manuring and three years of grass.[66] As land and natural resources dwindled, and land costs rose, it became almost uneconomic for planters to continue with the practices of the inter-war years when land was cheap and readily available. Tobacco farmers could no longer continually stump virgin land each year as virgin lands had disappeared on some of the old established farms.[67] Also, the land was now becoming too expensive to be worked extensively and left for long in an unproductive state. Thus, the rising cost of production began to shape tobacco farmers' conservation consciousness more than any state-led programme spontaneously and simultaneously.

In 1949, the Council of the RTA perturbed by the rising costs of tobacco production had sought the assistance of the chief agricultural economist of the Department of Agriculture to assess the extent of this rise. The chief agricultural economist after a cost of production survey noted that the structure of cost had risen significantly since the London

[65] Scott, 'The Tobacco Industry of Southern Rhodesia', 189–206. [66] Ibid.
[67] W. E. Haviland, 'Tobacco Farm Organisation, Costs and Land Use in Southern Rhodesia' *South African Journal of Economics*, 21, 4 (1953), 367–380.

Table 2.1 *Tobacco cost of production in Southern Rhodesia, 1947–1950*

Item	*Cost of Production %*
European Labour	27.0
Native Labour	27.0
Tractor work	4.0
Ox work	1.0
Fertiliser	6.0
Grading and Marketing	9.0
Transport	5.5
Land and Buildings	2.0
Sundries	7.5
Overheads	11.0

Source: NAZ, S983/2- Changes in Tobacco Production Costs 1947–1950, Chief agricultural economist to Secretary RTA, 21 January 1950.

Agreement of 1947, with wages having a significant bearing on the cost structure and contributing towards 54 per cent of the cost of production.[68] The absolute cost determined by this enquiry was 16s.3d/lb for the 1948/1949 crop on the basis of cost indices which had been established at 14s.2d/lb for the 1946/1947 crop, 15s.3d/lb in 1947/1948, 16s.3d/lb in 1948/1949 and 18s.8d/lb on the 1949/1950 crop.[69] Table 2.1 shows tobacco cost of production indices established by the survey in 1950.

While tobacco farming in most countries like the USA during this time was conducted on a smaller scale with employment of family labour, the Southern Rhodesian crop was grown on white-owned estates on a large scale.[70] It was thus impossible to grow tobacco properly without a large capital outlay as during the first decade after the war the price of land suitable for tobacco cultivation became five or six times higher, while wage and rations costs trebled.[71] At the same time the changing pattern of farming in Southern Rhodesia meant that

68 NAZ, S983/2- Changes in Tobacco Production Costs 1947–1950, Chief Agricultural Economist to Secretary RTA, 21 January 1950.

69 Ibid.

70 NAZ, S2505/TOB/1/1 Tobacco Marketing Board Members Correspondence 1954–1956, Report of the Chief classifier visit to the US tobacco markets, 1955. Also see, Scott, 'The Tobacco Industry of Southern Rhodesia', 189–206.

71 Barclays Bank, *Tobacco* (London,1961), 131.

tobacco growers were no longer able to draw on abundant resources of cheap land and inexpensive labour as they had done during the inter-war years and so increase production economically by merely increasing the acreage under cultivation.[72] The rising cost of labour was largely due to the acute labour shortages which were being experienced across the colony as demand outstripped supply.[73]

Also, while during the inter-war years any grower who had a crop to deliver to the auction floors was assured of high prices and he could even get by with a poorly produced crop, with the ever-rising costs, efficiency was becoming essential.[74] Machinery was much costlier than before, so was fertiliser and it was now increasingly uneconomical to have yields of around 600 lbs/acre.[75] Production costs rose substantially, not only because of wage increases but also because the production of the desirable leaf entailed the use of recommended fertilisers, approved pesticides and modern methods of farming. Consequently, confronted by this hard squeeze between relatively stable world prices and continually rising costs Rhodesian tobacco farmers had to invest millions of dollars into scientific research and modern methods of farming so that they could maintain a margin of profit.[76]

The director of the Rhodesian Tobacco Research Board (TRB) noted this important trend in 1953 when he observed that increasing land prices gave an advantage to those who 'could improve their farming fastest'.[77] This meant embracing crop rotations, manuring crops, improved fertilisation, growing disease resistant varieties and employing effective methods of pest control.[78] The rising costs of land, labour and equipment supplies exerted an influence on tobacco growing methods in Southern Rhodesia, such that it was now paying better to practise a rotation of crops than to break up new land each year. Much of the land that had been left to revert to natural shrub and forestry growth during the 1930s because farmers could not use it to advantage without undue labour and expenditure was now being appropriated.[79]

[72] Ibid., 40.
[73] Annual Report of the Secretary of Lands and Agriculture, 1948.
[74] *Rhodesia Herald*, 3 September 1955. [75] Ibid. [76] Ibid.
[77] F. A. Stinson, 'Research and Sound Farming', *Rhodesia Tobacco*, 1 (June 1953), 4.
[78] Ibid. [79] Ibid.

The significant improvement of research and extension in tobacco during the period greatly improved intensive agriculture. In June 1947, the Council of the RTA appointed Dr Keystone as director of research. His report made a diagnosis of the research activities and emphasised that tobacco culture was so dependent on soil and climatic conditions that it needed many lines of research investigations in the different soil climatic regions. These included field investigations, rotational cropping systems, pruning and topping methods, field trials of insecticides.[80]

As a follow up to the Keystone Report, in 1949, Professor Frank Engledow compiled his report on *Agricultural Teaching Research and Advisory Work in Southern Rhodesia* which pointed out the need for a research framework balancing the needs of research in tobacco culture with good husbandry methods.[81] In its evidence to Engledow, the RTA committed to fund research to the tune of £2 to every £1 provided by the government up to £60,000.[82] The list of items the RTA considered imperative in research were: the discovery of cheap methods to combat main tobacco pests, eelworm, cutworm, crickets and aphids, the discovery of economical methods to combat bacterial diseases, fungus, to find suitable rotation schedules for different soils, fertiliser experiments and the study of the economy of heating with relation to tobacco flue-curing, and labour saving devices such as planters.[83] The dissemination of this information on research and on tobacco generally was helped by the publication of a monthly magazine *Rhodesian Tobacco Journal*, the first issue of which appeared in February 1949. In April 1950, tobacco research was taken away from the hands of government and placed under TRB by an agreement in which the tobacco growers through the RTA would annually contribute £65,000 and the government £35,000 towards flue-cured tobacco research.[84]

Dr F. Stinson, previously head of the Soil Science Department of Ontario Agricultural College in Canada, was appointed the new director of TRB. Under his leadership there was a fresh impetus towards experiments focussed on improving suitable methods of tobacco fertilisation for the sand veld, improving methods of field practices,

[80] G. H. Tanser, 'A History of the Tobacco Research Board: The First 25 Years', *The Zimbabwe Agricultural Journal Technical Handbook*, 7 (1991), 29.
[81] Ibid. [82] Ibid., 33. [83] Ibid.
[84] Report of the Tobacco Research Board, 1950.

cultivation, and the control of pests – particularly eelworms.[85] Investigation on the use of soil fumigants for the control of eelworm in seed beds and tobacco lands was pursued vigorously with the result that soil fumigants such as ethylene dibromide (EDB) came into popular use.[86] Soil rotation was considered an important aspect since tobacco lands were more susceptible to eelworm infestations. The TRB recommended perennial grasses such as Katambora Rhodes grass (*Chloris gayana*), weeping love grass (*Eragrostis curvula*) and Guinea grass (*Panicum maximum*) as these grasses offered the best resistance to eel worm infestation and provided fodder for livestock.[87] In 1960, a writer for the American tobacco division Albert Davis who had spent years observing tobacco cultural practices in Southern Rhodesia appreciated the progress done in integrating biological conservation using grass rotations in tobacco fields and pointed out that grass was one of the most important crops grown on tobacco fields and grass rotations determined the amount of land that could be utilised for tobacco on most farms.[88] He added that:

> Grass occupy the tobacco lands for two to four years; after this they are ploughed under with tobacco plantings following. After being ploughed the field is left fallow for some time … this aid in control of nematodes. One of the main factors controlling the amount of tobacco grown each year is the amount of land tied up in rotation grasses on a typical Rhodesian tobacco farm, at one time.[89]

The result of this enthusiastic and effective research thrust was that it transformed several practices in tobacco culture, as farmers began to embrace scientific knowledge and apply it in a manner which contributed to conservation of the sand veld. It was now possible to establish permanent tobacco rotations without clearing virgin lands every year. The idea that there is no land as good as virgin land for the tobacco crop, which was popular during the inter-war years grew less popular as farmers began to understand that:

[85] NAZ, S983/2, Changes in Tobacco Production Costs 1947–1950, Tobacco Research, 30 December 1949.
[86] Ibid.
[87] 'Results of Experiments, 1949–1951', *Tobacco Research Bulletin* 1 (1952), 4.
[88] A. Davis, 'Tobacco Production and Marketing in Southern Rhodesia, Northern Rhodesia and Nyasaland', Foreign Agricultural Service, United States Department of Agriculture, (1964), 3.
[89] Ibid.

> If land is protected from erosion immediately after stumping and is cropped in rotation for three or four years before being reverted to grass, that land is not exhausted but is still in good heart, and when the time comes to plough out the grass and put in tobacco again, the land is to all intents and purpose as good as virgin.[90]

Efficient utilisation of land in tobacco rotations saw fallow land being used for feeding livestock by grazing, by cutting hay, or by making grass ensilage.[91] Working on this system it was possible to build up a considerable animal husbandry side to tobacco farming and integrate livestock production to tobacco farming.

Therefore, it is important to understand that biological conservation and the integration of livestock farming to field husbandry and farming if not in harmony with nature, then at least in concert with nature was slowly getting more established amongst tobacco farmers in Southern Rhodesia beginning from the late 1940s. This was because of the dynamic of capital, high land prices and the general exorbitant production costs that made extensive farming of tobacco unprofitable. The next section closely examines how these conservation ideologies were adopted and how they transformed the spatial appearance of the tobacco farms.

Mixed Farmers and Land Developers: Tobacco Farmers and Land Conservation, 1948–1960

A focus on the initial few years of the post-war tobacco boom in Southern Rhodesia can draw conclusions which though contextually valid ignore the long-term trickle-down effects of tobacco capital in changing the farming systems and positively changing the farming countryside. To this extent, it is important to note that while in the immediate post-war years, tobacco had created a notable disparity in capital distribution and concerns about the colony's food situation, this scenario was just a transitional stage as tobacco farming systems were evolving from planter communities into mixed farming. The Annual Report of the Secretary of Lands and Agriculture in 1948 pointed out to

[90] G. R. Hayman, 'Conservation on a Tobacco Farm', *Rhodesia Agricultural Journal*, (June 1953), 223–234.

[91] Hayman, 'Conservation on a Tobacco Farm', 223–234. Grass ensilage is fermented wet grass that is stored as fodder to feed livestock.

one changing aspect about tobacco production in the colony when it noted that:

> Tobacco is no longer regarded as an exploitative crop as it has commonly been considered in the past. Now it is financially the most important product in the colony, and it is realised the present prosperity of the colony is largely bound up with the future of the tobacco industry. Every effort must be made to expand the industry and improve the quality of the product.[92]

During that year, the department noted that the acreage under green crops was 99,449 acres and legumes for hay 70,140 acres making a total of 166,639 acres.[93] The report added that a further quantity of 36,069 tonnes of compost had been applied to 37,000 acres of crops, and the 203,639 acres under legumes and compost represented 38 per cent of total acreage under maize and other summer crops.[94]

Indeed, many of these conservation initiatives were described as 'politically neutral projects' that had limited value in pushing the wider policy issues involving land conservation.[95] However, it is critical to point out that significant progress in conservation *was* slowly taking place in white farms and constituting a progressive change in white farmers' attitudes towards land and natural resources. To this extent the notion of environmental transformation outside degradation conservation narratives is more relevant in framing these progressive conservation changes and efforts in the tobacco farms.[96] Much of this effort was being achieved through the Intensive Conservation Areas (ICAs) that had been established by the Natural Resources Act of 1942 but came to be operationalised in 1948.[97] Through these ICAs

[92] Annual Report of the Secretary of Agriculture and Lands, 1948. [93] Ibid.
[94] Ibid.
[95] Phimister, 'Discourse and the Discipline of Historical Context', 263–275.
[96] Beinart, *The Rise of Conservation in South Africa*, 390.
[97] Intensive Conservation Areas (ICAs) were modelled along the American conservation districts which were introduced in 1937 by the Standard State Soil Conservation District Law as a brainchild of M. L. Wilson, Undersecretary for Agriculture. The conservation districts were local units organised around local capacities to meet the needs of soil and water conservation with the technical and financial assistance of the Federal government. In Southern Rhodesia ICAs were established in white settler farming communities to engage in collective control of soil erosion and building of mechanical works. In 1944 the first ICA was created in the tobacco-producing area of Inyazura. The proclamation for the ICAs included a number of set conservation objectives which included to avoid cultivating any land less than 30 metres from the high flood level of any river, controlled burning of grass, avoiding unnecessary destruction of

much work was being done in intensive conservation programmes with the help of the Department of Conservation and Extension (Conex), which had been set up in 1948 to assist farmers with technical assistance in conservation works. Simeon Maravanyika in his case study of the Bromley ICA (which was a tobacco-producing area) notes the significant work which was being done in white farms towards soil and water conservation through the ICAs.[98] By 1949, the Bromley ICA had built eight dams with the capacity of three million gallons of water.[99]

Indeed, the construction of dams and the development of irrigation infrastructure was one of the most conspicuous features on the Rhodesian agricultural landscape between the late 1940s and the 1960s.[100] This period marked by the optimism of the tobacco boom and growing industrialisation witnessed an accelerated institutionalisation of water planning and dam construction for irrigating lands for food production.[101] In 1952, the Report on Large Scale Irrigation in Southern Rhodesia was published.[102] It prioritised water planning for extensive and intensive irrigation for food crop production. The construction of dams in the settler farms meant the restructuring of new landscapes in ways in which water conservation became linked to identity and belonging. David McDermott Hughes shows how dams served multiple purposes that transcended conservation and became fetishised symbols of white belonging, identity and claim to the land in Zimbabwe.[103] The new hydrological landscapes involved the imposition of new imaginations and experiences in a process evoked by white farmers' need to engrave belonging into physical landscapes and legitimate claims to ownership of land. Joost Fontein sees the dam construction and the concomitant irrigation revolution in Southern Rhodesia during the 1950s and 1960s as representing a re-imagined

indigenous trees, and where wood fuel was used to cure tobacco to ensure adequate supplies by adopting alternatives.

98 S. Maravanyika, 'Soil Conservation and the White Agrarian Environment in Colonial Zimbabwe, c.1908–1980' (PhD Thesis, University of Pretoria, 2013), 236.

99 Ibid., 237.

100 See, J. Fontein, *Remaking the Mutirikwi: Landscape, Water and Belonging in Southern Zimbabwe* (Suffolk, 2015).

101 Ibid.,173. 102 Ibid., 180–181.

103 D. M. Hughes, 'Farms Dams, Conservation, and Whiteness in Zimbabwe', *American Ethnologist*, 33, 2 (2006), 269–287.

future for Europeans during an era of rapid decolonisation – a restructuring of new futures and pasts through 'engineering the fabric of topology'.[104]

The restructuring of the landscape also happened through new contouring practices in tobacco farms as research on soil conservation and erosion intensified. In 1953, the Department of Conservation and Extension (Conex) set up a soil erosion research unit at Henderson in Mazowe to investigate the dangers of sheet erosion and the mechanics of this process. The erosion survey had identified tobacco as one of the problem crops since it provided the poorest protection to the soil, and this was exacerbated by the practice of ridging up and down the slope.[105] Field trials at Henderson revealed that while average soil losses per acre for maize and groundnuts was 8.7 tonnes per acre, the losses on tobacco fields amounted to 15.6 tonnes per acre.[106] In view of the serious erosion position and the importance of tobacco as a cash crop, tobacco lands were selected as a priority in the programme at Henderson research station. Members of Conex and field extension officers investigated the problem on farms and recommended that Conex should discourage the practice of ridging up and down the slope and promote ridging parallel to the contour, or in other words 'contour farming'.[107] The research findings of this survey were published in a technical report contained in a booklet entitled *'Conservation farming for tobacco growers'*. It recommended that conservation systems were efficient in reducing soil losses from gully and sheet erosion, and called on the need for suitable land preparation, planting and harvesting techniques so that the conservation model was an integral part of the whole farming system.[108] This idea was becoming very popular amongst tobacco farmers such that by 1956, Umvukwesi ICA had achieved 53 per cent adoption of contour farming by area and 54 per cent by numbers of farmers in the tobacco sector.[109] Mr. G. V. Jacks the director of the Commonwealth Bureau of Soil Sciences appreciated the significant progress during his visit in

[104] Fontein, *Remaking the Mutirikwi*, 174.
[105] NAZ, S3920, Natural Resources Board, Intensive Conservation Areas.
[106] N. W. Hudson, 'Soil Erosion and Tobacco Growing', *Rhodesia Agricultural Journal* (November–December 1957), 547–555.
[107] NAZ, S3920, Natural Resources Board, ICAs. [108] Ibid.
[109] Minutes of the Annual General Meeting of the Centenary West and Umvukwesi ICA, 4 September 1956.

1954 and remarked that soil conservation in Southern Rhodesia was 'as good as in America' adding that 'in some way you seem to have gotten to the root of the problem of soil conservation. You have realised that soil conservation is not merely a matter of building contour ridges and dams but of complete farm planning'.[110]

Thus, while Phimister describes the progress of biological conservation as 'lagging far behind' such dismissive cynicism and scepticism detracts from a critical appraisal of changes taking place on the use of good farming methods, water conservation for irrigation, the integration of field husbandry and livestock farming, the development of mixed farming and natural resource conservation as well as food crop production.[111] On the tobacco farms, this improvement and transition in landscape was becoming more conspicuous with changes in land use patterns and the general farm environment. This transition in scenery was more aptly captured by the Southern Rhodesia tobacco representative to London in 1949 who described the changes in the spatial patterns in the landscape taking place in the tobacco farms as constituting a 'healthy change in appearance of the farms', punctuated by general farming with fine herds, sheep and poultry, many new dams, and many contour ridges.[112] Overall, the tobacco farmer was moving from being a planter, into a mixed farmer practising intensive farming and rendering soil fertile for other agricultural enterprises and contributing to the colony's ideals of soil and water conservation.[113] In the tobacco farms, there were now many new dams, much contour ridging and good farm roads.[114] This new outlook was more intimately reflected in the *Rhodesian Tobacco Journal* by 'the roving reporter' who went around the tobacco farms and documented methods of agricultural production. He noted after visiting one farm:

> To those who contend that mixed farming cannot be allied to tobacco growing on the sand veld and that tobacco holdings of less than 3,000 acres are an uneconomic proposition, I recommend pay a visit to J. V. Danckwerts in the Arlington area ... He stresses the danger of over cultivation of sand veld country, and... to avoid overworking the land too much he has devised

110 *Rhodesia Herald*, 8 October 1954.
111 Phimister, 'Discourse and the Discipline of Historical Context', 263–275.
112 Annual Report of the Tobacco Representative, 1949. 113 Ibid.
114 Ibid.

a system of planting in place of tobacco maize, beans, nuts which also cuts down labour requirements ... Ample supplies of water for all purposes including irrigation of fodder crops are derived from three boreholes which at a cost of £2,000 has been a worthwhile investment. Mr Danckwerts drove me around and showed me excellent work which is being done in contouring and building dams.[115]

On another farm in Chikurubi owned by a Mr Ken Edward, he commented:

On the estate itself, a tremendous amount of afforestation had been carried out in conifers, gums and trees of many other varieties, and the lands are all sub divided, one from the other, by fine windbreaks which also provide valuable shade to lands themselves and thus help reduce the evaporation of soil moisture ... It interested me to learn that many of the lands in use have been rotation cropped for more than thirty years, yet some of the best yields in recent seasons have been obtained from the old lands. This is attributable to subsoiling, the large use of compost ... huge quantities of compost are made every year with saw dust litter from the cattle pens mixed with various types of green crops and natural grasses.[116]

On another farm owned by Winston Field in Marandellas, the farm owner explained how he had combined good husbandry and land management in his farm operations, doing afforestation work so much that he now had sufficient timber requirements for the next twenty years without having to have recourse to indigenous timber.[117] As a result of such efforts, the area planted alone to exotic *Eucalyptus* trees in the main tobacco growing areas showed an increase of 10 per cent during 1948 and 1949 bringing the total area to nearly 24,000 acres.[118] The conservation of trees featured most importantly amongst tobacco farmers as they began to use more fuel efficient and energy conserving furnaces, oil-curing furnaces and coal-fired heating and curing systems.[119] During 1949 and 1950, 14,420 tobacco furnaces were reported, 87 per cent of which being wood fired, 12 per cent coal

[115] 'Around the Farms by Our Roving Reporter', *Rhodesian Tobacco Journal*, April 1949.

[116] 'Individual Farming Methods: Chikurubi, Owned by Ken Edwards an Ideal Mixed Farm', *Rhodesian Tobacco Journal*, November 1949.

[117] Ibid. [118] Southern Rhodesia Legislative Assembly Debates, 26 April 1950.

[119] One such fuel-efficient furnace was the Gundry tobacco furnace which had been first publicised in 1934 and improved significantly over the years. Its important features were low fuel consumption.

burning and 1 per cent using oil.[120] Soil conservation was also becoming a key investment in most farms. As an item on normal farm production, it cost an average £40 annually between 1950 and 1952.[121] In its report of the activities for 1951, the NRB stated that some of the most advanced areas in relation to conservation were those where tobacco was grown:

> It is noteworthy that some of the most advanced areas from the conservation point of view are those in which tobacco production provides the main source of revenue, and it is commonly realised that the majority of the more experienced tobacco growers are utilising this revenue for the development of their properties on sound mixed farming lines and thus making a material contribution towards solving the problem of proper utilisation of the sand veld.[122]

After the post-war boom tobacco farmers were able to create mixed farming systems in the sand veld areas. The value of the tobacco crop to these areas was great as it opened more land for settlement and spurred investments in soil and water conservation. A writer for the *Rhodesia Herald*, Nigel Phillip, pointed this out:

> Our soil consists of 92 per cent sand veld, and where rainfall allows are most suitable for the production of tobacco. As virgin soils there are not suitable for foodstuffs but are greatly increased for this purpose in rotation with tobacco. Tobacco is not only an initiation crop but supplies the necessary early cash to enable farmers to finance their operations. In fact, where food farmers have sand veld they are encouraged to plant tobacco to assist them.[123]

In 1954, the chief agricultural economist pointed out that accelerating food production in the tobacco farming areas and reducing tobacco acreages would have negative effects for the Rhodesian economy.[124] He argued that the whole development of the sand veld areas of the country had been based on the capitalisation of these areas out of the incomes on tobacco. These areas comprising approximately 80 per cent of the total cultivable land under European occupation were

[120] Haviland, 'Tobacco Farm Organisation', 367–380. [121] Ibid.
[122] Annual Report of the Natural Resources Board, 1952.
[123] *Rhodesia Herald*, 3 April 1951.
[124] NAZ, 982/T/2F, Rhodesia Tobacco Association General 1 July 1954–13 March 1955, Chief agricultural economist, Notes on the effects of a decrease in demand for flue-cured Virginia tobacco.

largely incapable of sustaining any other form of crop production without the application of liberal quantities of fertiliser or rotation based on long periods under grass for subsequent ploughing and cultivation.[125] He noted that it was on these areas that the country was largely dependent for the development of its livestock industry and on which it has placed its only hopes of meeting the ever-increasing demand by the African labour population for large quantities of meat that they now insisted on as part of their normal diet.[126] He concluded that tobacco alone could finance the necessary development of these areas which entailed the provision of dams, widespread fencing and sinking of boreholes, and any material setback on tobacco was to result in retarding agricultural development.[127]

Mr Malone of the Board of the Tobacco Trade in London, who had visited Rhodesia in 1956 and toured thirty-six farms, chronicled that he had been impressed by the evidence he had seen of Rhodesia's dependence on tobacco, and most farmers he had spoken to pointed out that tobacco was the only crop that could finance the opening up of the country.[128] By 1956 tobacco farmers had more fully developed their lands so that 50 per cent of food production in Southern Rhodesia now came from tobacco growing areas.[129] Also, W. E. Haviland who was Southern Rhodesia's director of irrigation argued that the problem had not been that tobacco had taken away agricultural resources such as labour and capital from maize, but rather that tobacco expansion had provided more mouths to feed, and without a tobacco expansion, there would not have been such an influx of workers and increase in the demand for maize.[130] The total number of Africans employed on tobacco farms rose from 80,060 in 1945 to 92,640 in 1948 constituting over half of the total number of Africans employed in the agricultural industry.[131] Tobacco was also the only agricultural commodity that could bear the high cost of transport in a landlocked country and at the same time finance the development of the country in a pervasive spatial sense.[132]

125 Ibid. 126 Ibid. 127 Ibid.
128 NAZ, F114/473/E.8/8/ (473), Note on a Meeting held in the Commonwealth Relations Office on 26 October 1956 on Rhodesia Tobacco.
129 Ibid. 130 Haviland, 'Tobacco Farm Organisation', 367–380.
131 Annual Report of the Chief Tobacco Officer, January 1948.
132 Haviland, 'Tobacco Farm Organisation', 367–380.

Thus, hand in hand with tobacco production went the production of other key primary products vital to the life of Southern Rhodesia's community such as maize, cattle and dairy produce and timber as tobacco farmers made the most of the opportunities to develop their mixed farming activities. Large new areas of European occupation sprung up all over the colony, and vast tracts of land were being occupied, which could have taken hundreds of years to develop without the incentive of the flourishing tobacco industry.[133] Accordingly, while during the inter-war years the majority of tobacco farmers practised monoculture because they had to, after the tobacco boom 'every year tobacco income was used to fence the farms, to build paddocks for cattle, to build up beef and dairy herds, to provide irrigation for cultivated pastures, to experiment with new crops'.[134] As a result of tobacco expansion, the pattern of good land settlements spread further into remote areas, and the landscape became more pronounced and appealing as the soil was no longer vandalised but 'was occupied and mastered'.[135]

It is also important to note that the dominance of tobacco in the Southern Rhodesian agriculture was not constant but fluctuated. It had become smaller by the mid-1950s to constitute 51.8 per cent of all farm incomes while the importance of maize and cattle over the same period increased significantly.[136] Between 1949 and 1950, 77.3 per cent of all farms were diversified with maize, and of these 54.4 per cent had tobacco as the principal crop, 42 per cent of all farms in Southern Rhodesia reported tobacco as the principal crop, and of these only 1.8 per cent were completely specialised in tobacco farming.[137] A survey of white commercial agriculture in the colony issued by the Central Statistical Office showed that although the gross revenue of tobacco had been increasing steadily since 1950, the overall percentage of tobacco to farm earnings was dwindling.[138] While tobacco income was 67.1 per cent of all farm earnings during 1949/1950, it had dwindled to 58.1 per cent by 1955/1956, and to 51 per cent in

[133] *Industry and Commerce in Rhodesia*, December 1949.

[134] Clements and Harben, *Leaf of Gold*, 152. [135] Ibid.

[136] This figure is extrapolated from the data presented in Figure 2.5 which indicates gross output in monetary terms of European Agriculture in Southern Rhodesia between 1954 and 61.

[137] Haviland, 'Tobacco Farm Organisation', 367–380.

[138] Central Statistical Office of Southern Rhodesia, Agricultural Statistics, 1961.

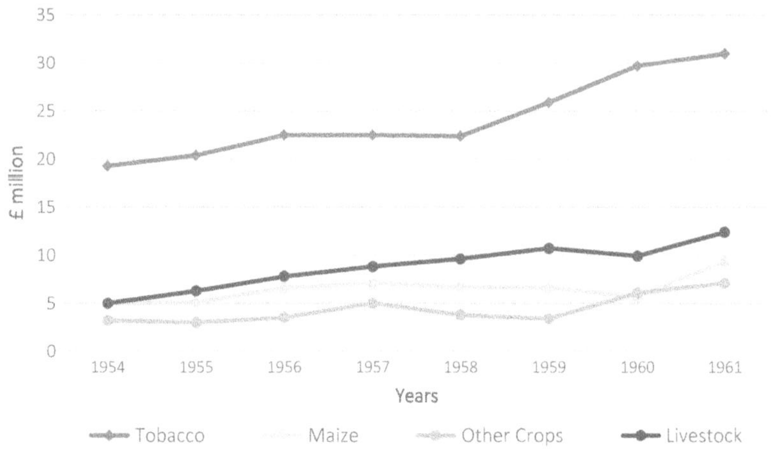

Figure 2.5 Gross output of European agriculture in Southern Rhodesia, 1954–1961

Source: Central Statistical Office of Southern Rhodesia, Agricultural Statistics, 1961.

1960.[139] At the same time, income from maize, dairy, cattle and other crops produced an increased share of total farm income.[140] Almost half of the flue-cured tobacco growers of Southern Rhodesia in 1961 had more than 100 head of cattle per farm, and over 80 per cent grew maize.[141]

The graph in Figure 2.5 shows that despite the dominance of tobacco, gross agricultural output from other crops and agricultural enterprises increased significantly between 1954 and 1961. Maize gross output rose from £5 million in 1954 to £9.3 million in 1961, while livestock production more than doubled in gross output from £6.0 million in 1954 to 12.4 million in 1961. This reflects that the dynamic of capital accumulation during the tobacco boom extended itself way beyond curtailing the growth of other agricultural sectors like maize production and livestock. On the other hand, this dynamic over time witnessed tobacco farmers investing in livestock, dairying and food production. The tobacco farmers had become more versatile. The RTA noted that 'the slightly better returns for tobacco has enabled

139 Ibid.

140 'How Tobacco Dominates the Southern Rhodesia Farm Scene', *Rhodesian Tobacco Journal*, March 1957.

141 Central Statistical Office of Southern Rhodesia, Agricultural Statistics, 1961.

these growers who are first and foremost tobacco farmers to put into practice theories about management of beef and dairy herds that they could never afford in the past'.[142] Officials statistics did show that in 1950, in seven of the thirty-three agricultural districts into which the colony was divided approximately 86 per cent of the flue-cured crop was grown by 83 per cent of the farmers, and in those areas 70 per cent of the colony's surplus maize was produced and 35 per cent of the cattle owned.[143] By 1961, the overall economic contribution of tobacco to the economy was so vast that it provided a livelihood for some 1,130,000 people in Southern Rhodesia.[144] The total number of male Africans working on European farms in Southern Rhodesia was 208,484 compared with 192,403 in 1957 and 194,327 in 1954.[145]

Conclusion

Therefore, in trying to understand the phenomenon of change on the Southern Rhodesian agrarian landscape during the post-war tobacco boom there is need to engage and further the existing historical debates on colonial conservation. Progressive conservation narratives are a helpful conceptual paradigm within which to understand the dynamic of environmental change as non-linear, fluid and kinetic. They gives scope to imagine and dramatise agrarian and environmental encounters beyond the post-war tobacco boom in vivid narratives that embrace change as a constant. Yet, this optimistic (indeed, occasionally Panglossian) progressivism sometimes exaggerates the smooth transitions of conservation ideologies from the late eighteenth century into higher forms of conservation management that arose at the beginning of the twentieth century. The pattern of progressive transitioning in the tobacco farms in Southern Rhodesia was not linear but a long drawn out, arduous journey across cyclical periods of financial depressions, overproduction, speculative production, unbalanced agricultural growth, retarded food production and un-contoured lands. But within this rugged terrain, at each stage new agronomic practices, conservation

142 *The Rhodesian Tobacco Grower*, August 1952.
143 *Rhodesia Herald*, 11 April 1951.
144 NAZ, F226/121/F2, Production Control 1964–1965, Memorandum by the Federal Ministry of Agriculture on Virginia Flue-cured tobacco production control policy.
145 Ibid.

ideologies, rotational principles were evolving. The post-war boom and tobacco capital unleashed the centripetal forces that spontaneously and simultaneously congealed all these formative biological practices into a conservation doctrine that slowly began to change the farming landscape and tobacco production systems in more positive ways than before. It was not a cataclysmic conservation revolution, but a subtle wave whose dialectical impulse generated a few negative signals in the Southern Rhodesian agricultural economy, but whose self-corrective long-term and medium-term dynamic led to wholesome environmental changes by 1960. There is also need to counterbalance declensionist interpretations of the tobacco boom in Southern Rhodesia by illuminating on the dynamic of environmental change and how colonial agrarian encounters in the 1930s and 1950s were not always hostile interactions between white settlers and the environment. The post-war tobacco boom significantly shaped agricultural development and conservation thinking in Southern Rhodesia. It provided the impetus through capital resources and exorbitant land prices for investments in intensive mixed farming systems, good land husbandry, soil and water conservation all of which altered environments and landscapes in white farms between 1947 and 1960.

3 A Silenced Spring? Exploring Africa's 'Rachel Carson Moment'

A Socio-environmental History of the Pesticides in Tobacco Production in Southern Rhodesia, 1945–1980

Can anyone believe it is possible to lay down such a barrage of poisons on the surface of the earth without making it unfit for all life? They should not be called 'insecticides', but 'biocides'.

Rachel Carson, 1962.

Introduction

In 1962, Rachel Carson, an American marine biologist, penned *Silent Spring*, a highly controversial book that revolutionised global perceptions of the widespread use of pesticides and chemicals in agricultural production.[1] In this book, Carson critiqued conventional views of organochloride persistent pesticides, particularly Dichlorodiphenyltrichloroethane (DDT) and their toxic effects on ecological systems, as well as plant and human life. She portrayed a dystopian civilisation teetering on the brink of self-imposed extinction because of the contamination of the air, rivers, forests and sea with chemical sprays that 'lie in the soil, entering into living organisms, passing from one to another in a chain of poisoning and death'.[2] *Silent Spring* became a contentious and contested text that put pesticide use within the domain of public debate and environmental policy globally. Although initially maligned by the defenders of the pesticide and chemical establishment, the book precipitated our contemporary discourse and debates over the ecological dimensions of pesticide use.[3]

[1] Rachel Carson, *Silent Spring* (London: Hamish Hamilton, 1963). [2] Ibid, 5.

[3] The book was heavily attacked by the defenders of the pesticide industry as being unscientific and a hysterical, apocalyptic fantasy. Environmental revisionists like David Ropeik also blamed her for fostering a set of accepted beliefs that actually caused much damage to the human and natural environment, http://blogs.discovermagazine.com/collideascape/2012/06/22/the-lessons-and-echoes-of-silent-spring/#.WzvC-RaxWEC, accessed 5 July 2018.

Silent Spring galvanised environmental activism and public policy in most countries as the problem of pesticides gained public notoriety and slowly became a subject of enquiry investigated by environmental scientists and, even more slowly, environmental historians.[4] However, concerning tobacco production, *Silent Spring* was reticent, noting only as an aside the permanent poisoning of the soil by tobacco chemicals.[5] This silence caused 'Big Tobacco' to receive the book less critically and even embrace it, as they had feared an overt critique might draw attention to the industry's own massive use of pesticides.[6]

Was there an African Rachel Carson? No, but Africa had its 'Rachel Carson moment(s)', as this chapter will show. Despite this, however, as well as over fifty years of considerable historical analysis of pesticides in the United States and the Global North, Africa has been neglected – there is a strange historiographical lacuna. Perhaps this omission could be explained by the distinctive quantitative disparities in pesticide use between the Global South and North. The World Health Organization (WHO) estimates that despite rising use since the 1940s, the Global South only consumes 25 per cent of total global pesticide production, while the North consumes a disproportionately higher 75 per cent.[7] More worryingly, however, and ironically within the context of the

[4] It is important to note that even before *Silent Spring*, environmental issues were already being made visible in public policy from the late 1950s by several other writers and practitioners in the global North. This movement, however, was not firmly entrenched, and it was Carson who gave much impetus to this wave. These early writers include the British–South African Sir Solly Zuckerman who coined the term 'environmental science' in 1959 and played a huge role in the establishment of the UK Natural Environment Research Council in 1964, and the American Lynton Caldwell who authored 'Environment: A Focus for Public Policy', in *Eikistics*, 17, 102 (May 1964). See Paul Warde, L. Robin and S. Sörlin, *The Environment: A History of the Idea* (Baltimore, 2018), 18–20.

Also see T. R. Dunlap (eds.), *DDT, The Silent Spring and the Rise of Environmentalism: Classic Texts* (Seattle, 2008); F. Graham, *Since Silent Spring* (London, 1972); A. Vinogradov and S. Petriashin, 'Chemical Industry, the Environment and Russian Provincial Society: The Case of Kokshan Chemical Works, 1850–1925', *Ambix*, 1, 26 (April 2018), 1–26.

[5] Rachel Carson discusses how tobacco chemicals then widely used in the United States, such as arsenic and benzene hexachloride, contaminate the soil and make it toxic for food crops such as carrots and sweet potatoes.

[6] Standard Schaeffer, 'The Greening of Big Tobacco', *Counterpunch Magazine*, https://counterpunch.org/2007/12/15/the-greening-of-big-tobacco/, accessed 10 July 2018.

[7] www.who.int/ceh/capacity/Pesticides.pdf, accessed 25 February 2019.

historiographical lacuna, 99 per cent of deaths due to pesticide use occur in the Global South![8] This inevitably begs the question whether *Silent Spring* represents a form of only European and Anglo-American environmentalism, which has been simply *projected* as a global movement. Is it because *Silent Spring* pontificates from the lofty parapets of a technologically modernistic, racially privileged society and fails to appeal to similar chemical calamities and disasters in the developing world that largely affect marginalised racial groups such as blacks, Asians and Latinos? This profoundly racially tinged accusation is, of course, a reminder that modern environmentalism is in itself the progeny of Western post-war cultures of prosperity and consumerism that ignited concerns about quality of life and other aesthetic values to which the natural environment became a public good, and which rested on perceptions of nature as being inseparable from humans.[9] This classed and raced identity of modern environmentalism has resulted in Carson's work not being fully appreciated or even investigated more robustly in the Global South.[10] Moreover, once a new wave of iconoclastic scholarship on environmental histories emerged in the 1990s, the universalism of environmentalism was challenged and a call was issued for more contextualised and nuanced interpretations.[11] These scholars argued that Northern environmentalism is not relevant to poor countries because of different development paths taken as well as differences in economic strength, socio-political structures and cultural attitudes between North and South explained (crudely) by poverty and weak democratic systems.[12] Under the banner of 'Environmental Justice' this scholarship further criticised the unfair

[8] 'Communities in Peril: Global Report on Health Impacts of Pesticide Use in Agriculture', Pesticide Action Network (September 2010), www.pan-germany.org/download/PAN-I_CBM-Global-Report_1006-final.pdf, accessed 25 February 2019.

[9] G. Kroll, 'The Silent Spring of Rachel Carson: Mass Media and the Origins of Modern Environmentalism', *Public Understanding of Science*, 10 (2001), 403–420.

[10] S. Miller, *An Environmental History of Latin America* (Cambridge, 2007), 206.

[11] Most outstanding in this regard is the work of Ramachandra Guha and Joan Martinez, which rejects a universal theory of modern environmentalism and contends that there are two different traditions of environmentalism for the North and South, all based on their unique historical trajectories. See, R. Guha and J. Martinez, *Varieties of Environmentalism: Essays North and South* (London, 1997), 12.

[12] Miller, *An Environmental History of Latin America*, 206.

and disproportionate impact of environmental policies along the lines of race, colour and class, even within the Global North.

This critical scholarly tradition seems to have evoked the derision for Carson in Africa and in the Global South, where environmentalism has struggled to connect with the historical problems of poverty, inequality and the legacies of colonialist and racist environmental violence. The ecocentrism of Carson's *Silent Spring* has been viewed by anthropocentric environmentalists as diametrically opposed to the more human-oriented environmentalism appropriate for Africa and the Global South.[13] Contemporary critics of her work have even called her a 'mass murderer' responsible for the death of millions of Africans from malaria due to her hyperbole and apocalyptic alarmism which led WHO to suspend the Global Malaria Eradication Programme in 1969 and to stop funding anti-malaria spray programmes in Africa.[14] However, African governments still remain opposed to the global 'ban' on DDT.[15] This background has clouded a critical understanding and historical reading of Carson in the contextualised realities of Africa, where *Silent Spring* has been approached by most critics of ecocentrism with a hostility almost amounting to hyperbolic.[16] This polemicisation

[13] See, P. Driessen, *Eco-Imperialism: Green Power, Black Death* (Bellevue, 2003). Driessen attacks the eco-centric environmental lobby groups from the Global North that value wildlife and ecology above human lives. He also further questions the scientific pedigree of the DDT claims in *Silent Spring*.

[14] D. Kinkela, *DDT and the American Century: Global Health, Environmental Politics and the Pesticide that Changed the World* (Chapel Hill, NC: University of North Carolina Press, 2011), 145. Also, US Senator Tom Coburn declared in 2007 that 'millions of people, particularly children under five, died because governments bought into Carson's junk science claims about DDT'. The bestselling novelist Michael Crichton in one of his novels, titled *State of Fear*, blames Carson for the DDT ban that 'killed more people than Hitler', and he puts the death toll at 50 million. See https://e360.yale.edu/features/rachel_carsons_critics_keep_on_but_she_told_truth_about_ddt, accessed 26 February 2019.

[15] In July 2013, the heads of state and government of the African Union adopted a resolution calling for the continued use of DDT for malaria eradication in the continent despite mounting concerns from some environmentalists in the Global North.

[16] As a result of propaganda from critics of ecocentrism and other localised experiences, most African governments continue to use DDT for the control of malaria and they have criticised the ban as being irrelevant in Africa where malaria kills millions of people every year and is a more serious threat than DDT environmental contamination. In 1996 for instance South Africa withdrew the use of DDT for malaria control and this resulted in a huge surge in malaria cases,

springs from the tension between what Ramachandra Guha and Joan Martinez have termed 'full stomach and empty belly environmentalism'.[17] Implicit in this dichotomisation is the racial legacy it reveals within the context of Africa's colonial history of racial domination, exploitation and subjugation. Subsequently, 'full stomach environmentalism' has been described as anti-human, elitist and driven by rich, white NGOs and wealthy nations which impose environmental agendas that are either irrelevant or actively harmful to Africa and black Africans.[18]

However, this chapter argues that it is imperative to go beyond strident polemics and attempt an historically contextualised understanding of Carson in Africa since the concerns she raised have continued to permeate current debates on the use of pesticides in agricultural production and the attendant human and ecological cost in the Global South. In the realm of tobacco farming, for example, Patricia Díaz Romo produced a 2011 documentary film that graphically portrayed the pesticide exposure of Huichol Indians who work as labourers in Mexico, exposing fatal poisonings, attendant poverty, vulnerability and reckless exploitation of labourers in the toxic zones that are Mexican tobacco farms.[19] There has also been increasing concern about the neuropsychiatric effects of pesticide exposure experienced by tobacco workers, with reports of incidences of depression and suicide linked to organophosphate pesticides.[20] More revealing in that regard is a study on Brazil's tobacco farms that found 48 per cent of workers suffered from pesticide-related health problems.[21] In Africa, the situation is equally disastrous. During a WHO

forcing the country to revert to DDT. Data for global use of DDT between 2000 and 2014 reveal that of the nineteen countries listed as still openly using DDT, fourteen are in sub-Saharan Africa. See, H. Van den berg et al., 'Global Trends in the Production and Use of DDT for Control of Malaria and Other Vector-borne Diseases', *Malaria Journal* 16, 401 (2017), 1–8.

17 Guha and Martinez, *Varieties of Environmentalism*, 12.

18 A. Ross, *Strange Weather: Culture, Science and Technology in the Age of Limits* (New York, 1991), 207–212.

19 P. Díaz Romo, 'Huicholes y Plaguicidas' [Huichols and Pesticides], www.youtube.com/watch?v=-5k7Xg8JuMI, accessed 11 April 2018.

20 T. Arcury and S. Quandt, 'Health and Social Impacts of Tobacco Production', *Journal of Agro-medicine*, 11, 3–4 (2008), 71–81.

21 R. M. Salvi et al., 'Neuro-psychiatric Evaluation in Subjects Chronically Exposed to Organophosphate Pesticides', *Toxicological Sciences*, 72, 2 (2003), 267–271.

public hearing on the Framework Convention on Tobacco Control (FCTC) in August 2000, a Kenyan member of parliament pointed out the scourge of pesticide use in tobacco farming in Africa and the impacts on poor black peasant farmers and the natural environment.[22] These include pesticide-related ailments, unexplained miscarriages, infant mortality and poisoned rivers.[23]

While there are several historical works on pesticides and pest control in Africa, most of these examine the problem from the perspective of colonisation of land and control of nature, particularly from an epidemiological perspective.[24] These studies focus on colonial pest control programmes for diseases such as trypanosomiasis, rinderpest, malaria and sleeping sickness that became popular in the discourses of colonial conquest and development from the 1930s. They, however, do not construct these histories within the narratives of environmentalism

[22] World Health Organization, 'Tobacco and Poverty: A Vicious Circle' (2004), 6. Kenya has approximately 55,000 tobacco farming households. Despite the narratives of prosperity of the smallholders, research has revealed that these farmers are poor, vulnerable and exposed to dangerous chemicals. An epidemiological study revealed that 26 per cent of tobacco workers in the country suffered from pesticide poisoning: see G. J. A. Ohayo-Mitoko et al., 'Acetylcholinesterase Inhibition as an Indicator of Organophosphate and Carbamate Poisoning in Kenyan Agricultural Workers', *International Journal of Occupational Environmental Health*, 3, 21 (1997),195–200. Also see, Q. Ling et al., 'The Economic Geography of Kenyan Tobacco Farmers' Livelihood Decisions', *Nicotine and Tobacco Research* (2019), 1–4.

[23] Statistics reveal that 86 per cent of global tobacco production is concentrated in the low- and middle-income economies (i.e., the Global South) where the use of agrochemicals imposes severe health and socio-environmental problems on the poor populations engaged in production. See, N. Lecours et al., 'Environmental Health Effects of Tobacco Farming: A Review of Literature', *Tobacco Control*, 21, 2 (2012), 191–196.

[24] These authors focus more on African colonial ecology, entomology and epidemiology and neglect pest control programmes in agricultural production. See, J. Ford, *The Role of Trypanosomiases in African Ecology: A Study of the Tsetse Fly Problem* (Oxford, 1971); J. Mackenzie, 'Empire and the Ecological Apocalypse: The Historiography of the Imperial Environment', in T. Griffith and L. Robin (eds.) *Ecology and Empire: Environmental History of Settler Societies* (Edinburgh, 1997), 215–228. Also see, J. Giblin, 'Trypanosomiasis Control in African History: An Evaded Issue?', *Journal of African History*, 31, 1 (1990), 59–80; K. A. Hoppe, *Lords of the Fly: Sleeping Sickness Control in British East Africa, 1900–1960* (Westport, 2003); I. Scoones, 'The Politics of Trypanosomiasis Control in Africa', STEPS Working Paper 57 (Brighton: STEPS Centre, 2014).

that were fashionable from the 1960s and put global scrutiny on some of the chemicals that were widely used for these large-scale pest and disease control projects.[25] There is also remarkably little research into southern Africa's historical reliance on pesticides. There has not been much research into the historical use of agricultural pesticides in Southern Rhodesia and Zimbabwe.[26]

In April 2018 the global human rights watchdog Human Rights Watch released a report focusing on child labour and other human rights abuses in the tobacco farms in Zimbabwe.[27] Even this report only glancingly alluded to the risks of nicotine poisoning and exposure of farm workers to tobacco chemicals.[28] This chapter takes this report

[25] Ford, although writing around 1970, simply provides a cursory mention of the use of these insecticides in pest control and argues that their effects were less durable than social control, but he ignores the environmental and public health debates about their use which had gained momentum during this time.

[26] The most recent work and perhaps the only truly historical work on the subject is Peter Uledi and Godfrey Hove's 2019 study on state responses to locust outbreaks in Southern Rhodesia between 1918 to the 1940s. The study examines the use of arsenic sprays to control locust swarms during the 1930s and 1940s and the impact of these sprays on the human and natural environment. The work is a good read on the development of the colonial pest control policies in Southern Rhodesia before the post-war pest control revolution. However, it doesn't extend into the post-war period to engage with the debates on environmentalism that emerged with the more widespread use of new pesticides such as DDT. See P. Uledi and G. Hove, 'a War of Man against Locust! Locust Invasions and Anti-locust Campaigns in Salisbury, Southern Rhodesia, 1918–1940s', *South African Historical Journal*, 70, 4 (2018), 689–707. Much of the other existing literature is largely from the agricultural and environmental sciences and focuses on the contemporary challenges of pesticide use in production from a technical perspective. See, B. Maumbe and S. M. Swinton, 'Hidden Costs of Pesticide Use in Zimbabwe's Smallholder Cotton' (unpublished paper), American Agricultural Economics Association Annual Meeting, California, 28–31 July 2002; H. Berg et al., 'DDT and Other Insecticides in Lake Kariba Ecosystem', *Ambio* 21, 7 (November 1992), 444–450; A. Mbanda and M. Zaranyika, 'DDT Residue in Terrestrial Environment in the Mount Darwin–Rushinga Area: Zimbabwe', *Journal of Applied Science in Southern Africa*, 7, 2 (2001), 83–96; Shepherd Ndlela, 'Phasing out Harmful/Hazardous Yet Effective Synthetic Insecticides: How Will the Tobacco Farmer Manage the Pesticide Intensive Tobacco Crop?', *TRB Technical Report* (April 2017).

[27] Human Rights Watch, 'A Bitter Harvest: Child Labour and Human Rights Abuses on Tobacco Farms in Zimbabwe' (April 2018), 48–57.

[28] The above report uses only oral interviews to look at the problem of nicotine and pesticide poisoning, thus relying exclusively on oral testimony not supported by documented cases of chemical poisoning. The interviews, though

back in time by offering an historical survey of the pesticide problem and the pest control infrastructure in tobacco production since 1945 when pesticide use started gaining its global reputation. The major challenge, however, is that until the 1960s much of the conversation on the use of pesticides in agricultural production generally reflected only utter obliviousness to the link between pesticides and the contamination of the human and natural environment. Consequently, official records and archival material afford us only scanty detail on the problem, and much that can be gleaned is from anecdotal data. This chapter hopes to open the floodgates for more surveys in future to understand the environmental costs of using chemical pesticides in agricultural production in Southern Rhodesia. In attempting this reconstruction, the chapter is informed by the dictum of Donald Worster that as environmental historians we should tell stories of the past that discourages 'irresponsibility in the present'.[29] Consequently in telling this story, this chapter invokes Carson's *Silent Spring*, reading it in an African context to show how the local and the global can interact within the broad spectrum of modern environmentalism – thus 'glocalising' and not 'globalising' *Silent Spring*.[30] In taking the context of the Global South seriously, this chapter bridges the neglected study of Carson with the ongoing attempts to understand environmentalisms that do not fall into the typical model offered by the Global North. Thus the chapter engages with the concept of 'slow violence': that is, ecological violence that unravels itself gradually, is subtly invisible and scattered in temporal space.[31] It also discusses the concept of the

important as windows into the social life of tobacco farm workers, neglect the prevalence of nicotine and pesticide poisoning. Consequently, many of the conclusions reached are superficially circumstantial, and an epidemiological study might be necessary to validate the findings of the report.

29 D. Worster, 'The Two Cultures Revisited: Environmental History and the Environmental Sciences', *Environment and History*, 2, 1 (February 1996), 3–14.

30 The term 'glocalisation' is used to denote a rejection of framing linear prescriptive global narratives around *Silent Spring*. Rather the chapter favours a more contextualised and ideographic framing based on a different set of social, economic and political local realities. This does not, however, delink the local from the global, but simply gives it a more comprehensible context. William Vogt's epoch-making book in 1948 *Road to Survival* written long before *Silent Spring*, was novel in its ability to illustrate this interconnectedness of global environmental histories and how local ecologies were integral to a larger global whole.

31 The concept of 'slow violence' caused by pesticide contamination and nuclear fallout is the chief motif in *Silent Spring*. For a more comprehensive

'environmentalism of the poor', which looks at environmentalism through the perception of livelihoods, necessity and survival as opposed to the 'environmentalism of the rich', which concentrates on aesthetics and quality of life.[32] The chapter further extends the class-based concept of the 'environmentalism of the poor' into illuminating how racial identity also created biases that led to discrimination in environmental policies and practices and the construction of 'environmental racism' in colonial Africa.[33] In this sense, Filomina Steady has underscored that 'environmental racism' is based on the 'structural expendability' of black Africans that is traceable to Western hegemonic proclivities derived from the history of the slave trade and colonialism in which Africans were reduced to 'no-humans' or subhuman to justify

conceptualisation of 'slow violence' see, R. Nixon, *Slow Violence and the Environmentalism of the Poor* (Cambridge, MA, 2011), 2.

32 Guha and Martinez popularised the concept in the 1990s. Nixon captures the term as signifying a condition where a new official landscape is formally imposed on a vernacular one. A vernacular landscape is one which is integral to the socio-environmental dynamics of the community, and an official landscape denotes a bureaucratically rewritten landscape devoid of existing socio-environmental norms. For further readings on the concept see J. Martinez-Alier, *The Environmentalism of the Poor: A Study of Ecological Conflicts and Valuation* (Cheltenham, 2002).

33 The concept of Environmental racism emerged from the 1960s during the American civil rights movement. It was connected to how race was at the heart of social policy in the urban environment where toxic waste was dumped in African American areas, leading to widespread protests in the late 1970s. These protests led to the publication of a seminal report by the Commission for Racial Justice entitled 'Toxic Waste and Race', which concluded that race was the most definitive variable in the location of waste facilities even more than poverty. See, R. D. Bullard, *Confronting Environmental Racism: Voices from the Grassroots* (Boston, MA: South End, 1993); C. Hudson-Weems, 'Environmental Racism: Black Landowners, and the Making of a New Hilton Head: An Emmett Till Continuum', in F. Steady (ed.), *Environmental Justice in the New Millennium: Global Perspectives on Race, Ethnicity and Human Rights* (New York, 2009); F. Steady, 'Environmental Justice Cross-Culturally: Theory and Praxis in the African Diaspora and in Africa', F. Steady (ed.), *Environmental Justice in the New Millennium*. In Africa and the Global South, environmental racism involved the deliberate pollution of the environment and settlements with toxic chemicals, leading to death and disease, and the physical dislocation from the natural environment through forced removals. See M. F. Phalane and F. Steady, 'Nuclear Energy Hazardous Waste, Health, and Environmental Justice in South Africa', in D. A. McDonald (ed.), *Environmental Justice in South Africa* (Cape Town, 2002); F. Khan, 'The Roots of Environmental Racism and the Rise of Environmental Justice in the 1990s' in D. A. McDonald (ed.), *Environmental Justice in South Africa*.

their oppression based on race and white privilege.[34] She further argues that the expendability of Africans and minority agricultural populations, built for many years on the basis of racial identity, still continues to shape the agenda of the contemporary neo-liberal global economy where African and Caribbean countries have been ruined by Northern chemical processes that destroy the environment and sustainable agriculture.[35] Although *Silent Spring* did not allude explicitly to race, class or any power dynamics, the chapter will show that it strongly connects with the 'environmentalism of the poor', 'slow violence' and 'environmental racism' because of its passionate activism against the power of big chemical companies and their toxic hold on the American subalterns.[36] The colonial pest control programmes in Africa were also much of a reflection of this intersection between science, power, race, ecology and politics, and this had significant leverage in shaping the intervention strategies and the impact on the human and natural environment.[37]

In contemporary postcolonial Africa, environmentalism has continued to be defined through the perceptions of the west to the detriment of local capacities and conditions.[38] Robert Nelson identifies a tendency where, under the banner of saving the African environment, African people have been subjected to a new form of 'environmental colonialism', and environmental activism in Africa has come to exhibit a neo-colonial character.[39] Paul Driessen categorises the ideological environmental movement from the North operating in the Global South as constituting a form of 'eco-imperialism'.[40]

[34] Steady, 'Environmental Justice Cross-Culturally', 49. [35] Ibid, 51.

[36] Nixon, *Slow Violence and the Environmentalism of the Poor*, xi.

[37] See, Ford, *The Role of Trypanosomiasis in African Ecology* and Scoones, 'The Politics of Trypanosomiasis Control in Africa', 11.

[38] In most cases pest control programmes for public health in Africa are run and sponsored by NGOs from the Global North who set the 'environmental agenda'. This agenda is usually influenced by global discourses and not vernacular experiences.

[39] R. Nelson, 'Environmental Colonialism: Saving Africa from Africans', *The Independent Review*, 8, 1 (2003), 65–86.

[40] Driessen, *Eco-Imperialism: Green Power, Black Death*. Also, Alfred Crosby uses the term 'ecological imperialism' to denote the changing face of vernacular ecologies as a result of European colonial settlement in North and South America, which introduced new human beings, new weeds, new animals, new pathogens and new diseases. See, A. W. Crosby, 'Ecological Imperialism: The Overseas Migration of Western Europeans as a Biological Phenomenon' in Donald Worster (ed.), *The*

Within the context of all this, therefore, this chapter contributes to the historiography of pesticide use in Africa and the framing of a more contextualised understanding of Carson's environmentalism within the Global South.[41] The chapter uses the lens of political ecology and environmental history to interrogate the use of pesticides in tobacco farming in Southern Rhodesia (now Zimbabwe) from 1945 to 1980, and their effects on the human body, the body politic and the natural environment. It traces the growth of pesticide use beginning with the end of World War II and explores the problems that arose with the use of these pesticides and connects this narrative with the various global debates on 'environmentalism' that arose in the 1960s, and how this impacted on the evolution of legislation and policies to curtail pesticide use in tobacco production in Southern Rhodesia.

The Post–World War II 'Pesticide Treadmill' and Pest Control in Southern Rhodesia, 1948–1964

The Second World War saw a prodigious growth of the pesticide and chemical industry.[42] During the development of chemical formulas to use as agents of chemical warfare, a substantial number of chemicals were created and stockpiled which had lethal potency to both humans and insects. These chemicals were being manufactured by big chemical companies such as the Swiss-based Geigy company which had subsidiaries in various countries in the Global North such as England, Canada and the United States.[43] It was in the United States, however, that the chemicals industry grew most substantially to meet the demands of the war effort.[44] The production of these synthetic pesticides in the United

Ends of the Earth: Perspectives on Environmental History (Cambridge, 1988), 111.

41 See also H. Twidle, 'Rachel Carson and the Perils of Simplicity: Reading Silent Spring from the Global South', *Ariel: A Review of English Literature*, 44, 4 (2014), 49–88. This is, however, an eco-critical analysis and frames *Silent Spring* as more a literary text, deploying textual criticism for its analysis. Nevertheless, Twidle juxtaposes the work of Arundhati Roy and Carson in trying to understand how Carson's ideas of ecology and toxicity carry meaning in the Global South.

42 C. D. Cook, 'The Spraying of America', *Earth Island Journal*, 20, 1 (Spring 2005), 34–38.

43 O. T. Zimmerman and I. Lavine, *DDT: Killer of Killers* (Rochester, New York, 1946), 39.

44 Between 1943 and 1944, fifteen American chemical companies were producing DDT and other chemicals for the armed forces.

States had reached 124,259,000 lbs in 1947.[45] When the war ended these chemicals slowly found wonder uses in agriculture where they were hailed as the saviours of mankind from pests and assumed an unparalleled global reputation. The most famous of these synthetic chlorinated hydrocarbons was DDT. It had been synthesised by a German chemist Othmar Zeidler in 1864 but became well known as an insecticide in 1939 due to the work of Swiss scientist and Nobel Prize winner Paul Hermann Müller. It was used extensively during the war to spray Allied soldiers against typhus in the Mediterranean and malaria in the tropics.[46] DDT catalysed an explosive revolution and expansion of the pesticide industry. This was largely a result of the lower costs and unprecedented effectiveness of the insecticide and other chlorinated hydrocarbon pesticides which led to their widespread use in the fields of agro-industry and public health.[47] The result of this monumental success was the expansion of the pesticide industry in general which was so widespread and rapid that it 'steamrolled' pest control technology as chemical pest control expanded in scale.[48] As development experts came to put their faith in the power of science and American capitalism to modernise backward communities in the post-war years, the large-scale use of DDT in the Global North was replicated in the Global South as an important technology 'to break the cycle of poverty, malnutrition and disease'.[49]

In Southern Rhodesia, DDT was registered for agricultural use in 1946, and by 1947 it was being used following an army worm outbreak in maize in early January (first in Gatooma before spreading to Victoria, Salisbury and Nyamandlovu districts).[50] DDT was found to be effective and was considerably cheaper than using gangs of African labour to

45 Carson, *Silent Spring*, 14.

46 W. Cronon, 'Silent Spring and the Birth of Modern Environmentalism', in Dunlap (ed.), *DDT, Silent Spring, and the Rise of Environmentalism*, xi.

47 R. Van den Bosch, *The Pesticide Conspiracy* (California, 1978), 21.

48 In the United States during the post-war period, public health and agricultural experts engaged in development projects to eradicate famine and disease through deployment of modern pest control technologies using DDT and other chlorinated hydrocarbons. Carson documents such several government-sponsored spray programmes. In 1954, the US Department of Agriculture started a spraying programme to eliminate the Japanese beetle in Illinois and applied dieldrin to 1,400 acres by air; in 1955 another 2,600 acres were treated similarly. In 1959, 27,000 acres in Michigan were dusted with pellets of aldrin.

49 Kinkela, *DDT and the American Century*, 9.

50 Report of the Division of Entomology, 1947.

physically pick up the worms; consequently, it formed the basis of tentative government recommendations for control in maize.[51] In 1947 the Pest Control Research Committee was set up by the Rhodesia Tobacco Association (RTA) to speed up research on tobacco pest control.[52] This followed the admission by the association in its report that year that work on the control of pests and diseases troublesome in Rhodesia had not progressed as far as could be wished. This pest and diseases control infrastructure became more important following the post-war tobacco boom that witnessed production increasing on the back of favourable market conditions and the entry of many new growers as discussed in the previous chapter. The government, through a subsidised scheme, agreed to cooperate with the RTA and a private company Pest Control Africa Ltd to investigate tobacco diseases. Spraying was to be carried out on various tobacco farms over four years starting from June 1947.[53]

Field spraying operations were conducted on an extensive scale on the tobacco farms, beginning in 1948.[54] In 1948 DDT was listed by Pest Control Africa as one of the new insecticides to be tested on tobacco, amongst other chlorinated hydrocarbons that included benzene hexachloride, chlorinated camphenes and Thiophos 3342.[55] By 1955, DDT and the organochlorine insecticide aldrin were being recommended by the Tobacco Research Board (TRB) and were also being widely used by many growers for the control of cutworm (*Agrotis ipsilon*) in both the nursery and field operations.[56] Not only was DDT being used in the field and nursery, it was also used in the cleaning of tobacco shades and applied as whitewash to leave a residual coating on the walls to control the tobacco beetle (*Lasioderma serricorne*) in cured leaf.[57] Nematocides and soil fumigants such as EDB and methyl bromide[58] for the control of eelworm and root knot nematodes were

[51] Ibid.
[52] NAZ, S25101/1, TRB Tobacco Pest Spraying Scheme, J. C. F. Hopkins, 'Field Spraying and the Control of Leaf Diseases on Tobacco: Review Report – 1948'.
[53] Ibid. [54] Ibid.
[55] NAZ, S2708/1, Pest Control and Plants, 1947–1952, E. Parry Jones (Managing Director Pest Control Africa), 'Research on Tobacco Pests and Diseases'.
[56] Tobacco Research Board, 'Recommendations for Flue-Cured Tobacco', 1955, 8.
[57] Ibid.
[58] EDB was first used in 1926 as an insecticide in the United States, although it was first commercially registered in 1946. In 1973, several studies showed that it was carcinogenic and caused birth defects, leading to its ban as a soil fumigant in the

also being recommended because of the dwindling supply of virgin lands.[59] Soil fumigation experiments were started at the tobacco research station in 1949.[60] By 1957, the TRB reported that soil fumigants were extensively used throughout the federation[61] both in seedbeds and in lands for the control of eelworms.[62] A 1961–1962 survey revealed that out of the total of 224,000 acres of tobacco planted in Southern Rhodesia that season the amount of land fumigated for nematode control was approximately 104,832 acres (46.8 per cent).[63] Carson identifies nematicides and other forms of soil treatment as being harmful as they eliminate the biological life in the soil.[64] She further posits that biological control of eelworm and nematodes through planting resistant crops such as marigolds was more helpful than chemical sprays.[65] In Southern Rhodesia during this time, although grass-ley rotations were used in tobacco to control eelworms, the use of nematicides on rotated lands was highly recommended by the TRB.[66]

By the 1960s, the proliferation of pests and diseases on the tobacco farms was becoming a growing concern to the state, especially since some of the insect pests were evidently becoming resistant to

United States in 1983. Methyl bromide is an organic bromide compound used as an insecticide. It first came into use in 1932 and was registered for use in the United States in 1961. It contains ozone layer-depleting chemicals and is highly toxic. For this reason, it was banned for use in tobacco fumigation and has been phased out in many countries, including Zimbabwe, by the 2005 Montreal Protocol.

59 Nematodes had been a recurring and perennial problem on tobacco farms since the expansion of tobacco production in the 1920s. Before the advent of nematicides in the 1940s, the only form of control was cultivating virgin lands, as tobacco grown on second-year lands would be badly affected.

60 H. Weinmann, *Agricultural Research and Development in Southern Rhodesia, 1924–1950* (Salisbury, 1975), 78.

61 Between 1953 and 1963, the three Central and Southern African British colonies of Southern Rhodesia, Nyasaland and Northern Rhodesia amalgamated into the Federation of Rhodesia and Nyasaland. The federation amalgamated most services under one authority and the TRB became a federal institution responsible for tobacco research in all the three territories.

62 'Chemical Control of Eelworm', *Rhodesian Tobacco Journal* (July 1957).

63 A. Daulton, 'Survey of Land Use and Plant Parasitic Nematodes Control', Rhodesian *Agricultural Journal* 59 (July–August 1962), 216–217.

64 Carson, *Silent Spring*, 65. 65 Ibid.

66 NAZ, F257/110/GEN, Tobacco General: Bulletins and articles 1963, R.C. Salmon (Officer in Charge Kutsaga Research Station), 'Some Thoughts on Second Year Tobacco'.

chlorinated hydrocarbons.[67] Organophosphate pesticides became more popular with farmers around the mid-to-late 1950s.[68] The pest control infrastructure that was developing in tobacco farms and the pest complex reflected the general trend in much of Africa from the late 1940s as colonial governments sought to expand the area of land available for occupation through pest eradication programmes.[69] In Rwanda-Burundi in the Rukwa Valley from August to November 1947 an experimental aerial 'hopper' campaign was launched at an estimated cost of £57,000.[70] A ground-dusting campaign was conducted in September and October using Messinger machines, DNOC dust and gammaxene.[71] In southern Africa the spraying campaigns became imperative as the numbers of new (white) settlers on the land increased following the post–Second World War settlement schemes and at a time when tsetse fly infestations were hampering expansion of settler agriculture and large-scale ranching.[72] In Southern Rhodesia, ground-spraying operations with dieldrin and DDT were conducted, beginning in 1950 on an extensive scale in both African and European areas to control tsetse flies, with huge numbers of native labourers mobilised to work in unsafe conditions while spraying large areas.[73] In South Africa, from the 1950s large quantities of a chlorinated hydrocarbon pesticide dieldrin mixed with fuel were sprayed in areas around Kruger National Park to control rinderpest.[74]

[67] 'Pests cost 20 million pounds every year', *Rhodesia Herald*, 18 February 1961.

[68] Chlorinated hydrocarbon insecticides are persistent and build up in the food chain and fatty acids of mammals; they are, however, less toxic to humans and animals. Organophosphate pesticides can easily be broken down and have no residual effect on the environment, but they are more lethal to humans and animals.

[69] The Anti-Locust Research Centre in London observed in 1948 that Africa's development was threatened by locust plagues as the hoppers would develop into dangerous pests as soon as suitable soils were found, and abundant food created by the clearing of forest areas and mechanised agriculture.

[70] *Record of Conference of the International Red Locust Control Service held in Salisbury on the 25th, 26th and 27th of May 1948* (Lusaka: Government Printer, 1948), 11.

[71] Ibid. [72] Scoones, 'The Politics of Trypanosomiasis Control in Africa', 12.

[73] Ibid., 13. For a comprehensive history of tsetse fly control in Southern Rhodesia, see, R. Pilossof, 'A Brief History of Tsetse Control Methods in Zimbabwe and Possible Effects of Climate Change on Their Distribution', *International Journal of African Development* 4, 1 (2016), 88–101.

[74] Scoones, 'The Politics of Trypanosomiasis Control in Africa' 13.

These spraying programmes were touted as depicting mastery over nature and constituting the colonial vision of modernising Africa expressed in such justificatory ecological catchphrases as 'taming the wilderness', 'conquering the fly' and 'pushing back disease'.[75] These ecological interventions were steeped in the notion of racial and cultural superiority under which European settlers perceived themselves to be the benchmark of progress and civilisation in Africa. White power and privilege formed the basis of this ideology which further casts blacks and other non-white racial groups as ignorant of and destructive to the environment, as well as being uncivilised.[76]

Environmental historians have, however, disparaged this racial bigotry as ahistorical in understanding the complex dynamics of colonial ecologies. Alfred Crosby in particular framed the colonial pest and pathogen epidemics which devastated much of the colonial Americas as 'exported' ecological disasters.[77] Orthodox Africanist scholarship has also challenged the narratives informing these colonial scientific interventions in African ecologies as being limited, disruptive and based on the logic of resource exploitation for settler gain.[78] Helge Kjekshus blames colonialism for the spread of diseases and epidemics such as tsetse fly and trypanosomiasis in Tanzania.[79] John McCracken, in his study of Malawi, was also highly critical of the role of experts in understanding the pest and ecological dynamics in cotton production.[80] Although focusing on the period before the end of the Second World War and the advent of large-scale chemical pest control programmes in Africa, these works' challenge to science and its utility in the reshaping of vernacular landscapes and ecologies share affinities

[75] J. Mackenzie, 'Empire and the Ecological Apocalypse; The Historiography of the Imperial Environment', in Griffith and Robin (eds.), *Ecology and Empire: Environmental History of Settler Societies*, 215–228. Also see, J. Giblin, 'Trypanosomiasis Control in African History – An Evaded Issue', 59–80 and Hoppe, *Lords of the Fly*. These works provide a framework for understanding how colonial pest control programmes were justified in the language of modernisation such as 'taming the wilderness', 'conquering the fly' and 'pushing back disease'.

[76] D. Anderson and R. Grove, *Conservation in Africa: People, Politics and Practice* (Cambridge, 1987), 4.

[77] Crosby, 'Ecological Imperialism', 112.

[78] Ibid.

[79] H. Kjekshus, *Ecology Control and Economic Development in East African History: The Case of Tanganyika, 1850–1950* (London, 1987).

[80] J. McCracken, 'Experts and Expertise in Colonial Malawi', *African Affairs*, 81, 322 (1982), 101–116.

with the environmentalism in *Silent Spring*, which questioned society's unflinching faith in the scientific control of nature.

Despite the prevalent scepticism of the utility of colonial knowledge systems in African ecologies, revisionist scholars in the 1990s came to view the colonial scientific and technological developments as being core to imperial development and playing a critical role towards the facilitation of effective exploitation of natural resources for agriculture and industry through environmental transformation.[81] In the case of Southern Rhodesian tobacco, the scientific knowledge of pest control, however, failed because the problem was linked to the increases in production which followed the post-war boom as tobacco overtook gold to become the principal export earner in 1947.[82] With increased acreages to meet the huge demands of the export market, the pest pressure also increased as a result of the changing production patterns which altered the natural ecosystem and created a pest explosion as a result of human ecological engineering.[83] This evokes Carson's prescient musing in *Silent Spring*; 'we are told that the enormous and expanding use of pesticides is necessary to maintain farm production. Yet is our real problem not one of over production?'[84]

There were several outbreaks of various tobacco diseases in most parts of the country.[85] An outbreak of tobacco rosette occurred in the Lomagundi area in December 1953, leading to total losses of seedbeds and November plantings.[86] Despite a determined effort by growers to spray with parathion, the disease was not checked, and by the end of

81 See, H. Tilley, 'African Environments and African Social Sciences: The African Research Survey, Ecological Paradigms and British Colonial Development', in W. Beinart and J. McGregor (eds.), *Social History and African Environments* (Oxford, 2003); W. Beinart, K. Brown and D. Gilfoyle, 'Experts and Expertise in Colonial Africa Reconsidered: Science and the Interpenetration of Knowledge', *African Affairs*, 108, 432 (July 2009), 413–433.

82 D. M. Rowe. *Manipulating the Market: Understanding Economic Sanctions, Institutional Change and the Political Unity of Southern Rhodesia* (Ann Arbor, Michigan, 2001), 69.

83 Southern Rhodesia's tobacco exports rose from an average of 14,000 metric tons during 1940–1945 to 121,000 metric tons in 1965 accounting for approximately one third of the free world's tobacco exports.

84 Carson, *Silent Spring*, 8.

85 Various outbreaks of tobacco anthracnose were reported in the *Rhodesia Herald* between 1953 and 1958 as having been prevalent in Marandellas, Karoi, Lomagundi and Banket districts.

86 NAZ, F149/TOB/360, Tobacco Diseases and Pests, 1956–1958, Tobacco extension officer to Senior tobacco extension officer, 21 April 1954.

February 1954 the disease was reported from all over the colony.[87] The failure of the spraying to contain the disease did little to dampen the firm faith in and conviction of the utility of chemical control. The TRB insect control programme for seedbed and field control under a government notice in 1958 recommended aldrin, dieldrin, parathion, DDT and malathion for routine pest control.[88]

In 1961, the President of the Pesticides Association of Rhodesia and Nyasaland, W. L. Cosker, lamented that the damage caused by pests to tobacco in Southern Rhodesia amounted to £10 million annually.[89] In 1960, there was a serious outbreak of 'bushy top disease', described as 'the biggest menace to the tobacco growing industry'.[90] The ravages of the bushy top virus were so severe that there was an urgent call by tobacco farmers exhorting the government to introduce legislation to force all growers to comply with TRB recommendations for regular sprayings.[91] Because of this huge surge in bushy top, systemic pesticides were now being recommended by the TRB for use on tobacco.[92] In 1960, the first systemic insecticide used in Southern Rhodesia, rogor 40,[93] was unveiled.[94] The TRB noted that the systemic insecticide would reduce the incidence of virus diseases in certain plants since it was more persistent than malathion and parathion.[95] In 1962, a second systemic pesticide (menazone) for the control of bushy top and tobacco rosette was recommended by the TRB.[96] For the first time, the TRB recommended field spraying of Turkish tobacco as a routine measure to give protection against white mould, rosette and bushy top diseases.[97]

87 Ibid.
88 NAZ, F149/TOB/360, Tobacco Diseases and Pests, 1956–1958, Federal Government Notice 1958: Plant Pest and Disease Regulations.
89 'Pests cost 20 Million Pounds Every Year', *Rhodesia Herald*, 18 February 1961.
90 Ibid.
91 'Urgent Call for Law to Force Growers to Curb Bushy Top', *Rhodesia Herald*, 29 March 1961.
92 Systemic pesticides work by being absorbed by the plant tissues and making the whole plant poisonous.
93 Rogor, also known as dimethoate in the United States and fosfamide in Russia, was introduced and patented in the 1950s by a US chemical company, American Cynamid.
94 'How to Use Systematics Recommended for Tobacco', *Rhodesia Herald*, 22 September 1960.
95 Ibid.
96 'TRB Releases New Systemic for Tobacco Virus Diseases', *Rhodesia Herald*, 15 November 1962.
97 Ibid.

By November 1962, therefore, tobacco farmers in Southern Rhodesia were armed with the deadly triad of chlorinated hydrocarbons, organophosphates and systemic poisons. The pesticide revolution had been completed, yet the war on pests continued and, despite the accumulating deadliness and toxicity of the chemicals which kept on escalating at each stage of the chemical evolution, the pest problem remained. Despite a surge in the use of hitherto unknown chemicals whose toxicity to human and natural life kept on escalating, no regulations were put in place to control pesticide usage in Southern Rhodesia, just as was the case elsewhere in the world at this stage. There were several risks of contamination and poisoning, particularly on the tobacco farms where all the work was done by African labourers who were politically largely powerless.[98] Rob Nixon, in discussing environmental 'slow violence', has shown how disempowered social groups are usually the casualties of environmental violence.[99] He points out that the poor suffer the challenge of invisibility and amnesia, and usually remain on the margins of official memory.[100] This 'slow violence' transcends defined boundaries in time and space and happens over extended geographical and technological displacements, which hides its severity and, in retrospect, the human and environmental costs.[101] Ian Scoones has demonstrated how power dynamics during the colonial period indelibly etched themselves on pest control programmes that followed a top-down technocratic approach.[102] This required mobilising a subservient African labour force in highly dangerous ground-spraying campaigns. Africans were the expendable race and, as one observer put it, 'under colonialism, you could tell people what to do without masks, without gloves, in the sheer heat of the dry season. Who cared because you could get the people? There were armies of people with knapsacks on their backs. They were used as slaves'.[103] This generic reference to the conditions under which pest control programmes were conducted in Africa and the plight of the disempowered African labourers is very much akin to the situation in

[98] The concept of power and class in environmentalism has received a great deal of scholarly attention since the entry of 'Environmental Justice' as a critical concept in ecocriticism and environmental history in the 1990s. See, R. Bullard, *Dumping in Dixie: Race, Class, and Environmental Quality* (Boulder, Colorado, 1990); A. Hurley, *Environmental Inequalities: Class, Race and Industrial Pollution in Gary, Indiana, 1945–1980* (Chapel Hill, 1995).

[99] Nixon, *Slow Violence and the Environmentalism of the Poor*, 2.

[100] Ibid., 6. [101] Ibid., 7.

[102] Scoones, 'The Politics of Trypanosomiasis Control in Africa', 5. [103] Ibid.

Southern Rhodesia where chemical field spraying was done by black workers. Although in some cases pest control was conducted using aerial sprays, these were expensive, and ground-spraying operations using knapsack sprayers and African labour were conducted on a more extensive scale on Southern Rhodesian farms. It is impossible to ascertain the magnitude of the slow chemical violence on the tobacco farms in Southern Rhodesia in the absence of much available evidence, but it may be that there were generations of silent casualties. After all, colonial authorities were notorious for their lack of concern for the health and safety of their black employees.[104]

Locating Southern Rhodesia in the Global Pesticide Regime and the Environmental Backlash, 1965–1970

From the 1960s, based on Carson's revolutionary ideas in *Silent Spring*, a nascent global movement had begun that interrogated the impact of pesticides on the environment. This movement, which started in the United States, focused primarily on the residual effects of chemical pesticides on the environment and the accompanying hazards to humans and wildlife. In 1962, Carson's book opened a floodgate. This trickle became a public stream that filtered into official discourses about the long-term effects of pesticides use in agricultural production. Carson's work reached policymakers, government agencies, environmental scientists and chemical manufacturers in the United States and elsewhere in the Global North.[105] It evoked a fierce and wide-ranging debate in the United States: Carson faced visceral opposition from the chemical industry who accused her of being an agricultural propagandist and, in a predictably sexist attack, a

[104] Ibid., 14.

[105] There is an extensive literature which acknowledges the contributions of Carson to the environmental movement. See, M. H. Lytle, *The Gentle Subversive: Rachel Carson, The Silent Spring and the Rise of the Environmental Movement* (New York, 2007); L. J. Lear, 'Rachel Carson's Silent Spring', *Environmental History Review*, 17, 2 (1993), 23–48; R. H. Lutt, 'Chemical Fallout: Rachel Carson's Silent Spring, Radioactive Fallout and the Environmental Movement', *Environmental History Review*, 9, 3 (1985), 210–225; L. Culver, 'Reading *Silent Spring* as a Challenge for Contemporary Environmentalism', *RCC Perspectives* 7 (2012), 31–34.

catastrophising 'spinster with an affinity for cats'.[106] Her work, however, culminated in pesticide use becoming a subject of agricultural policy intervention globally by the mid-1960s. The report of the President's Science Advisory Committee (PSAC) in the United States (1963) became the first official government critical evaluation of the hazards of pesticides.[107] Amongst other things it called for the need to monitor levels of pesticide residues in the environment and for the federal government to restrict wide-scale use of persistent insecticides.[108] The report went further and poignantly stated that, 'until the publication of *Silent Spring* by Rachel Carson, people were generally unaware of the toxicity of pesticides'.[109] The subsequent PSAC report (1965) concluded that environmental pollution by pesticides could be reduced significantly without losing efficiency.[110]

In North America, the environmental movement in the 1960s stemmed from the instigation of activists like Carson and drew much of its galvanising force from the power of the mass media and social movements that spoke to diverse national constituencies. But in the Global South such prodding emerged largely from the state under pressure from globalising influences from the Global North, and in most cases this environmentalism was usually a mere smokescreen to comply symbolically with global norms largely for the purposes of national economic interests rather than genuine environmentalism. This must be understood in the context of the dichotomy between the environmentalism of affluent societies and the environmentalism of poor and less developed polities. North American environmentalism was deeply rooted within the liberal agenda of the mid-1950s championed by Arthur M. Schlesinger and John Kenneth Galbraith.[111] The liberal

[106] Eliza Griswold, 'How "Silent Spring" Ignited the Environmental Movement', *New York Times*, 21 September 2012, www.nytimes.com/2012/09/23/magazine/how-silent-spring-ignited-the-environmental-movement.html, accessed 18 September 2018.

[107] For a full understanding of the import of the PSAC report see D. S. Greenberg, 'Pesticides: Whitehouse Advisory Body Issues Report Recommending Steps to Reduce Hazards to Public', *Science News Series* 40, 3569 (1963), 878–879.

[108] L. J. Lear, 'Bombshell in Beltsville: The USDA and the Challenge of Silent Spring', *Agricultural History*, 66, 2 (Spring 1992), 151–170.

[109] Lear, 'Rachel Carson's Silent Spring', 151–170.

[110] Graham, *Since Silent Spring*, 179.

[111] See A. Schlesinger, 'The Future of Liberalism: The Challenge of Abundance', *Reporter*, (3 May 1956), 8–11 and J. K. Galbraith, *The Affluent Society* (Boston: Houghton Mifflin, 1958).

agenda espoused during the period of post-war American affluence visualised the environment as a public good that was being defiled by overconsumption, and identified the need to expand the role of government in addressing its degradation.[112] The preservation of public spaces for aesthetic and amenity purposes thus framed the discourse of American environmentalism. Shawn Miller points out that for rich nations environmentalism is driven by the alienation of people from nature because of modernisation, while for poor countries it is motivated by the knowledge that livelihoods depend on nature for survival.[113] In other words: 'the first is driven by dreamy myth, the second by stark reality'.[114] While this binary generally holds true in explaining the contrast in environmentalisms between the North and the South, it is limited in its ability to unpack the various racialised nuances within the Global South where racial identity is a big factor and predetermines the different sites of location for blacks and whites within the environmental movement. Thus, in much of colonial Africa, the agenda of the mainstream environmental movement (just as in the Global North) appealed to the affluent white minority interests broadly centred on the preservation of nature and wildlife sanctuaries, while alienating black Africans who were often accused of degrading the environment.[115] The influence of environmentalism from the Global North thus percolated through racial lines, affecting and influencing the black Africans and Europeans in different ways, but largely in a configuration in which black Africans were the victims of the top-down technocratic interventions that were meant to protect the environmental and economic interests of settler society.

The board of the Southern Rhodesian Tobacco Advisory Committee (a body representing manufacturers and merchants in the United

[112] A. Rome, 'Give Earth a Chance: The Environmental Movement and the Sixties', *Journal of American History*, 90, 2 (September 2003), 525–554.

[113] Miller, *An Environmental History of Latin America*, 215. [114] Ibid.

[115] Khan, 'The Roots of Environmental Racism', 16. In Southern Rhodesia, this environmentalism based on aesthetics was much more visible through the displacement of Africans from their areas to pave way for the construction of dams such as Lake Kariba and Lake Mutirikwi (formerly known as Lake Kyle) during the 1950s and 1960s which were turned into centres for white recreational pleasure and playgrounds for Europeans. These became Europeanised landscapes within which whites viewed wildlife and engaged in boating, while Africans could not access these conservation landscapes. See, J. Fontein, *Remaking the Mutirikwi: Landscape, Water and Belonging in Southern Zimbabwe* (Suffolk, 2015), 215–229.

Kingdom) was the first in the country to react to the concerns stirred by Carson's work and lobbied the government of Southern Rhodesia on the need for regulation of the pesticide control of tobacco.[116] As this chapter will show, the motive behind this was largely to protect the reputation of the lucrative tobacco export leaf (as being free of pesticide contamination) rather than for any genuine environmentalism. The state was compelled to act accordingly and promptly launched a Pesticide Approval Scheme to guide growers in selecting suitable pesticides. The scheme emphasised the need for a handbook to inform farmers on how to apply pesticides safely and effectively.[117] The TRB noted that the Pesticide Approval Scheme was becoming more necessary as growers were getting confused by the 'increasing number and complexity of pesticides', and consumers had been alerted to the 'presence of pesticides in some agricultural produce by the recent publicity on the misuse of pesticides'.[118] This publicity was a result of Carson's work and the seismic waves it had stimulated in influencing governments of various states all over the world over the need for pesticide regulations, and it reflects the far-reaching influence *Silent Spring* had in propagating new narratives on pesticide use – even in Africa. These narratives were, however, scripted to meet local contexts.

In Southern Rhodesia, the TRB insisted that it had to be satisfied that the materials were safe and did not impart undesirable residues to the leaf, increasing health hazards to the consumers and endangering the export market.[119] Furthermore, for the first time all chemicals used in tobacco were supposed to carry triangle emblems signifying the level of their toxicity, colour-coded from green to purple.[120] Instructions for use and safe disposal, and procedures for treatment in the event of accidental poisoning were also supposed to be required in the labelling. The interests of these initiatives were of course disconnected from the concern about the environment, and more intensely attached to securing a global market for Rhodesian tobacco, hence this was more an imposed environmentalism emanating from concerns of British tobacco buyers and merchants. The TRB argued that 'the scheme protects the industry and assures potential buyers of Rhodesian leaf that the use of pesticides on Rhodesian leaf is controlled and responsible'.[121] These provisions

[116] 'How Pesticides Gain the Stamp of Approval', *Rhodesian Tobacco Journal* (May 1965).
[117] Ibid. [118] Ibid. [119] Ibid. [120] Ibid. [121] Ibid.

were gazetted under the Fertilisers, Farm Seeds and Remedies Regulations of 1965. During the same year the use of the herbicide maleic hydrazide on tobacco was banned in Southern Rhodesia following a report that had been published by the Department of Agriculture in the United States in May 1960 revealing that it changed the chemical composition and physical properties of the leaf in a way that would endanger cigarette smokers.[122]

Just as in the United States, the 1965 legislation marked only a superficial turning point in perceptions of the use of pesticides on tobacco farms as sporadic official voices began a conversation around the responsible use of these products. C. H. Cronin, the technical manager of a Salisbury pest control firm, issued a warning on the dangers to operators on tobacco farms of being exposed to methyl bromide when fumigating seedbeds.[123] He pointed out that methyl bromide was an extremely toxic substance. He warned:

> The effects of a single massive exposure are well known, but it has also been discovered that exposure to low concentrations over a long period of time may have severe prolonged effects on the human body. A number of such cases has been reported in the British medical literature … these cases underline the view that methyl bromide is highly toxic and that recommended safety precautions must be observed. It is disastrous for a labourer using methyl bromide whose clothing has become contaminated to either sleep in the garments in a poorly ventilated room or to take them off and leave them beside the bed.[124]

The TRB also advised growers that the modern chemicals used for the control of insects were highly toxic, and special precautions had to be taken by farmers and their labour force using them.[125] It advised against the drinking of alcoholic beverages before or during work as alcohol promotes the rapid absorption of organophosphates.[126] These conversations between officials and tobacco farmers were, however, largely limited to technical concerns, with little attempt to ensure limiting the exposure of the African workers who did all of the work on the tobacco farms, by making it compulsory through legislation for farmers to equip

122 NAZ, F256/TOB/260, Tobacco Soil and Leaf Analysis Reports.
123 'Tobacco Farmers Warned of Poisoning Danger', *Rhodesia Herald*, 22 April 1965.
124 Ibid.
125 Tobacco Research Board, 'Bulletin on Burley Tobacco Culture in Southern Rhodesia' (1970), 3.
126 Ibid.

labourers with the requisite protective clothing, creating exposure-free work environments and providing information to labourers on safe use. In the absence of consumer pressure from Britain targeting pesticide exposure of black workers, white farmers showed less regard and concern for that aspect.

Nevertheless, by the beginning of the 1970s, a range of diverse attitudes – from both state and farmers – to the need for responsible chemical use in tobacco farms in Southern Rhodesia were congealing into something resembling a coherent policy. This was reflected in the legislative manoeuvres and initiatives by the TRB. Just as in the United States, these initiatives underwent severe public and state scrutiny. This was particularly true in key turning points between 1968 and 1970 as global perceptions on chemical use gained remarkable consensus on the need for not only controlled use of some of the products, but also their total ban in several spheres of agricultural production. In 1968, for example, the US Government under pressure from the environmental lobby issued notices cancelling four uses for DDT: on shade trees, tobacco plants, around homes and on marshes except for control of disease carriers, before banning it eventually in 1972.[127] In West Germany, for example, the use of chlorinated hydrocarbon pesticides on foodstuffs had been banned, and there were considerations to extend the ban to its use on tobacco in 1973.[128] Meanwhile a German tobacco-buying company had announced in 1970 that it would no longer purchase tobacco that had been directly or indirectly treated with aldrin, dieldrin or heptachlor.[129] As these developments were happening elsewhere, they took centre stage in Southern Rhodesia where an impassioned debate between various government agencies took place. This debate pitted the state health department against the Ministry of Agriculture and reflected the unique and stark realities that had to be confronted in domesticating the American template of environmentalism in Southern Rhodesia.

The debate was the result of a report by the Acting Medical Officer of Salisbury in 1969 which had pointed out that toxic agricultural residues existed in food and called for the need for some form of legislation that

[127] Kinkela, *DDT and the American Century*, 145.
[128] NAZ, (unprocessed) 42-12-5F, Box number 126962, Pesticide control legislation, Minutes of the Meeting on Pesticides on Tobacco held 4 September 1970.
[129] Ibid.

could ban DDT and other persistent pesticides and replace them with less persistent sevin and malathion.[130] D. H. Saunders, the director of Research and Specialist Services, opposed the ban of synthetic chlorinated hydrocarbons as 'the total replacement of DDT, lindane, aldrin and dieldrin by malathion and sevin would result in increased expenditure by the farmer'.[131] He argued that sevin and malathion were not replacements for these chemicals and such a substitution would cause 'a most catastrophic breakdown in pest control with consequences on the economy, not only to the farmer, but the nation as a whole'.[132] As an alternative, he proposed a strict control on usage of these pesticides by a registration scheme which criminalised their sale and unlicensed distribution.[133]

Dr Timothy Stamps of the city of Salisbury health department noted on 14 April 1969 that pesticides such as dieldrin remain in the soil for many years after use and contaminate underground water supplies.[134] He added that research was being directed into the effects of residual chemicals on fish and plants in the dams, and the ecology of the country could be affected if nothing was done.[135] He also observed that vegetable growers had crops that were found with unacceptably high traces of dieldrin.[136] In response, the director of Research and Specialist Services countered with: 'we do not propose to ban DDT, or other more persistent chlorinated hydrocarbons such as dieldrin, but we shall seek to limit their use'.[137]

The Research Services department continued with their denial, pointing out that in Southern Rhodesia (where pest pressure was more intense than in the United States and other temperate countries) it was very difficult to see how a complete ban on the persistent hydrocarbons would even be possible.[138] In his correspondence with the Secretary of Agriculture, Saunders staunchly stated:

[130] NAZ, (Unprocessed) 42-12-5F, Box number 126962, Pesticide Control Legislation, D. H. Saunders cites the Report in his correspondence with the Secretary of Agriculture on 3 June 1969.

[131] Ibid. [132] Ibid. [133] Ibid.

[134] NAZ, (Unprocessed) 42-12-5F, Box number 126962, Pesticide Control Legislation Minutes of a Meeting to Consider Action on Control and Distribution of Pesticides Held on 14 April 1969 at 15 Cheshire Road Salisbury.

[135] Ibid. [136] Ibid.

[137] NAZ, (Unprocessed) 42-12-5F, Box number 126962, Pesticide Control Legislation, D. H. Saunders to Secretary of Agriculture, 20 August 1969.

[138] Ibid.

Aldrin, dieldrin and DDT all have a part to play in controlling the pest complex which prevails in this country, and although research work is proceeding in an endeavour to replace these chemicals with less persistent and toxic ones, it is doubtful if a complete ban will be realised in the near future. Nevertheless, the ministry of agriculture has under consideration new regulations for more effective control of the sale, possession of DDT and other substances will be subject to control which will prove adequate.[139]

The Minister of Agriculture shared similar views to the department of Research and Specialist Services on the need for more regulation and control, as opposed to a complete ban on these chemicals. During a debate in the Legislative Assembly on 29 August 1969, the minister observed that the most convenient policy initiative would be to amend the Farm Seeds, Pests and Remedies Act in conjunction with and simultaneous to the introduction of a Hazardous Substance Act, arguing, 'I believe that between these two pieces of legislation when they become law, the manufacture, distribution, packaging, sale, possession of DDT and other substances will be subject to control which will prove adequate'.[140]

The denialism of the Ministry of Agriculture on the need to ban the use of highly persistent pesticides such as DDT persisted even in the face of growing and terrifying evidence. On 17 December 1969, the Doma Intensive Conservation Areas (ICA) wrote a letter to the secretary of the Natural Resources Board (NRB), Mashonaland North, reporting that because of DDT spraying in the catchment area of a dam, subsequent rainfall had washed much of the spray down into the dam.[141] In this dam a white farmer had stocked black bass which died after the subsequent spraying and rains. The bream in the same dam were also dead. The letter went further:

The question arises on whether the water will be safe for humans and livestock and also what the effect will be if humans eat any of the dead fish or meat which has obviously been killed ... But it raises the question previously raised in other countries i.e. whether the use of DDT for field scale pest control is not altogether too risky, or whether it should be banned or severely curtailed.[142]

139 Ibid. 140 Legislative Assembly Debates, 29 August 1969.

141 NAZ, (Unprocessed) 42-12-5F, Box number 126962, Pesticide Control Legislation, Doma ICA District Secretary (R. N. Gallico) to Secretary Natural Resources Board, 17 December 1969.

142 Ibid.

NRB noted that the situation was potentially serious and had in fact posed serious problems.[143] Unsurprisingly, however, Saunders denied that the poisoning in the dam was a result of DDT spraying. In his letter to the Secretary of Agriculture he insisted that conventional application of DDT could never cause the death of large numbers of fish in a distant dam.[144] To him, current information was that once DDT was washed into the soil, it was very quickly absorbed by the soil particles and was not leached out, even in heavy rain. Even if washed into the dams, he argued, the DDT will only be slowly released from the soil particles, and it was highly unlikely that it would produce the observed massive kill of fish.[145] He concluded rather ambiguously:

> It is more likely that pollution of this type is due to the misuse of DDT for example: drift from the ground (mist blowers and aerial spraying), washing of spray equipment or tipping of excess DDT on the tributaries of the dam for the purposes of catching fish. Properly used on the crops there should be no health hazard and I would emphasize that most poisonings have arisen from misuse.[146]

Despite these denials, however, a vast amount of evidence was building up in different quarters. The Rhodesian Veterinary Association was raising its voice on the accumulation of pesticide residues in animal tissues used for human consumption,[147] the National Council of Women of Southern Rhodesia was also lobbying extensively about pesticide contamination of vegetables and it instituted its own investigation.[148] These pressures, however, failed to elicit a robust state pesticide policy and only resulted in the token withdrawal of DDT

143 NAZ, (Unprocessed) 42-12-5F, Box number 126962, Pesticide Control Legislation Natural Resources Board Secretary (D. J. S. Wilson) to director of Water Development, cc Secretary of Agriculture and Secretary of Health, 23 December 1969.

144 NAZ, (Unprocessed) 42-12-5F, Box number 126962, Pesticide Control Legislation, D. H. Saunders to Secretary of Agriculture, 6 January 1970.

145 Ibid. 146 Ibid.

147 The Rhodesian Veterinary Association had written to the Secretary of Health on 13 January 1970 voicing their concerns about the accumulation of pesticide residues in animal tissues used for human consumption. They noted that they had a collection of results from samples already analysed which showed high levels of such residues.

148 NAZ (Unprocessed), 42-12-5F, Box number 126962, Pesticide Control Legislation, National Council of Rhodesian Women to Minister of Health, 10 May 1970.

for domestic and garden uses in 1973, while it continued to play a bigger part in pest control in most crops (particularly maize, where it was used for the control of stalk borers).[149] During the 1970s, Southern Rhodesia is estimated to have used 1,000 tonnes of DDT per year, with 300 tonnes used on maize.[150] The story was, however, quite different in tobacco where a modicum of control was established, largely because the sector relied on the export market which was insisting on the need to regulate pesticide contamination and could little afford to ignore the economic ramifications of non-compliance to the global pest control template.[151]

'A Smokescreen of Environmentalism?' The Tobacco Pesticide Control Scheme, 1970–1980

Unlike other practitioners of agriculture in Southern Rhodesia, tobacco farmers relied more extensively on an export market for their crop. This export market had declined precipitously following the Unilateral Declaration of Independence (UDI) in 1965, as the white minority government severed political connection with Britain and illegally declared independence. Consequently, in 1966 the United Kingdom Government as a punitive measure started encouraging its manufacturers to boycott Rhodesian tobacco. The impact of this is fully discussed in Chapter 5 but the sanctions reduced tobacco exports by 76 per cent from 120,898 tonnes in 1965 to 28,959 tonnes in 1966 with a corresponding fall of 82 per cent in export receipts from R$93.9 million to a paltry R$16.7 million.[152] Thus, when news reached Rhodesia that most European countries (particularly West Germany, which had become an important export market for Rhodesian leaf after UDI) were planning to ban the import of tobacco treated directly

[149] This was legislated for under the Hazardous Substances Act of Southern Rhodesia, (1973).

[150] Ron Thomson, 'DDT: The Resurrection of an Old Threat to Africa's Wildlife', www.africahunting.com/threads/ddt-the-resurrection-of-an-old-threat-to-africa%E2%80%99s-wildlife.14737/, accessed 12 July 2018.

[151] The situation was different for other crops. For instance, the maize export consumer market was not making the same demands as the tobacco consumer market regarding pesticide contamination regulation, and also maize was largely grown for domestic consumption and was not a major export crop in Rhodesia.

[152] Rowe, *Manipulating the Market*, 74.

or indirectly with DDT or other hydrocarbon insecticides, it was imperative that they act promptly. From 1965, the TRB had operated an ill-defined and inchoate pesticide evaluation system. The scheme was largely voluntary and pesticide evaluation was done sporadically only for those growers who opted to be part of the pesticide monitoring programme.[153] There was also no technical and legal infrastructure for a comprehensive mandatory pesticide control scheme. The scheme, however, made some minor headway in eliminating some chemicals with unwanted residues that were on the list of recommended pesticides. At the end of July 1970, heptachlor and dieldrin, which were recommended applications for the soil, had been dropped in favour of aldrin, which was less persistent and resulted in lower levels of residue.[154] In addition, any recommendations for the application of DDT to the leaf in the field was eliminated and replaced by monocrotophos – a systemic poison (now banned for use in the country).[155] The international trends and opinions on DDT use and the need to give assurances to overseas buyers, however, played a bigger part in the setting up of the tobacco pesticide control infrastructure, more than any local concerns about curbing contamination of the environment or human poisoning. The scheme certainly eliminated unacceptable levels of residues from the export leaf but did little to control or even monitor the use of these chemicals on tobacco farms, and the accompanying human and natural hazards. It was a scheme based on the commercial interests of the Rhodesian tobacco industry. The environmental aspect of the programme was merely a smokescreen.

By September 1970 the key tobacco stakeholders in Southern Rhodesia considered that the best way to monitor the use of pesticides and create a deterrent in time for the 1970–1971 crop would be by means of a random sampling on the tobacco sales floors before selling took place.[156] They agreed on the need to set up legislation to enable this and ensure the confidence of the importing countries. They also agreed that the Tobacco Marketing Board (TMB) would invoke the

[153] Tobacco Research Board, 'Pesticides Use on Tobacco: A Review of International Trends and their Impact on Rhodesian Production', 31 August 1970.

[154] Ibid. [155] Ibid.

[156] NAZ, (Unprocessed) 42-12-5F, Box number 126962, Pesticide Control Legislation, Minutes of the Meeting on Pesticides on Tobacco held on 4 September 1970.

powers of the Tobacco Marketing and Levy Act to prohibit the sale of tobacco that had been treated with aldrin, dieldrin or heptachlor.[157] Where the levels of pesticide residues were above the permitted tolerances, or banned pesticides were detected, a full-scale investigation of the remainder of the crop on the farm would ensue.[158] An analytical unit worth R$7,000 and running costs of R$400 monthly was proposed as a preliminary budget.[159] The TMB noted with concern that although DDT was still recommended, it was highly suspect and there was a need to monitor its continued use to ensure that the West German standard of one part per million (ppm) was not exceeded.[160] The TRB also admitted that it had evidence of the presence of DDT in quantities in excess of this standard as a result of drift from cotton spraying.[161] By August 1970, the TRB had begun raising red flags over the use of DDT within tobacco grading and storage buildings, calling for a suitable replacement for pest control in stored tobacco.[162] Its director, Ian McDonald, agonised that 'there is a real danger of contamination of exposed leaf following contact with treated walls and floors'.[163]

Consequently, the Tobacco Pesticide Contamination Investigation Committee came into being in 1970 under the chairmanship of Mike Butler, President of the Rhodesian National Farmers Union, to consider all aspects of chemical contamination arising from crop spraying and to regulate the use of DDT and other banned substances.[164] Representatives on the committee included RTA, The department of Conservation and Extension, TRB and the cotton and grain commodity associations. The RTA noted that the purpose of the committee was to ensure that tolerance of toxic residues in tobacco remained lower than defined by legislation in other countries.[165] The Tobacco Marketing and Levy General Amendments Regulations Notice No. 3 of 1970 banned the use of DDT and other pesticides[166] for field

[157] Ibid. [158] Ibid. [159] Ibid. [160] Ibid. [161] Ibid. [162] Ibid.

[163] NAZ, (Unprocessed) 42-12-5F, Box number 126962, Pesticide Control Legislation, Ian McDonald to Head Branch of plant protection, 13 August 1970.

[164] 'Committee to Investigate Pesticide Contamination', *Rhodesia Herald*, 13 November 1970.

[165] Ibid.

[166] The other banned pesticides under the Government Notice included TDE (tetrachlorodiphenylethane), benzene hexachloride, CIC, dieldrin, arsenic, mendrin, endolsulfan and aldrin. The ban was to come into use as soon as

applications, but as a result of lack of satisfactory alternatives its use was retained in seedbeds and as a soil treatment following transplanting.[167] These control measures were adjudged to have been effective in containing the contamination of the tobacco leaf destined for export, so much so that in 1972, the Report of the TMB gloated glowingly that growers were using pesticides responsibly and every case of contamination was now proved to have arisen from accidental causes, either from applications in farm buildings before the introduction of the regulations in 1970, or from drift during aerial spraying.[168] The report further noted that as a result of investigations only four flue-cured and ten Burley crops were partially or entirely embargoed, resulting in the loss of 70,000 kg of tobacco.[169] By 1974, DDT had been 'eliminated' (although there were actually still sporadic incidences of its use despite the comprehensive ban) from tobacco production in Rhodesia and replaced by a new insecticide neotox, which the TRB said could be used 'more safely and effectively than DDT'.[170] It was also less persistent and less dangerous to wildlife, with a low dermal and inhalation toxicity.[171]

While the TRB pest control scheme played a greater part in limiting contamination of the tobacco export leaf on the white farms, the utility of this programme was a little weaker amongst black African Burley tobacco growers in the Tribal Trust Lands (TTLs). Amongst most African growers, DDT was being used indiscriminately, despite the 'ban' on its use on tobacco. In September 1975, the Acting Agricultural director of the TTLs, A. M. Coleman, wrote to the Provincial Agricultural Officer, Mashonaland West and Central, complaining about undesirably high levels of DDT found in leaf samples taken from African farmers in Mount Darwin, Karoi and Glendale.[172] During a meeting of the pesticide committee, the TRB director echoed this concern and observed that, as far as the TTL growers were concerned, there had not been much improvement, and in fact there

existing stocks in the shops were finished and these were expected to last until the end of the season.

167 Southern Rhodesia Government Notice No. 3 (1970).

168 Annual Report of the Tobacco Marketing Board, 1972. 169 Ibid.

170 'New tobacco pest control', *Rhodesia Herald*, 14 June 1974. 171 Ibid.

172 NAZ, S3700/44, Crop Pests Control, Use of Pesticides and Herbicides, October 1973–March 1977, Coleman to Provincial Agricultural Officer, Mashonaland West and Central, 15 September 1975.

had been some slight deterioration.[173] He pointed out that as long as DDT was still available to the black African grower he would continue to use it as *muti* (meaning 'magical medicine', referring here to a disinfectant chemical), and a great deal of African tobacco was stored in *kias* (African huts) which would have been dosed with DDT as a means of killing various household pests, including mosquitoes.[174] In addition, the use of the product by African farmers to spray their cotton caused problems of drift. The worst offenders in this regard were mentioned as the black farmers in the TTLs of Chiweshe and Chesa. To control the problem, the Secretary of Internal Affairs proposed the prohibition of purchases of 85 g packets of DDT in African areas.[175] This he viewed as effective since white farmers could buy this insecticide only in bigger packages of 1 kg or 50 kg.[176] Although DDT was still being used by both white and black cotton farmers for the control of cotton bollworms, the concern was that Burley tobacco was being accidentally contaminated by drift from cotton spraying in black African areas. The secretary of the Agricultural Pesticides Association pointed out that DDT was a cheaper alternative for the spraying of cotton, and to keep the spraying costs of African cotton within bounds, DDT still had to be used.[177] The problem, he noted, could only be solved by better extension advice and the right educational approach to the cotton grower rather than the removal of the pesticide from the market.[178]

In 1974, 28 per cent of African-grown Burley which was sampled by the Pesticide Control Committee revealed higher DDT residues as shown in Tables 3.1 and 3.2. In 1975, the figure went up to 31 per cent, but what was more worrying was the presence of much higher residues of over 2 ppm, constituting 15 per cent of the sample. In the

173 NAZ, S3700/44, Crop Pests Control, Use of Pesticides and Herbicides, October 1973–March 1977, Minutes of the Pesticide Control Committee held at the RTA (Salisbury), 13 October 1975.

174 Ibid.

175 NAZ, S3700/44, Crop Pests Control, Use of Pesticides and Herbicides, October 1973–March 1977, Secretary of Internal Affairs to Secretary Agricultural Pesticides Association, 8 March 1976.

176 Ibid.

177 NAZ, S3700/44, Crop Pests Control, Use of Pesticides and Herbicides, October 1973–March 1977, Secretary Agricultural Chemicals Industry (Mrs. P. A. Morgan) to Ministry of Internal Affairs, 4 May 1976.

178 Ibid.

Table 3.1 *Pesticide contamination of Burley tobacco grown in African areas, 1974*

DDT Amount Parts per million (ppm)	Number of Growers	Growers as %
Less than 0.5 ppm	94	51.4
0.5–0.9 ppm	15	8.4
1.0–1.5 ppm	37	20.2
1.6–2.0 ppm	16	8.0

Source: NAZ, (unprocessed) Records Centre collections C.32.15.11R, Box number 126959, Tobacco Burley Association. Rhodesia Tobacco Marketing Board, Monitoring Service for Pesticide. Residue in Tobacco: Report of Burley Sample, Tribal Trust Lands, 1974.

Table 3.2 *Pesticide contamination of Burley tobacco grown in African areas, 1975*

DDT Amount Parts per million (ppm)	Number of Growers	Growers as %
Less than 0.5 ppm	66	50.5
0.5–0.9 ppm	25	19.0
1.0–1.5 ppm	11	8.5
1.6–2.0 ppm	9	7.0
Over 2.1 ppm	20	15.0

Source: NAZ, (unprocessed) Records Centre collections C.32.15.11R, Box number 126959, Tobacco Burley Association. Rhodesia Tobacco Marketing Board, Monitoring Service for Pesticide Residue in Tobacco: Report of Burley Sample, Tribal Trust Lands, 1975.

white areas, the levels of contamination were remarkably lower. In 1974 for instance out of a sample of seventy-seven growers only two, 6.5 per cent, had crops with high levels of DDT, and in 1975 while 345 kg of black African tobacco was destroyed for containing higher levels of DDT, amongst the European growers no tobacco was destroyed.[179]

[179] NAZ, (unprocessed) Records Centre collections C.32.15.11R, Box number 126959, Tobacco Burley Association, TMB, Monitoring Service for Pesticide Residue in Tobacco, Pesticide Inspectors Report to the General Manager (TMB), 10 October 1975.

All in all, these comparative results reflect that there was heavier contamination by DDT in the TTLs which were black African areas. This contamination certainly left residues in the environment and food crops grown on the adjacent pieces of land as black African plots in the TTLs were smaller and crowded.[180] Unfortunately, this racialised dimension was never considered by the Tobacco Pesticide Scheme and the level of contamination of food crops, land and water in the TTLs by DDT can only be inferred from scientific evidence made available by later studies. A 1999 scientific study on samples from soil, rivers and dams found DDT residues in the terrestrial environment of the former TTLs of Mount Darwin and Rushinga, which was attributed to cumulative contamination over twenty years.[181] What this does reveal is how Carson's environmentalism operated unevenly along the lines of race and class in Southern Rhodesia, impacting black Africans and whites in distinctly different ways.

In the final analysis, the major lesson that can be drawn from the Tobacco Pesticide Control Scheme is that it was rarely about the safe use of chemicals to avoid environmental contamination and human poisoning. Instead, the scheme was about avoiding the contamination of the tobacco crop for the export market. Even then, by 1970, most farmers were unwilling to spend money on extending pesticide protection to include the safety of their labourers because of the costs involved. Increasing agricultural safety was estimated to cost farmers as much as R$2.1 million in 1971.[182] In 1972, the 'Kutsaga suit' was developed by the TRB for the safe and efficient application of pesticides to Burley tobacco.[183] This was a more effective suit than the protective suits available at the time of the jacket-and-trousers type that were not adequately protective against small particle penetration.[184] Despite this, most farmers were still not actually adopting safety practices for agricultural labourers using sprayers. The Ministry of Health in 1978 fretted that some Rhodesian farmers were far too casual with the use of

[180] The Tribal Trust Lands were largely overcrowded and a result of colonial racialised land policy that began with the 1930 Land Apportionment Act, which set up prescribed areas for African settlement.

[181] Mbamba and Zaranyika, 'DDT Residue in Terrestrial Environment', 83–96.

[182] 'New Safety Rules May Give Farmers a Shock', *Rhodesian Financial Gazette*, 15 January 1971.

[183] 'Applying Insecticides with a Knapsack Mist Blower', *Tobacco Forum of Rhodesia*, August 1972.

[184] Ibid.

highly toxic pesticides.[185] They noted that labourers using knapsack sprays were not protected against the chemicals used. Tanks were often refilled while still on the operator's back, and unless he was wearing protective clothing spillage would take place which would mean the chemical would be in contact with his skin.[186] As a result, several incidences of poisoning were reported.

A spokesperson for the government's Occupational Safety and Compensation department said that from April 1977 to March 1978 more than 100 cases of poisoning were reported. Of these, twenty-four involved pesticides, with twenty-two occurring in agriculture.[187] The spokesperson added that many more cases amongst black African agricultural labourers went unreported.[188] In one horrifying case, an African labourer was spraying pesticide on a tobacco crop in the Salisbury area when the hose became clogged. He tried to clear it by sucking with his mouth, swallowing the solution and dying.[189] In another case, African labourers were spraying chemicals on a tobacco crop at Kutsaga Research Station. The wind suddenly changed direction, blowing the toxic droplets into their unprotected faces, causing severe burns.[190] In yet another case, an African family was working on a tobacco farm where pesticide and water were stored in similar drums. A small daughter of the family drank from the wrong barrel and died.[191] In most instances, tobacco farm labourers exercised very little caution when using harmful chemicals as a result of ignorance. According to the testimony of one former farm worker, water containing DDT would be drunk by thirsty labourers, and some would even consume their food with unwashed hands after handling highly toxic organophosphate chemicals in tobacco nurseries, and there was very little concern on the part of the white farmers.[192] A survey by the Hazardous

185 'New Control on Pesticides', *Rhodesian Financial Gazette*, 3 March 1978.
186 Ibid.
187 'Poisonings Caused by Careless Handling', *Rhodesian Sunday Mail*, 18 December 1979.
188 Ibid. 189 Ibid. 190 Ibid. 191 Ibid.
192 Interview with Mrs Saizi (former farm worker, 74 years old), Westbury Farm, Centenary, Zimbabwe, 13 February 2019. Other former farm workers interviewed (Mr Ganizani, 68 years old, Westbury Farm, Centenary, 13 February 2019; Mr Kavhimbo, 71 years old, Mutwa Estate, Mount Darwin, 24 February 2019; and Mr Jimu, 63 years old, Avalon farm, Centenary, 15 February 2019) narrated horrendous tales of how chemical poisonings were common on the tobacco farms and resulted in the death of several workers, particularly those who worked in the tobacco nurseries, who often developed

Substances Inspectorate group of 378 farms revealed shockingly that less than half of the farmers throughout the country provided protective gear for their workers and on 72 per cent of the farms none of the workers interviewed knew the meaning of the purple and red triangle emblems on pesticide containers![193] Thus while the use of poisonous chemicals in agriculture was increasing there were no training facilities to teach black farm workers how to protect themselves, resulting in a high incidence of poisoning. Between January 1980 and July 1981 more than 120 cases of organophosphate poisoning were recorded on the white farms around Harare only, and the victims were all black Africans![194] On 10 July 1984, twelve tobacco farm workers from a farm in Centenary were admitted at Mvurwi district hospital and later transferred to a Harare hospital with organophosphate poisoning.[195] Upon inspection of the premises where the workers had been poisoned, the health assistant found:

> Five dangerous chemicals lying about on the shelf in a workshop where they should have been locked away. On the same shelf as the poisons, they found cups and a teapot as well as two mealie cobs. On the veranda of the workshop were a lot of other chemicals, new stock and old stock which were open.[196]

These sporadically reported instances of human poisoning on the tobacco farms are just a few of the many instances of the liminal losses and unseen sufferers that Nixon has argued are under-represented in both strategic planning as well as historical memory.[197] This marginalisation of the casualties of chemical poisoning is largely a result of what Mike Davis calls 'the dialectic of ordinary disaster', where a calamity is appropriated into history and made ordinary and forgettable because the burden of risk falls on the unsheltered poor.[198] Consequently, most such disasters are expunged from historical memory and policy

chronic conditions like tuberculosis, and eventually died after long illnesses. They also testified that protective clothing was not always provided, and in most cases farm workers sprayed these chemicals while exposed to drift spray.

193 'Farm Workers Exposed to Killer Sprays, Says Survey', *Sunday Mail*, 15 April 1983.

194 Ibid.

195 'Poisonous Chemicals Threaten Farm Workers', *The Herald*, 12 November 1984.

196 Ibid. 197 Nixon, *Slow Violence and the Environmentalism of the Poor*, 2.

198 M. Davis, 'Los Angeles After the Storm: The Dialectics of Ordinary Disaster', *Antipode* 27 (1995), 221–224.

planning by their framing as 'accidental and random'.[199] To this extent, therefore, the official figures on chemical poisoning of African labourers in Southern Rhodesia must be treated with scepticism.

Also, while the pesticide control scheme focused on the contamination of tobacco by these chemicals, many of them were still being used indiscriminately for other agricultural purposes, mostly within white farming areas. A scientific study carried out in 1972 covering most parts of the country revealed a massive build-up of DDT in lakes.[200] Many cases of fish poisoning by DDT, dieldrin, empty methyl bromide tins and tobacco scrap were also reported in most ICAs.[201] Reports were also published in the *Rhodesia Herald* (17 and 19 December 1975) on the use in the tobacco-producing districts of Karoi and Sinoia of non-selective poisons during a rodent plague, resulting in deaths all along the food chain, including natural predators such as owls and snakes.[202] The director of National Parks expressed concern over the use of highly toxic and long-lasting poisons as warfarin and nuvacron (also known as monocrotophos, a systemic tobacco pesticide) for the field control of rodents in the white farms.[203] In March 1975, J. J. Buitendag, the MP for Mhangula (another tobacco-producing district), wrote to the Minister of Lands and Agriculture complaining that farmers were using various poisons to combat rats and mice that were digging up and eating their maize seeds, and many predators were killed as a result.[204]

While forms of control had been established for the use of pesticides on tobacco and other crops, there were inadequate environmental control and policing mechanisms. Dr Hamilton Ritchie (a member of the Rhodesian Legislative Assembly) had posed the very 'Carson-esque' question to the Minister of Health in 1978 of whether he was satisfied with the policing systems stopping farmers from using too much pesticide which could then wash off into rivers and be detrimental to animal welfare and the biological chain.[205] The minister responded that it was

199 Nixon, *Slow Violence and the Environmentalism of the Poor*, 65.

200 R. J. Phelps and T. Billings, 'Pesticide Levels from Animals in Southern Rhodesia', *Transactions of Rhodesia Science Association* 55 (1972), 6–9.

201 'Wildlife Must Be Conserved', *Tobacco Today*, December 1974.

202 *Rhodesia Herald*, 19 December 1975. 203 Ibid.

204 NAZ, S3700/44, Crop Pests Control, Use of Pesticides and Herbicides, October 1973–March 1977, J. J. Buitendag to Minister of Lands and Agriculture, 5 March 1975.

205 'Control over Pesticides Difficult', *Rhodesia Herald*, 29 November 1978.

difficult to control the amount of pesticides farmers put onto their crops.[206] Cognisant of these problems, the NRB had created the Environmental Conservation Committee in November 1977 under the chairmanship of Professor Geoffrey Bond. The committee considered pesticide and herbicide usage in the country in detail, in particular that of DDT, by taking evidence from local 'experts' and informed by the global trends.[207] During the same period a number of local studies had begun to confirm through scientific data that DDT contaminated the environment.[208] The interim report of the Environmental Conservation Committee was the first comprehensive official study on the effects of pesticide poisoning on the environment in Southern Rhodesia.[209] The report was presented to the new government of independent Zimbabwe in late 1980. The new political context had little influence on the report as its findings were compiled over a long period of time. The report concurred with the global data that pesticide residues could accumulate in the environment, creating an insidious effect on the ecosystem.[210] It pointed out that although the threat to human life within the country had been negligible, there had been human fatalities through accidental overdose and suicide. In addition, certain bird species had been endangered.[211] The report further exhorted the NRB to consider the matter dispassionately from the point of view of what was best for the country.[212]

The report by the Environmental Conservation Committee thus confirmed what had already been articulated by sporadic official voices in Southern Rhodesia, including the Ministry of Health, since 1969 about the effects of pesticide residue on humans and the environment.

206 Ibid.

207 Under the supervision of the Ministry of Agriculture, a nationwide pesticide monitoring programme was started in 1979 to determine whether residues of chlorinated hydrocarbon poisons were present in dangerous quantities in the country. This came after repeated calls by conservationists for the banning of pesticides which had been recognised as dangerous to humans and wildlife. The monitoring programme was being carried out by the Ministries of Health, Agriculture and National Parks and Wildlife through sampling of water bodies, water life and soil.

208 Y. A. Greichus et al., 'Insecticides, Polychlorinated Biphenyls and Metals in African Lake Ecosystems II: Lake Chivero, Zimbabwe', *Bulletin of Environmental Contamination and Toxicology*, 19 (1978), 444–453.

209 Natural Resource Board, 'The Pesticide Dilemma', *Newsletter* no. 8 (September 1981).

210 Ibid. 211 Ibid. 212 Ibid.

A parallel can be made between the significance of the report and that of the American PSAC 1965 report, as it goaded the pesticide control agenda into the official policy corridors and called for relevant monitoring instruments, particularly through the NRB. For its part, the NRB noted that it was deeply concerned about the continued use of DDT in light of the adverse reports emanating from other parts of the world, mostly the developed world, in which several countries had banned this pesticide. It was concerned about the general misuse of pesticides and herbicides in the country, particularly the spraying of monocrotophos at two or more times the rate recommended for aphid control in tobacco for which it was registered.[213] The board noted that the pesticide was lethal to game birds such as guinea fowls, and a host of other birds, and as a result there had been a serious depletion of birdlife in some tobacco farming areas.[214] This perhaps evokes the eerie silence captured poetically by John Keats in 'La Belle Dame sans Merci', from which *Silent Spring* takes its title, two lines of which read:

> The sedge is wither'd from the lake,
> And no birds sing.[215]

From the 1980s, following the end of white colonial rule, the use of DDT fell under severe scrutiny in Zimbabwe, largely because of the build-up of evidence on its residual effects on wildlife and the environment. In 1982, the widespread use of DDT as an agricultural insecticide was banned by the newly independent government.[216] In 1985, DDT was declared a Group 1 hazardous substance, and its use was restricted to research purposes for malaria and tsetse fly control.[217] By 1991, it had been banned for outdoor control of malaria because of concerns over the contamination of tobacco.[218] Currently, DDT is being used only for indoor malaria control in the country.[219] However, concerns over the

213 Ibid. 214 Ibid.

215 J. Keats in M. H. Abrams, *The Norton Anthology of English Literature*, vol. 2 (New York, 1970).

216 S. M. Mpofu, 'DDT and Its Uses in Zimbabwe', *Zimbabwe Science News*, 21 (1987), 31–36.

217 M. E. S. Flint and M. J. S. Harrison, 'DDT Impact Assessment Project: Zimbabwe', *Department of International Aid, Evaluation Report*, 621 (December 1998), 9.

218 Flint and Harrison, 'DDT Impact Assessment Project', 9.

219 The current national spraying programme is largely funded by USAID under the President's Malaria Initiative Indoor Residual Spraying Project.

contamination of tobacco as a result of indoor DDT spraying have resurfaced in recent years, particularly with the entry of many black farmers into production after the Fast Track Land Reform Programme in 2000.[220] In 2018 there were concerns that the country's tobacco would face a ban over DDT residue contamination. Research findings by global tobacco merchants presented at the Cooperation Centre for Scientific Research Relative to Tobacco (CORESTA) showed that, of all producing countries, Zimbabwean tobacco was the only one contaminated by DDT.[221] Other highly toxic insecticides such as monocrotophos (warfarin and nuvacron) and methamidophos (tamaron) were banned for use in tobacco, but they have continued to be used by most black smallholder producers as they are easily available on the black market and cheaper than the recommended alternatives.[222]

Therefore, the history of pesticide use in Southern Rhodesia is a story of environmental pollution and contamination that has never been studied before by historians. Yet it is evident that the use of these chemicals posed serious hazards. Irresponsible and casual use of pesticides, because of lack of proper pest management and safety facilities, claimed a significant number of silent and silenced casualties – in both the human and natural environment. The story of this 'slow violence' and invisible deaths in tobacco farming does indeed conjure up Carson's Silent Spring. In fact, the local narrative connects with the global movement that Carson stirred, which brings us back to the question asked at the start: was there an African Rachel Carson? An engaged understanding of Carson in Africa needs to be understood in tandem with the triple concepts of 'slow violence', the 'environmentalism of the poor' and 'environmental racism', as this chapter has

220 There are over 165,000 smallholder tobacco producers registered for the 2018–2019 season. Some of these producers are in areas which have high incidences of malaria and they use DDT for indoor control. Consequently, their tobacco is contaminated from storage in the sprayed houses.

221 See, 'Zim Tobacco Faces Ban over DDT Residue Contamination', *AgriNews*, 14 December 2018, https://agrinews.co.zw/crops/2018/14/2153zim-tobacco-faces-ban-over-ddt-residue-contamination/, accessed 25 February 2019.

222 See, Doreen Badze, 'Farmers Still Using Banned Pesticide', *The Standard*, 11 December 2016, https://thestandard.co.zw/2016/12/11/farmers-still-usingbanned-pesticide/, accessed 25 February 2019. Other tobacco chemicals banned in the country include the soil fumigant methyl bromide, because of its negative effects on the ozone layer, and EDB, which was banned in the United States on 19 September 1983 because it was shown to cause cancer and birth defects.

argued. But this should not be an historiographical ending, rather a beginning of the quest for the African Carson moment. This chapter has not intended to write an environmental history epitaph or to rehabilitate Carson in Africa, but rather awaken an historiographical debate on Silent Spring as it relates to Africa. Already it is clear that Southern Rhodesia had its own 'Silent Spring' moment(s), but these moments were idiographic and vernacular encounters within a global environmental movement. While Carson sparked modern environmentalism and brought pesticide use into critical focus, her meaning within Africa must be critically understood within a strongly diachronic context. First, as argued in this chapter, Silent Spring did not invent environmental consciousness, but rather channelled it into a global environmental zeitgeist. It provided the impetus and vocabulary for a new kind of challenge post-1960. Second, this movement assumed new meanings and forms in Africa, where unique problems of technical innovation in agriculture, costs of harnessing new pest control management systems, economic and political inequalities, and the more hostile pest-prone climatic conditions required pragmatic approaches to pesticide control. To this end, the 'African Rachel Carson moment' must be seen as a vernacular experience drawing inspiration from its own local and global realities. Even in the United States, there never was a monolithic and homogenous 'Silent Spring'. Rather there were several silent springs. Finally, we must guard against the dangers of reading Carson in Africa in teleological terms; as historians, just as much as we need to reconstruct knowledge, we need to painstakingly reconstruct ignorance.

4 Beyond Agency

The African Peasantry, the State and Tobacco in Southern Rhodesia, 1900–1980

Is nothing to be left for natives to raise revenue on. Are they to be turned into criminals whenever they endeavour to raise taxes by disposing of a few pounds of tobacco grown on their old kraal sites...?

Native Commissioner Murehwa to Chief Native Commissioner (1936).

Introduction

Peasants are a fundamental part of African historiography, yet the historiographical debate has stalled in recent years. This stasis prompts the imperative to revisit African peasantries and locate their colonial encounters within the structural precincts of classical 'peasant agency' theory. There is a need to engage with how 'peasant agency' was constrained by structural factors in settler colonies such as commodity asymmetries, cash crop hierarchies, and global market forces. The scholarship of the 1960s and 1970s on peasant studies and colonial development and underdevelopment in Africa underestimated the role of peasants as historical actors and collapsed the complex processes of rural transformation into a single trajectory of 'strangulation' and collapse.[1] However, new approaches to African peasant studies foregrounded peasants' ingenuity in navigating the complex disruptive

[1] For comprehensive reading on scholarship and debates surrounding colonial Africa peasantries, see: W. Rodney, *How Europe Underdeveloped Africa* (London, 1972); A. G. Frank, *The Development of Underdevelopment* (Boston, 1966); G. Arrighi, 'Labour Supplies in Historical Perspective: A Study of the Proletarianization of the African Peasantry in Rhodesia', *Journal of Development Studies*, 6 (1970), 197–234; C. Bundy, *The Rise and Fall of The South African Peasantry* (London, 1979); I. Phimister, 'Peasant Production and Underdevelopment in Southern Rhodesia, 1890–1914', *African Affairs*, 73, 291 (1974), 217–228; R. Palmer, 'The Agricultural History of Rhodesia', in R. Palmer and N. Parsons (eds.), *The Roots of Rural Poverty in Central and Southern Africa* (London, 1977), 221–245; and W. Barber, *The Political Economy of British Central Africa* (London, 1963).

colonial infrastructure and highlighted 'peasant agency' to emphasise how enclaves of peasant production survived the colonial economic onslaught and fomented centres of rural resistance, rural entrepreneurship, and political consciousness.[2]

Nevertheless, although intently keen on demonstrating 'agency' this scholarship stressed the ubiquitous structural constraints under which peasants operated at various levels and how these constraints impinged on their limited choices.[3] John Lonsdale referred to this embedded pervasive precarity and intractable dilemma of African producers in hegemonic colonial and neo-colonial capitalist world systems as 'agency in tight corners'.[4] Thus, while there were moments of African prosperity and independent production of cash crops, these transient episodic booms were structured by and subject to the broader colonial relations and institutional arrangements that predisposed African peasantries to eventual collapse and failure. This chapter discusses cash crop and commodity asymmetries within the colonial economy as structural constraints on 'peasant agency'. Each cash crop or agricultural commodity occupied a unique space within the matrix of colonial economic and political power relations in Africa and these power asymmetries were based on the respective export value and the concomitant economic influence it bestowed upon white settler power.

A cursory perusal of agricultural archives reveals how settler colonial states in Africa systematically triaged cash crops and agricultural commodities into hierarchies. These were not only based on dispassionate economic calculations, but also invested with notions of what was 'right' and what was 'might' – what was fitting and what was hegemonic. In essence, they were invested with tacit ideologies of power and

[2] T. Ranger, *Peasant Consciousness and the Guerrilla War in Zimbabwe* (London, 1985), 54–96; W. Beinart and C. Bundy, *Hidden Struggles in Rural South Africa* (Berkeley, 1987); C. Van Onselen, *The Seed Is Mine: The Life of Kas Maine, A South African Sharecropper, 1894–1985* (London, 1987); S. Feierman, *Peasant Intellectuals: Anthropology and History in Tanzania* (London, 1990); P. Mosley, 'Agricultural Development and Government Policy in Settler Economies: The Case of Kenya and Southern Rhodesia, 1900–60', *The Economic History Review*, 35, 3 (1982), 390–408.

[3] Allen Isaacman's review article of Terence Ranger and the works of William Beinart and Colin Bundy contains a useful discussion of 'agency' and its structural constraints: A. Isaacman, 'Peasants, Social Protests and Africanists', *The Journal of African History*, 22, 4 (1989), 745–765.

[4] J. Lonsdale, 'Agency in Tight Corners: Narrative and Initiative in African History', *Journal of African Cultural Studies*, 13, 1 (2000), 5–16.

powerlessness, domination and subservience, knowledge and ignorance – evinced in their production and marketing. These commodity asymmetries concomitantly mediated 'peasant agency', accumulation patterns, and peasant options in the countryside. High value export cash crops and commodities such as coffee, tea, and tobacco, that were the basis of white economic power and privilege in settler colonies, were often subjected to more stringent production and marketing controls deliberately meant to exclude African producers and entrench specific paradigms of development that benefited white settler interests. In some instances, Africans were banned from participating in the production of high value export crops for much of the colonial period. Meanwhile, commodities with a low value in the hierarchy of colonial economic power relations, because of their lower unit returns on the global export market (such as cotton), were often used by the colonial state to entrench domination of peasantries through the stick of coerced production or, more often as time went by, the carrot of state subsidies to peasant producers.[5]

In settler colonies such as Kenya and Southern Rhodesia, export expansion targeted white farmers to create a monopoly in the cultivation of high value export crops while restricting Africans from those crops to ensure supply of labour to white farms. By the late 1940s though, with new global and local pressures such as festering nationalism, rural discontent, and post-war booms in agricultural commodity prices, colonial policy on high value export crops altered to allow a cautious and guided entry of African cultivators in a way that would not disrupt the status quo and imperil white settler agriculture.

This chapter engages with how cash crops were constructed in the colonial state and given a significance that controlled relations of production and the changing dimensions of African participation in commodity production that, in turn, impacted on the possibilities of 'peasant agency'. Using this framework, the chapter examines African

[5] During the first half of the twentieth century high prices for cotton forced European countries to shift their attention to African colonies. State subsidies were given to African peasants as inducement to grow cotton and cotton was viewed by colonial officials as a 'blackman crop': A. Isaacman et al., 'Cotton is the Mother of Poverty: Peasant Resistance to Forced Cotton Production in Mozambique, 1938–1961', *The International Journal of African Historical Studies*, 13, 4 (1980), 581–615; P. Nyambara, 'Colonial Policy and Peasant Cotton Agriculture in Southern Rhodesia, 1904–1953', *The International Journal of African Historical Studies*, 33, 1 (2000), 81–111.

tobacco producers in Southern Rhodesia chronologically across three distinct periods: a precolonial to early colonial period of independent production and boom (from the early 1900s to the late 1930s); an era of state curtailment of peasant modes of production and decline of African participation in the tobacco economy (from the 1930s to the 1950s); and, lastly, a period of colonial state-assisted African production of Turkish tobacco (from 1952 to 1980). The first period witnessed an ephemeral boom for African peasants because of the domestic market provided by emerging mining settlements and towns. The second period marked the collapse of production and trade in 'indigenous' African tobacco as the state systematically pushed Africans out of production through restrictive statutory interference in production and marketing as well as the introduction of Western cigarettes. The third period saw the initiation of African production of Turkish and Burley tobaccos, and their integration for the first time into the global export economy under the colonial state's modernistic agenda to transform African agriculture and cash crop production.[6]

There is also scant historical literature on the participation of Africans on tobacco production in Southern Rhodesia beyond their role as labourers on the white settler farms.[7] The only historical work on the subject is Barry Kosmin's early colonial study that ends in 1938 and misses the integration of peasant producers into the global export market between 1952 and 1980.[8] The chapter argues that, although

6 Turkish tobacco or oriental is an aromatic type of tobacco that is sun cured. Turkish tobacco is used as a blend in the manufacture of cigarettes because of its mild flavour and low nicotine content. Burley tobacco is air cured and is usually used for pipe smoking. Although Africans grew both Turkish and Burley tobacco beginning from 1952 and 1964 respectively, this paper focuses on Turkish tobacco only. However, state policy and motives for African cultivation were significantly similar for both crops.

7 F. Clements and E. Harben, *Leaf of Gold: The Story of Rhodesian Tobacco* (London, 1962); P. Scott, 'The Tobacco Industry of Southern Rhodesia', *Economic Geography*, 28, 3 (1952), 189–206; T. Mbanga, *Tobacco: A Century of Gold* (Harare, 1991); V. Machingaidze, 'The Development of Settler Capitalist Agriculture in Southern Rhodesia with Particular Reference to the Role of the State, 1908–1939' (unpublished PhD thesis, University of London, 1980); S. Rubert, *A Most Promising Weed: A History of Tobacco Farming and Labour in Colonial Zimbabwe, 1890–1945* (Athens, OH, 1998); and S. Ncube, 'Colonial Zimbabwe Tobacco Industry: Global, Regional and Local Relations, 1949–1979' (unpublished PhD thesis, University of the Free State, 2018).

8 B. Kosmin, 'The Inyoka Tobacco Industry of the Shangwe People: The Displacement of a Pre-colonial Economy in Southern Rhodesia; 1898–1938', in Palmer and Parsons, *The Roots of Rural Poverty*, 268–287.

colonial policy towards African tobacco producers shifted across the twentieth century from curtailment to encouragement, it was nevertheless enduringly informed by the imperative to restrict Africans to certain types of tobacco that would not challenge European tobacco farmers or lead to the rise of an independent African agrarian bourgeoisie that could compete with white settler farmers.[9] Thus, at all points during the colonial period, the African peasant producer was enmeshed within a complex global and local economic infrastructure in which he was susceptible to failure, and remained economically marginal and vulnerable.

From Incentives to Curtailment? The Rise and Fall of an African Tobacco Economy in Southern Rhodesia, 1904–1938

The cultivation of tobacco in Africa predates colonialism. By the end of the seventeenth century the crop had penetrated much of the continent as a result of Portuguese, French, English and Arabic trade networks.[10] The traditional species of tobacco cultivated in Africa was *Nicotiana rustica*.[11] In the area that came to be known as Southern Rhodesia, Africans began cultivating tobacco from at least the fifteenth century when it was introduced by Portuguese traders.[12] Its cultivation during the later parts of the precolonial period is well documented in historical accounts.[13] For example, Thomas Morgan Thomas of the London

[9] The categorisation of peasantries into the social hierarchy as to what constitutes a true rural bourgeoisie has always been challenging. Some Marxists like Lenin identified as many as six rural classes: the capitalist big landowners exploiting wage labour, the big peasants, the middle peasants, the small peasantry, and the agricultural proletariat obtaining livelihoods by working on the farms (V. I. Lenin, 'Preliminary Drafts on the Agrarian Question', in *Collected Works, Volume XXXI* [Moscow, 1966]).

[10] J. E. Philips, 'African Smoking and Pipes', *The Journal of African History*, 24 (1983), 303–319. For further reading on precolonial African tobacco cultures, see: C. Duvall, 'Cannabis and Tobacco in Precolonial Africa', *Oxford Research Encyclopaedia of African History*, (https://doi.org/10.1093/acrefore/9780190277734.013.44), 2017.

[11] There are dozens of species of *Nicotiana* but the two most important are *Nicotiana tabacum L.* (grown for commercial purposes) and *Nicotiana rustica L.* (produced for household consumption).

[12] H. Weinmann, *Agricultural Research and Development in Southern Rhodesia, 1890–1923* (Salisbury [Harare], 1972), 12.

[13] J. Wood, *Through Matabeleland: The Record of a Ten Months' Trip in an Ox Waggon through Mashonaland and Matebeleland* (Bulawayo, 1893); T. M. Thomas, *Eleven Years in Central South Africa* (Cardiff, 1873), 180–181.

Missionary Society, in memoirs of his adventures in southern Africa between 1864 and 1873, records that Ndebele people grew large quantities of tobacco: 'indeed I cannot remember seeing a single village around which there were no tobacco gardens'.[14] Tobacco was integral to the cultural rituals of the Ndebele people who took it as snuff and smoked it in *ingiti* (clay pipes) and *igudu* (smoking horns). Africans cultivated and irrigated patches of tobacco in their gardens for their own consumption, for barter, and for annual tribute to the king.[15]

Tobacco was the first important 'European crop' that was cultivated by the pioneer white settler farmers as early as 1893.[16] The British South African Company (BSAC) developed an interest in tobacco production for colonial economic growth and sampled 'indigenous' African tobaccos to ascertain their potential commercial value.[17] The Company concluded that this tobacco had no export value since its flavour was alien to British consumers.[18] Consequently, white settler farmers began to cultivate 'superior' varieties of *Tabacum* (flue-cured, Turkish, and fire-cured) from American seeds while Africans cultivated the 'inferior' *rustica* for the peripheral domestic market.[19] Africans could only interact with the 'European' types of tobacco as labourers, not as producers.[20] The growing of tobacco became particularly important from around 1908, when the colony's company administration launched a White Agricultural Policy (WAP).[21]

Tobacco became a symbolic agricultural commodity conveying white power and privilege.[22] Buoyed by the fortunes offered by the

[14] Thomas, *Eleven Years*, 179–180.

[15] National Archives of Zimbabwe, Harare (NAZ) AOH/59, Interview with Mudzongani Maodzwa, 8 August 1979.

[16] M. Rooney, 'European Agriculture in the History of Rhodesia, 1890–1907' (unpublished MA thesis, University of South Africa, 1968); Machingaidze, 'The Development of Settler', 183; H. Thomson, *Rhodesia and Its Government* (London, 1898), 67; and Clements and Harbern, *Leaf of Gold*, 70.

[17] NAZ A11/2/2/13, Tobacco 1904–November 1909, Professor Wyndham R. Dunstan, report on tobacco from Rhodesia received through the BSAC, June 1902.

[18] NAZ A11/2/2/13, Tobacco 1904–November 1909, Dunstan, report, June 1902.

[19] Clements and Harben, *Leaf of Gold*, 55.

[20] Department of Agriculture, *A Handbook on Tobacco Culture for Planters in Southern Rhodesia* (Salisbury [Harare], 1912), 92.

[21] The colony of Southern Rhodesia was founded on the hope of finding a second mineral Rand but when the hopes of a gold-based El Dorado faded, the Company administration had to reorient their priorities to support white settler agriculture from 1908.

[22] Clements and Harben, *Leaf of Gold*, 187–191.

Union of South Africa's market, white settler tobacco production expanded significantly. In 1914, 2.2 million lbs of tobacco were exported to the Union's market. This rose to nearly 10 million lbs in 1928.[23] The United Kingdom's granting of an imperial preference for empire tobacco from 1919 expanded the export market for Rhodesian tobacco prompting production to reach 14 million lbs in 1928 and resulting in white settler tobacco production contributing 42.7 per cent to agricultural export revenue.[24] Tobacco was second only to gold in aggregate value of all exports in Southern Rhodesia between 1916 and 1947 accruing nearly 43 million pounds sterling.[25]

While the settler export tobacco market expanded, the cultivation of 'indigenous' *Inyoka* tobacco amongst African peasants (who grew it together with other crops such as maize) continued. The exact size and scale of the precolonial *Inyoka* tobacco trade and economy cannot be ascertained because of limited records, but historical evidence does suggest that there was a significant manufacturing and tobacco trade economy.[26] This tobacco economy developed from around 1899, as European traders bought stocks of tobacco to resell on the mines, providing African peasants with money to pay taxes and accumulate wealth.[27] Indeed, the role of tobacco as a 'progressive crop' that provided economic opportunities for smallholder and peasant producers and prevented their proletarianisation into the colonial wage labour economy has received a lot of scholarly attention.[28] However,

[23] Ibid., 76. [24] Machingaidze, 'The Development of Settler', 183.

[25] This value greatly exceeded other major exports, such as beef, asbestos, iron, and maize. See, E. Frankema et al., *An Introduction to the African Commodity Trade Database, 1730–2010*, (https://doi.org/10.17026/dans-xt9-fzkw), 2017.

[26] Knight-Bruce, *Memories of Mashonaland*, 100; H. N. Hemans, *The Logs of a Native Commissioner* (Bulawayo, 1971), 168.

[27] Kosmin, 'The Inyoka Tobacco Industry', 274.

[28] J. McCracken, 'Planters, Peasants and the Colonial State: The Impact of the Native Tobacco Board in the Central Province of Malawi', *Journal of Southern African Studies*, 9, 2 (1983), 172–192; M. Prowse, 'A History of Tobacco Production and Marketing in Malawi, 1890–2010', *Journal of East African Studies*, 7, 4 (2013), 691–712; A. Kanduza, 'The Tobacco Industry in Northern Rhodesia: 1912–38', *The International Journal of African Historical Studies*, 16, 2 (1983), 201–229. For studies in peasant cash crop production in Latin America and Caribbean, see: P. A. Howard, *Black Labour, White Sugar: Caribbean Braceros and Their Struggle for Power in the Cuban Sugar Industry* (Baton Rouge, LA, 2015); M. Baud, *Peasants and Tobacco in the Dominican Republic: 1870–1930* (Knoxville, TN, 1995); and M. Baud and K. Koonings, 'A Lavoura dos Pobres: Tobacco Farming and the Development of Commercial

the resultant pecuniary gains to the prosperous peasant *Inyoka* tobacco economy restricted the flow of Africans into wage employment – which outraged some key colonial officials just when African labour was most desired for white settler tobacco production.[29] Between 1922 and 1938, this lucrative African tobacco economy declined precipitously as a result of the penetration of the African market by European cigarettes and lack of state support at a time when the state was subsidising the growing European tobacco sector.[30] The decline of the *Inyoka* tobacco economy was contemporaneous with the decline in African peasant production that happened in most African colonies and Southern Rhodesia during the 1930s as 'the further development of settler capitalism could no longer contain the very peasantries it had created'.[31] In Southern Rhodesia, the competitiveness of African producers was purposefully stymied through land alienation, and the state-imposed centralisation and conservation models codified more effectively by the 1930 Land Apportionment Act (LAA).[32] However, the early *Inyoka* tobacco industry remained outside much of this state centralisation and conservation injunction of the 1930s. The industry was a feature of the precolonial system and its cultivation methods were adapted to its environment.[33] The region where *Inyoka* was cultivated in southwestern Zimbabwe was dry, infested with tsetse flies, and lacking 'modernisation' such as water schemes or agricultural demonstrators in the production methods of their tobacco.[34] In essence, this tobacco economy remained outside the global export network, isolated from the white settler tobacco economy and the orbit of state agricultural policy in its marketing and production. Nevertheless, its autonomy was dependent on extraneous

Agriculture in Bahia: 1870–1930', *Journal of Latin American Studies*, 31, 2 (1999), 287–329.

29 The settler tobacco industry in Southern Rhodesia experienced cyclical labour crises from as early as 1899 and had to rely on migrant labour recruitment from Mozambique, Northern Rhodesia, and Nyasaland.

30 Kosmin, 'The Inyoka Tobacco', 279–284.

31 J. S. Saul and R. Woods, 'African Peasantries', in T. Shanin (ed.), *Peasants and Peasant Societies* (London, 1971), 106. For further readings on experiences of colonial African peasantries during the 1930s, see, D. Anderson and D. Throup, 'Africans and Agricultural Production in Colonial Kenya: The Myth of the War as a Watershed', *The Journal of African History*, 26, 4 (1985), 327–345.

32 G. Arrighi, *The Political Economy of Rhodesia* (Berkeley, 1967), 41.

33 Kosmin, 'The Inyoka Tobacco', 282.

34 NAZ S235/511/4, Report of NC Sebungwe district, 1933.

variables such as stable global market dynamics balancing with local production in white farms and averting the need to dispose of tobacco on the local market space where *Inyoka* thrived. This began to change after a 1914 glut precipitated a tobacco slump that ruined white growers.[35] The slump prompted the colonial government to prioritise securing the local market for poor grades of tobacco produced in white farms through the imposition of a cigarette tax on Rhodesian cigarettes sold on the local market. It was pointed out during the course of the debate on the tax by one of the directors of the BSAC, Earl Grey, that the tax would be paid for by the 'native' consumer and not the grower, since the habit of smoking cigarettes was growing amongst natives due to the availability of cheap locally made cigarettes in 'penny packets'.[36] The state's anxiety about the increasing supply of 'native' tobacco on the domestic market escalated in the 1930s, as a 1928–1930 tobacco export market slump destroyed European tobacco growers.[37] The slump was so severe that the contribution of tobacco to agricultural exports fell from 46.4 per cent in 1927 to 174 per cent in 1930.[38] Subsequently, an investigation into the 'native' position in the tobacco industry was initiated in 1931 so as to seek ways to promote local manufacturing for domestic consumption.[39]

Reports by native commissioners on 'native' tobacco during the 1930s all concurred that there was gradual collapse of the *Inyoka* tobacco industry from 1934, attributable to an African preference for European cigarettes.[40] These reports unanimously point to 'little trading of tobacco' by 'natives', and a decrease in the practice of smoking *Inyoka* tobacco in the mines, as Africans now preferred a cheap type of tobacco they could roll into cigarettes.[41] The decline in the smoking of *Inyoka* tobacco in Southern Rhodesia follows a trend found in most parts of colonial Africa, Asia, and America where the consumption of traditional tobacco products was disrupted by the

[35] Clements and Harbern, *Leaf of Gold*, 64. [36] Ibid.
[37] Kosmin, 'The Inyoka Tobacco Industry', 282.
[38] Machingaidze, 'The Development of Settler', 183.
[39] NAZ S1542/A4/2, Chief Native Commissioner (CNC) to NC Victoria district, 21 February 1934.
[40] NAZ, S235/511/4, Annual Report of NC Sebungwe district, 1933.
[41] NAZ S1542/A4/3, NC Victoria district to CNC, 4 April 1934; NAZ S1542/A4/3, NC Mvuma to CNC, 28 March 1934.

introduction of the modern cigarette industry during the twentieth century.[42] Demand for cigarettes amongst Africans was stimulated through their portrayal in advertisements as a class symbol of urban sophistication, and an escape from the countrified antediluvian living represented by coarse *Inyoka* tobacco as shown in commercials in Figure 4.1. The nucleus for the African tobacco market was built by creating demand and 'getting the African into the habit of smoking'.[43] This was done through the handing out of cigarettes as presents to African labourers, and the opening of retail shops on farms and mines which distributed cigarettes to whet the appetite amongst Africans.[44] Most white miner owners gave their African labourers weekly rations of tobacco for 'excellence of work' and added motivation.[45]

The consumption of tobacco amongst African mine workers was also popularised by a curiously widespread but erroneous medical opinion amongst white mine owners that smoking could cure scurvy.[46] It was believed that the disease was a mental affliction that could be disposed of 'as soon as a "boy" buys a six-penny pipe and learns to smoke'.[47] The increased popularity of cigarettes and European tobacco on mines significantly affected the indigenous tobacco economy over time (see Figure 4.2). *Inyoka* marketing statistics show that the amount of tobacco purchased by traders declined significantly from 7,980 lbs in 1934 to just 560 lbs in 1938, as a result of the promotion of domestic manufacture of cigarettes for local consumption by the state.[48] Simultaneously, tobacco sales from purchases by traders dropped precipitously in value from 234 to just 8 pounds sterling.

[42] J. Goodman, *Tobacco in History: The Cultures of Dependence* (New York, 1993), 96. For other discussion on how the modern cigarette disrupted traditional tobacco consumption in colonies see: G. Boudreau et al., 'Why the World Will Never Be Tobacco-Free: Reframing "Tobacco Control" into a Traditional Tobacco Movement', *American Journal of Public Health*, 106, 7 (2016), 1188–1195.

[43] 'Native smoking', *Vuka* (Salisbury [Harare]), September 1946.

[44] T. Burke, *Lifebuoy Men, Lux Women: Commodification, Consumption and Cleanliness in Morden Zimbabwe* (London, 1996).

[45] C. Van Onselen, *Chibaro: African Mine Labour in Southern Rhodesia, 1900–1933* (London, 1976), 172–173.

[46] Scurvy was endemic in most mines in colonial Zimbabwe because of poor diet lacking in vitamin C. See, I. Phimister, 'African Labour Conditions and Health in the Southern Rhodesia Mining Industry, 1893–1953, Part Three: Health', *The Central African Journal of Medicine*, 22, 9 (1976), 173–181.

[47] Ibid. [48] Kosmin, 'The Inyoka Tobacco Industry', 281.

Figure 4.1 Cigarettes' adverts in Southern Rhodesia portraying class and style
Source: *The Rhodesia Herald*, 15 July 1939; *The Bulawayo Chronicle*, 8 January 1941.

However, over the same period, the amount of tobacco hawked by the growers increased from 26,220 lbs to 51,000 lbs.[49] By 1938, the sale of the *Inyoka* tobacco by traders had ceased in the mines. Consequently, from 1939, the native commissioners' reports are silent on *Inyoka* production as it had receded into an informal almost black-market entity.[50]

[49] Ibid. [50] Ibid., 283.

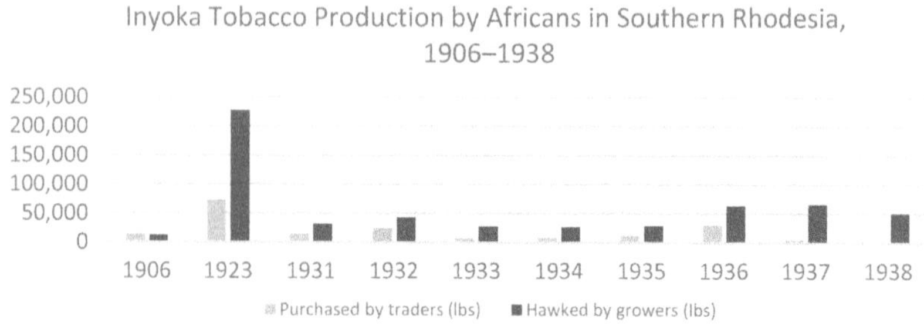

Figure 4.2 Inyoka tobacco production and trade in Southern Rhodesia, 1906–1938
Source: Kosmin, 'The Inyoka tobacco industry', 281.

While historians like Gary Blank have contended that the *Inyoka* tobacco industry prospered until the 1960s, there is no oral or archival evidence to support that inference.[51] In fact, the crop disappears from the official colonial sources thereafter, and Kosmin could only surmise that all the vestiges of its production had been virtually wiped out by the 1960s.[52] Also, as other sources have shown, the Shangwe area became famous for cotton production (and not tobacco) during the rest of the colonial period and, indeed, even up until today.[53] However, although Kosmin attributes the decline of the African tobacco economy to a shift in taste and preference for European cigarettes and the marketing infrastructure set up by the colonial state, there were other more disruptive legislative tools that were enacted to force Africans out of production. These policy regulations were constructed to

[51] G. Blank, 'Prosperity, Penury and Polarisation: Disaggregating the Peasantry in the Historiography of Colonial Zimbabwe', *African Journal of History and Culture*, 7, 1 (2015), 1–7.

[52] Kosmin surmises this based on a personal conversation he had with Reverend R. Peaden and the district commissioner of the area who had no knowledge or records of any tobacco industry. Such ignorance of this industry from sources living in the area during the mid-1970s further substantiates that it had collapsed so spectacularly into extinction from the late 1930s, leaving behind no vestiges of its existence. It further questions the credibility of sources that Blank used to conclude that the industry was prosperous well into the 1960s.

[53] P. Nyambara, 'A History of Land Acquisition, Commercialisation of Agriculture and Socio-economic Differentiation among Peasant Farmers in a Frontier Region: The Gokwe district of Northwestern Zimbabwe: c. 1945–1990s' (unpublished seminar paper, University of the Witwatersrand, 26 May 1997).

disrupt African tobacco producers and push them into the colonial labour market.

State Curtailment of African Peasant Tobacco Production in Southern Rhodesia, 1930s–1950

The 1930s had marked the low point for the agricultural viability of peasantries in Southern Rhodesia as African commodity production was severely curtailed to stem the tide of 'native' competition on European agriculture. Although the impact of this policy varied from crop to crop, the discrepancies between tobacco and other crops was particularly marked. While other commodities like beef and maize suffered the harsh effects of state curtailment policy in Southern Rhodesia during the 1930s, enclaves of peasant production still survived and even boomed during the 1940s, 1950s, and 1960s.[54] African cotton production under state subsidies flourished such that by 1949 peasant cultivators produced cotton with an export value of £156,650.[55] At the same time peasant grain production gained so much momentum that by the mid-1950s African farmers produced twice as much maize as European farmers![56] Other crops such as 'kaffir corn', *munga* (millet), groundnuts, and beans grown in African areas also expanded in production during the same period. Meanwhile amongst African peasants, tobacco was being cultivated on less than 1,000 acres of land.[57]

In 1936 the government emphasised the value of integrating African producers into world markets but insisted this had to be limited to 'those crops which Europeans cannot produce at world prices' and Africans had to be assisted only to produce 'certain crops' such as cotton, maize, and peanuts.[58] Consequently, crops that Europeans could produce at 'world prices' or produce for the export market profitably, such as tobacco, remained on the peripheries of African

[54] N. Samasuwo, 'There Is Something about Cattle' (unpublished PhD thesis, University of Cape Town, 2000), 68; A. A. Le Roux, 'African Agriculture in Rhodesia', *The Rhodesia Agricultural Journal*, 66, 2525 (1969), 85.

[55] Nyambara, 'Colonial Policy and Peasant', 81–111.

[56] A. A. Le Roux, 'African Agriculture in Rhodesia', The *Rhodesia Agricultural Journal*, 66, 2525 (1969), 85. For more on African grain production in Southern Rhodesia, see, M. Yudelman, *Africans on the Land* (Cambridge, 1964), 240.

[57] Ibid.

[58] 'World markets', *Rhodesia Herald* (Salisbury [Harare]), 28 November 1936.

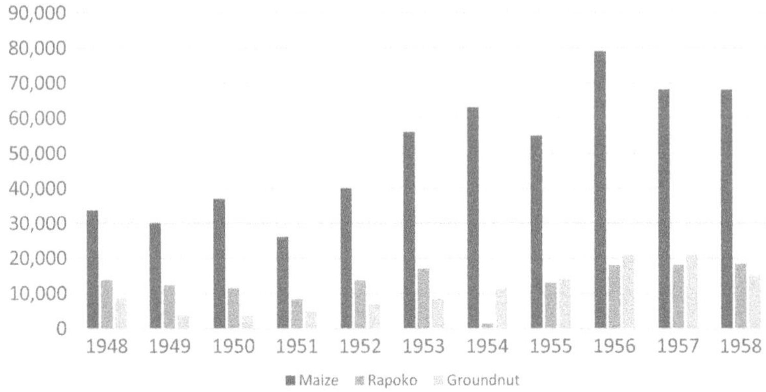

Figure 4.3 Crop production in African areas of Southern Rhodesia, 1948–1958 (in thousands of bags)
Source: Yudelman, *Africans on the Land*, 241.

peasant production. Resultantly, while crops such as maize, groundnuts, rapoko and cotton did relatively well in African areas, tobacco remained an almost invisible commodity within the production and marketing matrix of African peasants, as shown by Figures 4.3 and 4.4. Yet tobacco still occupied a higher place within the export hierarchy of agricultural commodities in Southern Rhodesia.[59] In 1940, tobacco accounted for 15 per cent of total exports, and in 1944 the crop contributed 54 per cent of the gross value of agricultural exports.[60] A post-war tobacco boom expanded the export market for Rhodesian tobacco, resulting in lucrative earnings, capital build-up, and an expansion of area under tobacco production on white settler farms.[61] By 1947, tobacco had overtaken gold as the colony's chief export, contributing more than a third to total export receipts.[62] By 1961, of the £55.6 million total value of agricultural production tobacco contributed 56 per cent, maize 13.8 per cent, beef 12.4 per cent and all other crops a combined 18.1 per cent.[63]

[59] I. Phimister, *An Economic and Social History of Zimbabwe* (London, 1988), 61, 131.
[60] K. Muir, 'Crop Production in Zimbabwe's Commercial Agricultural Sector, 1940–79' (unpublished working paper, July 1981), 2–3.
[61] Scott, 'The Tobacco Industry', 189–206. [62] Ibid.
[63] P. Mosley, *The Settler Economies: Studies in the Economic History of Kenya and Southern Rhodesia: 1900–1963* (New York, 1983), 171.

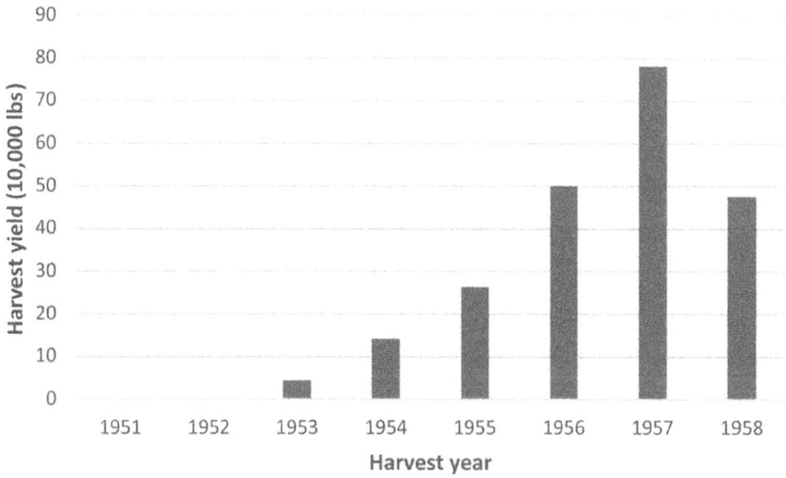

Figure 4.4 African production of Turkish tobacco in Southern Rhodesia, 1951–1958

Source: Yudelman, *Africans on the Land*, 241.

The significantly higher export value of tobacco comparative to other crops prompted the state to be more ruthless in curbing African peasant participation, through systematic marketing and production regulations to ensure white settler production hegemony. The state reckoned that the global export market could only be secured by an unsullied reputation of the quality of Rhodesian tobacco to overseas manufacturers to ward off competition from American producers. Entry of Africans was believed to compromise the export market through production of poor-quality tobacco. So to pre-empt this 'catastrophe', the state legislated against African production.[64] In 1933, the Tobacco Pest Suppression Act compelled all tobacco farmers to 'clean their lands' by uprooting stalks by the first of August of each year to control the spread of diseases.[65] Although this law had universal application to all farmers irrespective of race, it was used to target Africans' tobacco crops which were considered a risk to white growers because ostensibly they spread diseases and pests.[66] Police patrolled 'native areas' and were ordered to uproot and destroy all 'native crops' not grown in

[64] Clements and Harben, *Leaf of Gold*, 165. [65] Ibid., 118.

[66] H. Storey, 'Leaf Curl of Tobacco in Southern Rhodesia', *Rhodesia Agricultural Journal*, 29, 3 (1932), 186–192.

accordance with the law.[67] In Nyasaland, similar methods were used during the 1930s when the Department of Agriculture hired gangs to uproot African tobacco gardens to prevent overproduction.[68] Also, in Kenya the supposed threat of pests and diseases in African-grown coffee, endangering European-grown coffee and ruining the global credibility of Kenyan coffee, was used to justify the marginalisation of Africans from coffee production until the mid-1930s.[69]

Another statute that restricted African peasants' entry into tobacco production in Southern Rhodesia was the Tobacco Market and Stabilisation Act of 1936. Although touted as a panacea for the production and marketing chaos within the tobacco industry, this law actually forestalled the entry of Africans into commercial production of tobacco through a byzantine regulative regime. The act gave power to the Tobacco Marketing Board (TMB) to licence tobacco farmers, auction floors, and buyers, and centralised controlled sales.[70] The regulative framework established by this act discouraged Africans from getting into commercial export production by making it impossible for them to get growers' licences. The act was so antithetical to the interests of 'native' tobacco producers that one Native Commissioner described it as 'class legislation' that was solely crafted to marginalise African growers to stop them from raising taxes by selling their tobacco.[71] Although the law could not interfere with Africans as long as they did not enter commercial export production of European tobaccos, it was framed as a dormant deterrent to the existential threat of African competition in the production of European tobacco.[72] The restrictions to African participation in production of certain high value cash crops informed state policy in settler colonies and this was sometimes done through registration licences and administrative arrangements. In Kenya, for example,

[67] NAZ S1542/A4, Office of the Superintendent Fort Victoria to Staff police office, 3 September 1935; NAZ S1542/A4, Chief Entomologist to acting CNC, 18 September 1935.

[68] T. Woods, 'Why Not Persuade Them to Grow Tobacco? Planters, Tenants, and the Political Economy of Central Malawi, 1920–40', *African Economic History*, 21 (1993), 131–150.

[69] C. Barnes, 'An Experiment with African Coffee Growing in Kenya: The Gusii, 1933–1950' (unpublished PhD thesis, Michigan State University, 1976), 38.

[70] Clements and Harben, *Leaf of Gold*, 20.

[71] NAZ S1542/A4, NC Murehwa to CNC, 9 January 1936.

[72] NAZ S1542/A4, Secretary of the Department of Agriculture and Lands to CNC, 13 February 1936.

African production of pyrethrum and coffee was curtailed until the 1950s through levying of an expensive annual licence fee.[73]

The state in Southern Rhodesia was also always wary of the detrimental effects of 'native' production on the labour demands of settler tobacco producers but couched their anxieties in terms of black disease and white purity.[74] The labour crisis hit the mining and agricultural sectors in Southern Rhodesia severely during the 1930s, compounded by competition from South African gold mines offering higher wages.[75] Labour shortages and the 'labour question' had a significant impact: labour deficits of between 15 to 85 per cent were recorded in most farming districts of the colony during the 1930s.[76] By the war years, the state had to assuage the labour crisis in the white settler farms through coercive recruitment and compulsory conscription of African labour, since peasants were unwilling to abandon independent farming in the reserves. Similar concerns preoccupied the colonial state in Nyasaland, where land concentration by white tobacco estates' owners in the Southern region beginning in 1920 was used as a tool to control and coerce African labour through the notorious labour exploitation regime known as *thangata*.[77] The role of land tenure regimes and control over access to land for the prosperity of peasant

[73] Mosley, *The Settler Economies*, 40. For further reading on colonial measures to restrict African cultivation of high value export crops in Kenya, see, T. West, 'The History of the African Pyrethrum Industry', *Journal of the Royal Society of Arts*, 107, 5034 (1959), 423–441.

[74] G. Hove and S. Swart, '"Dairying Is a White man's Industry": The Dairy Produce Act and the Segregation Debate in Colonial Zimbabwe, c. 1920–37', *Journal of Southern African Studies*, 45, 5 (2019), 911–925.

[75] D. Johnson, 'Settler Farmers and Coerced African Labour in Southern Rhodesia, 1936–46', *The Journal of African History*, 33, 1 (1992), 111–128.

[76] Ibid.

[77] *Thangata* in Malawi has shifted: its pre-colonial meaning was linked to mutual aid in neighbours' fields. But after 1890 it came to mean exploitative unpaid agricultural labour in place of a cash rent on white-owned land. *Thangata* was formally abolished in 1962, but is sometimes still used for unfair labour on tobacco estates: see, J. A. K. Kandaŵire, 'Thangata in Pre-colonial and Colonial Systems of Land Tenure in Southern Malawi with Special Reference to Chingale', *Journal of the International African Institute*, 47, 2 (1977), 185–191. For readings on land concentration and tobacco production by white farmers in colonial Malawi, see: E. Green, 'Land Concentration, Institutional Control and African Agency: Growth and Stagnation of European Tobacco Farming in Shire Highlands c. 1900–1940', in E. Hillbom and P. Svensson (eds.), *Agricultural Transformation in a Global History Perspective* (New York, 2013), 229–252; and Prowse, 'A History of Tobacco Production', 681–712.

tobacco production has been highlighted in Latin American historical literature.[78] Abundance of land and low population densities in Latin American tobacco-producing areas meant that the state was unable to compel peasants to consolidate tobacco production or reform production techniques. This led to the emergence of strong, independent, and prosperous peasantries who could not be coerced into the wage labour economy, as was the case in Southern Rhodesia and Nyasaland.

Production of tobacco by Africans in Nyasaland *had* in fact jeopardised the smooth flow of migrant labour to Southern Rhodesia in the 1920s. In 1926, colonial labour recruitment officials announced worriedly that there had been a dramatic drop in the numbers of African migrant labourers crossing into Southern Rhodesia.[79] This was attributed directly to the cultivation of tobacco by Africans in Nyasaland, who were earning enough money to pay their taxes.[80] In Nyasaland, the state created the Native Tobacco Board in 1927 to regulate African production and save the European growers.[81] However, unlike in Southern Rhodesia (where the regulative act prevented Africans from growing European tobacco), in Nyasaland independent producers were able to flourish and obviate the Native Tobacco Board.[82] These disparities can be accounted for by the different institutional arrangements in tobacco production and marketing. In Nyasaland much of the settler tobacco production and marketing was controlled by companies. These companies would often buy African tobacco outside the Native Tobacco Board at cheaper and more exploitative prices to resell at a bigger profit.[83] From the early 1930s white growers in Southern Rhodesia were wary of how company-controlled production and marketing had ruined European growers and handed production to Africans.[84]

[78] Baud and Koonings, 'A Lavoura Dos Pobres', 287–329.
[79] NAZ, S238/49, Annual Report of the Supervisor of Facilities for Passage of Northern Natives, 1926.
[80] Ibid.
[81] McCracken, 'Planters, Peasants and the Colonial state', 172–192. For more reading on the work of the Native Tobacco Board in colonial Malawi, see, J. Smith and K. Lee, 'From Colonisation to Globalisation: A History of State Capture by the Tobacco Industry in Malawi', *Review of African Political Economy*, 45, 156 (2018), 186–202.
[82] McCracken, 'Planters, Peasants and the Colonial State', 172–192.
[83] Woods, 'Why not Persuade Them', 131–150.
[84] *The New Rhodesia* (Salisbury [Harare]), 29 September 1933.

Another unique feature of African production in Nyasaland, was the rise of visiting African tenancy and sharecropping in the central province from the late 1920s, as estate owners contracted landless Africans to produce tobacco on their farms.[85] Whether this system encouraged the rise of a more prosperous group of peasant growers than in the crown lands is debated.[86] However, it was still based on exploitative extraction of labour and was excoriated by African nationalists during the 1950s. It must also be remembered that the visiting African tenancy system in Nyasaland arose out of the collapse of settler plantation agriculture during the 1930s and the fractured nature of white settler tobacco farming due to lack of private technical assistance and state support. However, in Southern Rhodesia, the existence of economically stronger, better organised white settler tobacco farmers, actively supported by the state and controlling production and marketing, precluded the emergence of sharecropping and African tenancy. Meanwhile, in Northern Rhodesia from 1900 to 1937, Africans were simply banned from growing tobacco – although they were allowed to grow maize and other crops.[87] The Macdonell Reserves Commission of 1924 pointed out that flue-cured tobacco was 'beyond the scope of the native', as Africans had neither the capital nor the training for it.[88]

Therefore, state policy on tobacco production was predicated on creating a relationship of white planters as producers and Africans as labourers and consumers. A small thriving white planter community and a viable capitalist sector was established at the expense of the African peasantry. In Southern Rhodesia, this curtailment resulted in the collapse of African commercial production of 'indigenous' tobacco or, indeed, *any* tobacco from around 1938. This anomaly is more striking for one reason. The curtailment of African cash crop production by colonial officials from the 1930s was usually framed around the imperative not to completely vanquish or annihilate African production but to nurture enclaves of peasant production that were too weak to compete with the established white capitalist sector. This, as the economic historian Paul Mosley contends, was the cornerstone of the settler state policy for maize and beef production in Southern Rhodesia

[85] J. McCracken, 'Sharecropping in Malawi: The Visiting Tenant System in the Central Province, c. 1920–68' in J. McCracken (ed.), *Malawi: An Alternative Pattern of Development* (Edinburgh, 1984), 157–174.

[86] Woods, 'Why not Persuade Them', 131–150.

[87] Kanduza, 'The Tobacco Industry', 201–229. [88] Ibid.

(and Kenya): the European producer was supposed to be protected against the competition of the African *without hitting the African producer too hard* since there were influential sectors of the European economic sectors that benefited from African cheap supplies of grain and beef.[89] With other cash crops such as tobacco that occupied a higher value in the colonial export hierarchy, the state adopted a much more sustained and systematic curtailment policy, with the result that the African tobacco economy in Southern Rhodesia collapsed from the late 1930s. The integration of African tobacco producers into the export economy only began in 1952, at the behest of the colonial state during a time when the British imperial government was emphasising high modernism and state planning. But, even then, Africans could produce only those types of tobacco which least interested European farmers.

From Curtailment to Assistance? African Turkish Tobacco Production and the State in Southern Rhodesia, 1952–1980

During the 1940s and 1950s British colonial Africa initiated a series of programmes emphasising the merits of modernism, state planning, and increasing productivity through technical innovation.[90] Western science and top-down technical programmes became the fulcrum of state intervention in the agrarian landscape in most parts of British colonial Africa, tied to the desire to increase production for post-war reconstruction.[91] Beyond the rhetoric of development, high modernism and state planning had an international political aim of controlling rural populations in the countryside through market-led developmentalism and land tenure reform.[92] This was largely placatory within the context of the spread of communism, the rise of nationalism, and peasant unrest in most parts of Africa, Latin America, and Asia.[93] Thus, during

89 Mosley, *The Settler Economies*, 41.
90 J. C. Scott, *Seeing Like a State: How Certain Schemes to Improve the Human Condition Have Failed* (New Haven, 1998).
91 H. Tilley, *Empire, Development and the Problem of Scientific Knowledge, 1870–1950: Africa as a Living Laboratory* (Chicago, 2011), 115–168.
92 F. Araghi, 'The Invisible Hand and the Visible Foot: Peasants, Dispossession and Globalization', in A. Haroon Akram-Lodhi and C. Kay (eds.), *Peasants and Globalization – Political Economy, Rural Transformation and the Agrarian Question* (London, 2009), 124.
93 During the 1950s and 1960s the US government grappled with the problem of peasant societies because of the communist threats in Asia and Latin America. Their solution was to placate peasantries by co-opting them into national development programmes, import substitution industrial policies, and land reform programmes.

the 1940s and 1950s, colonial officials' position on peasant communities began to change, as the interests of white settlers shifted from demand for agricultural labour to the desirability of a settled industrial labour force, rural security, and a stable and productive but ultimately uncompetitive African peasantry.

Although much of the modernism rhetoric was expressed in the colonial jargon of 'rural development', 'peasant cash crop production', and soil conservation, the corresponding projects were tools for political control of rural populations. In Kenya, the Swynnerton Plan was launched in 1953, ostensibly to transform the African peasantry through land consolidation, soil conservation, and the encouragement of cash crop production.[94] It was espoused as the end of racial discrimination in agriculture, a joint enterprise of all races in the development of productive capitalist agriculture.[95] However, in reality, the political pressures brought by the Mau Mau uprisings and the state of emergency had compelled the colonial state on the expedient path of modernism. The colonial state implemented perfunctory and piecemeal rural reforms, aimed to consolidate a class of technologically progressive but politically conservative and quiescent African yeomen who might act as a buffer against subversive rural elements.[96] In 1944, the Native Trade and Production Commission in Southern Rhodesia recommended coercive enforcement of good husbandry methods in the native reserves to prevent land degradation, overstocking, and 'ruinous farming practices'.[97] These recommendations were later codified by the Native Land Husbandry Act (NLHA) in 1951, reconfiguring land tenure in African areas both spatially and politically.[98]

See: N. Cullather, *The Hungry World: America's Cold War Battle Against Poverty in Asia* (London, 2010).

94 N. E. Makana, 'Peasant Response to Agricultural Innovations: Land Consolidation, Agrarian Diversification and Technical Change: The Case of Bungoma district in Western Kenya, 1954–1960', *Journal of Third World Studies*, 27, 1 (2010), 155–170.

95 R. Van Zwanenberg, *The Agricultural History of Kenya to 1939* (Nairobi, 1972), 8–10.

96 For readings on land reform and rural development in colonial Kenya, see: J. Harbeson, 'Land Reforms and Politics in Kenya, 1954–70', *Journal of Modern African Studies*, 9, 2 (1971), 231–251; A. Thurston, *Smallholder Agriculture in Colonial Kenya: The Official Mind and the Swynnerton Plan* (Cambridge, 1987); and B. Berman, *Control and Crisis in Colonial Kenya: The Dialectic of Domination* (London, 1990), 366.

97 NAZ ZBJ 1/1/1, Report of the Native Production and Trade Commission, 1944.

98 For comprehensive historical literature on the Native Land Husbandry Act, see: V. Machingaidze, 'Agrarian Change from Above: The Southern Rhodesia

The implementation of modernisation meant that the colonial state had to find suitable agricultural commodities and cash crops that could be promoted in African areas, with the potential to generate capital investments and raise the standard of living. Peter Wagner conceived of the promotion of this policy as 'organised modernity' meant for the dual role of servicing post-war imperial self-sufficiency and metropolitan markets.[99] Ultimately, this new thrust in colonial agricultural policy realigned cash crop relations of production, as the colonial state became more amenable to Africans' participation in the agricultural export economy. As the apathy of the 1930s thawed, colonial governments started to encourage peasant cultivation of such crops as coffee, pyrethrum, tobacco, and tea to transform rural areas. On the other hand, export revenue from cash cropping would also conveniently pay for the coercive superstructure of post-war African administration. It was within this context that the state in Southern Rhodesia also altered its attitude to African production of tobacco. Suddenly, tobacco became the 'right crop' for African peasants to encourage new patterns of rural accumulations, land development, and soil conservation.

However, beyond the modernisation and technical side there were other factors that compelled the state in Southern Rhodesia to change its policy: global market forces and local production dynamics. During the 1950s there was a huge demand for Turkish tobacco on the international tobacco market, caused by the rising popularity of blended cigarettes such as Camels, Lucky Strikes, and Chesterfields. Concurrently, the post-war boom in flue-cured tobacco prices caused a significant decline in Turkish production amongst white growers.[100] Facing an uncertain future but still guaranteed a viable global market, the Turkish tobacco industry was rescued by encouraging African peasant production. Even then, the RTA, a body of exclusively white

Native Land Husbandry Act and African Response', *The International Journal of Historical Studies*, 24, 3 (1991), 557–588; I. Phimister, 'Rethinking the Reserves: Southern Rhodesia's Land Husbandry Act Reviewed', *Journal of Southern African Studies*, 19, 2 (1993), 225–239; and W. R. Duggan, 'The Native Land Husbandry Act of 1951 and the Rural African Middle Class of Southern Rhodesia', *African Affairs*, 79, 315 (1980), 227–240.

99 P. Wagner, *A Sociology of Modernity: Liberty and Discipline* (London, 1993).

100 In 1947 London tobacco manufacturers assured Southern Rhodesia that they would absorb two thirds of their total flue-cured tobacco production each year for five years. As a result, Turkish production fell from 11,811 acres in 1946 to 326 acres in 1951.

growers, was perturbed by the initiative to encourage Turkish production in African areas and noted with concern that 'the great inflow of cash to the reserves would deplete the already scanty labour supply'.[101]

So, in 1952, the state launched a pilot scheme for Turkish tobacco production in the Musengezi Native Purchase Area (NPA) with twenty pioneer African farmers growing the crop on half-acre plots.[102] Native Purchase Areas, set up in 1931 under the LAA to encourage 'progressive African farming', had better land and were less congested than native reserves.[103] In 1954 the scheme was further extended to cover seventy African farmers in four other NPAs.[104] Predictably, there was no attempt to encourage African production of Virginia flue-cured tobacco, ostensibly because 'the capital costs involved would be a big deterrent to the farmer'.[105] The 1962 report on African agriculture pointed out that Virginia flue-cured tobacco was grown almost entirely by white farmers (with the exception of just three African farmers) because of the high fixed and working capital required, and the large area of suitable soil needed for rotations.[106] Confronted with the high cost of production, poverty, lack of credit facilities, tobacco-curing barns, and technical assistance, Africans could not venture into production of flue-cured Virginia tobacco, and instead grew lower value tobaccos such as Turkish and Burley.

The Turkish tobacco scheme was a colonial initiative to harness cash cropping in adaptation to ecological marginalisation and land scarcity in African areas. The Turkish crop could thrive in the drier parts of the country with poor sandy soils, into which Africans had been forced by the racist land segregation policies. Turkish tobacco was also ecologically ideal for the African farmer in the native reserves, as it did not denude natural resources like woodlands and did not require firewood for curing like flue-cured Virginia.[107] Officials also felt that Turkish tobacco fitted

101 'Turkish for Africans', *Rhodesian Tobacco Grower and Food Producer* (Salisbury [Harare]), September 1952.

102 'Growing of Tobacco by Natives', *Rhodesia Herald*, 11 November 1954.

103 G. Kay, *Rhodesia: A Human Geography* (London, 1970), 93. 104 Ibid.

105 Ibid.

106 J. Phillips et al., *Report of the Advisory Committee of the Economic Resources of Southern Rhodesia with Particular Reference to the Role of African agriculture* (Salisbury [Harare], 1962), 193.

107 Tobacco Export Promotion Council of Rhodesia and Nyasaland (TERPCORN), *The Tobacco Industry of Rhodesia and Nyasaland* (Salisbury [Harare], 1963), 58.

within the NLHA template of soil conservation and cash crop production.[108] Experiments growing Turkish tobacco on over-worked and poor soils in rotation with other crops such as maize, sunn hemp, and *rapoko* (finger millet), in an effort to improve soil fertility, were initiated by the Department of Native Agriculture in the Native Reserves (later called Tribal Trust Lands, or TTLs, when the NLHA was repealed in 1962) of Chinhamhora.[109] In 1956, production extended to other native reserves. During the 1959–1960 season, out of a total Turkish harvest of 1,878,000 lbs in Southern Rhodesia, 618,000 lbs were produced by 4,444 African growers.[110] By 1958, production by Africans spanned 150 acres.[111] Between 1957 and 1960, the average gross output value from Turkish tobacco ranged from £38.12s/acre to £58.12s.11d./acre, a figure between five and six times the yield of low unit value crops in the African areas.[112] However, the adoption of Turkish tobacco production amongst African farmers was slowed by high transportation costs, high labour costs, and limited capital investments for farm expansion, all of which made the crop too costly to grow.[113] In the end, Turkish tobacco production by African peasants remained marginal in the 1950s. Figure 4.5 shows one of the few successful African tobacco farmers.

Turkish tobacco production generated class differentiation amongst peasants as some accumulated capital and investments that altered the agricultural landscape in African areas. This was most conspicuous in the NPAs and, particularly, in Musengezi NPA, which became one of the 'most progressive farming areas in the country'.[114] By 1965, fifty-three farms in Musengezi NPA were fully fenced and subdivided into

108 Phimister, 'Rethinking the Reserves', 225–239.

109 'Government Helps Natives to Grow Tobacco', *Rhodesia Herald*, 19 October 1955. The Department of Native Agriculture had been set up in 1926 under agriculturalist E. D. Alvord to oversee the implementation of good husbandry methods in African areas. In 1969 it was changed to the Department of Agricultural Development to provide extension advice to communal farmers.

110 'Oriental Tobacco: A Crop with a Promising Future', *Tobacco Forum of Rhodesia*, May 1965.

111 NAZ 42-13-3R, Box 126958, 'Record of a meeting on the marketing of Turkish tobacco held on Friday 27 January 1961'.

112 Yudelman, *Africans on the Land*, 173.

113 A. Shutt, 'Squatters, Land Sales and Intensification in Marirangwe Purchase Area', *The Journal of African History*, 43, 3 (2002), 473–498.

114 'African Farmers Turn to Modern Methods', *Rhodesia Herald*, 18 January 1965.

Figure 4.5 A Purchase Area farmer and his wife standing with his tobacco bales in 1974
Source: *Tobacco Forum of Rhodesia*, 3, 1974.

paddocks enclosing 18,000 acres of rotational grazing.[115] These developments on African farms were now possible as the average income of each NPA farmer from tobacco was estimated to be around £300–400 gross, with a few individuals earning £1,000 or more. One of the model African farmers, Mr Griston Mungofa, practiced intensive farming, putting under twenty acres of tobacco and twenty acres of maize a year while practising rotation to integrate grazing.[116]

The income and class differentiation precipitated by Turkish tobacco in the NPAs prompted the state to integrate the crop within its new

[115] Ibid. [116] Ibid.

'native administration' outlook during the 1960s, as it abandoned the coercive approach of 'high modernism' in pursuit of the much more integrative policy of community development.[117] Community development was predicated on the integration of African systems into colonial administration and encouraging Africans to stay on the land at a time of simmering nationalism and rampant urban protest. Expanding cash crop production to TTLs and raising rural incomes could forestall rural political discontent.[118] Thus, from the 1960s, the state expanded the Turkish tobacco endeavour to most poor and dry TTLs in Fort Victoria province (Gutu, Zimuto, and Bikita TTLs), the Midlands, and Manicaland provinces. African Turkish tobacco farmers were given seedlings from the African Loan Fund, set up in 1958 to grant loans to peasants.[119] Technical assistance was deployed using state-trained tobacco officers to help and encourage participation and cooperation of peasants in arable conservation, maintenance of contours, soil fertility, and grazing management.[120]

However, despite this, the gross returns in most of the TTLs were poor, amounting to a mere £5 per acre, while production costs hovered around £18 to £20 per acre.[121] The poor remuneration saw the acreage planted fall drastically between the 1967–1968 and 1968–1969 seasons, from 1,100 to 213 acres, respectively. Reservations began to be expressed on the commercial value of the enterprise particularly in the poor sand soils of the TTLs. The Secretary for Internal Affairs pointed out that the extremely low profit margins of the crop in the TTLs made it impossible to continue with government support. In fact, he recommended the abandonment of the project:

> It seems to me that with the possible exception of very few Purchase Area Farmers who may be making something out of the crop. There is no attraction

[117] For a comprehensive discussion on 'community development' policy, see, J. Alexander, *The Unsettled Land: State Making and the Politics of Land in Zimbabwe, 1893–2003* (Oxford, 2006), 65–72.

[118] NAZ 42-13-3R, Box 126958, 'Minutes of the meeting of members of the Tobacco Marketing Board held on 13 June 1967'.

[119] A. Weinrich, *African Farmers in Rhodesia: Old and New Peasant Communities in Karangaland* (London, 1975), 27.

[120] NAZ S3700/29, Secretary External Affairs to all provincial agricultural officers, 14 August 1973.

[121] NAZ 42-13-3R, Box 126958, Secretary of Internal Affairs to Secretary for Agriculture, 8 July 1969.

in the crop at the present price of 25d. . .. In the circumstances I must support the recommendation that government support for the crop be dropped.[122]

When the state decided to withdraw support for the Turkish tobacco production, new entities emerged to fill the void. The Tribal Trust Lands Development Cooperation (TTLDCOR), formed in 1968 to develop TTLs with European private capital, stepped in to underwrite the production of 150,000 lbs to 200,000 lbs of Turkish tobacco during the 1969–1970 season and ensuing years. This was a result of a steady increase in local consumer demand for the Turkish tobacco used in toasted cigarette brands, such as Gunston and Texas.[123] As a result, Turkish tobacco prices rose from under R$1 to R$1.35 (Rhodesian dollars) per kilogram over three years beginning in 1974.[124] The rise in prices nevertheless failed to raise production of Turkish tobacco in African areas, as acreages under cultivation decreased. In Victoria district, the number of growers had declined because of lack of watering facilities for seedlings and poor financial returns from the crop.[125] In the Midlands, Turkish tobacco was overtaken by cotton.[126] The Turkish tobacco interim survey of 1975 concluded that under the prevailing standards of management, tobacco production in the TTLs was not sufficiently profitable to encourage significant further expansion.[127] The survey noted that the only way yields – and concomitantly profits – could be raised would be through an effective extension system and field management involving fumigation, adequate pest control, and fertilisation of soils.[128]

The collapse of commercialised production of Turkish tobacco within the TTLs created new opportunities for cultivation by women. From 1975, there was an interesting shift in the gender of the farmers – as much of the tobacco farming was now being done by women, or so-called 'farmers' wives' – in their backyards.[129] This was possible because the processes of Turkish cultivation such as reaping, curing,

122 Ibid.
123 NAZ 42-13-3R, Box 126958, G. D. Cox for Secretary Agriculture to Secretary Internal Affairs, 1 October 1969.
124 Ibid.
125 NAZ S3700/22, Promotion of oriental tobacco policy meeting, Victoria district report, March 1975.
126 NAZ S3700/22, Senior agricultural officer to Secretary Internal Affairs, 18 October 1974.
127 NAZ S3700/22, Oriental tobacco survey, 1975.
128 Ibid.
129 Ibid.

and cultivation required less physical strength and were therefore deemed more suited to women and children.[130] However, the district commissioner[131] of Inyanga noted that these women growers could not even be qualified as real tobacco growers because they did not see the crop as a cash crop, but just as a trivial effort to make 'pocket money'.[132]

Tobacco Production: A Model for Conservation and Development in African Areas or a Political Tool?

The African Turkish tobacco initiative in Southern Rhodesia reveals how crop hierarchies – a pyramid based not only on economic rationale but on the political ideology of control – helped institutionalise patterns of white settler dominance in the countryside and agrarian economy. White settler cash crop hegemonic ideologies shaped colonial development paradigms in African areas and the nature of African participation in the agricultural economy. Even within the new colonial development narratives of modernisation and technical intervention during the late 1940s and 1950s, African cash crop production remained pigeon-holed within the hegemonic imperatives of servicing white settler interests and agricultural export growth for administrative and political expediency. Predictably, the Turkish tobacco drive failed to have any significant positive impact on improving the physical environment and African accumulation patterns – particularly within TTLs and had limited successes in the NPAs. This was because post-war policy intervention in the rural areas had a much broader political objective than the much-touted modernist and technical rationale of transforming African export agriculture through encouraging cash crop production. The rise of nationalism and the tide of decolonisation imperilled most settler colonies and threatened the status quo of white farmers in the countryside, precipitating the need for rural reforms. Within this context, it is important to note that the crop hegemonic status quo that had hitherto impinged on African peasants and the

[130] 'Turkish Tobacco Is a Good Crop for African Farmers', *Rhodesia Herald*, 15 November 1956.

[131] In 1969, the control of African agriculture in Southern Rhodesia passed to district commissioners.

[132] NAZ S3700/22, C. des Tombe (District Commissioner, Inyanga), Oriental Production in Inyanga, 5 March 1975.

structural constraints to their participation in the global export production were not dismantled but, instead, shifted to accommodate new colonial priorities and new idioms of control and authority. Notably, the post-war imperial project of encouraging cash crop production by African peasants was foisted upon a settler state that implemented piecemeal rural reforms. These reforms were not intended to create a real rural bourgeoisie, but rather a quiescent class of African farmers who might serve as a political buffer. The overwhelming logic was to construct a black farmer with a stake in the political economy and make him an ally against subversive rural elements.[133] In the end, the state's drive to encourage African cultivation of Turkish tobacco was part of a political project to impose political control and extend colonial authority in a way that could not lead to the emergence of a strong African agrarian bourgeoisie to disrupt white settler farmer privilege.[134] Tobacco was still, therefore, a hegemonic crop, as its cultivation was used to control patterns of accumulation in African areas in ways that could contain rural discontent and preserve white settler dominance. While tobacco was a high value crop that transformed rural livelihoods and created a strong agricultural middle class in Latin America, its cultivation was controlled by the colonial state to preclude the same from happening for Africans in Southern Rhodesia. The cultivation of tobacco was limited to a containment strategy for threats to rural stability. During the late 1970s, at the height of the War of Liberation, the Rhodesian state conscripted African farmers to grow Burley tobacco in abandoned white farms under the guise of combating land denudation and soil erosion as well as raising rural incomes.[135] However, this measure was part of a broader counter-insurgency strategy to create buffer zones against guerrilla incursions as vacant farms were becoming breeding grounds for African

[133] Berman, *Control and Crisis*, 366.

[134] For more on the making of the black bourgeoisie, see: A. Shutt, 'Purchase Area Farmers and the Middle Class of Southern Rhodesia, c. 1931–1952', *The International Journal of African Historical Studies*, 30, 3 (1997); and M. West, *The Rise of an African Middle Class: Colonial Zimbabwe, 1898–1965* (Bloomington, IN, 2002).

[135] Many white-owned tobacco farms were abandoned at the height of the Liberation War during the late 1970s creating the problem of vacant farms. The Rhodesia Tobacco Association (RTA) began promoting the settlement of African smallholder tobacco producers in these vacant farms deserted by Europeans because of the war.

nationalist fighters and tobacco farms were seen as the first line of defence.[136] The enduring objective and design of state policy on tobacco production remained to relegate African producers to second-class farmers in a white-dominated tobacco farming sector, producing those low-profit tobacco types unwanted by white farmers and sustaining the domestic demands for Turkish tobacco.

In the long run, the colonial project failed at tackling the glaring problems of the African rural economy such as lack of capital, poor soils, and inability to invest in technical services and infrastructure. This became more conspicuous in the years after the Unilateral Declaration of Independence (UDI) in 1965, as state expenditure for African agriculture fell from 2.8 per cent of total spending between 1966 and 1969 to a mere 1.2 per cent in the years 1975 to 1976.[137] The economic sanctions imposed by the United Kingdom on Rhodesia in 1966, in response to the UDI, severely crippled white settler agriculture and hit tobacco farming hardest. Tobacco export receipts dwindled by a massive 82 per cent from 93.9 million to 16.7 million Rhodesian dollars between 1965 and 1966.[138] The state had to intervene with the tobacco support programme to subsidise white tobacco farmers, with this assistance amounting to 22 million Rhodesian dollars in 1970. Thus, much of the state funding for African agriculture was withdrawn in order to subsidise white farmers during the UDI.[139] This affected African Turkish production as government technical support went down, amid falling tobacco prices induced by the tobacco embargo. Bereft of subsidies (unlike white tobacco farmers), and confronted by a drastic cut in funding, African Turkish tobacco farmers were unable to remain competitive producers and their enterprises inevitably collapsed. This case was different to Kenya where African coffee producers were relatively more successful and even outcompeted European growers. This was because unlike in Southern Rhodesia, the colonial state in Kenya was obliged to sacrifice incompetent European producers to support competitive African farmers to

[136] Ncube, 'Colonial Zimbabwe Tobacco Industry', 127–128.

[137] A. Shutt, 'We Are the Best of the Poor Farmers' (unpublished PhD thesis, University of California, 1995), 198.

[138] D. Rowe, *Manipulating the Market; Understanding Economic Sanctions, Institutional Change and the Political Unity of White Rhodesia* (Ann Arbor, MI, 2001), 74.

[139] A. Astrow, *Zimbabwe: A Revolution That Lost Its Way?* (London, 1983), 65.

ensure the survival of the coffee export sector.[140] In Kenya, the state actually reduced its financial assistance to white farmers and, when coffee prices plummeted, settler farmers could not compete with low cost African cultivators.[141] The role of 'off-farm incomes' in the success of rural cash cropping in colonial Africa has also been emphasised by Mary Tiffen, Francis Gichuki, and Michael Mortimore in their work on Kenya.[142] In Southern Rhodesia, restrictions on black urban employment meant that there was limited off-farm investments to supplement meagre capital resources from cash cropping.[143]

Indeed, there were very few African farmers who were 'success stories' in these state programmes – mostly those in the NPAs with access to relatively better land and capital opportunities.[144] However, amongst most African farmers, these state initiatives did little to stimulate positive change in the environmental and economic landscapes. State financial assistance was very little, African plots too small, and the soils so poor that tobacco cultivation accelerated erosion.[145] A state agricultural official highlighted in 1978 that the efforts made in the TTLs had not succeeded in raising the standard of living for the so-called 'tribesmen', or in slowing down the rate of deterioration in the country's natural resources.[146] Even the state's own Five Year Plan in 1979 admitted that land pressure in most TTLs caused livelihood insecurity and poverty amongst Africans and was destroying the land.[147]

In the final analysis, peasant 'agency' and autonomy in tobacco production by Africans in Southern Rhodesia was severely limited by the state and white growers, so that there was never a truly independent

140 D. Hyde, 'Paying for the Emergency by Displacing the Settlers: Global Coffee and Rural Restructuring in Late Colonial Kenya', *Journal of Global History*, 4, 1 (2009), 81–103.

141 Ibid.

142 M. Tiffen, M. Mortimore, and F. Gichuki, *Population Growth and Environmental Recovery: Policy Lessons from Kenya* (Chichester, 1994).

143 For statistics on African urban employment in Southern Rhodesia from 1904–1974, see: M. Smout, 'Urbanization of the Rhodesian Population', *Zambezia*, 4, 2 (1975), 79–91.

144 *The Rhodesian Financial Gazette* (Salisbury [Harare]), 18 July 1975.

145 This is based on interviews carried out in December 2017 with Africans who grew tobacco during the late colonial period in the Chiweshe Tribal Trust Lands.

146 'TTL Development a Failure', *The Rhodesian Financial Gazette*, 19 May 1978.

147 'TTLs Reform a Priority', *The Rhodesian Financial Gazette*, 30 March 1979.

peasant producer class during the colonial period. Even during episodes of so-called booms in rural commodity production, the pervasive precarity of African peasant economies was evident in their subordination to larger forces such as the interests of settler agrarian capitalism and global commodity market dynamics. Within this colonial leviathan, the agency of the peasant tobacco producers was hamstrung by the broader colonial objectives: to maintain labour supplies, create a domestic market for settler tobaccos, and preserve security in the countryside through piecemeal encouragement of cash crop production and guided rural accumulation. Thus, the hegemonic value of tobacco as an important export crop for white settler power and survival in Southern Rhodesia constructed the narrow and constricted 'tight corners' within which peasant agency and autonomy was negotiated and navigated under shifting structural factors. While there were complex variables at play like global market forces, political contexts, and social demographics, the constant was the hegemonic imperative to control and curtail African participation in the export economy. The aim was to confine Africans to modes of agrarian development amenable to coercive political and economic control without disrupting the hegemonic centres of white power.

Conclusion

African tobacco production in Southern Rhodesia, just like colonial peasant production elsewhere, must be understood within the context of shifting colonial state priorities constructed around power relations revolving around commodity production, the global export forces and the changing dynamics of the commodity value chain. The hierarchy of commodities was instrumentalised in various ways to control African peasantries depending on the changing patterns of global economic and political pressures. But eventually, it was the colonial state that structured not only factors of productions, but relations of production amongst producers on the land and the imperative to prop up settler capital always defined the state's response to peasant production. This chapter has joined the debate on the impact of colonial state policy on African peasant producers. It has argued that while there was certainly evidence of peasant initiative in circumnavigating the restrictive colonial regulations as most scholars have shown, it is imperative to move beyond agency and locate other centres of historical change in colonial peasantries, which involve subtle but symbolic political processes constructed over international commodity networks, local economic processes and power relations. These of course were not stagnant but shifted over time. They evoked colonial revisionist programmatic interventions in African agriculture, but essentially the colonial project on African peasantries was to create a malleable and tractable class of African producers. Each crop and agricultural commodity produced by Africans had a unique colonial encounter and context. These encounters and contexts were shaped by how colonialist viewed the crops *themselves*, their value to the basis of white settler economic power and how native cultivation of such crops would impinge on and challenge that power and with it the whole institutions of colonial hegemony. Tobacco in Southern Rhodesia was thus a hegemonic crop, solidifying the precincts of white economic dominance and for that reason African production had to be more significantly curtailed than in other commodities (like maize, beef, small grains and cotton). Even when the state encouraged such production, as from 1952 to 1980, it was with the condescending benevolence that only allowed Africans to cultivate the 'inferior tobaccos', while flue-cured tobacco remained a preserve of Europeans until independence. Finally, the value of a specific crop in the hierarchy of power hegemonies in the colonial state determined the extent and level of peasant curtailment, control and decline. Thus, while 'agency' has palpable conceptual utility in colonial African peasant studies, moving beyond it to engage power asymmetries and disparities amongst agricultural commodities within the colonial economy affords a new understanding of the pervasive and enduring constraints of white settler power on peasant autonomy and independence.

5 'The Threat of Soil Erosion Is Far More Permanent Than the Threat of Sanctions'

The Unilateral Declaration of Independence, War, and Ecological Change in Tobacco-Farming Landscapes in Southern Rhodesia, 1960–1980

No longer is the weed the magic crop for opening new lands and creating closer settlement. Some profit may remain in tobacco, but no satisfaction and no future.

RTA President and tobacco farmer Gordon Hoskins Davies, 1966.

It is obvious that the degree of intensification and diversification of land use practiced on many farms is such that it cannot be tolerated with safety by the prevailing land, soil and climatic conditions – as evidenced by the increasing incidences of erosion.

The director of conservation and extension (Conex). J. H. Lowrens, 1970.

Introduction

Three major events shaped the Southern Rhodesian tobacco industry between 1960 and 1980. These were the global public health controversies over smoking and cancer, the end of the Federation that precipitated the Unilateral Declaration of Independence (UDI) and the Rhodesian 'Bush war'.[1] The Federation of Rhodesia and Nyasaland ended in 1963, after widespread African political agitation against the doctrine of 'racial partnership'; paving way to the granting of black

[1] The nomenclature of the war is political: 'bush war' is a term that was often used by the white minority government in Southern Rhodesia to describe the armed struggle and probably originates from the condescending view of guerilla bush tactics as opposed to modernised conventional warfare. Whereas 'liberation war' was used by the nationalists to emphasise their political objectives of liberating Africans from colonial oppression.

majority rule to Nyasaland and Northern Rhodesia in 1964.[2] For Southern Rhodesia the end of Federation triggered a series of political disturbances between 1963 and 1964 that led to the emigration of 20,000 whites.[3] In 1962, the radical white minority Rhodesian Front (RF) party had come to power backed by a bloc of white farmers (most of whom were tobacco farmers). These tobacco farmers comprised the 'rural backbone of the party'.[4] In November 1965, the Rhodesian Premier, Ian Douglas Smith, unilaterally declared independence – severing Southern Rhodesia's political and imperial ties with Britain.[5] The response from the British government was a punitive economic embargo and sanctions that momentously impacted the political and economic institutions of white Rhodesian society.[6] For the tobacco sector, the sanctions ruined much of the gains made since the 1947 London Agreement. The effect of this on the country's economy was more pronounced as tobacco occupied 19 per cent of the total European cropland and contributed a third of national export revenue in 1965.[7] The state was forced to intervene through production controls and compelled tobacco farmers to diversify into other agricultural enterprises – under mostly unsuitable ecological conditions. The war that broke out in 1972 exacerbated this agricultural crisis in the tobacco countryside as farms were abandoned and land conservation

[2] The federal project that amalgamated the three colonial territories of Southern Rhodesia, Northern Rhodesia and Nyasaland in 1953 had been conceived as a partnership of black Africans and whites. African nationalists criticised the doctrine as representing the partnership relationship between a horse and his rider.

[3] P. Godwin and I. Hancock *'Rhodesians Never Die': The Impact of War and Political Change on White Rhodesia, c.1970–1980* (Oxford, 1993), 17.

[4] D. M. Rowe, *Manipulating the Market: Understanding Economic Sanctions, and the Political Unity of White Rhodesia* (Ann Arbor, 2001), 63.

[5] It is worth noting that the first leader of the party and Prime Minister of Southern Rhodesia between 1962 and 1964, Winston Field, was a tobacco farmer and former president of the Rhodesian Tobacco Association (RTA). His successor Ian Douglas Smith was also a tobacco farmer, cattle rancher and maize grower.

[6] See, G. V. Stephenson, 'The Impact of International Economic Sanctions on the Internal Viability of Rhodesia', *Geographical Review*, 65, 3 (1975), 377–389; R. McKinnell, 'Sanctions and the Rhodesian Economy', *Journal of Modern African Studies*, 7, 4 (1969), 559–591; J. Mtisi, M. Nyakudya and T. Barnes, 'Social and Economic Developments During the UDI', in B. Raftopolous and A. S. Mlambo (eds.), *Becoming Zimbabwe: A History From the Precolonial Period to 2008* (Harare, 2009).

[7] Stephenson, 'The Impact of International Economic Sanctions', 377–389.

practices were discontinued because of the worsening security and conditions.

While there is substantial literature on the ramifications of the UDI and Rhodesian 'Bush war' on white identity, politics and the economy, there is nothing on how the sanctions and war affected the agrarian countryside and ecological conditions particularly on the tobacco farms which as – this chapter will show – weathered much of the storm from the resultant economic embargo.[8] Existing historical works do not examine the impact of production changes enforced by sanctions and the war on the land, natural resources and physical landscapes on tobacco farms. Furthermore, the history of the tobacco industry of Southern Rhodesia between 1960 and 1980 has so far been under-researched. This period is only covered by two notable historical works: by David Rowe and very recently by Sibanengi Ncube.[9] Rowe examines the changing political dynamics and grower-state relations unleashed by the 1966 tobacco embargo that brought the new state-directed paraphernalia of tobacco marketing.[10] He argued that the heightened interventionistic role of the state in regulating production quotas and marketing institutions during the UDI weakened the political influence

[8] There is a huge corpus of literature on the UDI and settler society which focuses on the economic and political conditions of white farmers. See, Hancock and Godwin, *Rhodesians Never Die*; R. Pilossof, 'The Unbearable Whiteness of Being: White Farming Voices in Zimbabwe and their Narration of the Recent Past, c.1970–2004' (Unpublished Ph.D. thesis, Sheffield University, 2010); J. Mtisi, M. Nyakudya and T. Barnes, 'Social and Economic Developments during the UDI'; M. Rukuni, 'The Evolution of Agricultural Policy: 1890–1990', in M. Rukuni et al. (eds.), *Zimbabwe's Agricultural Revolution Revisited* (Harare, 2006), 45–46; J. A. McKenzie, 'Commercial Farmers in the Governmental System of Colonial Zimbabwe' (DPhil thesis, University of Zimbabwe, 1989); S. Ncube, 'Colonial Zimbabwe's Tobacco Industry: Regional and Local Relations, 1949–79' (Unpublished PhD thesis, University of the Free State, 2018); S. Ncube, 'We Must Adapt to Survive: International Sanctions, Settler Politics, and White Tobacco Farmers' Struggles for Economic Survival in Rhodesia, 1966–79', *African Economic History*, 48, 2 (2020), 67–91. This literature, however, although examining the economic and political impact of the UDI on the white agrarian environment does not interrogate how the economic and political conditions of the UDI impacted on the natural landscape in the white farms and conservation.

[9] Rowe, *Manipulating the Market*, 63–95; Ncube, 'We Must Adapt to Survive', 67–91. Another notable work on the period is by Trish Mbanga which, however, is a general populist work and thus cannot be treated as a critical historical text. See T. Mbanga, *Tobacco: A Century of Gold* (Harare, 1991).

[10] See, Rowe, *Manipulating the Market*, 63–95.

of tobacco farmers into an unprecedented position of docility and acquiescence.[11] Ncube challenged Rowe's assumptions about the capture of the Rhodesian tobacco industry by the state during the UDI and contends that the RTA still had significant leverage over the state and benefitted through preferential price-support subsidies after UDI.[12] Ncube further examined the internal dynamics of tobacco politics during the 1960s and 1970s, the impact of the war of liberation on the cohesive identity of tobacco growers and grower-state relations.

However, although Ncube and Rowe offer engaging readings on the political and economic dynamics of the tobacco industry from the 1960s to 1980 including the post-UDI dispensation and the tobacco embargo, they miss the triumvirate of key points that this chapter addresses. First, their engagement of grower-state politics and relationship during this period is too confined in showing power symmetries embedded in domination and capture of either the state by the tobacco farmers, or the tobacco farmers by the state. Recent literature on the tobacco industry has shown that the relationship between the tobacco industry and the state is not usually a matter of capture or corruption but 'associational state building' – as state bureaucracies and the industry often work together to seek new markets and expand demand for tobacco.[13] Second, they fail to locate and link the Rhodesian tobacco industry to the global public health debates on tobacco smoking and cancer that arose during the mid-1950s, and how these impacted on production-control policies and agrarian change from around 1962. Third, they did not discuss how the politics and economics of the UDI led to transitions in land use and landscapes within the tobacco farms.

Simeon Maravanyika's 2013 work on soil conservation has broken fresh ground and was the first to contextualise the post-UDI era within

[11] Ibid., 84–92.

[12] Ncube, 'Colonial Zimbabwe's Tobacco Industry', 123–124.

[13] See, S. Milov, *The Cigarette: A Political History* (Massachusetts, 2019), 9, 58. Milov identifies this new form of partnership in the USA beginning in the 1930s with the New Deal where tobacco growers were recruited into the state bureaucratic institutions for price support and production control under the Federal Tobacco Program. With the post-war global proliferation of cigarettes, tobacco growers in the USA sponsored a bill that led to the creation of tobacco export promotion organisations called Associates whose role was to promote consumption of American tobacco abroad. Ncube discusses a similar institutional form of 'associationalism' in Southern Rhodesia under the Tobacco Export Promotion Council of Rhodesia (TEPCOR).

environmental history. His work revolved around the argument that the economic embargo that resulted from the UDI slowed down the pace of land conservation in the white agrarian environment since 'conservation was closely linked to the issue of productivity'.[14] However, his focus was on the bureaucratic dimension of conservation instead of the ecology of production dynamics after UDI. Furthermore, he offered only a generalised narrative of the environmental impact of sanctions on settler agriculture despite the fact that different sectors were affected differently by UDI and crops such as maize and non-exporting beef actually did well.[15] The impact of sanctions at an economic and ecological level was most severe on tobacco farmers: they were forced to diversify within the sand veld environs that could not sustain any other crop or agricultural enterprise on a large scale apart from tobacco. This led to rapid land degradation because of environmentally unsound cropping systems. In addition, this chapter examines the scale of environmental degradation on the tobacco farms at a micro-level by focussing on tobacco-farming conservation data from ICAs in the Centenary and Umvukwesi area. The chapter takes a new approach, unlike previous Southern Rhodesia's agrarian and tobacco histories of the 1960s to 1980s, by using the environment as a prism through which to observe political and economic change.

The chapter embraces Ellen Stroud's challenge to reject the mere gesture towards environmental histories by mainstream historical texts that shove environmental histories into marginalia – introductions, sidebars and footnotes – as secondary to 'real' political, social and economic histories.[16] Concerns over the natural environment can offer better tools to tell stories about power and society, by inviting historians to join in the 'attention to the physical and biological, ecological nature of dirt, water, air, sea, trees and animals to uncover new answers and questions about the past'.[17] Changes to environmental ecosystems have a history of their own that is as equally important as the political and

[14] S. Maravanyika, 'Soil Conservation and the White Agrarian Environment in Colonial Zimbabwe, 1908–1980' (Unpublished PhD thesis, University of Pretoria, 2013), 283.

[15] Selby, 'Commercial Farmers and the State', 91.

[16] Ellen Stroud, 'Does Nature Always Matter? Following Dirt through History,' *History and Theory*, 42, (December 2004), 75–81.

[17] Stroud, 'Does Nature Always Matter?', 75–81.

social history simultaneously unfolding with them.[18] Stroud and others' compelling call for historians to pay attention to 'dirt' and nature has conscripted a whole new wave of historical scholarship that emphasises the materiality of physical geographies over political and economic narratives.[19] Previous environmental histories for this period in Southern Rhodesia have not drawn on this scholarship – so this chapter tries to embrace this approach and showcase the new results it yields.

The Spectre of Tobacco-Production Control in Southern Rhodesia, 1962–1965

The overall effect of the cancer scares during the 1950s and 1960s (to be discussed in the next chapter) on limiting global tobacco consumption was insignificant as consumption trends remained buoyant. However, the transient dips in global cigarette sales had a conspicuous effect on production trends. Figures supplied by the Tobacco Export Promotion Council of Rhodesia and Nyasaland (TEPCORN) revealed that global tobacco consumption and the expansion of cigarette output had declined from 5 per cent per annum between 1956 and 1961 to 2.4 per cent in 1962 as a result of global health concerns.[20] Therefore, global stocks of tobacco were at record high levels and these totalled 972 million lbs in January 1963 representing 30 per cent of annual global flue-cured tobacco.[21] The Terry Report released in early 1964 had added fresh impetus to the smoking and public health issues and prompted widespread reductions in cigarette sales in the first half of 1964 by up to 20 per cent.[22] The result of this dynamic was that acreage allotments under the Federal Tobacco Program in the USA were reduced

[18] This point is made more strongly by William Cronon who argues that the environment is much more than a stage on which history unfolds, but an actor on its own. See W. Cronon, *Changes in the Land: Indians, Colonists, and the Ecology of New England* (New York: Hill and Wang, 2003).

[19] See, T. Cole, 'Nature Was Helping Us: Forests, Trees, and Environmental Histories of the Holocaust', *Environmental History*, 19, 4 (2014), 665–686. Cole devoted his article to a riveting history of the Jewish holocaust by focusing on trees and forests and how survivors interacted with nature. Also, see C. Pearson, *Mobilizing Nature: The Environmental History of War and Militarization in Modern France* (Manchester, 2012).

[20] National Archives of Zimbabwe (NAZ) Harare, F226/1211/F2, Production Control 1964 to 1965, Tobacco Export Council of Rhodesia, 1964 to 1965 crop recommendations.

[21] Ibid. [22] Ibid.

in most farms by 10 per cent making 639,861 acres available down from the 710,191 acres that had been planted in 1963.[23] The repercussions of these global pressures in Southern Rhodesia were fears that the 1963 tobacco crop of 280 million lbs would leave a carry-over of 50 to 70 million lbs.[24] In light of this, it was therefore considered prudent to restrict the 1964/1965 seasonal production to only 200 to 210 million lbs to avoid overproduction and a glut.[25] The council of the RTA authorised a working committee to investigate overproduction and the position of the 1964/1965 crop and look for ways to enforce domestic control and to hear the different views of the growers.[26] The committee recommended that any scheme of voluntary control by individual farmers would fail, and there was need for a comprehensive and global control system.[27]

Under Government Notice No. 16 of 1964 of the Tobacco Marketing Levy Act the total amount of tobacco to be sold in Rhodesia during the 1965 selling season was not to exceed 250 million lbs.[28] Each registered grower was to be allotted a basic quota. In the case of a new grower using new facilities a production quota of 40,000 lbs was allocated, for a new grower on old facilities previously used for tobacco production, a weight of tobacco equal to the greatest weight sold by the registered grower who previously used such facilities in the selling season in the three years prior to 1965, and in the case of old growers the quota was the weight equal to the greatest weight sold by the grower in the three seasons prior to 1964.[29] All tobacco to be produced in excess of the approved quotas was to be destroyed. In a press statement, the Minister of Agriculture lauded the control scheme as a measure which would effectively lead to greater diversification and intensive use of land in the tobacco-growing areas. He pointed out; 'I hope that the limitation to be imposed on tobacco production will hasten the diversification that I and previous ministers have for so long advocated. To mention the more

[23] 'USDA Announces Changes for 1964 Crop', *Flue-Cured Tobacco Cooperative Stabilisation Cooperation Newsletter*, 2 December 1963.

[24] NAZ, F226/1211/F2, Production Control 1964 to1965, Tobacco Export Council of Rhodesia, 1964 to 1965 crop recommendations.

[25] Ibid.

[26] NAZ, F226/121/F2, Production Control 1964 to 1965, RTA Production Control: Report of the Working Committee.

[27] Ibid. [28] The Tobacco Marketing and Levy (Marketing Quota) Order, 1964.

[29] Ibid.

obvious lines to fill the gap, I would mention cattle first, cotton second, monkey nuts third and sheep fourth.'[30]

While the control scheme had been initially received by growers with mild enthusiasm, opposition to it grew until there was a marked degree of protest amongst most farmers, particularly the smaller, not well-established farmers who argued that it only served to protect the big growers and made it impossible for new growers to enter the industry.[31] Tobacco farmers from Bindura, in their letter to the Secretary for Lands and Agriculture, pointed out that 40,000 lbs were uneconomic as many growers had been handicapped in their expansion by the shortage of available land, an obstacle that they hoped would be overcome in future by purchasing more land and developing it. The farmers argued that 'by cutting their production many of them would be forced to leave the land as they represented in the main the developing farmer'.[32] The other argument against control was that there were very good tobacco areas in the country which were not yet fully developed and which under the control scheme could be underutilised. Production would tend to be frozen in present areas and thus prevent a shift to the best areas.[33]

On its part, the RTA was adamant that production control was the only mechanism which would guarantee the stability of the tobacco industry in the face of global volatile marketing conditions.[34] Its President E. H. Jeffreys told an angry gathering of tobacco farmers that he was determined to go on with the control scheme. He argued that without the scheme the industry would be plunged into a state of chaos and made a laughing stock by other global producers.[35] Farmers' associations protested the control scheme and protest meetings were held across the country. However, the dissatisfaction with the control scheme was largely confined to the fringe tobacco-growing areas in the newly resettled places like Tengwe, Gadzema, Mrehwa,

[30] NAZ, F226/1211/F2, Production Control 1964 to 1965, Press Statement by Minister of Agriculture on tobacco-production control. The press statement is undated but happened around September 1964.

[31] *Rhodesia Herald*, 17 October 1964.

[32] NAZ, F226/1211/F2, Control of production 1964 to 1965, Bindura farmers to Secretary Agriculture, 27 September 1964.

[33] Ibid.

[34] 'Chief Is Determined to Implement Quota Plan', *Rhodesia Herald*, 14 October 1964.

[35] Ibid.

Mutoko, and Centenary.[36] These farmers presented the argument that their farm holding consisting of 500 to 700 acres of arable land gave limited scope for diversification under the present accepted farming practices.[37] The Tengwe Farmers' Association noted that most farmers in their area were settled based on cultivating 60 acres of tobacco to make a living of £1,500 per annum. Their geographical and financial position as well as the lack of capital to diversify, and the capital already poured into the 60-acre portions precluded seeking revenue from other farm enterprises.[38] Votes of no confidence in the leadership of the RTA were passed during those meetings.[39] Consequently, as a result of these protests, the government was forced to abandon the mandatory tobacco control scheme and settled for a voluntary scheme which was implemented during the 1965 selling season. Nevertheless, the tobacco-production control scheme was a harbinger for things to come as it put into focus two main issues that were to shape tobacco production during the UDI period: state-regulated production and marketing and tobacco farm diversification to meet the existential threat of collapsing markets.

Tobacco Farms, Diversification, Ecological Change in Southern Rhodesia, 1966–1980

On 11 November 1965, the RF government of Southern Rhodesia unilaterally severed its political attachments to Britain and declared independence. The response from the British government was a raft of economic restrictions and sanctions banning the import of Rhodesian mineral products, the sale of petroleum products and the imposition of a boycott on Rhodesian tobacco.[40] The effects of the boycott on the tobacco industry were tellingly disastrous. The tobacco embargo stripped Southern Rhodesia off at least 50 per cent of its traditional tobacco market.[41] It was apparent that in light of limited marketing opportunities the state had to once again raise the spectre of production control to cushion the white farmers from the disaster of depressed prices and overproduction starting from the 1966 season.

[36] NAZ, F226/1211/F2, Production Control 1964–1965, Memorandum of Tengwe Farmers Association on the Tobacco Quota, 3 October 1964.
[37] Ibid. [38] Ibid.
[39] 'RTA Stand Sparks Protests', *Rhodesia Herald*, 20 October 1964.
[40] Rowe, *Manipulating the Market*, 60. [41] Ibid., 73.

So the state set up the Tobacco Cooperation in 1966, a statutory entity whose task was to dispose of the tobacco crop and create the requisite marketing framework.[42] The Cooperation's terms of reference included ensuring continuity of supplies to external markets, supporting growers' production and maintaining the existing auction system.[43] In terms of the law, the Cooperation became the sole monopoly body that could buy, export and regulate tobacco in Southern Rhodesia in a manner reminiscent of a communist command economy.[44] Each farmer was allocated a basic quota calculated on the basis of weight sold by him during the 1965 season which was then reduced to a production quota by a percentage designed to equate the total crop to meet marketing requirements.[45] The control scheme came into effect on 15 July 1966, and the seasonal national quota was put at 200 million lbs.[46] However, the 1966/1967 season was a marketing nightmare that left a huge glut of 80 million lbs unsold.[47] Consequently, during the 1967/1968 season the national quota was revised down to 132 million lbs – in acreage terms this was a reduction of 56,700 acres from 166,700 acres in 1966 to 110,000 in 1967.[48] Despite the reduction, the Tobacco Cooperation

42 D. Losman, 'Rhodesia: A Decade under Sanctions', *Il Politico*, 43, 2 (1978), 321–340.

43 For a more detailed discussion of the Tobacco Cooperation, its membership, broader statutory obligations, terms of reference and funding see, Rowe, *Manipulating the Market*, 73–74.

44 Southern Rhodesia considered itself the last bastion on the fight against communism in southern Africa. In his memoirs, Ian Smith (who was Southern Rhodesia's Prime Minister between 1964 and1980) pointed out that southern Africa faced the threat of communist imperialism that was being worsened by 'unbridled black nationalism'. See I. Smith, *Bitter Harvest: The Great Betrayal and the Dreadful Aftermath* (Johannesburg, 2001), 124–125.

45 'The Production Control Scheme', *Tobacco Forum of Rhodesia, August* 1966. There was a lot of reticence concerning tobacco production and marketing from the government during the UDI: so much that some of the statistics put in the public domain may not be very accurate. Tobacco marketing and production figures were a heavily guarded secret and Prime Minister Smith said that the open tobacco auctioning system had to come to an end in 1966 since British spies were trying to identify buyers and influence the marketing of the crop. See Smith, *Bitter Harvest*, 118.

46 'Tobacco Control Scheme Details Sent to Growers', *Rhodesia Herald*, 16 July 1966.

47 'Flue-Cured Tobacco Growers and a Reduced Marketing Quota', *Rhodesian Tobacco Journal*, December 1967.

48 Ibid.

had further difficulties in disposing of the crop and during the 1969 season, unsold stockpiles of tobacco stood at 300 million lbs.[49]

The financial implications of this for tobacco growers was a reduction in incomes, as the value of Rhodesia's tobacco exports fell precipitously by 82 per cent from R$93.9 million to R$16.7 million (Rhodesian dollars) in 1965 and 1966 respectively.[50] Gross incomes of tobacco farmers fell down as they could not meet overhead expenditure and personal living expenses.[51] The situation was so desperate that Mr. Gordon Hoskins Davies, former RTA President and Sinoia farmer, agonised that 'no longer is the weed the magic crop for opening up new lands and creating closer settlement'.[52] He added, 'some profit may remain in tobacco, but no satisfaction and no future'.[53] Most farmers surrendered their production quotas because they could not profitably grow and dispose of the crop. By December 1967, of the 68 million lbs target reduction imposed by the government for the season, 50 million lbs had been voluntarily surrendered by producers to the government at the cost of 6d/lb payable to the growers.[54] By early 1968, about 900 white farmers had been driven out of tobacco by sanctions.[55] There was also a corresponding sharp drop in the number of Asian and European people employed in agriculture from 4,700 before UDI to 3,800; the number of African employees dropped from 300,000 to 218,000.[56]

In the light of these adverse economic conditions, the state pushed forward agricultural diversification as a relevant tobacco-farming policy.[57] The state brought in a farm irrigation fund which allocated

[49] Losman, 'Rhodesia: A Decade under Sanction', 321–340.

[50] Rowe, *Manipulating the Market*, 74.

[51] 'Flue-Cured Tobacco Growers and a Reduced Marketing Quota', *Rhodesian Tobacco Journal*, December 1967.

[52] 'Surrendered Tobacco Quotas now 2.8 million', *Rhodesia Herald*, 27 July 1967.

[53] Ibid.

[54] 'Flue-Cured Tobacco Growers and a Reduced Marketing Quota', *Rhodesian Tobacco Journal*, December 1967.

[55] *The Star*, 8 March 1968. [56] Ibid.

[57] In Agricultural sciences, diversified farming systems are farming units that grow several crops and engage in other non-crop agricultural activities such as livestock or fish farming. Diversified farms constitute farming landscapes which stimulate biodiversity within the soil through mixed cropping systems, rotation of crops and rotational livestock grazing. At the landscape scale diversified farming systems include such other physical farm landforms as fallows, fields, pastures, woodlot plantations, marshes, streams, rivers and lakes.

financial grants to 211 white tobacco farmers and put 12,631 acres under irrigation to grow other crops between 1966 and 1967.[58] During 1966, 300 tobacco farmers used this facility, bringing over 8,000 hectares of land under irrigation to grow wheat under a state wheat subsidy support scheme.[59] The President of the RTA, Mr Carol Heurtley appealed to tobacco growers to diversify their exploits into other ventures. He urged them:

> Increase the lines you know can be profitable, remember your soil and your future on the farms. There were signs well before UDI that our economy was too dependent on one or two products. Tobacco accounted for half of the agricultural production and a third of all the value of exports ... too many Rhodesian farmers are over specialised and hence subject to excessive risk.[60]

Tobacco farmers turned – in large numbers – to other crops and enterprises such as cotton. Cotton became a particularly important diversification crop as it had a ready domestic market provided by the growing Rhodesian textile industry and it could also be exported to South Africa.[61] The diversification drive, however, created serious ecological problems within the tobacco sand veld environment. Faced with the necessity to continue an all-out effort to produce as much as possible from alternative crops to compensate for the loss of income from tobacco production, farmers were cultivating larger acreages, leading to over cropping well above the inherent capability of the land.[62] This was so because where tobacco production was discontinued, it was replaced by at least twice the acreage of cotton, with the result that the total area planted in the sand veld more than doubled making it necessary for changes in rotational practices to accommodate the increased cropping acreages.[63] Previously cropping for tobacco on the sand veld soils had been planned based on a rotational system involving two crops of tobacco followed by maize, and then followed by three years rotational pasture planted to indigenous grasses. This rotational practice ensured that for every acre of tobacco cropped, at least double the

58 'Tobacco Cut Back Has Had Its Credit Speeding up Farm Diversification', *Rhodesia Herald*, 6 July 1967.
59 Rukuni, 'The Evolution of Agricultural Policy', 46.
60 'Tobacco Farmers Urged to Retain Employees', *Rhodesia Herald*, 7 July 1967.
61 Stephenson, 'The Impact of International Economic Sanctions', 377–389.
62 W. R. Robertson, 'Cotton Rotations on Sand Veld Farms', *Rhodesia Agricultural Journal*, 66 (1969), 2–6.
63 Ibid.

amount of land had lain under pasture or grass fallow.[64] Thus, for every 100 acres of cropping on a tobacco farm, there would be a minimum of 200 acres under pasture or fallow, requiring in all some 300 to 400 acres of arable land.[65] This rotation with long periods under grass was desirable for the restoration of organic matter and the depression of soil pests such as the common root nematode. However, cotton produced very small quantities of crop residues owing to it being woody, and the continuous cultivation of cotton as replacement for tobacco could not provide enough organic matter to replace the soil fertility.[66]

As a result, the soil structure in the tobacco farms became poorer. Cotton also gave poor cover in the earlier part of the rainy season, had longer growing periods and continued to fruit long after the end of the rains resulting in abnormally dry soils which precluded early planting of the following crop.[67] It also reduced the infiltration rate and permeability of the soil and produced greater soil and water losses than tobacco.[68] Consequently in 1968, during a special congress, the RTA President lamented this ecological breakdown and pointed out with despair that for the vast majority of the remaining 1,700 white tobacco growers, the limits of diversification had been reached as the types of soils, annual rainfall, and general ecological situation on most tobacco farms made it virtually impossible for the cultivation of other crops other than the commodity for which they were originally developed.[69]

While taking note of these challenges, the director of Conex Mr. J. H. Lowrens pointed out during the annual conference of ICA committees: 'it is obvious that the degree of intensification and diversification of land use practiced on many farms is such that it cannot be tolerated with safety by the prevailing land, soil and climatic conditions – as evidenced by the increasing incidences of erosion'.[70] He also highlighted that there was a general slackening of concern for the mechanical protection of soil in arable areas. There had also been a considerable decrease on the number of dams built and their total capacities compared with previous years.[71] Diversification also required sound sand veld management

[64] Ibid. [65] Ibid. [66] Ibid. [67] Ibid.

[68] J. M. Cormack, 'Efficient Utilisation of Water Through Land Management', *Rhodesia Agricultural Journal*, 69, 1 (March 1973), 12.

[69] RTA Presidential Speech at the Special Congress held on 22 April 1968.

[70] 'Farmers Warned of the Consequences of Over-Cropping', *Rhodesia Herald*, 30 July 1970.

[71] Ibid.

techniques to incorporate new crops. This was not being practiced on a sound basis such that by March 1970 only 1,070 (8,666,700 acres) farms had been planned and this represented only 19.7 per cent of the forty-four million acres in the European and Native Purchase Areas.[72]

The result of these ecological problems was that the diversification drive was too slow to change the fortunes of many tobacco growers who were frustrated and unable to adapt to the changing production environment. Mr Hoffman of Lee Farm in Inyazura wrote a letter to the Prime minister in 1970 complaining that the future of the grower was 'bleak and dismal, one of woe, and regrets and financial ruin, and eventual evacuation of rural areas'.[73] Young men disillusioned by the diversification scheme and unable to meet their financial commitments were already throwing in the towel and leaving the tobacco-growing districts.[74] The Mrehwa-Mutoko Farmers Association wrote to the Minister of Agriculture noting that although most of them had planted cotton and acquired a few cattle, 'the cotton had proved to be difficult and damaging' to their ecological conditions.[75] In much of Mashonaland, the

[72] Ibid.

[73] NAZ, (Unprocessed) C.32.15.11R, Box number 126959, Tobacco Burley Association, 1962–1970, Tobacco Sales Quota and General, 12 March /1970 to 21 September 1971, Mr. Du Toit Hoffman to PM Ian Smith, 3 March 1970.

[74] The tobacco farmers were furious and mostly united in clamouring against what they thought was state ineptitude in addressing their plight. During an annual Congress of the RTA in 1969, the tobacco farmers expressed their lack of confidence in the government's handling of the problems relating to the tobacco industry, which they said were ruining the industry and causing a security problem due to abandoned farms. They blamed the refusal of the government to pay a guaranteed 25d/lb support price. Rowe presents much of this political bickering between tobacco farmers as being very unsubstantial in shoring up the combined political power of the growers against the state during the UDI. The state was able to use its control of the institutions of tobacco marketing and production control to influence tobacco farmers much more effectively than the now disparate RTA. While Rowe's interpretation might be true at a political level in understanding the relationship between tobacco farmers and the state, it fails to appreciate the significant leverage tobacco farmers still commanded that was decisive in compelling the state to make a lot of sacrifices to alleviate the impact of the sanctions on the growers. This was because tobacco farmers were a significant pillar of its political support. In 1970, close to R$22.8 million was spent on the tobacco support programme and only a paltry R$ 3.6 million was allocated to a combined crops subsidy for cotton, soya beans, and maize.

[75] NAZ, (Unprocessed) C.32.15.11R, Box number 126959, Tobacco Burley Association, 1962 to 1970, Tobacco Sales Quota and General, 12 March 1970 to 21 September 1971, Mrehwa-Mutoko farmers association to Minister of Agriculture, 22 April 1970.

diversification into cotton was proving to be a disaster as cotton in the sand veld had thrown up a number of unexpected problems. The most serious of these problems was the tendency of the cotton plants to develop tap root problems when two or three inches high, as well as the higher incidences of weeds and insect pests such as eelworm.[76] This was attributed to the lengthy wet spells and the lack of hot weather. As a result of these ecological impediments, most tobacco farmers abandoned cotton production as a viable diversification alternative.

The diversification drive was given further impetus by the expansion of Burley tobacco production, which had begun during the 1956/1957 season on a trial basis to meet the huge demand of the American blended cigarette market. Although Burley tobacco had been grown in the 1930s, its production had ceased during the war years as a result of limited markets.[77] Burley had the advantage of supplementing flue-cured Virginia, as Virginia required sandy soils while Burley did best in heavier soils.[78] Burley could also fit well with maize rotations since it required fewer imported materials like fertiliser, and the heavier soils within which it was grown retained soil fertility for the next crop rotations.[79] From 1968, most white tobacco farmers appreciative of the erosion hazard engendered by the diversification of the sand veld particularly on small farms, were adopting Burley tobacco.[80] The expansion of Burley tobacco in European farms, however, remained restrained because of the lower returns per acre compared to Virginia. By 1973, Burley was grown by 416 European growers across the 21 tobacco-producing districts of Southern Rhodesia and sold at an average price of 51.79 cents/kg.[81] Despite this, however, the President of RNFU, Mike Butler, noted that the profitability and diversity following the decline in tobacco markets were difficult for most growers.[82]

[76] 'Sand Veld Tobacco Growers May Drop Cotton Production', *Rhodesia Herald*, 15 May 1969.

[77] 'Burley: An Outline of Its History and a Look into the Future', *Tobacco Forum of Rhodesia*, November 1969.

[78] 'Burley – The Crop with a Big Future', *Tobacco Forum of Rhodesia and Nyasaland*, August 1963.

[79] Ibid.

[80] NAZ, (Unprocessed) C.32.15.11R, Box number 126959, Tobacco Burley Association, 1962 to 1970, Chairman Centenary Farmers Association to Minister of Agriculture, 21 March 1968.

[81] '1973 Burley Sales', *Tobacco Today*, December 1973.

[82] Ibid.

The situation was made worse by the rising costs of inputs such as fuel and fertilisers that were imported and which were now expensive because of the sanctions.[83] By 1972, the number of European tobacco growers in Rhodesia had fallen from 2,500 in 1965 to 1,666 as a result of these hardships.[84]

Diversification was not easy. Most tobacco farmers had invested their capital in land suitable for the exclusive production of the crop. Compared with land for general cropping and livestock, most tobacco farms were relatively smaller and had become expensive to their owners largely because income from one acre of tobacco generally equalled that of four acres of other crops.[85] The common size of a sand veld farm was between 1,500 and 2,000 acres of which roughly 40 per cent could be classified as arable.[86] The arable land was further subject to a loss of 25 per cent in arable land taken up by roads, buildings, small unusable areas, and soil conservation works. Eventually, this would leave only 450 to 500 acres available for cropping rotations on a 1,500 acre farm.[87] A survey of land use in the Mazowe valley revealed that there was a steady drop in the area of fallow land from 11,480 acres between 1968 and 1969 to 9,800 acres between 1970 and 1971 (31 per cent of total arable).[88] The number of farms with fallow land also decreased from sixty-seven to fifty-five.[89] The problem, then of growers shifting from highly intensive tobacco production on limited acreages to general farming requiring large of areas of land became more glaring.[90]

Low-profit margins compounded the problem. Prices from the other crops were very low compared to tobacco; for instance, cotton gave a return of R$20 per acre against R$70 per acre for tobacco.[91] A survey of forty tobacco farms in the northern fringe of Mashonaland (Karoi, Tengwe, Doma, Raffingora, Centenary, Umvukwesi, and Spolilo) revealed that between 1969 and 1970, all the farms had made an

83 Rowe, *Manipulating the Market*, 79.

84 'The Rhodesian Tobacco Grower since 1965', *Tobacco Forum of Rhodesia*, February 1972.

85 'Toil and Sweat, but Success', *Rhodesia Herald*, 25 November 1971.

86 Robertson, 'Cotton Rotations on Sand Veld Farms', 2–6. 87 Ibid.

88 M. H. Buttress, 'Agricultural Land-Use in the Mazowe Valley during the Period 1966–1971', *Rhodesia Agricultural Journal*, 70, 5 (April 1972), 105.

89 Buttress, 'Agricultural Land-Use in the Mazowe Valley', 105.

90 'Toil and Sweat, but Success', *Rhodesia Herald*, 25 November 1971.

91 Rowe, *Manipulating the Market*, 79.

average loss of R$628.[92] An economic survey by the RTA during 1972 and 1973 showed that out of a sample of 222 farmers, 50 were in the red.[93] The worsening economic crisis in 1975 hit tobacco farmers most hard.[94] The financial crisis was a result of unfavourable exchange rates, poor harvest as a result of the 1974/1975 drought, overseas marketing competitions, the higher input costs and falling prices.[95] A third of tobacco farmers recorded a loss during the 1974/1975 season, and several were highly in debt with growers owing R$120 million in short-term credits by March 1975.[96] The precarious financial condition of most tobacco farmers thus slowed down investments in land conservation and farm planning.

In November 1972, H. A. Ellwell from the department of Conex complained that the result of UDI had been that the survival of tobacco soil was threatened. Indeed, he argued, 'the reality of soil erosion was far more permanent than the threat of sanctions'.[97] He noted with regret that many of the steep tobacco lands were irreparably damaged by soil erosion because of the neglect of long grass ley rotations.[98] This was because tobacco soils were notoriously shallow, gravel, infertile subsoils of decomposing rock which once exposed had to be abandoned:

> Remember the days of the long grass ley rotations. These old rotations were based on the knowledge that tobacco soils are highly erodible and require special treatment if they are to remain productive. The detrimental influence of an erosion-prone crop like tobacco was diluted by several years of a very erosion resistant crop like grass pasture ... the cutback in tobacco has put increased pressure on the land and farmers on the small tobacco farms are fighting for economic survival ... the safe rotations have gone to the board, tobacco followed by maize and back to tobacco is not an uncommon rotation on most farms.[99]

He pointed out that the higher erosion rates in the tobacco lands had a profound effect on the efficiency of conservation works as the soil eroded from the land between the contours was deposited in the contour channels.[100] While before UDI farmers could have 'gotten away' with such practices since there was enough land to practice long

92 'Low-Profit Margins in the Mashonaland Fringe Areas', *Rhodesia Herald*, 9 February 1973.
93 'More Tobacco Growers Are in the Red', *Rhodesia Herald*, 27 June 1975.
94 Godwin and Hancock, *Rhodesians Never Die*, 132. 95 Ibid. 96 Ibid.
97 'Protect the Future of Tobacco', *Rhodesian Tobacco Journal*, November 1972.
98 Ibid. 99 Ibid. 100 Ibid.

ley rotations and it could be rested, the reduced area under tobacco changed all that.[101] Indeed, a writer in the *Rhodesian Tobacco Journal* pointed out that under the prevailing cropping systems tobacco farms were losing soils at an alarming rate:

> Tobacco is still our valuable cash crop. Tobacco soils are therefore the foundations and backbone of the economic viability of many of our farms ... valuable assets demand and deserve great care and consideration. Contour farming ensures that soils are given attention not only does contour farming decrease the rate of erosion and thereby protect the future of the industry, but it also offers the prospects of more economic all-round farming.[102]

Within the Sinoa group of ICAs for instance, there was a general concern over the mechanical conservation works. The Group Conex officer Mr W. D. Nicolli pointed out that the problem was more serious within the ICA because 49 per cent of the cropping area was in the sand veld and most sensitive to soil erosion that was hastened by the construction of tobacco ridges up and down the slope, which was now being aggravated by over cropping and incorrect rotation systems adopted during the UDI.[103] In the Centenary ICA, NRB noted in 1976 that of the ninety farms only thirty-nine had been planned.[104] The board also complained that mechanical conservation was still an issue, with only 43 per cent of the farmers using parallel ridging in 1975.[105] A survey done by Conex in December 1975 on conservation practices on tobacco lands in the Umvukwesi group of ICAs revealed that of the total 3,421 acres of tobacco planted only 848 acres (26.9 per cent) were conserved by modern methods as shown in Table 5.1.[106]

[101] Ibid.

[102] 'Largest Concentrations of Farming Units in Rhodesia', *Rhodesian Tobacco Journal*, January 1973.

[103] 'Soil Erosion Aggravated', *Rhodesian Financial Gazette*, 15 April 1976.

[104] 'Controlled Conservation of Arable land', Centenary East and West ICA Newsletter, no. 6, June 1976.

[105] Ibid.

[106] Minutes of the 15th AGM of the Centenary ICA held on Friday 17 September 1976.

Table 5.1 *Adoption of conservation by tobacco farmers in the ICAs in Southern Rhodesia, 1975–1976*

AREA	*Umvukwesi ICA%*	*Horseshoe ICA%*	*Centenary West ICA%*	*Centenary East ICA%*
Tobacco farmers applying conservation new practices by area 1975–1976	58.80	49.40	24.80	21.60
Tobacco farmers applying new conservation practices by area 1976–1977	67.0	68.70	38.70	17.60
Tobacco farmers applying new conservation practices by a number of farms, 1975–1976	53.80	56.80	26.90	19.00
Tobacco farmers applying new conservation practices by number of farms, 1975–1976	67.30	73.50	42.50	15.00

Source: Centenary East and West ICA *Newsletter*, 6 (June 1976).

The Rhodesian Bush War and Agrarian Change in the Tobacco Farms, 1972–1980

The impact of the Rhodesian civil war on farming had been neglected in historical literature until the works of Rory Pilossof and Angus Selby put fresh focus on the plight of white farmers and farming in general.[107] Ncube's recent study added a new layer to this existing historiography on war and agriculture by emphasising how tobacco farming

[107] See, Pilossof, 'The Unbearable Whiteness of Being'; Selby, 'Commercial Farmers and the State'.

and farmers were at the frontier of the defences against incursions by freedom fighters.[108] He emphasises that the war affected tobacco farming in many ways that included destruction of farm properties, intimidation and murder of farm workers, the disruption of farming operations and the killing of white farmers. However, Ncube's focus was on the political impact of the war on tobacco grower's cohesiveness and the political economy of production and not on how the war specifically shaped and changed the physical landscape on the farms.

The deterioration of the security situation in the Rhodesian countryside had begun as early as 1966 as the result of a surge in nationalist activities sparked by the UDI.[109] This escalated from 1972, particularly in the northern parts of the country in such areas as Tengwe, Karoi, Guruve, Centenary and Mount Darwin – areas that were largely tobacco-producing – where more white farmers' lives were lost.[110] In Mutoko district, incursions by freedom fighters resulted in the exodus of a third of white farmers.[111] One farmer, for example, was compelled to leave in 1977 after his farm had been attacked several times and his tobacco crops and barns destroyed.[112] However, not all tobacco-farming areas suffered desertions and abandonment. The desertion of farms usually happened in the less profitable and marginal tobacco-growing areas such as Mrehwa and Mutoko, while in the lucrative tobacco-producing areas like Centenary most farmers stayed on the land.[113] The lifting of the tobacco quota between 1973 and 1974 and the restoration of the tobacco auction system, which improved tobacco prices, witnessed a wave of young tobacco farmers moving into the

108 Ncube, 'Colonial Zimbabwe Tobacco Industry', 127–128.

109 In 1965 there were widespread reports of the destruction of tobacco plants in the Karoi area leading to the arrest of several African youths from the Hurungwe Tribal Trust Lands.

110 Pilossof, 'The Unbearable Whiteness of Being', 26. Pilossof points out that the area lost more than eighty members during the war. Godwin and Hancock add that 50 per cent of tobacco growers farmed in or near these security-sensitive areas. The nationalist leaders changed their strategic conduct of the liberation war in 1972 from conventional warfare against a well-equipped Rhodesian army into politicising and mobilising the rural populace and launching guerrilla warfare. This phase meant that many of the rural areas were now infiltrated with guerrilla units who attacked white farms and farmers. See, D. Martin and P. Johnson, *The Struggle for Zimbabwe: The Chimurenga War* (London, 1981), 2–3, 13.

111 Godwin and Hancock, *Rhodesians Never Die*, 132.

112 Ibid., 256.

113 Godwin and Hancock, *Rhodesians Never Die*, 132; Selby, 'Commercial Farmers and the State', 80.

lucrative growing areas as demand for tobacco farms around these areas increased.[114] These tobacco farmers who stayed on the land were to become a critical component of territorial defence and important buffers for localised defence to repel guerrilla raids.[115]

Nevertheless, the security situation led to the problem of vacant farms across the country, which was blamed on the 'townie farmer' who remote-controlled the management of his farm.[116] In 1977, just within the rich tobacco-producing Karoi area, there were fifty such farms.[117] In Mtoko district by 1979, only fifty of the ninety-three farms were still occupied, thirty-three were completely abandoned and ten were being run by caretakers.[118] 'Townie farmers' and caretakers cared less about maintaining the costly business of land conservation in the midst of political and economic volatility. To make matters worse some of these farmers had their tobacco crops and seed beds plucked out and burnt by the freedom fighters.[119] In 1978, the Chairman's report of the Centenary west ICA lamented that tobacco farmers were tending to mine their farms, and rotation had gone by the board because of the war situation.[120] He, however, chastened growers:

> You are reminded that it is still your land and you will not find any area in Rhodesia like this one. Just because conditions are such that you might not always be in possession of land is no excuse – you might be here and if world markets improve you could lose out.[121]

He said that the results of the year with regards to conservation were very poor as only six growers had their contour up to standard, and only eleven out of ninety-two farmers had a satisfactory bank.[122] The Kutsaga tobacco research station pointed out in 1978 that because of the war there were no grass ley rotations on tobacco farms, and this trend had been discernible over the past seven or eight years.[123] They argued:

114 Losman, 'Rhodesia: A Decade under Sanction', 321–340.
115 *Rhodesia Herald*, 27 September 1972.
116 Pilossof, 'The Unbearable Whiteness of Being', 26.
117 'Vacant farms Causing Concern', *The Rhodesia Herald*, 30 September 1977.
118 Godwin and Hancock, *Rhodesians Never Die*, 290.
119 Centenary East and West ICA Newsletter, No.9, October 1979.
120 Minutes of the AGM of the Centenary West ICA, 20 October 1978: Chairman's Report.
121 Ibid. 122 Ibid.
123 Natural Resources Board (NRB) Newsletter no.4, April 1978, 3.

There appears to be a growing body of thought that says, hammer the land and to hell with next year. From this same philosophy comes the very dangerous practice of continuous tobacco cropping. The trend is alarming and knowledgeable conservationists predict that it could be a disaster parallel to the rapidly declining TTLs. If farmers are custodians of the land, then many of them are highly negligent in their duty.[124]

In 1977 with the escalation of the security situation, the government instituted mandatory call-ups for young men to serve in the military. The military call-ups were deemed by the RTA to be more severe on growers between the ages of twenty-four and thirty-five, most of whom it reckoned would not be able to continue production.[125] In these conditions, the gender roles of production in the tobacco farms also changed as farmers' wives came to be more involved in farming and other duties on the farm. Margaret Strong, wife of a former RNFU President, pointed out during the RNFU annual congress in 1979 that while farmers' wives had in the past 'ran the home, shouted at the children and arranged the flowers', they were now assuming active roles in farm management while their husbands were on call-ups.[126] For the first time, tobacco farmers' wives and daughters took part in various tobacco courses organised by the RTA. In 1974 a three-day course on fumigation, seedbed mulching, watering and pest, and diseases for 'farmers' wives' was conducted.[127] In 1976, white women in Burma Valley, a low-lying area on the border between Zimbabwe and Mozambique, attended another cause hosted by the TRB and Conex on top dressing in the lands.[128] The objectives of these courses were not to make these 'wives' expert growers, but to give them some understanding of tobacco so that they could take care of the farming temporarily when their husbands were away.

A Well Disguised Blessing? Diversification and the New Tobacco-Farming Landscapes

Despite its bleak prospects, the diversification initiative, however, had begun to achieve significant successes particularly from the late 1970s

124 NRB Newsletter no.4, April 1978, 3.
125 'RTA Council Report: Call up Proposals', *Tobacco Today*, February 1977.
126 Godwin and Hancock, *Rhodesians Never Die*, 292.
127 'Courses for Farmers' Wives', *Tobacco Today*, May 1974
128 'Burma Valley: Ladies Course and Field Day', *Tobacco Today*, November 1976.

as farm incomes improved. The number of cattle held by white farmers increased by 54 per cent since UDI from 1.6 million to 2.5 million in 1970.[129] This increase was largely because many tobacco farmers produced some beef prior to UDI under a crop rotation in which tobacco was grown one year followed by 3 to 5 years of planted grass. Thus, when tobacco production was curtailed, the response by some of the farmers with bigger farms was to raise beef by allocating resources to livestock production.[130] Smith argued in his autobiography that the Tobacco Cooperation was a 'magnificent success' and tobacco farmers streamlined production methods and increased efficiency – establishing irrigation schemes and creating food self-sufficiency and surplus for the export market.[131] Maize production increased reaching 1.2 million tonnes in 1970, while production of cotton lint increased over ten-fold from an annual average of 3,000 tonnes between 1961 and 1965 to 36,000 tonnes between 1966 to 1970.[132] White farmers also increased their share of food production from 30 per cent in 1960 to 75 per cent in 1978.[133] A 1977 survey revealed that the gross value of tobacco production had dropped from 50 per cent in 1965 to 27 per cent of total European agricultural production, with the remaining 73 per cent being distributed amongst maize, beef, cotton, sugar, dairying and coffee.[134] By 1977 tobacco farmers also produced 45 per cent of maize, 29 per cent of groundnuts, 52 per cent of fodder crops, 17 per cent of wheat, 13 per cent of cotton and they owned 21 per cent of the national beef herd, and 16 per cent of the dairy herd.[135] Resultantly, while the country had only produced 2 per cent of its annual wheat requirements prior to 1965, by 1971 Southern Rhodesia could meet 75 per cent of its domestic wheat needs and in 1976 it was self-sufficient and a net importer of wheat.[136]

Diversification also led to greater use of coal furnaces.[137] Bush timber had been the traditional source of fuel for curing flue-cured tobacco since

[129] 'UN Sanctions against Rhodesia Brings Changes in Farm Production', *Rhodesian Tobacco Journal*, November 1972.
[130] Ibid. [131] Smith, *Bitter Harvest*, 118.
[132] 'UN Sanctions against Rhodesia brings changes in farm production', *Rhodesian Tobacco Journal*, November 1972.
[133] Selby, 'Commercial Farmers and the State', 69.
[134] 'Spotlight on Tobacco', *Rhodesia Herald*, 16 December 1977. [135] Ibid.
[136] Rukuni, 'The Evolution of Agricultural Policy', 47.
[137] 'Wankie Gives $10,000 to the Tobacco Training Institute', *Rhodesia Herald*, 23 December 1977.

suitable soils for tobacco culture in Mashonaland supported fair to heavy growths of indigenous trees that had to be cleared and stumped to permit cultivation; its cost was considered negligible in new and developing farms.[138] In view of the rotational cropping requirements of tobacco culture, no pressing demand for an alternative fuel had arisen. However, during the UDI large areas of land were opened up to alternative crops and indigenous timber was suddenly and rapidly destroyed.[139] Within the older tobacco-growing areas dating from World War II, large unbroken tracts of land in the open rolling country had been put to the plough and the natural timber resources almost entirely depleted many years before. This evoked the need to find alternative fuel sources and heat efficient furnaces. Constant efforts had been made since 1948 to improve heating efficiency of wood-fired furnaces beginning with the Gundry furnace, then the TRB furnace and the Townsend furnace.[140] All these furnaces functioned through heating by combustion particularly through the partial provision of air to the firebox. Improved designs were being made by Wankie Colliery from the 1960s for conversion of these wood furnaces into coal systems. These efforts were important since natural timber in the tobacco farms was useful as a natural cover for wildlife, for aesthetic reasons and in the interests of soil conservation.[141] With coal being readily available farms were encouraged by the TRB to switch to coal. As a result, by 1976, 40 per cent of tobacco farmers were using coal for all or part of their curing programme, with growers spending R$5 million annually on getting coal to their farms.[142] Most of the tobacco barns from the 1970s used coal steam curing technology. Figure 5.1 shows a commercial in a farmers' magazine exhorting the use of coal steam curing technology.

As a result of increasing costs of coal and transportation, growers were also beginning to look for alternative renewable energy sources such as the growing of *Eucalyptus* in tobacco-growing districts. Compared with indigenous wood which was a once and for all yield, *Eucalyptus* was a continuous productive process yielding 7.2 cubic metres per hectare per annum against 0.70 cubic metres per hectare per annum for indigenous wood.[143] Seedlings were provided by the Rhodesian Forestry Commission at a cost of R$25 per 1000

[138] E. P. du Toit, 'Timber as a Tobacco Curing Fuel', *Rhodesia Agricultural Journal*, 70, 5 (1974), 107–110.

[139] Ibid. [140] Ibid. [141] Ibid.

[142] 'Gum Trees or Coal', *Tobacco Today*, October 1976. [143] Ibid.

Figure 5.1 An advert in a farmers' magazine encouraging the use of coal and a coal steam curing barn that was popular on most tobacco farms in Southern Rhodesia in the 1970s
Source: *Tobacco Today*, October 1973.

seedlings.[144] As a result of these initiatives, the total fuel wood consumption in Zimbabwe as estimated by the Whitsun foundation in 1980 stood at 4,974,000 cubic metres annually, with the tobacco industry consuming 7 per cent of the national aggregate.[145] Around the same time, in other African tobacco-producing countries forestry resources were under threat as a result of the axing of trees for tobacco

[144] Ibid.
[145] A. Fraser and R. C. D. Bowles, *The Use of Wood by the Tobacco Industry in Zimbabwe* (Edinburgh: International Forestry Science Consultancy, December 1986), 23.

drying, which was contributing to 'the poor man's energy crisis'.[146] In Kenya, Tanzania and Malawi tobacco production was threatening wood scarcity and desertification with 2,000 hectares of forest being axed each year by the tobacco industry in Kenya alone.[147] In Southern Rhodesia, the use of alternative energy sources for the curing of tobacco reduced the aggregate demand on forestry resources. In 1986, the International Forest Science Consultancy concluded that there was no serious problem in meeting future wood fuel requirements for curing tobacco, and the gradual switch to coal was reducing demand.[148] The report went further and pointed out that there was no evidence that any environmental degradation could be attributed to tobacco growing since the amount of wood consumed by the tobacco sector was small in proportion to total wood consumption.[149] This, of course, was to change from the late 1990s and early 2000s with the entry of many smallholder black farmers into tobacco farming who relied on indigenous woodlands for curing tobacco as the next chapter will show.

Conclusion

Between 1960 and 1980, three major events played a key role in shaping the tobacco farm physical environment in Southern Rhodesia – the global smoking and public health debates, the UDI economic embargo imposed by the British government in 1966 and the so-called Bush War that intensified from 1972. The first event ushered in a transient global tobacco consumption recession that caused a glut in 1963 and raised the spectre of production control in Southern Rhodesia. However, its impact on agrarian change on the tobacco farms was negligible as it did not significantly affect production models and systems or lead to reduction of acreages. The second brought an economic slump that ruined many tobacco farmers, led to severe production cuts and diversified cropping systems in the sand veld. The result was a break down in sand veld ecologies and limited

146 'Death Knell for Kenyan Forests', *The London Observer News*, 28 October 1981.
147 Ibid.
148 Fraser and Bowles, *The Use of Wood by the Tobacco Industry in Zimbabwe*, 23.
149 Ibid., 24.

investment in land conservation. The third simply accentuated the effects of the second. Ultimately, there is need to look at political and economic events in history as complex forces helping shape new geographies on the land, reprocessing the soil granules and crafting new ecological encounters. But equally the environmental impacts also define political and economic institutions. This chapter has extended the economic history of Southern Rhodesia during the UDI by showing how production systems shifted between 1966 and 1980 and the consequence of this on settler agriculture. The chapter argues that the UDI and the so-called Bush War not only affected the economy and politics of the country, but they also significantly altered the environment on the white tobacco farms. It *visibilises* the environment and physical landscapes from their obscurity in historiographical terrains populated with dominant political and economic narratives of war and sanctions in Southern Rhodesia during this period.

6 Tobacco-Control Discourses and the Tobacco Industry in Southern Rhodesia and Zimbabwe, 1953–2020

It is just not good enough to say that tobacco is responsible for lung cancer. For example, tobacco grown in one part of the world may produce an entirely different effect on health than tobacco grown in another part of the world. People in Southern Rhodesia and south of the Limpopo are relatively heavier smokers, yet the incidence of lung cancer amongst them is much smaller than in Britain or the UK.

Dr H. M Webster, Southern Rhodesian Secretary for Health, 1964

I have always argued that WHO has got its priorities wrong. I may be wrong, but I take my own country as an example. I do not know how many people have died of nicotine here, lung cancer, but I know that very many more, almost on a weekly basis, have died of too much alcohol.

Former Zimbabwean President, Robert Mugabe, 1994

The Cigarette Century and the Global Tobacco Epidemic

The twentieth century has been dubbed 'the cigarette century' by tobacco historians. The cigarette was an epoch-defining invention in the history of tobacco bringing in new methods of cultivation, curing, manufacturing, a new commercial and consumer culture and the rise of tobacco co-operations and trust companies that influenced global political and economic institutions during the last hundred years. The 'cigarette century' witnessed the globalisation of the epidemic of tobacco-related diseases such as lung cancer that claimed an estimated 100 million human casualties during the last century.[1] WHO estimates that one billion people will die of tobacco-related ailments during the twenty-first century and 80 per cent of these deaths will occur in low and middle-income countries where tobacco use has been on the

[1] World Health Organization (WHO), 'Report on the Global Tobacco Epidemic', Geneva, 2008.

increase since the 1990s.[2] Between 1995 and 2000, tobacco consumption in low and middle-income countries and Sub-Saharan Africa rose by 2.7 per cent and 3.2 percent respectively.[3] Consequently, the United Nations (UN) and other international organisations declared tobacco a threat to the socio-economic development of low and middle-income countries.[4] The rising use of tobacco in low and middle-income countries has caused mortalities and a concomitant loss of productivity that has negatively affected national economies and burdened healthcare systems. For example, in 2003, the annual cost of treating tobacco-related sicknesses in Egypt was estimated to be as high as US$455 million.[5] African healthcare systems already strained by HIV/AIDS, Tuberculosis (TB), Malaria and other diseases are significantly pressured towards collapse. The addictive nature of cigarettes also makes smoking a costly habit that drains incomes and threatens livelihoods, access to food, education and other necessities in families, creating a vicious cycle of poverty. During 2010, Morocco's expenditure on tobacco almost equalled education expenditure, and in Egypt 10 per cent of household income was spent on tobacco.[6]

This contemporary 'tobacco epidemic' is a progeny of the historical changes in tobacco consumer culture, the globalisation of tobacco corporations and the rise of 'political tobacco' that began as early as 1900. The changes in tobacco consumption from chewing, snuffing and pipping to cigarette smoking during the beginning of the twentieth century exacted a huge influence on tobacco farming, manufacturing and the overall organisation of the industry on a global scale.[7] The first cigarettes were manufactured in 1869 by F. S. Kinsey company in the USA using the bright flue-cured tobacco. These were hand rolled and largely produced by female labour.[8] In 1881, cigarette manufacturing

[2] 'Report on the Global Tobacco Epidemic', 2008.

[3] See African Union Commission, 'The Impact of Tobacco Use on Health and Socio-economic Development in Africa: A Status Report', (2010), 4.

[4] 'The Impact of Tobacco Use.'

[5] WHO, 'Tobacco and Poverty: A Vicious Cycle', (2004), 7.

[6] 'The Impact of Tobacco Use', 9.

[7] For a fuller discussion on the rise of the cigarette See A. M. Brandt, *The Cigarette Century: The Rise and Fall of the Deadly Persistence of the Product That Defined America* (New York, 2004); N. M. Tilley, *The Bright Tobacco Industry* (Chapel Hill, 1948).

[8] J. Goodman, *Tobacco in History: The Cultures of Dependence* (London, 1993), 229.

took on a revolutionary turn with the invention of the Bonsack machine by James Duke of the American Tobacco Company.[9] The discovery of a mechanical means of mass production of cigarettes from the traditional hand rolling methods witnessed a huge increase in cigarette production while lowering costs. The result of this was mechanisation and mass consumption.[10] With the rise in mass production and mass consumption came new methods of marketing, particularly packaging and advertising that popularised the cigarette. The result was the creation of enormous monopolistic tobacco trust companies that integrated various facets of the tobacco value chain and spent millions in marketing. For instance, the marketing expenditure for one of the big global tobacco brands of the twentieth century R. J. Reynolds was US$10 million by 1925.[11] The American Tobacco Company marketing expenditure also tripled between 1925 and 1932 to reach US$24 million.[12] Tobacco advertising revolutionised consumption through targeting specific social audiences and arousing need and desire for cigarettes by appealing to various fashion and tastes.[13]

While the rise of the cigarette marked a turning point in the history of tobacco consumerism, the social and public health effects of smoking had begun to attract a lot of attention from as early as the beginning of the twentieth century. Cigarette smoking was heavily maligned and attacked by moral reformers, scientists, evangelical Christians and eugenics at the turn of the twentieth century.[14] The anti-smoking movement in the USA castigated cigarettes for social vices such as juvenile delinquency, indolence and moral degeneracy.[15] Smoking was vilified as a serious threat to the moral fabric and considered responsible for the degeneracy in citizens and even national indolence. Businesspeople and industrialist of the time such as Henry Ford were strongly opposed to cigarette use and considered smokers less productive than non-smokers.[16] Smoking was considered a threat

[9] For a detailed discussion of James Duke and the activities of the American Tobacco Company in cigarette manufacturing and trade see, Sarah Milov, *The Cigarette: A Political History* (Massachusetts, 2019), 15–21.

[10] Goodman, *Tobacco in History*, 228. [11] Ibid., *105*. [12] Ibid.

[13] See, A. M Brandt, 'Engineering Confidence in the Twentieth Century' in S. L Gilman and Z. Xun (eds.), *A Global History of Smoking* (London, 2004), 332–343.

[14] Milov, *The Cigarette*, 23. [15] Ibid. [16] Ibid., 25.

to the moral and social fabric of society, a habit that squandered family resources while reducing national output. Consequently, between 1893 and 1930, fifteen states in the USA had enacted laws that banned the sale, manufacture, use or possession of cigarettes.[17] There were also several anti-smoking organisations in other parts of the world. These included the British Anti-Tobacco Society, the Anti-Tobacco Legion and the Scottish Anti-Tobacco Society.[18] By the twentieth century most anti-smoking organisations such as the British Lads anti-Smoking Union and the International Anti-Cigarette League focussed on opposing smoking amongst children.[19]

However, the First World War popularised the cigarette and smoking culture as major tobacco-producing and manufacturing countries in the world conscripted the tobacco industry within their bureaucratic machinery to expand global markets for cigarettes. In the USA the growth of the post-war cigarette and tobacco economy was a result of the alliance between farmers, tobacco merchants and the state in a mutual relationship of what Sarah Milov calls 'tobacco associational state-making'.[20] Tobacco Associates – products of private-public partnership – emerged as powerful vehicles for foreign tobacco export marketing and were complicit in globalising the tobacco epidemic. The Associates' export links and connection to the US government after World War II were so big that out of the US$13 billion Marshal Aid package for European countries, US$1billion went towards the procurement of tobacco.[21]

However, by the end of the Second World War concerns about smoking and cancer had come to populate global scientific medical discourses. In the USA there was a rise in lung cancer mortality rates from 4,000 in 1935 to 11,000 in 1945.[22] In Britain, the scientific works of Richard Doll and Austin Bradford Hill published in the *British Medical Journal* in 1950 concluded that smoking was a factor in causing lung cancer.[23] In 1953, the American Cancer Society (ACS)

[17] Ibid., 24.
[18] J. Welshman, 'Smoking, Science and Medicine' in S. L. Gilman and Z. Xun (eds.), *Smoke: A Global History of Smoking* (London, 2004), 327.
[19] Welshman, 'Smoking, Science and Medicine', 327.
[20] See Brandt, *The Cigarette Century*, 9. [21] Ibid., 79–95.
[22] Welshman, 'Smoking, Science and Medicine', 328.
[23] R. Doll and A. B. Hill, 'Lung Cancer and Other Causes of Death in Relation to Smoking: A Second Report on the Mortality of British Doctors', *The British Medical Journal*, 2, 5001 (1956), 1071–1081.

released research findings that linked tobacco smoking to lung cancer.[24] By the mid-1950s most researchers and clinicians were convinced and had reached consensus that indeed smoking caused cancer of the lung and tobacco was a health risk.[25]

The revelation of this new scientific evidence linking smoking to serious risk of disease rattled the tobacco industry to its core as negative publicity arose.[26] The result of this negative publicity was a dramatic fall in the global consumption of tobacco products. For the first time, cigarette consumption in the USA, which had been rising since the days of the Depression in the 1930s, slumped from 394.1 million cigarettes in 1952 to 386 million cigarettes in 1953 and 368 million cigarettes in 1954.[27] The tobacco companies responded with more aggressive marketing strategies, advertising and sponsoring their own parallel scientific research to counter the public health outcry.[28] In 1953, the Tobacco Industry Research Council (TIRC) was formed as the main public relations front for the industry, responsible for sponsoring and disseminating research information on smoking and cancer. Between 1954 and 1957 TIRC spent US$300 million on funding and trafficking researches on smoking and cancer that vindicated tobacco from the public health scares.[29] The 1961 report of the Committee concluded that there was no link between smoking and cancer.[30] Another innovative strategy used by the tobacco industry during the 1950s to obviate the public health scrutiny was the introduction of a series of tobacco products that were presented as much safer and

[24] Two American researchers Dr E. Cuyler Hammond and Daniel Horn from the Cancer Society conducted a study that surveyed 187,000 men between the ages of fifty and seventy. They concluded that there was a link between smoking, lung cancer, and heart diseases. The report of their findings was published at the American Medical Association conference in 1954 and drew a widespread response in the mass media such as *The Times*, *World Report* and *US News*. The report opened an avalanche of other global studies that vindicated their findings and put smoking under the spotlight of global public health discourse.

[25] Brandt, *The Cigarette Century*, 156.

[26] *The Times* produced an article entitled 'Beyond Any Doubt' in November 1953 that vouched for the credibility of scientific evidence linking cancer to smoking. *Reader's Digest* had circulated a piece titled 'Cancer by the Carton' in November 1952.

[27] 'US Cigarette Firms Are Worried about the Threat of a New Anti-smoking Campaign', *Rhodesia Herald*, 27 March 1962.

[28] Brandt, *The Cigarette Century*, 159–207. [29] Milov, *The Cigarette*, 111.

[30] 'US Cigarette Firms Are Worried about the Threat of a New Anti-smoking Campaign', *Rhodesia Herald*, 27 March 1962.

marketed as part of smokers' health protection.[31] These innovative products included filter-tipped and low tar and nicotine content cigarettes. By 1955, 257 filter brands were on the market in 29 different countries and 10 per cent of total cigarette sales in the USA were in filter brands as opposed to less than 1 per cent in 1951.[32] The output of filter-tipped cigarettes further rose by 130 per cent between 1956 and 1961 and accounted for 54 per cent of the market by 1961.[33] This upward trend continued such that by the mid-1970s filter-tipped production had a 90 per cent stake in the global cigarettes' market.[34]

However, in 1964, the American Surgeon General's report (commonly known as the Terry report) solidified the existing scientific medical consensus about smoking and health and ended many lingering doubts about the harmfulness of smoking.[35] The Surgeon General's report generated a key watershed moment towards the regulation of tobacco and the beginning of a global conversation towards universal tobacco control. The immediate effect of the report was a transient fall in cigarette sales in the USA by between 15 per cent and 20 per cent during the first half of 1964.[36] Ironically, in 1965, there was a huge boom of per capita cigarette consumption that generated the biggest ever profits for the industry.[37] Nevertheless, the report became an important document in the history of public health. Several regulations were enforced in several countries after the report. In the USA in 1965, the Cigarette Labelling and Advertising Act made health warning labels compulsory on cigarette packs.[38] In Britain and

[31] Benson, *Tobacco Capitalism*, 45.

[32] NAZ, F114/473/E.8/8/ (473) Tobacco economic section 1955–1957, Major Peter Spearing (Agricultural Adviser), Report No.40 of 1955, 26 September 1955, 1. Also see, Brandt, *The Cigarette Century*, 244.

[33] 'US Cigarette Firms Are Worried about the Threats of a New Anti-smoking Campaign', *Rhodesia Herald*, 27 March 1962.

[34] Brandt, *The Cigarette Century*, 244.

[35] United States Department of Health, Education and Welfare, 'Smoking and Health: Report of the Advisory Committee to the Surgeon General of the Public Health Service', Public Health Service Publication No. 1103, (Washington D.C., 1964). This report is also referred to as the 'Terry report' after the then Surgeon General of the United States Luther Leonidas Terry (1961–1965).

[36] Brandt, *The Cigarette Century*, 237.

[37] Milov, *The Cigarette*, 2.

[38] Brandt, *The Cigarette Century*, 256. However, the ambiguous language used on the cigarette packets to frame the health risk of smoking as a 'possibility' despite the Surgeon report having established that as a 'certainty' drew a lot of criticism to the Act. *The New York Times* described it as 'a shocking piece of special interest legislation.'

Canada, the government had already started circulating a report titled 'smoking and cancer' which warned the public on the dangers of smoking.[39] In Denmark, the Danish National Society for the Combating of Cancer issued a report urging the government to restrict or abolish all persons under sixteen years from smoking in public.[40] The 1972 Surgeon General's report referenced concerns over public exposure to air pollution from tobacco smoke and concluded that second-hand smokers were exposed to more concentrated levels of tobacco smoke pollutants such as tar, nicotine, carbon monoxide than smokers.[41] Although not yet confirmed as thoroughly scientific, this validation brought in a new public health narrative that focussed on non-smokers. By the mid-1970s, smoking was also becoming less socially acceptable in the USA.[42] Non-smokers inspired by the environmental crusades and the civil rights movement rallied under the banner of 'non-smokers' rights and succeeded in having smoking banned from several public places. In 1972, interstate buses were required to restrict smoking to the rear seats and coaches, parlour cars and dining cars were required to allocate space for non-smokers.[43] The non-smokers activism also prompted most airlines to allocate space for non-smoking passengers. In 1973, the Arizona State legislature introduced the first state-wide law in the USA restricting smoking in some public places such as elevators, libraries and theatres.[44] Subsequently, smoking rates across America had decreased to 37 per cent in 1970 from 42 per cent in 1965.[45]

Smoking and Public Health Narratives in Southern Rhodesia, 1953–1980

While this anti-smoking movement was galvanising support and dominating the conversations on public health and tobacco consumption in the USA and Global North, in Southern Rhodesia the conversations on the social controversies of tobacco and public health were dominated by the tobacco interests' groups. Already there was close cooperation and a cohesive relationship between the tobacco industry (farmers, merchants) and the state as they worked together to secure export

[39] 'US Cigarette Firms Are Worried about the Threats of a New Anti-smoking Campaign', *Rhodesia Herald*, 27 March 1962.
[40] Ibid. [41] Milov, *The Cigarette Century*, 192. [42] Ibid., 2.
[43] Ibid., 167. [44] Ibid., 196. [45] Ibid., 150.

markets abroad. This cooperation was conducted through the Tobacco Export Promotion Council of Rhodesia and Nyasaland (TEPCORN), an organisation established in 1958 to amalgamate the interests of growers, buyers and the state to secure tobacco markets abroad.[46] In 1961, TEPCORN was given statutory identity and played a bigger role in marketing, public relations and monitoring global smoking trends. Unsurprisingly, no one in Southern Rhodesia 'was too bothered by cigarettes' and despite the American Surgeon General's report on the effects of smoking, tobacco remained an important local crop.[47] Local tobacco interests' groups aided by state support spearheaded research to counter the scientific evidence linking smoking and lung cancer. In 1962, one of the tobacco merchants in Southern Rhodesia and a Russian expatriate, Elia Salzman put up £50,000 towards the construction of a tobacco research institute for the study of tobacco smoke to be placed at the disposal of the University College of Rhodesia and Nyasaland.[48] To show the close links between the tobacco industry and its political support, Prime Minister of the Federation of Rhodesia and Nyasaland Sir Roy Welensky was given the honour of full life patronage of the Tobacco Institute.[49] Salzman vociferously criticised the global scientific reports linking smoking and lung cancer as 'vicious propaganda' aimed at discrediting the industry and protecting interests in the oil and motor industries.[50] He further claimed cancer occurred more frequently in urban areas with heavy concentration of traffic with diesel and ordinary motor pollution.[51]

The tobacco growers' interests through RTA were also part of the public relations infrastructure of the industry. In 1962, the growers association proclaimed confidently that the attitude of the country towards smoking was supposed to be positive as 'exhortation, curbing cigarette publicity or fear campaigns' were not going to have any lasting effect on the cigarette smoking habit.[52] The association declared that the only realistic strategy for the Rhodesian tobacco industry was to passionately embrace smoking as a 'pleasant and permanent worldwide practice' while researching on ways through which lung cancer could be

[46] For a reading on TEPCOR's core business see, Ncube, 'Colonial Zimbabwe Tobacco Industry', 82–89.
[47] Godwin and Hancock, *Rhodesians Never Die*, 33.
[48] '£50,000 Tobacco Institute for Salisbury', *Rhodesia Herald*, 29 March 1962.
[49] Ibid. [50] Ibid. [51] Ibid.
[52] 'Rhodesia Should Help Fight Cancer', *Rhodesia Herald*, 23 March 1962.

curbed.[53] This endeavour, the association reckoned, would make the tobacco industry in Southern Rhodesia gain both 'morally and practically'.[54] This approach of deflecting the risk of tobacco into a factor that could be managed through technology and scientific research was one of the strategies used by the tobacco industry globally to avoid the public health backlash.[55]

The state bureaucracy in Southern Rhodesia also cooperated in the tobacco industry's publicity campaigns to sanitise tobacco as a harmless product. In 1964, while responding to the Surgeon General's report, the Southern Rhodesia Secretary for Health Dr. H. M Webster noted that Rhodesian tobaccos contained less carcinogenic substances than tobacco smoked in other parts of the world.[56] He pointed to the low cancer death rates recorded in Southern Rhodesia (23 deaths per 100,00) as compared to Britain's (50 deaths per 100,000) as vindicating his conclusions that the causes of cancer could be linked to the effects on health of tobacco grown in other parts of the world.[57] He argued:

> It is just not good enough to say that tobacco is responsible for lung cancer. For example, tobacco grown in one part of the world may produce an entirely different effect on health than tobacco grown in another part of the world. People in Southern Rhodesia and south of the Limpopo are relatively heavier smokers, yet the incidence of lung cancer amongst them is much smaller than in Britain or the UK. An investigation on the question of whether Rhodesian or South African tobaccos contain less cancer producing substances than American tobacco should produce more interesting results particularly in view of the heavy consumption of American tobaccos in the northern hemisphere.

He concluded that in Southern Rhodesia, the incidences of lung cancer were higher in urban areas than in rural areas and therefore air pollution was more suspect than tobacco. Another research in Rustenburg South Africa, sponsored by a tobacco firm concluded that air pollution was the main cause of the disease.[58] The research noted that in Rustenburg

[53] Ibid. [54] Ibid.

[55] This approach involved replacing the object of eliminating tobacco with the 'biopolitical goal' of enhancing the probabilities of life. See Benson, *Tobacco Capitalism*, 42.

[56] 'Southern Rhodesia Lung Cancer Is Half That of Britain', *Rhodesia Herald*, 14 January 1964.

[57] Ibid.

[58] 'Air Pollution Has Main Cancer Danger, Says Tobacco Men' *Rhodesia Herald*, 14 January 1964.

where most of South Africa's tobacco was grown there was not even a single case of cancer per year. Yet in Bloemfontein, an average of four Europeans died annually because of lung cancer and in highly industrialised Durban the rate was forty-eight deaths per year. This was attributed to more concentrated levels of pollution in Durban. In 1963, the senior chemist of the Tobacco Research Board (TRB) Dr G. H. Wiltshire concluded that Rhodesian leaf lacked carcinogenic properties when compared to American tobaccos.[59] Interestingly, scientific studies in Southern Rhodesia at the time revealed a causal relationship between *Carcinoma of the Bronchus* and smoking. Research on the smoking habits of Rhodesian African males in 1968 showed that 87.5 per cent of patients with lung cancer were cigarette smokers.[60] The study ruled out atmospheric pollution as a causative factor in the aetiology of cancer amongst Rhodesian Africans. However, despite this, Southern Rhodesia remained fixated on protecting the interest of its national tobacco industry by funding research that emphasised the uniqueness of Rhodesian tobacco brands as superior and harmless when compared to other global brands.

In June 1971, the *Rhodesian Tobacco Journal* – a tobacco farmers' mouthpiece – dismissed the new evidence based on experiments on dogs and chimpanzees that had confirmed smoking caused cancer.[61] In 1975, the Bulawayo City Council banned smoking in the cinemas to conform to the global norms of protecting non-smokers' rights and harm from second-hand smoke. However, the move was met with a huge public backlash.[62] The tobacco industry successfully mobilised thousands of signatures across all races to mount a formidable petition in opposition. Subsequently, when legislator Hilary Squires moved a motion in the legislative assembly for the prohibition of smoking in confined public places to reduce the risk of second-hand smoke to non-smokers, he was opposed on grounds that the cinema industry would lose money.[63] One of the legislators who spoke against the motion and hailed from a tobacco-growing constituency, Ian Sanders argued that the evidence

59 'Rhodesia and USA Virginia Tobaccos: What Chemical Analysis Reveal', *Tobacco Forum of Rhodesia and Nyasaland*, August 1963.

60 M. Gelfand, A. Graham and E. Lightman, 'Carcinoma of the Bronchus and the Smoking Habits of Rhodesian Africans', *British Medical Journal*, 3, 5616 (1968), 468–469.

61 *Rhodesian Tobacco Journal*, June 1971.

62 Godwin and Hancock, *Rhodesians Never Die*, 139–140.

63 Ibid., 140.

by WHO on smoking and cancer was based on 'foreign tobacco' and not Rhodesian tobacco, which he vouched was 'entirely safe for people to smoke'.[64] The motion was eventually passed in Parliament – but was ignored by cabinet.[65]

The Post-colonial State, Contemporary Public Health and Tobacco-Control Narratives, 1980–2020

The close relationship between the state and the tobacco industry in Southern Rhodesia continued into the post-colonial period after the country gained independence in 1980. During the 1980s most African countries lacked the infrastructure for government-backed public health and anti-smoking campaigns.[66] Government-backed anti-smoking campaigns found in the west were not found in Africa where smoking was relatively 'tolerated'.[67] As a result there was a rise in tobacco use that prompted concerns from global public health officials that Africa would be home for the next tobacco epidemic. While cigarette consumption between 1979 and 1984 had been lower in Britain, America, France and Germany, it had risen by 17 per cent during the same period in Africa compelling WHO to prognosticate that smoking diseases would appear in the third world before communicable diseases.[68] By the early

64 Ibid.

65 From the 1970s the debates on smoking and public health broadened from the personal health impact to the social impact as a result of pollution caused by second-hand smoke to non-smokers. Cigarette smoke came to be viewed as an environmental toxin affecting innocent victims. The impact of smoking on non-smokers transformed the regulation and cultural perception of the cigarette in ways which led to smoking prohibitions in public places as well as tobacco advertising in the public media. In April 1970, the United States Congress passed a law, the Public Health Cigarette Smoking Act that outlawed cigarette advertising on the radio and television. From 1971 several airlines had put up segregated sections for smokers and non-smokers. In 1990 legislation was introduced to ban smoking aboard all domestic flights in the USA and in 1992 the Environmental Protection Agency (EPA) classified tobacco smoke as group A carcinogen, opening floodgates for its ban at the workplace.

66 S. Chapman et al., 'Smoking Control in Africa: Problems and Prospects', *Health Policy and Planning*, 13, (1986), 222–231.

67 In 1984, while addressing the World Tobacco Symposium Secretary General of the International Tobacco Information Centre (INFOTAB) a public relations machinery of the world tobacco industry named Africa as the only continent where governments and public opinion tolerated smoking.

68 'Smoking Control Strategies in Developing Countries', Report of a WHO Expert Committee, (Geneva, 1983), 7.

1980s incidences of tobacco-related diseases in Africa were on the increase. Lung cancer increased six-fold and five-fold amongst men and women respectively between 1971 and 1982 in Natal, South Africa.[69] Studies in southern Africa also revealed higher lung cancer incidences amongst smokers. Retrospective research in 1994 on the incidences of cancer in Southern Rhodesia between 1963 and 1977 identified tobacco use as associated with increased risk of lung cancer and oesophagus cancer amongst Africans.[70] Incidences of oesophageal cancer amongst blacks were also amongst the highest in the world in Zimbabwe and South Africa during the 1980s.[71]

In Zimbabwe, tobacco consumption rose from 2.4 billion cigarettes to 2.7 billion cigarettes between 1979 and 1981.[72] This corresponded with a massive growth of the tobacco export economy. In 1982, Zimbabwe's flue-cured tobacco exports accounted for 14 per cent of total global export volumes, third to only USA and Brazil.[73] By 1983, tobacco provided 23.2 per cent of all export earnings.[74] Effectively, this placed tobacco interests groups at the centre of policy formulation on the tobacco smoking and public health agenda in Zimbabwe. In 1984, the Zimbabwe Tobacco Association (ZTA) in cahoots with other five tobacco-producing countries formed the International Tobacco Growers Association (ITGA) a lobby group to push for continued tobacco production and use in the third word and to combat what it considered hostile WHO propaganda against tobacco multinational corporations.[75] In 1993 the Chairman of the Zimbabwe TRB and former Chairman of ITGA agreed to involve the Zimbabwean tobacco industry in the wars to counter the anti-smoking lobbies.[76] Beyond its

69 A. Taha and K. Ball, 'Smoking in Africa: The Coming Epidemic', *World Smoking Health*, 7, 2 (1982), 25–30.

70 D. M. Parkin et al., 'Cancer Patterns and Risk Factors in the African Population of Southwestern Zimbabwe, 1963-197', *Cancer Epidemioliogy Biomarkers Prevention*, 3 (1994), 537–547.

71 Taha and Ball, 'Smoking in Africa', 25–30.

72 Chapman, 'Smoking Control in Africa', 222–231.

73 'The Economic Significance of Tobacco', Food and Agricultural Organisation, (FAO, Rome, 1983).

74 Tobacco and its Economic Contribution to Zimbabwe, *Tobacco International*, 21 September 1984: 18–26.

75 See, www.industrydocuments.ucsf.edu/tobacco/docs/#id=pxxh0203, accessed on 15 August 2020.

76 G. Woelk, S. Mtisi, J. P. Vaughan, 'Prospects for Tobacco Control in Zimbabwe: A Historical Perspective', *Health Policy*, 57, 3 (2001), 179–192.

international clout in the global tobacco wars, the ZTA had significant leverage and influence in the making of national tobacco policy.

During the 1990s global concerns about environmental tobacco, tobacco pollution and the effects of second-hand smoke on non-smokers increased, creating negative publicity on tobacco production and threatening viability of the Zimbabwean tobacco industry. The state in Zimbabwe strongly sided with the tobacco industry to counter proposals by WHO for a multilateral treaty to curb production, consumption and distribution of tobacco in all its forms. In 1994, while addressing ZTA, President Robert Mugabe retorted rhetorically that WHO had no business trying to regulate tobacco smoking as this was a matter of personal choice.[77] He extoled Zimbabwe tobacco as being of 'high quality' and viscerally concluded that more people in the country died from alcohol consumption rather than cancer:

> I have always argued that WHO has got its priorities wrong. I may be wrong, but I take my own country as an example. I do not know how many people have died of nicotine here, lung cancer, but I know that very many more, almost on a weekly basis, have died of too much alcohol.[78]

The Zimbabwean government further insisted that revenue from tobacco taxes and levies was funding the health sector whose condition would deteriorate if WHO tobacco regulations and proposals from the anti-tobacco lobby were to be implemented.[79] The Minister of Health Dr Timothy Stamps argued that tobacco brought in a lot of money into the country which sustained the health ministry, and banning tobacco would be like 'cutting our own throat'.[80] However, as a token of acquiescence to the new cigarette pollution concerns to non-smokers, smoking was banned in hospitals and health clinics, theatres, cinemas, supermarkets, local flights and most public transport in 1992.[81] ZTA and other stakeholders in the industry cited that the WHO tobacco-control proposal would imperil the country's economy and harm the tobacco industry. In 1996, out of every hundred people in Zimbabwe six depended on the tobacco industry for their livelihood, out of every

[77] 'Leave It to the Individual – Mugabe', *Tobacco News*, October 1994.
[78] Ibid.
[79] 'Tobacco Levy Boost Ailing Health Sector', *The Herald*, 4 July 1998.
[80] 'Despite Lobby Tobacco Still the Biggest Forex Earner', *The Herald*, 15 January 1998.
[81] Woelk et al., 'Prospects for Tobacco Control in Zimbabwe', 179–192.

hundred workers, twelve were employed in the tobacco industry and out of every Z$100 (US$9.13) non-gold exports Z$20 dollars (US$1.82) came from the sale of tobacco.[82] In 1996, the government introduced a 10 per cent tobacco levy. A sum of Z$561(US$61,445,783) million was subsequently raised from the levy and the government claimed that the bulk of the revenue had been disbursed towards the Ministry of Health's budget allocation.[83] A 1999 World Bank report pointed out that Zimbabwe was one of the countries that had much to lose from curbing the tobacco epidemic as its economy strongly relied on the fortunes of the tobacco industry.[84] By 2000 tobacco contributed 38 per cent to the country's physical trade, US$663 million in export earnings, and was the single largest employer of labour accounting for 11.3 per cent of all formal employees.[85] The ZTA noted that the proposed tobacco-control convention would be an unprecedented challenge to the tobacco industry's 'freedom to continue doing business'.[86] The association argued that the voice of tobacco growers and the economic impact of the convention to national economies had received little attention from WHO and the Free Tobacco Initiative (FTI). The Zimbabwean delegation to the WHO public hearings on the convention in Geneva led by Ambassador Chidyausiku joined the stance of other tobacco-producing countries such as Malawi, China, Brazil and Argentina that called for tobacco control to seriously take into account the economies of affected countries.[87] BAT- Zimbabwe added its weight to the lobby against WHO convention by saying that the framework was fundamentally flawed and driven by a coalition of anti-tobacco advocates in violation of the principles of good public policy formulation and it undermined governments' self-determination.[88] A visiting European cigarettes manufacturing official at the ZTA congress in 1996 Mr John Lepere criticised the WHO propaganda campaign on the cigarette.[89] The Chief

[82] 'The Late 20th Century Tobacco Controversy', *The Herald*, 19 July 1996.
[83] 'Tobacco Levy Boosts Ailing Health Sector', *The Herald*, 4 July 1998.
[84] World Bank, 'Curbing the Tobacco Epidemic: Governments and the Economics of Tobacco Control', Washington DC, 1999.
[85] 'Zim Protests at WHO Tobacco Convention' *The Herald*, 7 April 2000.
[86] 'Zimbabwe Tobacco Industry Faces New Threat From WHO', *The Herald*, 17 March 2000.
[87] 'Zim Protests at WHO Tobacco Convention' *The Herald*, 7 April 2000.
[88] 'WHO Framework Convention for Tobacco Control Fundamentally Flawed', *BAT Supplement Independent Extra*, 28 July 2000.
[89] 'The Late 20th Century Tobacco Controversy', *The Herald*, 19 July 1996.

Executive of the TIRC claimed WHO had been hijacked by anti-tobacco lobbyist and that the scientific evidence on the harmful effects of passive smoking on non-smokers was not conclusive.[90]

In 2005, the Framework Convention on Tobacco Control (FCTC) came into effect. The convention obligated members to put in place tobacco-control measures that reduced demand and supply for tobacco products.[91] These included protection of exposure from tobacco smoke, regulation of contents of tobacco products, packaging and labelling, and eliminating trade in illicit cigarettes. Zimbabwe refused to accede to the convention until 2014. The result has been very weak tobacco-control regulation in the country and government widespread support for the tobacco industry. Following the Fast-Track Land Reform Program in 2000 the state has taken a more active interest in tobacco farming which has become an arena for nationalist politics and black empowerment. In 2015, President Mugabe publicly gloated that western isolation and sanctions on the Zimbabwean economy had resulted in a shift of the tobacco market to China where the Chinese habit of over indulgence in smoking had been a blessing to the Zimbabwean tobacco industry.[92] Sadly, tobacco-related diseases are one of the major cause of deaths amongst the Chinese, killing 500,000 people in 1996 and projected to kill 2,000,000 people between the ages of thirty-five and sixty-nine by 2025.[93] Mugabe further made fun of tobacco-control policies by erroneously pointing out that the organisation advised people 'against over-smoking, and not against growing the crop', adding that if people over-smoked Zimbabwe would keep on growing more tobacco to sustain the habit.[94]

Zimbabwe has one of the lowest cigarette excise duties in Africa. Its excise duty at 40 per cent is way lower than the FCTC recommended rate of 75–80 per cent for demand reduction.[95] Consequently, cigarettes

90 Ibid.

91 World Health Organization Framework Convention on Tobacco Control (Geneva, 2003).

92 'Zimbabwe grows tobacco for China', www.youtube.com/watch?v=EHPmtI8VJYk, accessed on 22 October 2019.

93 Brandt, *The Cigarette Century*, 454.

94 'Zimbabwe Grows Tobacco for China'. www.youtube.com/watch?v=EHPmtI8VJYk, accessed on 22 October 2019.

95 See I. Madanhire and C. Mbohwa, Impact of Smoking in a Tobacco-Growing Developing Country: A Review, Available on http://dx.doi.org/10.5772/intechopen.85959, accessed 14 August 2020.

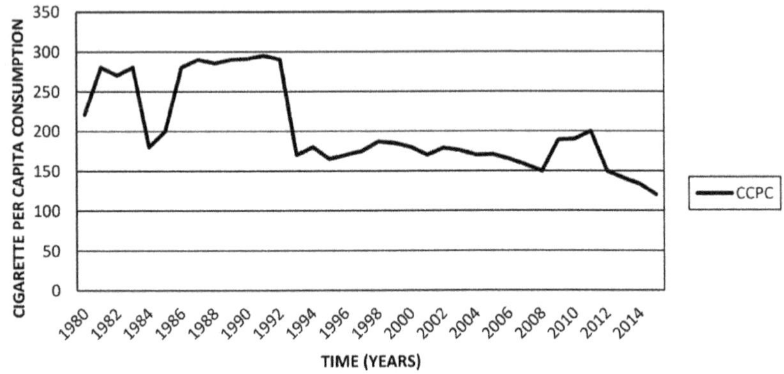

Figure 6.1 Cigarette consumption per capita in Zimbabwe, 1980–2015
Source: Zimbabwe Statistical Services, 2015.

are cheaper, readily available and smoking is prevalent. Also, there is a huge amount of coarse cured leaf from tobacco farms (*chimonera*) readily available for free and sometimes sold on the informal market way more cheaply. In 2014, Zimbabwe's biggest cigarette manufacturers British American Tobacco (BAT)-Zimbabwe and Savanna Tobacco produced 3 billion cigarettes for the local market which translates to 10 million cigarettes per day.[96] Although cigarette consumption per capita in Zimbabwe has decreased significantly from 1980 as shown by Figure 6.1, there is still a high prevalence of smoking.

In 2006, prevalence of tobacco use in the country amongst adults between the ages of 15–49 years was 21.3 per cent among men and 0.4 per cent amongst females.[97] Estimates by the International Tobacco Atlas in 2016 established that there were 970,000 adult smokers, 6,000 child smokers and 8,300 deaths per year from tobacco-related causes.[98] The prevalence amongst adult males was 30.7 per cent. Although the prevalence of smoking has been declining gradually, there has been a worrying increase in the rate of underage smoking

[96] 'Tobacco Use in Spotlight as Companies Target Africa', Available at www.voazimbabwe.com/a/zimbabwe-cigarette-smoking/2860085.html, accessed on 16 August 2020.

[97] Report Card on the WHO Framework Convention for Tobacco Control for Zimbabwe (2006), Available on www.afro.who.int/sites/default/files/2017-09/Zimbabwe_report_card_0.pdf, accessed on 10 August 2020.

[98] See https://tobaccoatlas.org/country/zimbabwe/.

and tobacco use amongst youths.[99] A WHO survey in 2015 revealed that 20 per cent of youths between the ages of thirteen and fifteen were smokers; of these 12.5 per cent began smoking from as early as seven years.[100] Tobacco-control initiatives to reduce smoking amongst school children and young people have not been successful because of lack of information on the dangers of tobacco. This has raised concerns amongst the country's public health experts on the social and economic burden of illnesses and negative lifestyles. The Minister of Health pointed out in 2016 that while tobacco made huge financial contributions to the economy, 'it was harmful to health' as the increasing prevalence of tobacco use in the country was contributing to a rise in non-communicable diseases and placing a burden on the already collapsing public health facilities.[101] The economic crisis in the country and rising rates of youth unemployment since 2000 has further exacerbated the tobacco epidemic amongst youths who have been forced into smoking and drugs.[102] Exposure to environmental tobacco is also high as the country does not enforce the 100 per cent smoke-free policy. The 2013–2017 National Cancer Prevention and Control Strategy for Zimbabwe pointed out that 24.7 per cent of youth in the country were exposed to second-hand smoke.[103] It further expressed dismay on the stranglehold that powerful commercial tobacco production, manufacturing and distribution companies had in exploiting people's dependency on tobacco. Although the exact net social impact of increasing

[99] For detailed discussions on the smoking trends and prevalence amongst the youths in Zimbabwe see, UNICEF Report, 'Results on the Global Tobacco Youth Survey in Zimbabwe, Harare and Manicaland Regions, 1999–2000'; T. Bandason and S. Rukasaniko, 'Prevalence and Associated Factors of Smoking among Secondary School Students in Harare Zimbabwe', *Tobacco Induced Diseases*, 8,12 (2010), 1–9.

[100] 'Underage Smoking Zimbabwe's New Headache', Available at www.aa.com.tr/en/africa/underage-smoking-zimbabwe-s-new-headache/1859629, accessed on 20 August 2020.

[101] 'Schools Tobacco Shocker as 1 in 5 Pupils Smoke, Says Health Minister', available at www.herald.co.zw/schools-tobacco-shocker-1-in-5-pupils-smokes-says-health-minister/, accessed 13 August 2021.

[102] 'Waking up to Teenage Smoking in Zimbabwe', Available at www.dw.com/en/waking-up-to-teenage-smoking-in-zimbabwe/a-19026965, accessed on 16 August 2020.

[103] Ministry of Health and Child Welfare, 'The National Cancer Prevention And Control Strategy For Zimbabwe , 2013–2017', 21, Available at www.iccp-portal.org/sites/default/files/plans/CANCER%20STRATEGY%20FINAL%202013%202017.pdf, accessed 25 August 2020.

tobacco consumption amongst youths and adults cannot be ascertained by existing scientific data, the social impact to the collapsing health care infrastructure is palpable. Decreasing health expenditure because of a shrinking economy has weakened the capacity of health institutions in the country to cure such tobacco-related diseases as cancer. In April 2022, there were reports that the country's public health institutions did not have a single functioning cancer treatment machine.[104]

The opaque regulation of the Zimbabwe tobacco industry and its links to institutions of state power has perpetuated illicit trafficking and trade by big tobacco companies that have political connections. Zimbabwean cigarette manufacturers have been implicated in the illicit trade of tobacco and linked to nefarious criminal activities, organised crime, patronage politics and smuggling. Several Zimbabwean tobacco companies have been fingered in a multi-million-Rand cigarette smuggling syndicate into neighbouring South Africa. This has contributed to corruption, tax evasion, organised crime and the erosion of state institutions in both countries.[105] Zimbabwean-manufactured cigarettes are estimated to constitute 57 per cent of the illicit tobacco trade in South Africa.[106] One of the Zimbabwean cigarette companies identified in this scam, Savanna Tobacco, is owned by Adam Molai who is married to former President Mugabe's niece; and the company is alleged to have channelled rents towards the Mugabe regime.[107] It is also alleged that proceeds from illicit tobacco smuggling could have funded Mugabe's state machinery during much of the 'crisis years.' Another notorious cigarette smuggler is the late John Bredenkamp, politically connected to the ZANU PF ruling party in Zimbabwe, an arms dealer with a murky history that involves sanctions-busting for the Rhodesian regime, looting diamonds during the Second Congo War and supporting the Zimbabwean coup in November 2017.[108] Bredenkamp's company

[104] 'Chin'ono sparks debate on state of cancer treatment in Zimbabwe', available at https://zero.pindula.co.zw/chinono-sparks-debate-on-state-of-cancer-treatment-in-zimbabwe/ , accessed on 14 April 2022.

[105] S. Hayson, 'The Illicit Tobacco Trade in Zimbabwe and South Africa: Impacts and Solutions', Working Paper, Atlantic Council, March 2019, 5–8.

[106] See, 'The illicit tobacco trade in Zimbabwe and South Africa', Available at www.atlanticcouncil.org/in-depth-research-reports/issue-brief/the-illicit-tobacco-trade-in-zimbabwe-and-south-africa/, accessed on 12 August 2020.

[107] Hayson, 'The Illicit Tobacco Trade', 5–8.

[108] J. Van Loggerenberg, *Tobacco Wars: Inside the Spy Games and Dirty Tricks of Southern Africa's Cigarette Trade* (Cape Town, 2019), 113–117.

Masters International which manufactures the Mega brand of cigarettes was busted in South Africa in 2006 for illicit trade in tobacco and subsequently liquidated.[109] The illicit cigarettes trade in both South Africa and Zimbabwe has also created a criminal underworld involving state officials in corrupt scams benefitting tobacco co-operations and corrupting state institutions. TIRC estimates that the illicit cigarette trade in South Africa cost the country more than 48 billion Rands (US$3,1 billion) in lost taxes between 2018 and 2019.[110] In 2021, an investigative report by a credible BBC source revealed that BAT negotiated for political settlements between US$300,000 and USD$500,000 to bribe the ruling ZANU PF party towards the contested 2013 harmonised general elections.[111] The company also allegedly bribed custom officials, police officers and the Forensic Security Services (FSS) to illegally spy on their rivals.[112]

Beyond the political and economic impact, tobacco smuggling has also been identified as a public health issue by WHO.[113] Illicit cigarette trade brings in cheaper and more affordable tobacco into the market, stimulating consumption and increasing the rate of tobacco-related diseases. In March 2020, the South African government imposed a covid-19 lockdown regulation banning the sale of cigarettes. Subsequently, there was a heavy influx of smuggled tobacco products from Zimbabwe through the Beitbridge–Musina border.[114] In September 2020, the Free Trade Independent Tobacco Association (FITA) a group of South African cigarette manufacturers ejected Zimbabwean Golden Leaf Tobacco after accusations of illicit trading in cigarettes.[115] The tax revenue flows to government coffers from

[109] Ibid., 117.

[110] 'South Africa tobacco ban greeted with cigarette smuggling boom', Available on www.theguardian.com/global-development/2020/jun/26/south-africa-tobacco-ban-greeted-with-cigarette-smuggling-boom, accessed on 16 August 2020.

[111] 'British American Tobacco negotiated bribe for Mugabe, new evidence suggest', available at www.bbc.com/news/world-58517339, accessed 5 January 2022.

[112] Ibid. [113] See WHO, 'Tobacco and Poverty', 7.

[114] 'South Africa's tobacco ban greeted with cigarette smuggling boom', available at www.theguardian.com/global-development/2020/jun/26/south-africa-tobacco-ban-greeted-with-cigarette-smuggling-boom, accessed 18 November 2020.

[115] 'Tobacco group ejects Zimbabwe's Golden Leaf after accusations of dealing in illicit trade', available at www.news24.com/fin24/Companies/Agribusiness/tobacco-group-ejects-zimbabwes-gold-leaf-after-accusations-of-dealing-in-illicit-trade-20200929, accessed 18 November 2020.

tobacco companies and cigarette sales has also restrained the pursuit of much enthusiastic tobacco-control governance in the country. Big multinational tobacco companies such as BAT make immense financial contributions to the fiscus. In 2021, for instance, BAT more than doubled its tax remittances to the Zimbabwean government to ZWL 2.1 billion (US$19,3337,010) after a 1327 per cent growth and an after-tax profit of ZWL 1.4 billion (US$12,891,340).[116]

New Farming Landscapes and New Livelihoods? Tobacco Farming in Post-colonial and Post–Land Reform Zimbabwe, 1980–2020

At independence in 1980, the post-colonial state in Zimbabwe inherited a tobacco-farming landscape dominated by white commercial farmers and a handful of marginal African producers as discussed in Chapter 4. However, after independence the post-colonial government initiated concerted efforts to encourage African participation in tobacco cultivation as one of the ways to develop the rural areas and empower economically marginalised rural communities.[117] Tobacco training and settlement schemes were set up for African farmers by the state with assistance from tobacco merchants and ZTA.[118] These new farming settlement schemes called 'family farm units' based on the allocation of land to African families for production of Burley tobacco and maize were structured along the Malawian peasant tobacco-farming model.[119] The most famous of these formative tobacco farm settlements in post-colonial Zimbabwe was the Tabex scheme set up in Mount Darwin district, Mashonaland Central province in 1981. The scheme initially resettled 100 African peasants and former commercial farm labourers for tobacco production.[120] Nevertheless, the post-colonial government inherited colonial prejudices concerning the types

[116] 'BAT pours 2 billion in taxes', available at www.newsday.co.zw/2022/04/bat-pours-21bn-in-taxes/ , accessed 10 April 2022.

[117] See, D. Magadlela, 'A Smoky Affair: Challenges Facing Some Small-Holder Burley Tobacco Producers in Zimbabwe', *Zambezia*, XXIV, i (1997), 13–30; 'Spread Tobacco Farming to Rural Areas', *Sunday Mail*, 5 July 1981; 'Move into Cash Crops, Kangai Tells Peasants', *The Herald*, 16 July 1981.

[118] The two most important tobacco merchants in this regard were Tabex and Carrington Michaux Tobacco Private Limited.

[119] 'Tobacco Plan for Settlers', *The Herald*, 16 May 1981.

[120] 'Peasants Start a New Life at Model Scheme', *The Herald*, 27 February 1982.

of tobacco most suitable for African cultivation and touted Burley and Turkish as 'ideally suited' for small-scale production because of their simpler cultivation management as compared to flue-cured tobacco. Thus, much of the state's agricultural and technical assistance to African tobacco farmers through the department of Agricultural Technical and Extension Services (Agritex) in the communal and resettlement areas emphasised the promotion of Turkish and Burley.[121] By 1983, 3,000 African farmers in the communal areas were participating in the cultivation of Burley tobacco. As a result, national Burley output more than doubled from 2 million kilograms during the 1980/1981 season to 5 million kilograms in 1982/1983.[122] The entry of African farmers to Burley production after independence grew steadily such that by 1995, the number of African Burley farmers had surpassed 7,000.[123]

Meanwhile, in the much drier parts of the country such as Gutu, Murehwa, Mutoko, Nyanga, Zvimba, Makoni, Kwekwe, Chivhu and Bikita, the post-colonial government resurrected the colonial Turkish tobacco drive to support local Turkish tobacco demand for cigarette manufacturing.[124] Turkish was envisaged as the 'backbone of the communal farmers' cash income' bringing in gross returns of Z$211–Z$292 (US$220–US$304) as compared to Z$172 (US$179), Z$12 (US$12,50), Z$9 (US$9,38) and Z$17 (US$17,70) for maize, groundnuts, rapoko and *nyimo* respectively.[125] From around 1995, however, prices of Burley tobacco tumbled, forcing many African farmers to switch to flue-cured tobacco.[126] Concurrently, ZTA and Farmers Development Trust (FDT) had begun a tenant scheme in the 1990s to stimulate African smallholder production of flue-cured tobacco.[127] This model to train African farmers into small-scale commercial farmers was one of the biggest influences towards the accelerated production of flue-cured tobacco by African farmers in resettlements and communal areas after independence. The FDT targeted technological empowerment of previously marginalised African smallholder producers into commercial

121 Agritex replaced the colonial Department of conservation and extension (Conex) at independence in 1980.
122 'Burley's Purse Bursting out', *The Herald*, 21 January 1983.
123 *The Herald*, 14 September 1995.
124 'Oriental Good as Cash Crop for Peasants', *The Herald*, 30 December 1983.
125 Ibid.
126 'Burley Tobacco Growers Shift to Flue-Cured', *The Herald*, 10 November 1995.
127 'Small Holder Tobacco Farmers Impress', *Financial Gazette*, 16 June 1996.

farmers through collaborative effort harnessing government, Commercial Farmers Union (CFU), Tobacco Trade Association (TTA) and ZTA. Their programme included courses in sustainable agricultural management at their training centres, provision of inputs and facilitating the access to financial resources and markets. During the 1996 season, fifty-eight African farmers who had graduated under the programme received total income of Z$90 million (US$2,484,129) after selling their flue-cured tobacco.[128] The expansion of African smallholder flue-cured tobacco production extended to other areas so that by 1998, there were 3,481 African flue-cured farmers in the communal areas.[129] Nevertheless the number of African commercial farmers remained strongly subdued because of prohibitive land costs and high interest loans from banks. Subsequently, only 450 African farmers had managed to break into commercial tobacco farming by 1999 while the rest of the 3,500 African producers of flue-cured tobacco were smallholder farmers in communal and resettlement areas.[130]

Also, between 1980 and 2000 the white commercial tobacco-farming sector had further intensified the diversification of their farm systems to include other crops such as wheat, maize, soya beans, groundnuts and horticultural products. From the mid-1990s most of the white tobacco farms had fully diversified into high value crops such as export roses and horticultural enterprises so that 80 per cent of all horticultural exports were now grown on tobacco farms.[131] Although tobacco was the backbone of most white commercial farms, its coverage on land use was modest constituting only 2.3 per cent of the total area on large-scale farmland as 86.4 per cent of the land was not cultivated and allocated towards beef production for the important European export market.[132] There was also extensive investment in farmland and water conservation, building of dams, installation of

[128] Ibid.

[129] 'Flue-Cured Tobacco Takes Giant Leap into Communal Areas', *The Herald*, 30 January 1998.

[130] 'Woes Threaten Small Scale Tobacco Farmers' Production', *The Herald*, 6 January 1998; The Herald, 27 November 1999.

[131] J. C. Keyser, 'Crop Substitution and Alternative Crops for Tobacco', Study conducted as a technical document for the First Meeting of the Ad Hoc Study Group on Alternative Crops Established by the Conference of the Parties to the WHO Framework Convention on Tobacco Control, February 2007, 21.

[132] I. Scoones et al., 'Tobacco, Contract Farming and Agrarian Change in Zimbabwe', *Journal of Agrarian Change*, 18,1 (2018), 22–42.

irrigation infrastructure and the establishment of nature-based tourist landscapes on tobacco farms.[133] By the year 2000, white commercial tobacco farms accounted for 87 per cent of the area planted to tobacco in Zimbabwe and 95 per cent of the total harvested crop.[134]

In 2000, the government of Zimbabwe implemented the Fast-Track Land Reform Program (FTLRP) which deracialised the country's land ownership structure and resolved the long-standing and institutionalised historical agrarian inequalities. The land reform transferred over 10 million hectares of land from white commercial farmers to 146,000 hitherto landless black smallholder farmers.[135] It was perhaps the biggest redistributive agrarian revolution in the history of post-colonial Africa with far-reaching effects on the agrarian structure, agrarian relations and the whole edifice of the country's agricultural super structure and the political economy. The land reform dismantled much of the tobacco-farming landscapes dominated by 2,000 large-scale white commercial farms and supplanted them with black smallholder farmers in the newly established resettlement farms and traditional communal areas. Predictably, the immediate result of this land transfer was a drop in tobacco output as the more capitalised white commercial sector collapsed. However, there was a post–land reform tobacco boom for black indigenous smallholder farmers as many started growing tobacco leading to the 'peasantisation' of tobacco production.[136] Also, many smallholder farmers switched from cotton and maize to tobacco as a result of this boom and the subsequent higher prices paid to tobacco.[137] The post–land reform tobacco boom generated new livelihoods, accumulations patterns and new relations of productions and has been hailed as one of the biggest success stories of smallholder agrarian transitions in Africa. It created opportunities for accumulation from below as peasant growers earned tobacco cash incomes and

[133] D. M. Hughes, 'Farms Dams, Conservation, and Whiteness in Zimbabwe', *American Ethnologist*, 33, 2 (2006), 269–287.

[134] Keyser, 'Crop Substitution', 20.

[135] S. Moyo, 'Three Decades of Agrarian Reform in Zimbabwe', *The Journal of Peasant Studies*, 38, 3 (2011), 493–531.

[136] See, Y. Sakata, 'Reactions of Peasants to Global Capital in Zimbabwe: A Case Study of Tobacco Contract Farming in Mashonaland East Province', in H. Chitonge and Y. Mine (eds.), *Land, the State and the Unfinished Decolonization Project in Africa* (Bamenda, 2019).

[137] *The Herald*, 14 March 2014.

invested in tractors, cars, trucks, motor bikes, oxcarts, water pumps, solar panels and other household goods.[138]

The boom was accompanied with a phenomenal rise in the numbers of flue-cured tobacco farmers from 8,500 in 2000 to 31,700 in 2005, then to 106,372 in 2014 and 140,895 in 2018.[139] In particular, the contribution of communal area farmers and smallholder farmers has by far outstripped output from the commercial sector contributing 91 per cent to the 2018 national harvest.[140] Export earnings from tobacco has fluctuated across the years from an all-time low of USD$157 million in 2008 to US$847 million during the 2017 season, US$908 million in 2018 and US$782 million in 2020 as shown on Table 6.1.[141] Much of the tobacco grown in Zimbabwe is exported to China. China is the biggest importer of Zimbabwean tobacco accounting for 33 per cent of total exports in 2019.[142] Other prominent export destinations include Belgium, South Africa, United Arab Emirates and Indonesia.[143]

Although the land reform signalled a boom for smallholder tobacco production in Zimbabwe, the period after 2000 was accompanied by economic collapse, capital flight and the imposition of economic sanctions on the country by the West for violation of human rights and the political violence that had accompanied the Land Reform Program.[144] The tobacco sector was hit hard as the financial infrastructure for funding commercial production fell apart at a time government did not have adequate resources to finance smallholder

[138] Scoones et al., 'Tobacco, Contract Farming', 22–42.

[139] Tobacco Industries and Marketing Board (TIMB) Annual Report, 2018.

[140] TIMB Annual Report 2017.

[141] TIMB Annual Report 2019; See also TIMB Annual Report 2017.

[142] TIMB Annual Report 2019.

[143] Belgium used to be the main destination for Zimbabwe's tobacco during the early post-land reform era until it was overtaken by China. In 2014, China bought 22.3 million kgs of tobacco worth US$187.6 million, Belgium took up 22.1 million kgs worth US$104 million, South Africa 11.2 million kgs worth US$44.7 million, UAE imported 8.4 million kilograms worth US$25.8 million and Indonesia 4.02 million kgs worth US$24.1 million. Other peripheral export destinations for Zimbabwean tobacco are United Kingdom, Philippines, Spain, New Zealand, Montenegro and Russia. See 'China Reclaims Top Virginia Tobacco Importer', *The Herald*, 1 January 2015.

[144] After the 2000 land invasions there was heightened political violence as the ruling party sought to contain the challenge of the opposition. In 2001, the United States Congress passed the Zimbabwe Democracy Recovery Act (ZIDERA) that put restrictions on trade with Zimbabwe and placed several Zimbabwean businesses on embargo.

Table 6.1 ***Flue-cured tobacco production statistics in Zimbabwe, 2000–2019***

Year	Number of growers	Area (Ha)	US$/Kg	US$ Gross value	ZW$ Gross value	Mass (Kgs)
2000	8,537	84,857	1.69		19,266,709	236,946,295
2002	14,353	74,295	2.27		59,576,224	165,835,001
2005	31,761	57,511	1.61		1,666,410,523	73,376,990
2008	35,094	61,622	3.21	156,663,816		48,775,178
2010	51,685	64,054	2.88	355,572,326		123,503,681
2012	60,047	76,359	3.65	527,805,943		144,565,253
2014	106,372	88,627	3.17	685,244,013		216,196,683
2015	97,616	104,816	2.95	586,544,231		198,954,849
2017	98,927	110,816	2.96	737,603,251		188,920,313
2019	154,926	146,000	2.03	526,732,734		259,492,611

Source: TIMB Annual Report, 2019.

producers. Commercial banks could not offer loans to African smallholder farmers as most of them did not have collateral. The new land tenure regime after land reform stripped land of its market value and replaced title deeds with 99-year lease agreements which are not acceptable as security for bank loans The challenges of financing tobacco farming from local capital resources led to the inception of contract tobacco production in 2003. Tobacco-contracting companies such as Tian Ze, Zimbabwe Leaf Tobacco (ZLT) and BAT became major players in the financing of smallholder tobacco production. Contract farming has become a major component of smallholder tobacco production in Zimbabwe and contract companies provide financing for inputs and other production expenses as well as marketing facilities for the crop.[145] In 2015, there were sixteen registered tobacco-contracting companies operating in Zimbabwe and during 2017/2018 the number of registered contracting companies had grown to 30 servicing a clientele of 106,667 tobacco growers.[146] Essentially, tobacco contractors have an unassailable monopoly in the marketing and production of the crop in Zimbabwe controlling a disproportionately huge chunk of the sector. For instance, during the 2017 season, 157 million kilograms of tobacco (constituting 84 per cent of total output) were grown and marketed under the contract system and sold at an average price of US$2,98/kg.[147] In 2018, 86 per cent of the tobacco produced in Zimbabwe (217 million kgs) was grown under the contract system.

While the contract system has been exalted as a success story by Ian Scoones and other agrarian scholars who extol it as signifying new relations between agribusiness, capital and the state, there have been concerns over exploitation of small-scale tobacco farmers by these companies through unfair pricing and high interest rates on the loans.[148] Tobacco contractors have also been heavy-handed on loan

145 L. Sachikonye, 'Old Wine in New Bottles? Revisiting Contract Farming after Agrarian Reform in Zimbabwe', *Review of African Political Economy*, 43,1 (2016), 86–98.

146 TIMB Annual Report 2018.

147 F. Mazwi, W. Chambati and G. Mudimu, Tobacco Contract Farming in Zimbabwe: Power Dynamics, Accumulation Trajectories, Land Use Patterns and Livelihoods, *Journal of Contemporary African Studies*, 38,1 (2018), 55–71.

148 See, 'Zimbabwe tobacco boom but farmers are complaining of debt', Available on https://abcnews.go.com/International/wireStory/zimbabwes-tobacco-booms-black-growers-complain-debt-77855755, accessed 24 July 2021.

defaulters by seizing their properties and sometimes sending some to jail.[149] The Human Rights Watch report on tobacco farming in Zimbabwe observed that tobacco-contracting companies abuse smallholder farmers through opaque contract arrangements in which tobacco farmers are neither availed with copies of the agreements nor educated on the legal implications.[150] For most tobacco farmers, the contract system entraps them in a vicious cycle of debt and exploitation as each year after the selling season and paying off the tobacco companies they are left with not much income to buy inputs and fund the next agricultural season.[151] This compels them to enter into contract farming each and every year. Most small-scale farmers point out that the contract system is not the ideal funding arrangement, and its inefficiency is underlined by the fact that it has made them 'capital-bereft dependent producers'.[152] This is perhaps one of the biggest weakness of the post–land reform tobacco boom in Zimbabwe, that it is virtually premised on the capital, funding and infrastructure of transnational tobacco companies and not local capital and financial resources. Consequently, the capacity of smallholder producers to build up capital resources and become independent producers has been constrained. The dependency of smallholder producers in the third world on the financial and institutional resources of transnational tobacco companies often result in disruptions to rural economies when such resources are withdrawn or there are changes within global production dynamics. For instance, in Honduras, the dependency of rural communities within the Copan valley on BAT contract tobacco production between 1952 and 1995 resulted in the breakdown of the rural economy when BAT cancelled its contracts with growers and left during the late 1990s.[153] Also, in Zimbabwe the collapse of the contract cotton

149 This is based on personal experiences where I have witnessed several farmers in my farming area being subjected to this kind of treatment after failing to pay what they owed contracting companies usually after a bad crop or some other mishap beyond their control.

150 'A Bitter Harvest Child Labor and Human Rights Abuses on Tobacco Farms in Zimbabwe', Human Rights Watch Report (2018), 12.

151 This is based on interviews conducted with tobacco farmers in Muzarabani district between August 2018 and December 2020.

152 Ibid.

153 W. M. Loker, 'The Rise and Fall of Flue-Cured Tobacco in the Copán Valley and Its Environmental and Social Consequences', *Human Ecology*, 33, 3 (2005), 299–327.

production system during the 2000s ruined cotton farmers and destroyed the industry serving as an illustration of the pitfalls of relying on contract production.

At the ecological level, the post–land reform tobacco boom in Zimbabwe has escalated the destruction of forestry resources, woodlands and natural ecosystems in many tobacco-growing areas. Before the land reform coal and electricity were the main sources of energy for curing tobacco but with the rise of smallholder farmers estimates suggests that 90 per cent of tobacco grown in Zimbabwe is cured using wood fuel.[154] Large tracts of land have been depleted at alarming rates. During a period stretching for over twenty years, from 1992 to 2020 I directly experienced transitions in tobacco-farming landscapes and forestry resources in a tobacco-growing district (Centenary/Muzarabani) which is my home area. The boom in flue-cured tobacco production from the mid to late-1990s and the Land Reform Program during the 2000s ushered in a frenetic frenzy to cash in on the accumulation opportunities offered by higher priced flue-cured tobacco. Tobacco became a ubiquitous crop, covering every stretch of arable land, dominant and imposing. Every farmer grew tobacco, everyone had a small plot of tobacco. Even within the same family, children or wives could have separate pieces of tobacco plots outside the main family field to earn personal income. Literally everyone grew tobacco as it was the only crop that had a higher return and offered opportunities for accumulation. My father raised much of my school fees to attend boarding school from tobacco farming. It was a lucrative venture as the villages and resettlement areas buzzed under the golden glow of tobacco income. Televisions, water pumps, booming radios, assorted household furniture, cars, motorbikes, scotch carts and even tractors were purchased.

But, slowly and imperceptibly at first forest began to dwindle as tobacco farmers chopped trees each year to use as wood fuel. The common forests were exhausted and the remaining shrubs were cleaned out, leaving vast grasslands with no tree cover.[155] Thick forests disappeared, leaving barren lands covered in shrubs and grass. Each

[154] 'European Countries Can't Resist Zimbabwe Tobacco', *The Herald*, 24 March 2014.

[155] This is based on personal observations of changes in forestry and landscapes by the author in the Fast-track land resettlement areas of Muzarabani and Mount Darwin districts.

year hundreds of cords of firewood were cut and stacked to grow tobacco. In most of the tobacco-growing areas swathes of forests have been hewed out and there is already a crippling shortage of wood fuel even for domestic use, let alone for curing tobacco.[156] Housewives complain of the burden they now face to look for wood for cooking because the communal forestry supplies have been exhausted.[157] Most small-scale tobacco farmers now resort to buying wood fuel or poaching wood from neighbouring forested areas or commercial farms. During my last year of growing tobacco in 2016, I had to buy wood fuel from about 20 kilometres away because the forests in my area had been stripped bare. When my supplies of wood fuel ran out, we would creep out during the night and bribe guards at neighbouring commercial farms to let us in to cut firewood. Wood shortages in some of the tobacco-growing areas have created a thriving black market for firewood and the cost of curing fuel is a significant item on the expenditure list of tobacco farming. A scotch cart load of firewood can cost as much as US$5 and a scotch cart can barely last a night during the peak of curing. Some of the tobacco farmers I interviewed are contemplating moving away to new forested farming areas in search of wood fuel.[158] Others have already done so.

The changes in the landscape as a result of tobacco farming are conspicuous, and the figures below represents what was once a scenic landscape around 1995; a dam that had fish and was surrounded by overhanging trees with birds' nests and water ducks teeming on its shores, beyond it a thicket of bush that obscured the horizon. Now, twenty-three years later, it is just a muddy puddle stripped of all beauty, the birds' nests are gone, the fish disappeared and the trees around it cut down for curing fuel. Figures 6.2 and 6.3 show what was once a thriving dam with biodiversity, but now a silted marsh choked with weeds feeding on run-off fertilisers and chemicals from adjacent tobacco fields. Figure 6.4 shows a wood furnace used for curing

[156] This is based on interviews conducted with tobacco farmers in Muzarabani and Mount Darwin districts.

[157] Interview with Ms Tera, 28 year-old tobacco farmer, Avalon farm, Centenary district, 12 June 2021.

[158] Interviews with Mr Tsenzi, 54 year-old tobacco farmer, Stanmore farm, Centenary district, 6 June 2021; Interview with Mr Chikore, Interview with Chikore, 37 year-old tobacco farmer, Dhabi village, Centenary district, 8 June 2021; Interview with Mr Chakona, 46 year-old tobacco farmer, Hopi village, Mt Darwin district, 10 June 2021.

Figure 6.2 A barren landscape deforested by tobacco farming and a silted dam
Source: Author fieldwork files.

tobacco and Figure 6.5 depicts a typical small-scale tobacco-farming field. Satellite images on Figures 6.6 and 6.7 show in a much broader scale the changes that happened in forestry and vegetation landscapes between 2000 and 2019 in the Centenary tobacco-farming district.

Figure 6.3 Siltation and eutrophication of a dam due to erosion from adjacent tobacco fields
Source: Author fieldwork files.

What is conspicuous is the significant loss of forestry areas over the nineteen-year period, most of which is linked to the small-scale tobacco boom and the Land Reform Program.

The national forestry conservation body, the Forestry Commission of Zimbabwe (FCZ) acknowledges the impact of the post–land reform tobacco boom on forestry resources and estimates that the tobacco sector destroys about 50,000 acres of forest across the country every year.[159] This amounts to 15 per cent of the total (330,000 hectares) forest cover the country is losing annually to deforestation.[160] Indeed, there have been measures by the government and tobacco companies to limit and control tobacco-related deforestation but these have not been effective.

In 2012, the government passed a statutory instrument to control timber movement and trade (Control of Timber and Forests Produce Regulations) and to encourage the sustainable production of flue-cured

[159] *The Herald*, 23 June 2016. [160] *The Herald*, 23 June 2016.

Figure 6.4 A common wood fuel curing furnace used by small-scale tobacco farmers
Source: Author fieldwork files.

tobacco.[161] The law also requires tobacco farmers to establish a hectare of fast-growing *Eucalyptus* for every ten hectares of tobacco grown – a requirement that still remains unenforceable. On their part, the tobacco merchants and contracting companies formed the Sustainable Afforestation Association (SAA) in 2013 with the ambitious strategic objective of planting at least 40,000 hectares of *Eucalyptus* within seven years countrywide.[162] In 2015, the government set up the Tobacco Afforestation Levy to meet the costs of afforesting tobacco-growing areas with 1.5 per cent deductible from tobacco farmers' earnings during the first year and 0.79 per cent thereafter. However, the

161 www.cfuzim.com/wp-content/uploads/2012/07/si11612firewood1.pdf, accessed on 11 August 2021.
162 'Tobacco Industry Moves to Reverse Crop's Ecological Footprint', *The Herald*, 24 August 2015.

Figure 6.5 Tobacco field of a small-scale farmer in Centenary district
Source: Author fieldwork files.

Figure 6.6 Map of Centenary district showing forestry cover and vegetation in 2000
Source: Cartography by Isaac Meat.

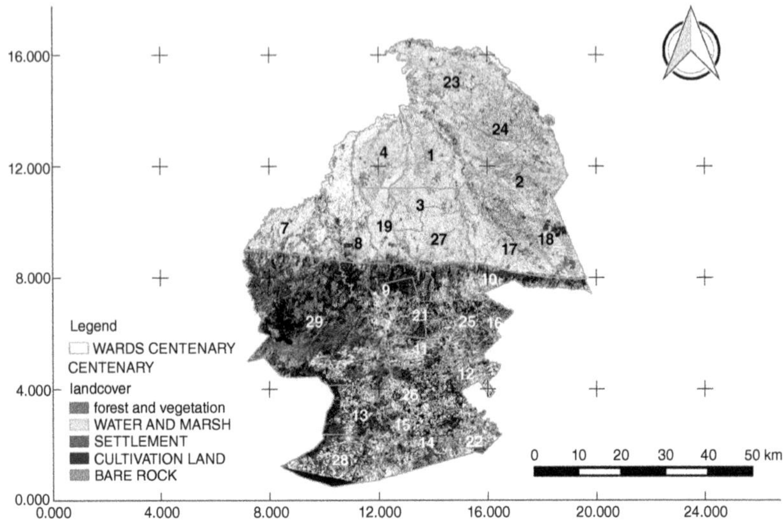

Figure 6.7 Map of Centenary district showing forestry cover and vegetation in 2019
Source: Cartography by Isaac Meat.

implementation of this programme has been problematic. By 2019, the US$23 million collected under the levy had not been disbursed towards afforestation as a result of administrative bottlenecks.[163] In 2020, a Chinese tobacco-contracting company Tian Ze launched the Sustainable Tobacco Program (STP) in support of sustainable development goals and to improve tobacco farming economically, environmentally and socially.[164] However, many of these afforestation projects are green-washing public relations stunts that are very insignificant in limiting deforestation in the country's tobacco-growing areas. These programmes are rarely visible on the ground and most tobacco-farming communities where I did field research are not part of these initiatives and the impact of tobacco afforestation programmes has been overstated by tobacco public relations institutions. In the more than twenty years there has not been a significant tobacco afforestation project by either government or tobacco companies in the research area. At best farmers receive packets of *Eucalyptus* seeds and the few who had gone

[163] '21 million Tobacco Levy Lies Idle', *The Herald*, 23 April 2019.
[164] 'Sustainable Tobacco Program Launched', *The Herald*, 4 March 2020.

on to implement the programme have established very scant and insignificant woodlots in comparison to the damage already done and is still happening. The area devoted to these afforestation projects is way less than what is lost annually to deforestation. For instance, SAA claims to have planted 11,000 hectares of fuel wood plantation between 2013 and 2020, an area way less than their ambitious target of 40,000 hectares and the 50,000 hectares of forestry cover lost annually to tobacco farming.[165] The TRB has come up with several innovations and inventions to limit deforestation such as the use of biogas, solar, electricity, coal and energy-efficient curing barns.[166] However, much of the infrastructure for alternative energy sources are beyond the economic reach of many small-scale farmers and there is a very low uptake of these new tobacco-curing technologies and it is impossible to envisage a transition of small-scale tobacco farmers to these technologies.

New social relations have also etched themselves within the post–land reform tobacco-farming landscape and altered the relations of production and the dynamics of labour immensely. Before the land reform white commercial tobacco farmers and some black smallholder tobacco producers were able to utilise large pools of landless and unemployed Africans in the communal areas. Consequently, most tobacco farmers were able to operate with relatively lower labour costs and make huge profits. The conditions of labour in most commercial farming tobacco farms were grotesque with lengthy hours of work including weekends with no overtime.[167] Leave was usually restricted to two or three days a year and was usually unpaid.[168] Labour control was rigid and highly autocratic with workers treated as ganged labourers. Women and children were used as wage-cutting options. Land allocations to workers for production of their own foodstuffs was to the most unsuitable parts of the farms. Farm workers' accommodation was highly centralised like during the colonial days and consisted of grass and dagga huts with no amenities such as water and sanitation.[169] Education was very poor and most children who grew up on tobacco farms did not attend any schooling. In 1997, at least 70 per cent of farm labourers were below the poverty

[165] See, www.saazimbabwe.org/, accessed 10 September 2021.
[166] 'TRB Develops New Tobacco Barn', The Herald, 20 May 2019.
[167] R. T. Garvin, 'The Management of Labour on Zimbabwe's Flue-cured Tobacco Farms', *Agricultural Administration*, 12 (1983), 195–206.
[168] Ibid. [169] Ibid.

datum line while average monthly wages were 51 per cent of the poverty datum line.[170]

The Land Reform Program shrank the formal labour economy within the tobacco commercial farms, but the labour market did not collapse as new forms of labour organisation and transactions arose based on informal networks within the production process.[171] Labour remains an important item in tobacco production but the locus of production has shifted into new circuits of productive relations concentrated on the use of family labour and other informal conduits within tobacco-farming communities. This shift has more importantly evoked concern over the use of child labour in the production of tobacco. This is the enduring heritage of the tobacco crop because of the high cost of labour and the intensive labour demands. Child labour is prevalent and widespread in tobacco farming with reports suggesting that more than 50 per cent of small-scale tobacco farmers in Zimbabwe employ children under the years of eighteen on their farms as hired or family labour.[172] This has contributed to absenteeism from school, high rates of school dropouts and exposure of children to harmful chemicals and Green Tobacco Sickness (GTS).[173] Figure 6.8 shows children manning a tobacco-curing furnace and Figure 6.9 depicts the poor working conditions that pose health hazards in a tobacco-grading shed.

Child labour exploitation is a big problem in post–land reform tobacco farming in Zimbabwe. High labour costs often compel small-scale farmers to rely exclusively on family labour during much of the season and this burden is much heavier on smaller families with fewer children. Bigger families can pull together the labour resources and the burdens are in most cases mitigated. Consequently, marrying many wives and having many children is considered a huge capital

170 G. Kanyenze, 'Zimbabwe Labour Relations Policies and Implications for Workers' in Amanor-Wilks (ed.), *Zimbabwe Farm Workers: Policy Dimension* (Lusaka, 2001), 86–114.

171 For comprehensive reading on labour in post–land reform Zimbabwe see, W. Chambati, 'Changing Forms of Wage Labour in Zimbabwe's New Agrarian Structure', *Agrarian South: Journal of Political Economy*, 6,1 (2017), 79–112; T. Shonhe, I. Scoones and F. Murimbarimba, 'Agricultural Commercialization and Changing Labour Regimes in Zimbabwe', *Journal of Contemporary African Studies*, 10.1080/02589001.2021.1933397.

172 'A Bitter Harvest', 28.

173 'A Bitter Harvest',30.

Figure 6.8 Children tending to tobacco curing and managing a furnace
Source: Author fieldwork files.

resource by some tobacco farmers as it saves on labour costs.[174] Seasonal workers are hired during the peak labour periods to perform such task as weeding, harvesting and grading to complement family labour. Tobacco-contracting companies only give farmers around US$100/ha to meet labour costs during the harvesting season, and this leaves a huge deficit that must be met by mobilising family labour and hiring seasonal labourers usually during the harvesting period.[175] The cost of labour usually fluctuates across the season depending on the demand and supply dynamics but is often US$2 per day during the rest of the season rising to US$3/day when harvesting and US$4 when there

[174] These opinions were expressed during Interviews with Mr Goma, 62-year-old tobacco farmer, Westbury farm, Centenary district, 13 February 2019 and Mr Jata, 37-year-old tobacco farmer, Mutwa Estate, Mount Darwin district, 22 June 2021.

[175] Interview with Mr Goma.

Figure 6.9 A poorly lit and aerated tobacco-grading shed
Source: Author field work files.

is a serious demand at the peak of harvesting.[176] Children carry out all sorts of tasks on tobacco farms including dangerous work such as the handling of chemical sprays, curing tobacco and harvesting. Labour transactions are not only monetary but involve non-monetary payments such as land and inputs for tobacco farming, groceries, clothing and mealie meal. Sometimes, labour is acquired in advance with payments to be made at the end of the season when the crop would have been sold. The labour regimes in post–land reform tobacco farming have become much more flexible and less paternalistic, less rigid and less autocratic. There is now less treatment of workers as 'ganged labourers' as the social networks and relations of production linking farmers and labourers are more intimate and fluid. A tobacco farmer

[176] This is based on a survey carried out by the author on labour conditions in tobacco farms around Muzarabani and Mount Darwin districts.

can also be a labourer, and a labourer can also be a farmer and that distinction is very blurred. Some of the tobacco farmers sometimes work as labourers for other farmers when they have little workload on their plots. Nevertheless, the conditions of workers in tobacco farms remain deplorable with very low wages inadequate to cover their basic needs and most of them are not employed on a permanent basis. The General Agricultural and Plantation Workers Union of Zimbabwe (GAPWUZ) revealed in 2013 that much of the workforce in the tobacco farms consists of women and children from poor backgrounds who are only hired when need arises for payments of between US$2 and US$3 for eight hours of hard labour for cultivating and applying chemicals in the field.[177] The Union further noted that children from poor backgrounds were frequently employed in tobacco farming to provide family income. Thus, while income opportunities have arisen with tobacco production for small-scale farmers, the social landscape remains very rugged with labour abuses and exploitation of children.

[177] 'Tobacco: Development or Disease?', *The Herald*, 31 May 2014.

Conclusion

Confronting the harmful social and environmental legacy of tobacco and its use is one of the biggest challenges of the twenty-first century. Yet, this challenge, though contemporary and requiring present interventions calls for holistic and transcendental insights into how the 'tobacco epidemic' is part of the globalisation and institutionalisation of cultures of production, cultivation, marketing and consumption of the crop across historical time. The tobacco epidemic is a historically constructed leviathan linking various centres of power and institutions of governance to big tobacco in a grand profit-making scheme, exploitation and plunder of human bodies, ecologies and landscapes for private gain and profit. The stranglehold that the tobacco industry wields today over progressive tobacco-control regimes and attempts to limit tobacco's harm is a heritage of this complex relationship between the industry, the state and tobacco farmers forged across more than a century from 'jungle tobacco farms' in colonial America and colonial Africa to more organised production systems during the mid to late twentieth century. This book has shown how the colonial state in Southern Rhodesia gave tremendous succour to the development of the white settler tobacco industry and facilitated land expropriation and plunder of indigenous natural resources, coercive recruitment and exploitation of African labour within the tobacco farms, and promoted the marketing of tobacco to increase consumption and exports. This complex relationship perpetuated itself into the post-colonial state and the tobacco industry is still the most unregulated and rogue sector of the Zimbabwean agricultural economy whose interests are intimately protected by the state. In the end, political tobacco still has a pervasive, insidious and ubiquitous grapple hold on every sphere of society, and this complicates national tobacco-control governance.

In March 2019, one of the tobacco contracting companies in the country Golden Leaf Tobacco owned by Simon Rudland, allegedly a notorious cigarette smuggler, who has been implicated as a major player in the illicit trade of cigarettes in South Africa, availed a ZWLS$1 million (USD$385,000 million) sponsorship deal per season to the biggest football club in the country Dynamos FC in return for the sales and marketing of his company's Remington brand of cigarettes during football matches.[1] This gesture violates Article 13 of the Framework Convention on Tobacco Control (FCTC) which Zimbabwe is party to and that binds states to ban advertisements and promotion of any form or sponsorship by tobacco companies. In September of the same year another tobacco company Tian Ze donated uniforms to a school.[2] In March 2021 Ethical Leaf Tobacco donated an assortment of medical equipment to a clinic in Bindura.[3] These examples reflect the deeply institutionalised pitfalls that confront regulating the tobacco industry in Zimbabwe towards compliance to FCTC norms in order to eradicate the cycle of disease, death and environmental degradation. Tobacco corporations have spread their tentacles and secured lucrative government-backed contracts to expand tobacco production for export revenues. Resultantly, tobacco-control oversight has been very opaque and tame to monitor infractions on the use of child labour in tobacco farming, illicit trading and use of tobacco, the social burden of tobacco use and the negative environmental impacts. Therefore, contemporary farming landscapes in Zimbabwe resemble the colonial tobacco terrains that thrived on institutionalised social violence, mining of soils, stripping of forests, chemicalisation of landscapes and despoliation of human bodies. Problematically, the state and tobacco interest groups have made these historical transgressions less visible and conveyed mythological and triumphalist narratives of tobacco as the '*golden leaf*' and the fountain of the prosperity of both the colonial and post-colonial economic state-building projects. *Golden leaf* narratives are not only myths, but they are essentially a disruptive ideologue and dislocate the writing of a very objective and critical history of the Rhodesian and Zimbabwean tobacco industries. It is the ultimate responsibility of the environmental historian to prick fantasy bubbles, to be a doomsayer, and 'to spout a kind of black armband history' which exposes that not all that glittered

[1] Dembare strike deal, available on www.herald.co.zw/dembare-strike-deal/, accessed 1 June 2020.

[2] 'Tian Ze Donates $216,000 to School', *The Herald*, 16 September 2019.

[3] 'Tobacco Firm Bails out Clinic', *The Herald*, 15 March 2021.

in history was golden.[4] Indeed, tobacco was an important agricultural commodity that sustained colonial economic growth and provided the impetus for agrarian transformation and land conservation in colonial Zimbabwe and beyond but its cultivation at most points restructured social encounters and landscapes in much more cataclysmic and spasmic ways that reproduced temporal displacements and disorientations of geographic spaces and human lives.

Social violence was enduringly inscribed in the production models of tobacco farming in both Southern Rhodesia and Zimbabwe. During the colonial period social violence in tobacco farming was constructed much along racial lines but with redistributive agrarian policies during the post–land reform period, social violence has been deracialised. However, production regimes and cultural practices that propped up colonial tobacco farmers are still intact and entrenched. Child labour, the slow violence of chemical exposure, labour exploitation, the plunder of natural resources and social inequality are still commonplace. Tobacco's 'slow violence' continues unabated and festers insidiously. The human cost and ecological toll of this violence across more than a hundred years of the industry has not been widely reflected upon and much scholarly work has endeavoured to highlight this as the golden century enamoured with export earnings, indices of economic growth and development, growers' cohesion and ingenuity, political acumen and financial strategy.

There has to be a shift in national tobacco-farming discourse away from the euphoric and celebratory paradigms that lionise the crop. Indeed, there has been a wave of new literature on tobacco farming and the land reform in Zimbabwe that has engaged with the ecological and social crisis. But this scholarship, much of it from the social sciences is trapped in short-term apocalyptic paradigms that do not connect the processes of environmental degradation to cultures embedded in history. Ultimately, to these narratives, the post–land reform tobacco boom generated a unique environmental crisis that must be investigated and resolved separately. This book tries to address the deficit in historicising patterns of land degradation, social violence, and the deforestation crisis in contemporary tobacco-farming systems in the country.

[4] D. Garden, 'Catalyst or Cataclysm? Gold Mining and the Environment', *Victoria Historical Journal*, 72, 1–2 (2001), 28–44.

The deeply entrenched hegemonic position of tobacco within the national body politic and the economy since the early colonial days has precluded the pursuit of a comprehensive tobacco-control agenda. It is imperative that a new tobacco-control governance outlook is needed, and part of this book's ultimate objective is to help frame new perspectives into tobacco production that provokes thoughts on how to effectively regulate the industry and protect the environment, growers and society from big tobacco interest groups. The expansion of multinational tobacco companies into the third world and Africa since the end of the last century makes it urgent to safeguard public health, society and the environment from the deleterious effects of the twenty-first-century 'tobacco epidemic'. The nature and scale of this epidemic is likely to transcend the last epidemic as patterns of global climatic shifts caused by environmental decline have made tobacco farming much more than just a public health threat but a catastrophe to forests, biodiversity and rainfall patterns contributing to the contemporary global climate crisis. The challenges of the contemporary tobacco epidemic require transcendental evaluations of national and global tobacco-control regimes that effectively integrates public health governance, environmental regulatory regimes, climate change action and tobacco farmers into conversations and discourses of cooperation towards areas of concern.

The deeply entrenched and institutionalised historical role of big tobacco companies and interest groups in tobacco production in Zimbabwe has to be dismantled by handing regulatory and policing powers on tobacco control to public health institutions, environmental civil societies and government agencies. Tobacco companies cannot be expected to regulate themselves under frameworks created by their own public relations networks. But this can only be done if the intimate links between the state and tobacco interest groups in Zimbabwe can be severed and if there is a willingness on the part of the government to dismantle 'political tobacco' and democratise tobacco-farming landscapes to allow a more active process of transition and change. Since colonial times, tobacco-farming landscapes have always been politicised terrains within which the state, tobacco farmers and tobacco merchants forged relationships to control land, power and inscribe authority on subject bodies and physical geographies. These landscapes imbued power to settler growth and iconised white identity in the countryside forging the colonial Rhodesian state into a formidable political behemoth and regional economic powerhouse. Tobacco capital structured agrarian encounters, determined patterns of growth, land settlement and conservation in the farmlands. It knitted the fabric of the topology and configured spatial changes in farm landscapes across time.

Contemporary tobacco-farming landscapes in Zimbabwe still carry these idioms of politics and power etched within new spaces of authority and control but still constructed along similar exploitative and predatory production models that connect the state, farmers and tobacco interests' groups in an unholy triad of social and environmental impunity. The political stakes of stringently regulating farmers are much higher now in a terrain where tobacco-farming areas constitute huge constituencies of the rural support for the ruling ZANU PF party. In this regard, tobacco control is seen as disruptive to the state's centres of power as it will take away livelihoods and the means for black economic empowerment which has been the fulcrum for the state elites' political mobilisation. Tobacco farming is one of the few sectors in the Zimbabwean economy that still earns much-needed foreign currency and whose revenue has propped the ailing fortunes of the political leadership for over two decades. Therefore, the expediencies for regime survival negates the pursuit of a more robust tobacco-control policy in Zimbabwe and makes it difficult to envisage a different policy outlook unless the political and agrarian relations in the countryside shift. The socio-environmental politics of tobacco control in Zimbabwe are a complex set of scenarios that preclude rigorous regulatory regime and the articulation of an honest and sincere stakeholder dialogue on tobacco farming's harm to social and physical landscapes. The contemporary tobacco-farming agenda needs a much broader national platform for policy making than the state, growers and tobacco companies. This broad platform must include labour organisations, environmental activist, anti-tobacco civil societies, youth organisations and public health groups who hitherto have been peripheral voices in structuring national response strategies to tobacco farming's social and ecological damage. National scientific studies have to be carried out to document the scale of ecological disruption in tobacco-growing areas, epidemiological surveys on the impact of tobacco chemical exposure to farm workers and the social costs of tobacco use on young people and families. The net social and environmental bill of tobacco farming has to be quantified concretely to inform the urgency of proactive tobacco control.

Whither Tobacco Farming in Zimbabwe's Agrarian Future?

It is palpable that winds of change have always been blowing across tobacco farmlands in Zimbabwe since the early colonial period days in many different ways. From the economic and ecological pressures during the 1930s and the crisis of overproduction to the post-war tobacco boom and agricultural imbalance and the global public health scrutiny from the 1950s and 1960s to the tobacco embargo after the UDI and the diversification drive during the 1970s. At each point in time the colonial tobacco economy had to be restructured to meet the new challenges and survive. New cultural and agronomic practices had to be invented, novel production and marketing institutions had to be set up to address changing production contexts and shifting environmental and social landscapes. This innovation lay at the core of the survival and memorialisation of the Rhodesian tobacco industry. Similarly, today new winds of change in the form of global tobacco-control pressures, public health concerns and threats to forestry resources and the environment are blowing across tobacco farmlands not only in Zimbabwe but across the world. The stakes for survival are higher and the long-term viability of tobacco farming stands under perilous scrutiny from these pressures. This prompts new strategies for survival and alternative and mitigatory models from various players within the tobacco value chain. For transnational tobacco companies the adaptation and transition will be much smoother as they continue to appropriate, control and shift narratives of tobacco's harm within their public relations machinery and still make millions of dollars. Governments and the tobacco industry have already spent much, ostensibly on altering smoking patterns of citizens, limiting production, consumption and managing the environmental risks of tobacco production but they have not addressed the supply-side imperatives such as reducing cigarette manufacturing, distribution and sales.[5] Subsequently, tobacco dependency for third world economies has grown as tobacco tax revenue support economic growth and tobacco incomes are pillars for agricultural stability. In this volatile environment, the fate of tobacco farmers and how to confront the challenges

[5] P. Benson, *Tobacco Capitalism: Growers, Migrant Workers, and the Changing Face of a Global Industry* (Princeton University Press: Princeton and Oxford, 2012), 261.

to farm incomes and livelihoods outside tobacco farming hangs precariously in the balance.

In Zimbabwe, agricultural diversification and the shift into other alternative crops such as cannabis has been espoused as one of the routes for protecting tobacco farmers but has not been given much prodding in the strategic framing of tobacco-farming policy which is actually predicated on expanding and not limiting current production and manufacturing capacity. In 2021, the Zimbabwean government launched the Tobacco Value Chain Transformation Plan. This policy framework actually aims at incrementally transforming the tobacco value chain from its current value of US$1 billion into a US$5 billion industry by 2025 through accelerated local financing of production, increased production, value addition and cigarette exports.[6] The strategic objectives of this plan include raising production from the national all-time production high of 262 million kilograms realised during 2018/2019 season to 300 million kilograms by 2025 and increasing the levels of value addition of tobacco from the current 2 per cent to 30 per cent of the total produced.[7]

Ultimately, investment in diversification of tobacco-farming systems is much neglected and there has been very limited progress in that regard. While doing field research in Muzarabani district most tobacco farmers I interacted with are not so enthusiastic about the prospects of shifting from tobacco to other alternative crops and insist there is no future for smallholder production outside tobacco. The farmers contend that while tobacco incomes have dwindled over the years and most of the forests depleted and their soils exhausted, tobacco is the only viable crop that can support sustainable livelihoods within their ecological zones. Other crops such as maize and cotton pay way less per hectare and other enterprises such as horticulture, poultry and dairying are either too capital-intensive or do not have a guaranteed market. So, farmers have to eke an existence out of the fragile ecosystems pushing them to the limits each year to grow tobacco. The barren landscapes, pale over-used soils and drying dams that litter farmlands in most tobacco-farming areas in Zimbabwe tell the story of an enterprise that is on the brink of collapse, but most are willing to cut the last

[6] 'Plan to Turn Tobacco Sector into US$5 Billion Industry Approved', *The Herald*, 8 September 2021.

[7] Ibid.

tree and choke the last stream to grow the golden leaf. The elephant in the room is how to transition these rural tobacco-farming landscapes into diversified agricultural zones with rehabilitated ecologies to improve rural livelihoods.

This transition requires integrating tobacco-farming communities into the tobacco-control initiatives so they understand the global pressures, public health and environmental concerns much more effectively to avoid resistance to change. Resistance to implementation of tobacco-control measures and the FCTC by the state and tobacco industry in Zimbabwe and the symbolic acquiescence to new global norms to limit tobacco use have institutionalised a risky denialism on the socio-ecological liability of tobacco farming. Millions of dollars have been invested by tobacco companies and government into downscaling the social and environmental damage of tobacco production, but this has not halted the onslaught. It is perhaps critical to invest not in new technologies of curing, or wood saving technology and creating a dangerous cult of social responsibility but instead to direct funding towards building the resilience of rural farmers to diversify away from tobacco into other crops.

Indeed, current tobacco production models in Zimbabwe are not sustainable and will inevitably collapse from the sheer weight of ecological, economic and social pressures. Tobacco is effectively an endangered crop and must not be used as a fulcrum for agricultural development in Zimbabwe, or for any agrarian strategic planning. To this end agricultural policy must focus on building mixed farm systems in the tobacco-growing areas, investing in irrigation infrastructure and looking for alternative crops that have prospects of replacing tobacco and are suitable for each ecological region within which tobacco is grown. Policy framing must also understand that ad hoc, reactive and forced diversification of tobacco farm systems is not the best option and in the era of rapid climate change, ecological prudence must always inform all relevant policy options. Considering these challenges ameliorating the socio-environmental impact of tobacco farming becomes key. While most of the current socio-environmental challenges of tobacco are difficult to address more comprehensively in Zimbabwe as a result of the economic significance and political nature of the crop, it is important that environmental lobby groups and human rights civil society engage tobacco stakeholders and policymakers to create workable long-term strategies for sustainable tobacco production. Ironically, the long-term future of the tobacco industry in Zimbabwe lies in developing agricultural systems that will eventually phase out the crop before a crisis point is reached and the social and environmental burden triggers an ecological and economic implosion of rural livelihoods and communities.

Select Bibliography

Archival Sources: National Archives of Zimbabwe (NAZ)

NAZ (unprocessed), 42-12-5F, box number 126962, Pesticide Control Legislation.

NAZ (unprocessed), C.32.15.11R, box number 126959, Tobacco Burley Association, 1962–1970.

NAZ (unprocessed), 42-12-9R, box number 126959, Tobacco Burley Production Quotas.

NAZ (unprocessed), 42-13-3R, box number 126958, Tobacco Oriental Marketing and Production.

NAZ, 982/T/2F- Rhodesia Tobacco Association General, 1 July 1954–13 March 1955.

NAZ, A11/2/2/13 Tobacco, 1904–November 1909.

NAZ, AOH/51, Interview with Musonzi Paurosi, 18 April 1979.

NAZ, AOH/59, Interview with Mudzongani Maodzwa, 8 August 1979.

NAZ, F114/473/E.8/8/ (473), Tobacco Economic Section 1955–1957

on 26 October 1956 on Rhodesia Tobacco.

NAZ, F149/TOB/360, Tobacco Diseases and Pests, 1956–1958.

NAZ, F226/121/F2, Production Control 1964–1965.

NAZ, F226/1215/F3, Turkish Tobacco Marketing and Production 1960–1961.

NAZ, F226/1217/F22/3, Tobacco United States Newsletters, 1961–1964.

NAZ, F226/1218/F3, Burley Tobacco Marketing and Production, 1960–1964.

NAZ, F257/110/GEN, Tobacco General: Bulletins and Articles.

NAZ, L2/1/108, Tobacco Culture and Land Settlement.

NAZ, L2/1/114, The Inyoka Rhodesia Tobacco Company.

NAZ, ORAL/QU2, Interview with H. J. Quinton, May 1977–May 1978.

NAZ, S1189/9, Rhodesia Cooperation Limited: Settlement of the Land.

NAZ, S1193/T3/5, Memorandum on Proposed Tobacco Cesspool Legislation, L. M. Hastings, President RTA.

NAZ, S1194/1217, Tobacco: Restrictions of Output Legislation, 1934–1935.

NAZ, S1194/201/1, D. D. Brown to Secretary, Department of Agriculture and Lands, 27 June 1932.

NAZ, S1215/1710/1, Fertilisers General.
NAZ, S1246/5/30 (C), Evidence of Farmers on the Farming Enquiry, 1933.
NAZ, S1246/530 (B), Complete Evidence of Witnesses to the Farming Enquiry: Government Officials, 1933.
NAZ, S1246/530(E), Statements Forwarded by Those Unable to Give Evidence to the 1934 Farming Enquiry.
NAZ, S138/255, The Native Juveniles Employment Act, 1926–1928.
NAZ, S138/40, Labour Recruitment, 1924–1928.
NAZ, S1542/A4, Annual Reports for Developments in the Native Areas and Reserves.
NAZ, S1827/1245/3, Tobacco Cultural Practices, 1931–1941.
NAZ, S1828/PP/20A, Tobacco Alternaria, 1937–1944.
NAZ, S1828/PP60, Conservation Officer to Irrigation Department.
NAZ, S235/473, Report of the Native Labour Committee, 1927–1928.
NAZ, S235/508, Annual Reports of District Native Commissioners.
NAZ, S235/511/4, District Native Commissioner Sebungwe District Annual Report, 1933.
NAZ, S2371/1/1, Land Settlement, 'Closer Settlement', Department of Agriculture, Paper Read at the Laboratory on 5 January 1925.
NAZ, S238/49, Forced Recruitment of Women and Juveniles.
NAZ, S2505/TOB/1/1, Tobacco Marketing Board Members Correspondence, 1954–1956.
NAZ, S25101/1, TRB Tobacco Pest Spraying Scheme.
NAZ, S2532/1080/1/1, Darwendale ICA, Petition for the Declaration of an ICA by Darwendale Farmers.
NAZ, S2570, Tobacco 1946–1950.
NAZ, S2708/1, Pest Control and Plants, 1947–1952.
NAZ, S3700, Production and Marketing of Oriental Tobacco, October 1975–July 1976.
NAZ, S3700/29, Farming Competitions Policy.
NAZ, S3700/44, Crop Pests' Control, Use of Pesticides and Herbicides, October 1973–March 1977.
NAZ, S3920, Natural Resources Board, Intensive Conservation Areas.
NAZ, S482/108/39, Turkish Tobacco 1944–1948.
NAZ, S482/114/39, Tobacco, 1936–1939.
NAZ, S482/114/39/1, Tobacco, May 1934–January 1935.
NAZ, S482/20/42, Food Production Committees, FPC Meetings.
NAZ, S482/32/42, Control of Production, Tobacco, 1942–1946.
NAZ, S7878, Reports on the Summer Crop Returns, 1926–1928.
NAZ, S955/22, Food Production Local Committees.
NAZ, S983/2, Changes in Tobacco Production Costs, 1947–1950.

NAZ, S987/1, Oral Evidence; Farming Enquiry, 1942.
NAZ, S989, The Natural Resources Act, 1941.
NAZ, ST0014, TIMB Annual Reports 1939–1940 and 1945–1946.
NAZ, ZCF 1/1/1, Report of the Native Labour Supply Committee, 1921.

Published Primary Sources

Official Reports

'Child Labour, Commercial Agriculture and the Role of Tobacco', International Labour Organisation Report, Geneva, 2009.
Annual Report of the Natural Resources Board, June 1952.
Annual Report of the Supervisor of Facilities for Passage of Northern Natives, 1926.
Annual Reports of the Tobacco Representative in London, 1948–1949.
Annual Report of the Secretary of Lands and Agriculture, December 1948.
BDO Zimbabwe Chartered Accountants, 'Tobacco Industry and Marketing Board Study into Cost of Tobacco Production in Zimbabwe', 2015.
'A Bitter Harvest: Child Labour and Human Rights Abuses on Tobacco Farms in Zimbabwe', HRW Zimbabwe, 2018.
BSAC Co., Directors Reports, 1907.
BSAC, Company Reports, 1903–1905.
'Curbing the Tobacco Epidemic: Governments and the Economics of Tobacco Control', World Bank, 1999.
Davis A., 'Tobacco Production and Marketing in Southern Rhodesia, Northern Rhodesia and Nyasaland', Foreign Agricultural Service, United States Department of Agriculture, 1964.
'Global Resources Assessment: Country Report: Zimbabwe', Food and Agricultural Organisation, Rome, 2014.
Hayson Simeone, 'The Illicit Tobacco Trade in Zimbabwe and South Africa: Impacts and Solutions', Working Paper, Atlantic Council, March 2019, 5–8.
The Impact of Tobacco Farming on Deforestation, Forestry Commission of Zimbabwe, Harare, 2013.
The Impact of Tobacco Use on Health and Socio-economic Development in Africa-A Status Report, African Union Commission, 2010
Ndlela Shepherd, 'Phasing Out Harmful/Hazardous Yet Effective Synthetic Insecticides: How Will the Tobacco Farmer Manage the Pesticide Intensive Tobacco Crop?', TRB Technical Report, April 2017.
Odlum G. M., 'The Culture of Tobacco', BSAC, Department of Agriculture, 1905.

Record of Conference of the International Red Locust Control Service Held in Salisbury on the 25th, 26th and 27th of May 1948 (Lusaka: Government Printer, 1948).

Report for the Native Commissioner Darwin District, 1927.

Report of the Agriculturalist, Native Development Department, 1929.

Report of the Central Statistical Office of Southern Rhodesia, Agricultural Statistics, 1961.

Report of the Commission of Enquiry into the Conservation of the Colony's Natural Resources, 1939.

Report of the Commission of Enquiry into the Economic Position of the Agricultural Industry, 1934

Report of the Committee set up by the Minister of Agriculture to Investigate the Need for Change in the Methods of Turkish tobacco, 1960.

Report of the Native Labour Committee, 1927–1928.

Report of the Native Labour Supply Committee (1921).

Report of the Native Production and Trade Commission, 1944.

Report of the Proceedings at the 24th Annual Congress of the Rhodesian Agricultural Union held on 14–18 September 1926.

Report of the Tobacco Research Board, 1936, 1950.

Report on Agricultural Teaching, Research and Advisory Work in Rhodesia, 1949.

Report on the Global Tobacco Epidemic', WHO, Geneva, 2008.

Reports of the Department of Agriculture, 1903, 1920, 1927.

Reports of the Division of Entomology, December 1937, 1947.

Results on the Global Tobacco Youth Survey in Zimbabwe, Harare and Manicaland Regions, 1999–2000, UNICEF, 2000.

Rhodesia Tobacco Marketing Board, Monitoring Service for Pesticide Residue in Tobacco: Report of Burley Sample, Tribal Trust Lands, 1974.

Rhodesia Tobacco Marketing Board, Monitoring Service for Pesticide Residue in Tobacco: Report of Burley Sample, Tribal Trust Lands, 1975.

Smoking Control Strategies in Developing Countries', Report of a WHO Expert Committee, 1983.

'A State of Fear: Human Rights Abuses in North Carolina's Tobacco Industry', Oxfam Report, 2011.

The 2019 National Budget Statement by Hon. Prof. Mthuli Ncube Minister of Finance and Economic Development, 22 November 2018.

TIMB Annual reports 1939, 1940, 1945–1946, 1972.

TIMB Annual Statistical Report, 2018.

Tobacco Research Board, 'Bulletin on Burley Tobacco Culture in Southern Rhodesia' 1970.

Tobacco Research Board, 'Pesticides Use on Tobacco: A Review of International Trends and Their Impact on Rhodesian Production', August 1970.
Tobacco Research Board, 'Recommendations for Flue-Cured Tobacco', 1955.
Tobacco Research Board, 'Recommendations for Flue-Cured Tobacco', 1961.
'Will the Tobacco Farmer Manage the Pesticide Intensive Tobacco Crop?', *TRB Technical Report* (April 2017).

Parliamentary Debates

Southern Rhodesia Legislative Assembly Debates, 8 April 1913
Southern Rhodesia Legislative Council Debates, 9 October 1914
Southern Rhodesia Legislative Assembly Debates, 2 May 1919.
Southern Rhodesia Legislative Council Debates, 2 November 1928.
Southern Rhodesia Legislative Assembly Debates, 26 April 1950.
Legislative Assembly Debates, 29 August 1969.

Newspapers and Magazines

Centenary East and West ICA Newsletter
The Countryside
The Financial Gazette
Flue-cured Tobacco Cooperation Stabilisation Newsletter
Foreign Affairs
The Herald
Industry and Commerce in Rhodesia
The London Observer News
Natural Resources Board Newsletter
The New Rhodesian
The Patriot
Rhodesia Herald
Rhodesia Tobacco Today
The Rhodesian Financial Gazette
The Rhodesian Sunday Mail
Rhodesian Tobacco Grower and Food Producer
Rhodesian Tobacco Journal
The Rhodesian Tobacco Quarterly
The Star
The Sunday Mail
Sunday Times

Tobacco Forum of Rhodesia and Nyasaland
Tobacco News
Tobacco Today
Vuka
The Zimbabwean Independent

Internet Sources

Albaugh, Janine M., Dye, Peter J., and King John S., 'Eucalyptus and Water Use in South Africa', *International Journal of Forestry Research*, (2013) available online at http://dx.doi.org/10.1155/2013/852540.

Badze, Doreen, 'Farmers Still Using Banned Pesticide', *The Standard,* 11 December 2016, https://thestandard.co.zw/2016/12/11/farmers-still-usingbanned-pesticide/.

'British American Tobacco Negotiated Bribe for Mugabe, New Evidence Suggests', available on www.bbc.com/news/world-58517339.

Chingono, Nyasha, South Africa's Tobacco Ban Greeted with Cigarette Smuggling Boom', available at .www.theguardian.com/global-development/2020/jun/26/south-africa-tobacco-ban-greeted-with-cigarette-smuggling-boom.

'Chin'ono Sparks Debate on State of Cancer Treatment in Zimbabwe', available at https://zero.pindula.co.zw/chinono-sparks-debate-on-state-of-cancer-treatment-in-zimbabwe/.

'Communities in Peril: Global Report on Health Impacts of Pesticide Use in Agriculture', Pesticide Action Network (September 2010), www.pan-germany.org/download/PAN-I_CBM-Global-Report_1006-final.pdf.

Conniff, Richard, 'Rachel Carson's Critics Keep On, But She Told Truth About DDT', https://e360.yale.edu/features/rachel_carsons_critics_keep_on_but_she_told_truth_about_ddt.

Doro E., 'An Environmental History of Tobacco Pests and Diseases in Southern Rhodesia, 1893–1940', Environment & Society Portal, *Arcadia*, 31 (Summer 2019), Rachel Carson Center for Environment and Society. www.environmentandsociety.org/node/8766.

Frankema E. et al., *An Introduction to the African Commodity Trade Database, 1730–2010*, DANS, doi.org/10.17026/dans-xt9-fzkw.

Glenza, Jessica, 'Tobacco Companies Tighten Hold on Washington under Trump', available on www.theguardian.com/world/2017/jul/13/tobacco-industry-trump-administration-ties.

Gogo, Jeffrey, 'Zimbabwe's Tobacco Industry Seeks to Cure Addiction to Fuel Wood', http://news.trust.org//item/20140501090447-tjohm/.

Government, BAT Sign MoU', available at www.herald.co.zw/govt-bat-sign-mou/.

Griswold, Eliza, 'How "Silent Spring" Ignited the Environmental Movement', *New York Times*, 21 September 2012, www.nytimes.com/2012/09/23/magazine/how-silent-spring-ignited-the-environmental-movement.html.

Human Rights Watch, "Hellish Work" Exploitation of Migrant Tobacco Workers in Kazakhstan', www.hrw.org/report/2010/07/14/hellish-work/exploitation-migrant-tobacco-workers-kazakhstan.

Kloor, Keith, 'The Lessons and Echoes of Silent Spring', http://blogs.discovermagazine.com/collideascape/2012/06/22/the-lessons-and-echoes-of-silent-spring/#.WzvC-RaxWEC.

Madanhire, Ignatio and Mbohwa, Charles, Impact of Smoking in a Tobacco-Growing Developing Country: A Review, Available on http://dx.doi.org/10.5772/intechopen.85959.

McLaughlin Mark, 'Counterbalancing Declensionist Narratives in Environmental History', Network in Canadian History and Environment (NiCHE), 3 February 2016, available at http://niche-canada.org/2016/02/03/counterbalancing-declensionist-narratives-in-environmental-history/.

Mlambo, Elias, 'Tobacco Farmers Fuel Deforestation', *The Zimbabwe Independent*, 28 March 2014, available at www.theindependent.co.zw/2014/03/28/small-scale-tobacco-farmers-fuel-massive-deforestation/.

Muzi, Luca and Tondo Lorenzo, 'I Had Pain All over My Body': Italy's Tainted Tobacco Industry', www.theguardian.com/global-development/2019/may/31/i-had-pain-all-over-my-body-italys-tainted-tobacco-industry.

'Pesticides: Children's Health and the Environment', www.who.int/ceh/capacity/Pesticides.pdf

Philip Morris International, 'Eliminating Coal from Tobacco Curing', World Business Council for Sustainable Development, available at www.wbcsd.org/Programs/Redefining-Value/Business-Decision-Making/Measurement-Valuation/Business-Examples/Philip-Morris-International-Eliminating-coal-from-tobacco-curing.

Report of the World Commission on Environmental Development: Our Common Future, available at www.un-documents.net/our-common-future.pdf.

Romo, Patricia Díaz, 'Huicholes y Plaguicidas' [Huichols and Pesticides], www.youtube.com/watch?v=-5k7Xg8JuMI

Standard Schaeffer, 'The Greening of Big Tobacco', *Counterpunch Magazine*, https://counterpunch.org/2007/12/15/the-greening-of-big-tobacco/

'The Secret Bribes of Big Tobacco', www.bbc.com/news/business-34964603, accessed 10 July 2023.

Thomson Ron, 'DDT: The Resurrection of an Old Threat to Africa's Wildlife', www.africahunting.com/threads/ddt-the-resurrection-of-an-old-threat-to-africa%E2%80%99s-wildlife.14737/.

Thornycroft, Peter, 'Tobacco Prices Go up in Smoke', available at www.businesslive.co.za/fm/features/africa/2019-06-13-tobacco-prices-go-up-in-smoke-in-zimbabwe/.

'Tobacco Farmers Cry Foul over Forex Payments', www.zbc.co.zw/farmers-cry-foul-over-pricing-of-golden-leaf/.

Tobacco Group Ejects Zimbabwe's Golden Leaf after Accusations of Dealing in Illicit Trade', available at www.news24.com/fin24/Companies/Agribusiness/tobacco-group-ejects-zimbabwes-gold-leaf-after-accusations-of-dealing-in-illicit-trade-20200929.

'Tobacco Politics', www.who.int/tobacco/en/atlas24.pdf?ua=1.

World Rainforest Movement, 'Mounting Pressure Against Eucalyptus in Kenya Described as a Water Guzzler', World Rainforest Movement, Bulletin 147, October 2009, available at https://wrm.org.uy/articles-from-the-wrm-bulletin/section2/mounting-pressure-against-eucalyptus-in-kenya-described-as-the-water-guzzler/.

'Zim Tobacco Faces Ban over DDT Residue Contamination', *AgriNews*, 14 December 2018, https://agrinews.co.zw/crops/2018/14/2153zim-tobacco-faces-ban-over-ddt-residue-contamination/.

'Zimbabwe Government Dismisses HRW Report on Child Labour', available on www.voanews.com/africa/zimbabwes-government-dismisses-hrw-report-child-labor

'Zimbabwe Grows Tobacco for China', www.youtube.com/watch?v=EHPmtI8VJYk.

'Zimbabwe Tobacco Production Hits Record High', available at www.zbc.co.zw/zims-tobacco-production-hits-record-high/.

'Zimbabwe Tobacco Sector Booming but Farmers Growing It Are Not', Voice of America, 30 May 2017, available at www.voanews.com/africa/zimbabwe-tobacco-booming-farmers-growing-it-are-not.

Marufu, Livingstone, 'Zimbabwe Tobacco under Threat', *The Herald*, 24 January 2018, available at www.herald.co.zw/zimbabwe-tobacco-under-threat/.

Mutsaka, Farai, 'Zimbabwe tobacco boom but farmers are complaining of debt', Available on https://abcnews.go.com/International/wireStory/zimbabwes-tobacco-booms-black-growers-complain-debt-77855755.

Oral Interviews

Interview with Chakona, 46 year-old, tobacco farmer, Hopi village, Mt Darwin district, 10 June 2021.

Interview with Chikore, 37 year-old, tobacco farmer, Dhabi village, Mukwengure ward, 8 June 2021.

Interview with Mr Barnabas, 32 year-old, tobacco farmer, Mutwa Estate, Mount Darwin district, 22 June 2021.

Interview with Mr Chavhakaira, 69 year-old, African tobacco farmer, Bare, Chiweshe, 13 December 2017.

Interview with Mr Ganizani, former farm worker, 68 year-old, Westbury Farm, Centenary, 13 February 2019.

Interview with Mr Goma, 62 year-old, tobacco farmer, Westbury farm, Centenary district, 13 February 2019.

Interview with Mr Jata, 37 year-old, tobacco farmer, Mutwa Estate, Mount Darwin district, 22 June 2021.

Interview with Mr Jimu, 63 year-old, Avalon farm, Centenary, 15 February 2014.

Interview with Mr Kavhimbo, 71 year-old, Mutwa Estate, Mount Darwin, 24 February 2019

Interview with Mr Makanjera 74 year-old, African tobacco farmer, Karuyana, Mt Darwin, 18 December 2017.

Interview with Mr Masekeni 67 year-old, African tobacco farmer, Bare, Chiweshe, 12 December 2017.

Interview with Mrs Saizi former farm worker, 74 year-old, Westbury Farm, Centenary, Zimbabwe, 13 February 2019.

Interview with Ms Tera, 28 year-old, tobacco farmer, Avalon farm, Centenary district, 12 June 2021.

Interview with Tsenzi, 54 year-old, tobacco farmer, Stanmore farm, Mukwengure ward, 6 June 2021.

Secondary Sources

Theses and Dissertations

Barnes C., *An Experiment with African Coffee Growing in Kenya: The Gusii, 1933–1950* (PhD thesis, Michigan State University, 1976).

Chivheya R. V., *Indigenous Forest Level of Deforestation, Forest Dependency and Factors Deserving Willingness to Participate in Indigenous Forestry Conservation: Evidence from Resettled Farmers in Shamva* (PhD thesis, University of Fort Hare, 2016).

Chivuraise C., *Economics of Small Holder Tobacco Production and Implications of Tobacco on Deforestation in Hurungwe District of Zimbabwe* (MSc thesis, University of Zimbabwe, 2011).
Elliot J. A., *Soil Erosion and Conservation in Zimbabwe: Political Economy and Environment* (DPhil thesis, Loughborough University of Technology, 1989).
Graen L., *Opening Malawi's Tobacco Black Box* (DPhil thesis, Martin Luther University of Halle-Wittenberg, 2012).
Hove G., *The State, Farmers and Dairy Farming in Colonial Zimbabwe (Southern Rhodesia), C.1890–1951* (PhD thesis, Stellenbosch University, 2015).
McGregor J., *Woodland Resources: Ecology, Policy and Ideology: An Historical Case Study of Woodlands Use in Shurugwi Communal Area, Zimbabwe* (PhD thesis, Loughborough University of Technology, 1991).
Machingaidze V. E. M., *The Development of Settler Capitalist Agriculture in Southern Rhodesia with Particular Reference to the Role of the State, 1908–1939* (PhD thesis, University of London, 1980).
McKenzie J. A., *Commercial Farmers in the Governmental System of Colonial Zimbabwe* (PhD thesis, University of Zimbabwe, 1989).
MacKenzie J. M, *African Labour in South Central Africa, 1890–1914, and Nineteenth Century Colonial Labour Theory* (PhD thesis, University of British Columbia, 1969).
Mudimu E., *The Impact of Environmental Change on Rural Livelihoods in Zimbabwe, The Case of Hurungwe District Ward 13, 2006–2014* (BA Hons thesis, Midlands State University, 2014).
Madimu T., *Farmers, Miners and the State in Colonial Zimbabwe, c. 1895–1961* (PhD thesis, University of Stellenbosch, 2017).
Maravanyika S., *Soil Conservation and the White Agrarian Environment in Colonial Zimbabwe, 1908–1980* (PhD thesis, University of Pretoria, 2013).
Masocha S., *Tobacco Research Board: A History with Special Reference to the Flue-Cured Virginia Tobacco Industry, 1935–1965* (BA Hons thesis, University of Zimbabwe, 1996).
Mhike M., *An Evaluation of the Impact of Tobacco Farming on Livelihoods and Land Degradation: A Case Study of Mount Bokoto Ward 24, Murehwa District, 2000–2013* (BA Hons thesis, Midlands State University, 2014).
Ncube S., *Colonial Zimbabwe Tobacco Industry: Global, Regional and Local Relations, 1949–1979* (PhD thesis, University of the Free State, 2018).

Ndomba H., *A History of Peasant Tobacco Production in Ruvuma Region, Southern Tanzania, c. 1930–2016* (PhD thesis, Stellenbosch University, 2018).

Pilossof R., *The Unbearable Whiteness of Being: White Farming Voices in Zimbabwe and Their Narration of the Recent Past, c. 1970–2004* (PhD thesis, Sheffield University, 2010).

Pophiwa N., *Settler Planter Interests and Encouragement of African Turkish Tobacco Production in Southern Rhodesia, 1954–1962* (BA Hons thesis, University of Zimbabwe, 2004).

Punt E., *The Development of African Agriculture in Southern Rhodesia with Particular Reference to the Inter-War Years* (MA thesis, University of Natal, 1979).

Rooney M. G. B., *European Agriculture in the History of Rhodesia, 1890–1907* (MA thesis, UNISA, 1968).

Samasuwo N., *'There Is Something about Cattle': Towards an Economic History of the Beef Industry in Colonial Zimbabwe, with Special Reference to the Role of the State, 1939–1980* (PhD thesis, University of Cape Town, 2000).

Selby A., *'Commercial Farmers and the State: Internal Group Politics and Land Reform in Zimbabwe* (PhD thesis, University of Oxford, 2006).

Shutt A., *'We Are the Best Poor Farmers': Purchase Area Farmers and Economic Differentiation in Southern Rhodesia, c. 1925–1980* (PhD thesis, University of California, 1995).

Conference and Seminar Papers

Babere Kerata Chacha, 'From Pastoralist to Tobacco Peasants: The BAT and Socio-ecological Change in Kuria District Kenya, 1969–1999' (unpublished paper).

Keyser J. C., 'Crop Substitution and Alternative Crops for Tobacco', study conducted as a technical document for the First Meeting of the Ad Hoc Study Group on Alternative Crops Established by the Conference of the Parties to the WHO Framework Convention on Tobacco Control, February 2007.

Matibiri A., 'Tobacco Production and Marketing Trends in Zimbabwe in the Last Two Decades', Coresta conference paper, Victoria Falls, 2 April 2019.

Maumbe B., and Swinton S. M., 'Hidden Costs of Pesticide Use in Zimbabwe's Smallholder Cotton' (unpublished paper), American Agricultural Economics Association Annual Meeting, California, 28–31 July 2002.

Nyambara P. S., 'A History of Land Acquisition, Commercialisation of Agriculture and Socio-economic Differentiation among Peasant

Farmers in a Frontier Region: The Gokwe District of Northwestern Zimbabwe: c. 1945–1990s', seminar paper presented in the Richard Ward Building, University of the Witwatersrand, 26 May 1997.
Scoones I., 'The Politics of Trypanosomiasis Control in Africa', STEPS Working Paper 57 (Brighton: STEPS Centre, 2014).

Books and Chapters in Books

Akehurst B. C., *Tobacco* (London, 1981).
Alexander J., *The Unsettled Land: State Making and the Politics of Land in Zimbabwe, 1893–2003* (Oxford, 2006).
Anderson D., and Grove R., *Conservation in Africa: People, Politics and Practice* (Cambridge, 1987).
Araghi F., 'The Invisible Hand and the Visible Foot: Peasants, Dispossession and Globalization', in A. Haroon Akram-Lodhi and C. Kay (eds.), *Peasants and Globalization: Political Economy, Rural Transformation and the Agrarian Question* (London and New York, 2009).
Arrighi G., *The Political Economy of Rhodesia* (Mouton, 1967).
Astrow A., *Zimbabwe: A Revolution That Lost Its Way?* (London, 1983).
Athearn R. G., *The Mythic West in 20th Century America* (Kansas, 1986).
Badger A. J., *Prosperity Road: The New Deal, Tobacco, and North Carolina* (Chapel Hill, 1980).
Barber W. J., *The Political Economy of British Central Africa* (London, 1963).
Baud M., *Peasants and Tobacco in the Dominican Republic: 1870–1930* (Knoxville,1995).
Beinart W., *The Rise of Conservation in South Africa: Settlers, Livestock, and the Environment, 1770–1950* (Oxford, 2003).
Beinart W., and C. Bundy, *Hidden Struggles in Rural South Africa* (Berkeley, 1987).
Bennett H., *Soil Conservation* (New York, 1939).
Benson P., *Tobacco Capitalism: Growers, Migrant Workers, and the Changing Face of a Global Industry* (Princeton, 2012).
Berman B., *Control and Crisis in Colonial Kenya: The Dialectic of Domination* (London, 1990).
Berry T., *The Dream of the New Earth* (New York, 1990).
Billington R. A., *Frontier and Section: Selected Essays of Frederick Jackson Turner* (New Jersey, 1961).
Bonnifield P., *The Dust Bowl: Men, Dirt and Depression* (Albuquerque, 1979).

Brandt A. M., *The Cigarette Century: The Rise, Fall, and Deadly Persistence of the Product That Defined America* (New York, 2007).

Brooks J. E., *The Mighty Leaf: Tobacco throughout the Centuries* (Boston, 1952).

Bullard R. D., *Confronting Environmental Racism: Voices from the Grassroots* (Boston, MA, 1993).

Dumping in Dixie: Race, Class, and Environmental Quality (Boulder, 1990).

Bulman M. E., *The Native Land Husbandry Act of Southern Rhodesia: A Failure in Land Reform* (Tribal Areas of Rhodesia Research Foundation: Salisbury, 1975).

Bundy C., *The Rise and Fall of The South African Peasantry* (London, 1979).

Burke T., *Lifebuoy Men, Lux Women: Commodification, Consumption and Cleanliness in Modern Zimbabwe* (London, 1996).

Carson R., *Silent Spring* (London, 1963).

Clements F. and Harben E., *Leaf of Gold: The Story of Rhodesian Tobacco* (London, 1962).

Coetzee J. M., *White Writing: On the Culture of Letters in South Africa* (New Haven, Cape Town, 1988).

Cole D. L and Cole J. S., 'Tobacco Research and Development' in M. Rukuni and Eicher C. K eds., *Zimbabwe's Agricultural Revolution*, (Harare, 1994).

Craven A., *Soil Exhaustion as a Factor in the Agricultural History of Virginia and Maryland, 1606–1860* (Urbana, 1925).

Cronon W., *Changes in the Land: Indians, Colonists, and the Ecology of New England* (New York, 2003).

'Silent Spring and the Birth of Modern Environmentalism', in Dunlap T. R (ed.)., *DDT, The Silent Spring and the Rise of Environmentalism: Classic Texts* (Seattle, WA, 2008).

Crosby A. W., *Ecological Imperialism: The Biological Expansion of Europe, 900–1900* (Cambridge, 1986).

'Ecological Imperialism: The Overseas Migration of Western Europeans as a Biological Phenomenon' in Worster D. (ed.)., *The Ends of the Earth: Perspectives on Environmental History* (Cambridge, 1988).

Cullather N., *The Hungry World: America's Cold War Battle against Poverty in Asia* (London, 2010).

Daniel P., *Breaking the Land: The Transformation of Cotton, Tobacco, and Rice Cultures since 1880* (Urbana, 1985).

Degroot D., *The Frigid Golden Age: Climate Change, the Little Ice Age, and the Dutch Republic, 1560–1720* (New York, 2018).

De Kock E. P., *Various Outspans* (Bloemfontein, 1948).

Department of Agriculture, *A Handbook on Tobacco Culture for Planters in Southern Rhodesia* (Southern Rhodesia, 1905).

A Handbook on Tobacco Culture for Planters in Southern Rhodesia (Southern Rhodesia, 1913).

Driessen P., *Eco-Imperialism: Green Power, Black Death* (Bellevue, WA, 2003).

Earle C., 'The Myth of the Southern Soil Miner: Macrohistory, Agricultural Innovation, and Environmental Change', in W. Donald (ed.)., *The Ends of the Earth: Perspectives on Environmental History* (Cambridge, 1988).

Feierman S., *Peasant Intellectuals: Anthropology and History in Tanzania* (London, 1990).

Fontein J., *Remaking the Mutirikwi: Landscape, Water and Belonging in Southern Zimbabwe* (Suffolk, 2015).

Ford J., *The Role of Trypanosomiases in African Ecology: A Study of the Tsetse Fly Problem* (Oxford, 1971).

Fraser A., *The Use of Wood by the Tobacco Industry and the Ecological Implications* (Edinburgh, 1986).

Fraser A. and Bowles R. C. D., *The Use of Wood by the Tobacco Industry in Zimbabwe,* (Edinburgh,1986).

Galbraith J. K., *The Affluent Society* (Boston, 1958).

Gann L. H., *A History of Southern Rhodesia: Early days to 1934* (London, 1965).

Gilman S. L. and Xun Z., *Smoke: A Global History of Smoking* (London, 2004).

Godwin P. and Hancock I., *'Rhodesians Never Die': The Impact of War and Political Change on White Rhodesia, c.1970–1980* (Oxford, 1993).

Goodland R. J. A, Watson C. and Ledee G., *Environmental Management in Tropical Africa* (Boulder, 1984).

Goodman J., *Tobacco in History: The Cultures of Dependence* (New York, 1993).

Graham F., *Since Silent Spring* (London, 1972).

Gray L. C., *History of Agriculture in the Southern States to 1860* (Gloucester, 1958).

Green E., 'Land Concentration, Institutional Control and African Agency: Growth and Stagnation of European Tobacco Farming in Shire Highlands *c*.1900–1940' in E. Hillbom and P. Svensson (eds.), *Agricultural Transformation in a Global History Perspective* (New York, 2013), 229–252.

Grove R., *Green Imperialism: Colonial Expansion, Tropical Island Edens and the Origins of Environmentalism, 1600–1860* (Cambridge, 1996).

Guha R. and Martinez J., *Varieties of Environmentalism: Essays North and South* (London, 1997).

Hartz L. (ed.)., *The Founding of New Societies: Studies in the History of the United States, Latin America, South Africa, Canada, and Australia* (San Diego, CA, 1964).

Harvey W., *On the South African Frontier: The Adventures and Observations of an American in Mashonaland and Matabeleland* (New York, 1899).

Hays S. P., *Conservation and the Gospel of Efficiency: The Progressive Conservation Movement 1890–1920* (Cambridge, 1959).

Hemans H. N., *The Logs of a Native Commissioner, Reprint of the 1935 Edition* (Bulawayo, 1971).

Hewes L., *The Suitcase Farming Frontier: A study in the Historical Geography of the Central Great Plains* (Lincoln, 1973).

Hodder-Williams R., *White Farmers in Rhodesia: A History of the Marandellas District, 1890–1965* (London, 1983).

Hofstadter R., *The Progressive Historians: Turner, Beard and Parrington* (New York, 1968).

Hollerman H., *Dust Bowls of Empire: Imperialism, Environmental Politics, and the Injustice of "Green" Capitalism* (New Haven, 2018).

Hone P. F., *Southern Rhodesia* (London, 1909).

Hoppe K. A., *Lords of the Fly: Sleeping Sickness Control in British East Africa, 1900–1960* (Westport, CT, 2003).

Howard P. A., *Black Labour, White Sugar: Caribbean Braceros and Their Struggle for Power in the Cuban Sugar Industry* (Baton Rouge, 2015).

Hudson-Weems C., 'Environmental Racism: Black Landowners, and the Making of a New Hilton Head: An Emmett Till Continuum', in F. Steady (ed.)., *Environmental Justice in the New Millennium: Global Perspectives on Race, Ethnicity and Human Rights* (New York, 2009).

Hurley A., *Environmental Inequalities: Class, Race and Industrial Pollution in Gary, Indiana, 1945–1980* (Chapel Hill, 1995).

Hurt D., *Dust Bowl* (Chicago, 1981).

Iliffe J., *Agricultural Change in Modern Tanganyika* (Nairobi, 1971).

Isaac R., *The Transformation of Virginia, 1740–1790* (Chapel Hill, 1982).

Kanyenze G., 'Zimbabwe Labour Relations Policies and Implications for Workers' in Amanor-Wilks (ed.), *Zimbabwe Farm Workers: Policy Dimension* (Lusaka, 2001), 86–114.

Keats J. in Abrams M. H., *The Norton Anthology of English Literature*, vol. 2 (New York, 1970).

Khan F., 'The Roots of Environmental Racism and the Rise of Environmental Justice in the 1990s' in D. McDonald (ed.)., *Environmental Justice in South Africa* (Cape Town, 2002).

Kinkela D., *DDT and the American Century: Global Health, Environmental Politics and the Pesticide That Changed the World* (Chapel Hill, NC, 2011).

Kjekshus H., *Ecology Control and Economic Development in East African History* (London, 1987).

Knight-Bruce G. H. W., *Memories of Mashonaland* (London, 1895).

Kosmin B., 'The Inyoka Tobacco Industry of the Shangwe People: The Displacement of a Pre-colonial Economy in Southern Rhodesia', in R. Palmer and N. Parsons (eds.)., *The Roots of Rural Poverty in Central and Southern Africa* (London, 1977).

Krishnamurthy B. S., 'Economic Policy, Land and Labour in Nyasaland, 1890–1914', in B. Pachai (ed.)., *Early History of Malawi* (London, 1972).

Laws B., *Fifty Plants That Changed the Course of History* (New York, 2010).

Lenin V., 'Preliminary Drafts on the Agrarian Question', in *Collected Works*, Vol. XXX1 (Moscow, 1966).

Lowitt R., *The New Deal and the West* (Bloomington, 1984).

Lytle M. H., *The Gentle Subversive: Rachel Carson, the Silent Spring and the Rise of the Environmental Movement* (New York, 2007).

Mackenzie J., 'Empire and the Ecological Apocalypse: The Historiography of the Imperial Environment', in T. Griffith and L. Robin (eds.), *Ecology and Empire: Environmental History of Settler Societies* (Edinburgh, 1997).

Magnan A., *When Wheat Was King: The Rise and Fall of the Canada-UK Grain Trade* (Vancouver, 2016).

Martin D. and Johnson P., *The Struggle for Zimbabwe: The Chimurenga War* (London, 1981).

Martinez-Alier J., *The Environmentalism of the Poor: A Study of Ecological Conflicts and Valuation* (Cheltenham, 2002).

Mbanga T., *Tobacco: A Century of Gold* (Harare, 1991).

McCracken J., 'Sharecropping in Malawi: The Visiting Tenant System in the Central Province, c. 1920–68' in J. McCracken (ed.), *Malawi: An Alternative Pattern of Development* (Edinburgh, 1984), 157–174.

Miller S., *An Environmental History of Latin America* (Cambridge, 2007).

Milov S., *The Cigarette: A Political History* (Massachusetts, 2019).

Mitchell D., 'Women and 19th Century Images of Smoking', in L. G. Sander and X. Zhou (eds.)., *Smoke: A Global History of Smoking* (London, 2004).

Mosley P., *The Settler Economies: Studies in the Economic History of Kenya and Southern Rhodesia, 1900–1963* (Cambridge, 1983).

Mulwafu O., *Conservation Song: A History of Peasant State Relations and the Environment in Malawi, 1860–2000* (Cambridge, 2010).

Murray D. J., *The Governmental System in Southern Rhodesia* (Oxford, 1970).

Nixon R., *Slow Violence and the Environmentalism of the Poor* (Cambridge, 2011).

Oreskes N. and Conway E. M., *Merchants of Doubt: How a Handful of Scientists Obscured the Truth on Issues from Tobacco Smoke to Global Warming* (New York, 2010).

Palmer R., 'The Agricultural History of Rhodesia', R. Palmer and N. Parsons (eds.)., *The Roots of Rural Poverty in Central and Southern Africa* (London, 1977).

Land and Racial Domination in Southern Rhodesia (London, 1977).

Pearson C., *Mobilizing Nature: The Environmental History of War and Militarization in Modern France* (Manchester, 2012).

Phalane M. F. and Steady F., 'Nuclear Energy, Hazardous Waste, Health, and Environmental Justice in South Africa', in D. A. McDonald (ed.)., *Environmental Justice in South Africa* (Cape Town, 2002).

Phimister I., *An Economic and Social History of Zimbabwe, 1890–1948: Capital Accumulation and Class Struggle* (London, 1988).

Price A. G., *White Settlers and Native Peoples* (Melbourne, 1950).

White Settlers, in the Tropics (New York, 1978).

Ranger T., *Peasant Consciousness and Guerrilla War in Zimbabwe* (London, 1985).

Ross A., *Strange Weather: Culture, Science and Technology in the Age of Limits* (New York, 1991).

Rowe D. M., *Manipulating the Market: Understanding Economic Sanctions, Institutional Change and the Political Unity of White Rhodesia* (Ann Arbor, 2001).

Rubert S., *A Most Promising Weed: A History of Tobacco Farming and Labour in Colonial Zimbabwe, 1890–1945* (Athens, 1998).

Rukuni M., 'The Evolution of Agricultural Policy,1890–1990', in M. Rukuni and E. K. Eicher (eds.)., *Zimbabwe's Agricultural Revolution* (Harare, 1993).

Saul J. S. and Woods R., 'African Peasantries', in T. Shanin (ed.)., *Peasants and Peasant Societies* (University of Michigan, 1971).

Scott J. C., *Seeing Like a State: How Certain Schemes to Improve the Human Condition Have Failed* (New Haven, 1998).

Showers K., *Imperial Gullies: Soil Erosion and Conservation in Lesotho* (Athens, 2005).

Siegel F. F., *The Roots of Southern Distinctness: Tobacco and Society in Danville, Virginia,1780–1865* (Chapel Hill, 1987).
Smith H. N., *Virgin Land: The American West as Symbol and Myth* (Cambridge, 1970).
Smith I., *Bitter Harvest: The Great Betrayal and the Dreadful Aftermath* (Johannesburg, 2001).
Sondley F. A., *A History of Buncombe County, North Carolina* (Spartanburg, SC, 1977).
Steady F., 'Environmental Justice Cross-Culturally: Theory and Praxis in the African Diaspora and in Africa', F. Steady (ed.)., *Environmental Justice in the New Millennium: Global Perspectives on Race, Ethnicity and Human Rights* (New York, 2009).
Thomas T. M., *Eleven Years in Central South Africa* (Cardiff, 1873).
Thomson H. C., *Rhodesia and Its Government* (London, 1898).
Thurston A., *Smallholder Agriculture in Colonial Kenya: The Official Mind and the Swynnerton Plan* (Cambridge, 1987).
Tiffen M. et al., *More People, Less Erosion: Environmental Recovery in Kenya* (London, 1994).
Tiffen M, Mortimore M. and Gichuki F., *Population Growth and Environmental Recovery: Policy Lessons from Kenya* (Chichester, 1994).
Tilley H., 'African Environments and African Social Sciences: The African Research Survey, Ecological Paradigms and British Colonial Development', in W. Beinart and J. McGregor (eds.)., *Social History and African Environments* (Oxford, 2003).
Empire, Development and the Problem of Scientific Knowledge, 1870–1950: Africa as a Living Laboratory (Chicago, 2011).
Tilley N. M., *The Bright Tobacco Industry, 1860–1929* (Chapel Hill, 1948).
Tobacco Export Promotional Council of Rhodesia and Nyasaland, Rhodesia's Golden Harvest: A Special Review of the Tobacco Industry of Rhodesia and Nyasaland (Salisbury, 1963).
Tropp J. A., *Natures of Colonial Change: Environmental Relations in the Making of the Transkei* (Athens, 2006).
Turner F. J., *The Frontier in American History* (New York, 1921).
Turrell R., 'Kimberly: Labour and Compounds, 1871–1888,' in S. Marks and R. Rathbone (eds.), *Industrialisation and Social Change in South Africa: African Class Formation, Culture, and Consciousness, 1870–1930* (Essex, 1982).
Van den Bosch R., *The Pesticide Conspiracy* (Berkeley, CA, 1978).
Van Loggerenberg J., *Tobacco Wars: Inside the Spy games and Dirty Tricks of Southern Africa's Cigarette Trade* (Cape Town, 2019).

Van Onselen C., *Chibharo, African Mine Labour in Southern Rhodesia, 1900–1933* (London, 1976).

The Seed Is Mine: The Life of Kas Maine, a South African Sharecropper, 1894–1985 (London, 1987).

Wagner P., *A Sociology of Modernity: Liberty and Discipline* (London, 1993).

Warde P., Robin L. and Sörlin S., *The Environment: A History of the Idea* (Baltimore, 2018).

Webb W. P., *The Great Frontier* (Cambridge, MA, 1951).

Weinmann H., *Agricultural Research and Development in Southern Rhodesia, 1890–1923* (Salisbury, 1972).

Agricultural Research and Development in Southern Rhodesia, 1924–1950 (Salisbury, 1975).

Weinrich A. K. H, *African Farmers in Rhodesia: Old and New Peasant Communities in Karangaland* (London, 1975).

Welshman J., 'Smoking, Science and Medicine' in S. L. Gilman and Z. Xun (eds.), *Smoke: A Global History of Smoking* (London, 2004).

West M., *The Rise of an African Middle Class: Colonial Zimbabwe, 1898–1965* (Bloomington, 2002).

Wood J. G., *Through Matabeleland: The Record of a Ten Months' Trip in an Ox Waggon through Mashonaland and Matebeleland, Reprint of 1893 edition* (Bulawayo, 1974).

Worster D., 'Doing Environmental History', in D. Worster (ed.), *The Ends of the Earth: Perspectives on Modern Environmental History* (Cambridge, 1988).

Dust Bowl: The Southern Plains in the 1930s (Oxford, 1979).

Nature's Economy: The Roots of Ecology (San Francisco, 1972).

Rivers of Empire; Water Aridity and the Growth of the American West (New York, 1985).

Under the Western Skies: Nature, History and the American West (Oxford, 1982).

Yudelman M., *Africans on the Land: Economic Problems of African Agricultural Development in Southern, Central and East Africa with Special Reference to Southern Rhodesia* (Cambridge, 1964).

Zwanenberg R. V., *The Agricultural History of Kenya to 1939* (Nairobi, 1972).

Journal Articles

African Explosives and Industries Limited, 'Rhodes Grass for the Rhodesian Tobacco Grower', *Rhodesia Agricultural Journal,* 32, 10 (October 1935), 700.

Algeo K., 'The Rise of Tobacco as a Southern Appalachian Staple: Madison County, North Carolina', *South-eastern Geographer*, 37, 1 (May 1997), 46–60.

Anderson D. and Throup D., 'Africans and Agricultural Production in Colonial Kenya: The Myth of the War as a Watershed', *The Journal of African History*, 26, 4, *World War II and Africa* (1985), 327–345.

Anderson D., 'Depression, Dust Bowl, Demography, and Drought: The Colonial State and Soil Conservation in East Africa during the 1930s', *African Affairs*, 83, 332 (1984), 321–343.

Arcury T. and Quandt S., 'Health and Social Impacts of Tobacco Production', *Journal of Agro-medicine*, 11, 3–4 (2008), 71–81.

Arrighi G., 'Labour Supplies in Historical Perspective: A Study of the Proletarianization of the African Peasantry in Rhodesia', *Journal of Development Studies*, vi (1970), 198–233.

Aylen D. and Roberts H. R., 'Soil Erosion Technical Bulletin', *Rhodesia Agricultural Journal,* (February 1937), 64.

Bandason T. and Rukasaniko S., 'Prevalence and Associated Factors of Smoking among Secondary School Students in Harare, Zimbabwe', *Tobacco Induced Diseases*, 8, 12 (2010), 1–9.

Baud M. and Koonings K., 'A Lavoura dos Pobres: Tobacco Farming and the Development of Commercial Agriculture in Bahia: 1870–1930', *Journal of Latin American Studies*, 31, 2 (1999), doi.org/10.1017/S0022216X99005295.

Beinart W., 'Academic Amnesia and the Poverty of Polemics', *Journal of African History,* 46, 1 (2005), 127–134.

Beinart W., Brown K. and Gilfoyle D., 'Experts and Expertise in Colonial Africa Reconsidered: Science and the Interpenetration of Knowledge', *African Affairs*, 108, 432 (July 2009), 413–433.

'The Politics of Colonial Conservation', *Journal of Southern African Studies*, 15, 2 (January 1989), 143–162.

'Soil Erosion, Conservationism and Ideas about Development: A Southern African Exploration, 1900–1960', *Journal of Southern African Studies*, 15, 1 (October 1984), 52–83.

Bennett E. P., 'Dubious Heritage: Tobacco, History, and the Perils of Remembering the Rural Past', *Agricultural History,* 86, 2 (Spring 2012), 23–40.

Bennet H. H., 'The Relation of Grass Cover to Soil Erosion Control', cited in *Rhodesia Agricultural Journal,* 32, 6 (June 1935), 385–394.

Berg H. et al., 'DDT and Other Insecticides in Lake Kariba Ecosystem', *Ambio* 21, 7 (November 1992), 444–450.

Blank G., 'Prosperity, Penury and Polarisation: Disaggregating the Peasantry in the Historiography of Colonial Zimbabwe', *African Journal of History and Culture*, 7, 1 (January 2015), 1–7.

Braje T. J., 'Earth Systems, Human Agency, and the Anthropocene: Planet Earth in the Human Age', *Journal of Archaeological Research*, 23, 4 (December 2015), 369–396.

Brown D. D., 'The Economics of the Rhodesia Tobacco Industry: Marketing and Disposal of the Crop', *Rhodesia Agricultural Journal*, 30, 7 (July 1933), 538–563.

'Tobacco Culture', *Rhodesia Agricultural Journal,* 29, 11 (November 1931), 1036.

Buttress M. H., 'Agricultural Land-Use in the Mazowe Valley during the Period 1966–1971', *Rhodesia Agricultural Journal*, 70, 5 (April 1972), 105.

Caldwell L., 'Environment: A Focus for Public Policy', in *Eikistics*, 17, 102 (May 1964).

Chambati W., 'Changing Forms of Wage Labour in Zimbabwe's New Agrarian Structure', *Agrarian South: Journal of Political Economy,* 6,1 (2017), 79–112.

Chapman S. et al., 'Smoking Control in Africa: Problems and Prospects', *Health Policy and Planning,* 13, (1986), 222–231.

Chavunduka D. M., 'African Attitudes to Conservation', *Rhodesia Agricultural Journal,* 75, 3 (May–June 1978), 61–63.

Chingosho R., Dare C. and Van Walbeek C., 'Tobacco Farming and Current Debt Status among Smallholder Farmers in Manicaland Province in Zimbabwe', *Tobacco Control*, 30, 6 (2021), 610–615.

Chung-Hall J. et al., 'Impact of the WHO FCTC over the First Decade: A Global Evidence Review Prepared for the Impact Assessment Expert Group', *Tobacco Control*, 28 (2018), 119–128.

Cole T., '"Nature Was Helping Us": Forests, Trees, and Environmental Histories of the Holocaust', *Environmental History*, 19, 4 (October 2014), 665–686.

Collins J. C., 'Tobacco Eelworm', *Rhodesia Agricultural Journal*, 35, 4 (April,1938), 264–278.

Cook C. D., 'The Spraying of America', *Earth Island Journal*, 20, 1 (Spring 2005), 34–38.

Cormack, J. M., 'Efficient Utilisation of Water through Land Management', *Rhodesia Agricultural Journal*, 69, 1 (March 1973), 12.

Cruitzen J. P. and Stoermer E. F., 'The Anthropocene', *Global Change Newsletter*, 41 (2000), 17–18.

Culver L., 'Reading *Silent Spring* as a Challenge for Contemporary Environmentalism', *RCC Perspectives*, 7 (2012), 31–34.

Daulton A., 'Survey of Land Use and Plant Parasitic Nematodes Control', *Rhodesia Agricultural Journal*, 59 (July–August 1962), 216–217.

Davis M., 'Los Angeles after the Storm: The Dialectics of Ordinary Disaster', *Antipode*, 27 (1995), 221–224.

Doro E. and Swart S., 'A Silenced Spring? Exploring Africa's 'Rachel Carson Moment': A Socio-environmental History of the Pesticides in Tobacco Production in Southern Rhodesia, 1945–80', *International Review of Environmental History*, 5, 2 (November 2019), 5–39.

Diogo M. P, Louro I. and Scarso D., 'Uncanny Nature: Why the Concept of Anthropocene is Relevant for Historians of Technology', *Icon*, 23 (2017), 25–35.

Doll R. and Bradford H. A. B., 'Lung Cancer and Other Causes of Death in Relation to Smoking: A Second Report on the Mortality of British Doctors', *The British Medical Journal*, 2, 5001 (November 1956), 1071–1081.

Downie J. W., 'Control Boards and Their Functions', *Rhodesia Agricultural Journal*, 28,10 (October 1931), 899–902.

Drinkwater M., 'Technical Development and Peasant Impoverishment: Land Use Policy in Zimbabwe's Midlands Province', *Journal of Southern African Studies*, 15, 2 (January 1989), 287–305.

Du Toit E. P., 'Timber as a Tobacco Curing Fuel', *Rhodesia Agricultural Journal*, 70, 5 (1974), 107–110.

Duggan W. R., 'The Native Land Husbandry Act of 1951 and the Rural African Middle Class of Southern Rhodesia', *African Affairs*, 79, 315 (April 1980), 227–239.

Duvall C. S., 'Cannabis and Tobacco in Precolonial Africa', Oxford Research Encyclopaedia of African *History*, (March 2017), 1–32.

Editorial, *Rhodesia Agricultural Journal* (December 1933), 106.

Rhodesia Agricultural Journal, 3 (February 1908), 153–159.

Federico G., 'Not Guilty? Agriculture in the 1930s and the Great Depression', *Journal of Economic History*, 65,4 (2005), 949–978.

Fite G., 'The Pioneer Farmer: A View Over Three Centuries', *Agricultural History*, 50, 1 (1976), 275–289.

Flint M. E. S. and Harrison M. J. S., 'DDT Impact Assessment Project: Zimbabwe', Department of International Aid, *Evaluation Report*, 621 (December 1998).

Floyd B. N., 'Land Apportionment in Southern Rhodesia', *Geographical Review*, 52, 4 (1962), 566–582.

Foltz R. C., 'Does Nature Have Agency? World History, Environmental History, and How Historians Can Help Save the Planet', *The History Teacher*, 37, 1 (2003), 9–28.

Froude M., 'Veld Management in the Victoria Tribal Areas', *Rhodesia Agricultural Journal*, 71, 2 (March–April 1974), 29–33.

Gamlin B., 'My Eyes Are Red from Looking and Looking: Mexican Working Children: Perspectives on How Tobacco Affects Their Bodies', *Vulnerable Children and Youth Studies*, 6, 4 (December 2011), 339–345.

Garden G., 'Catalyst or Cataclysm? Gold Mining and the Environment', *Victoria Historical Journal*, 72, 1–2 (2001), 28–44.

Garvin R. T., 'The Management of Labour on Zimbabwe's Flue-cured Tobacco Farms', *Agricultural Administration*, 12 (1983), 195–206.

Geist H. J., 'Global Assessment of Deforestation Related to Tobacco Farming', *Tobacco Control,* 8, 1 (Spring 1999), 18–28.

Gelfand M., Graham A. and Lightman E., 'Carcinoma of the Bronchus and the Smoking Habits of Rhodesian Africans', *British Medical Journal*, 3, 5616 (1968), 468–469.

Giblin J., 'Trypanosomiasis Control in African History: An Evaded Issue?', *Journal of African History*, 31, 1 (1990), 59–80.

Good K., 'Colonialism and Settler Colonialism: A Comparison', *Australian Outlook*, 33, 3 (1979), 339–351.

Gottschalk L. C., 'Effects of Erosion and Navigation in Upper Chesapeake Bay', *Geographic Review*, 35 (1945), 219–238.

Green G. P., 'The Political Economy of Flue-cured Tobacco Production', *Rural Sociology*, 52, (1987), 221–241.

Greenberg G. S., 'Pesticides: Whitehouse Advisory Body Issues Report Recommending Steps to Reduce Hazards to Public', *Science News Series* 40, 3569 (1963), 878–879.

Greichus Y. A et al., 'Insecticides, Polychlorinated Biphenyls and Metals in African Lake Ecosystems II: Lake Chivero, Zimbabwe', *Bulletin of Environmental Contamination and Toxicology*, 19 (1978), 444–453.

Grier B., 'Invisible Hands: The Political Economy of Child Labour in Colonial Zimbabwe, 1890–1930', *Journal of Southern African Studies*, 20, 1 (March 1994), 27–52.

Grove R., 'Scottish Missionaries, Evangelical Discourses and the Origins of Conservation Thinking in Southern Africa, 1820–1900', *Journal of Southern African Studies*, 15, 2 (1989), 163–184.

Harbeson J., 'Land Reforms and Politics in Kenya, 1954–70', *Journal of Modern African Studies*, 9, 2 (1971), doi.org/10.1017/S0022278X00024915.

Haviland W. E., 'The Use and Efficiency of African Labour in Tobacco Farming in Southern Rhodesia', *The Canadian Journal of Economics and Political Science*, 20, 1 (February 1954),100–106.

'Tobacco Farm Organisation, Cost and Land Use in Southern Rhodesia', *The South African Journal of Economics*, (December 1953), 367–380.

Hayman G. R., 'Conservation on a Tobacco Farm', *Rhodesia Agricultural Journal*, (June 1953), 223–234.

Heald S., 'Agricultural Intensification and the Decline of Pastoralism: A Case Study from Kenya', *Journal of the International African Institute*, 69, 2 (1999), 213–237.

'Tobacco, Time and the Household Economy in Two Kenyan Societies: The Teso and the Kuria', *Comparative Studies in Society and History*, 33, 1 (January 1991), 130–157.

Holm P. et al., 'Collaboration between the Natural, Social and Human Sciences in Global Change Research', *Environmental Science and Policy*, 28 (2013), 25–35.

Horwitz R., 'White Settlement in Africa', *African Studies*, 5,1 (1946), 63–66.

Hove G., 'Creating Order and Stability? The Dairy Marketing Board, Milk (over)production and the Politics of Marketing in Colonial Zimbabwe, 1952–1970s', *Historia*, 58, 2 (November 2013), 119–156.

Hudson N. W., 'Soil Erosion and Tobacco Growing', *Rhodesia Agricultural Journal*, (November–December 1957), 547–555.

Hughes D. M., 'Hydrology of Hope: Farm Dams, Conservation, and Whiteness in Zimbabwe', *American Ethnologist*, 33, 2 (May 2006), 269–287.

Hyde D., 'Paying for the Emergency by Displacing the Settlers: Global Coffee and Rural Restructuring in Late Colonial Kenya', *Journal of Global History*, 4, 1 (2009), doi.org/10.1017/S1740022809002964.

Ingold T., 'The Temporality of Landscapes', *World Archaeology*, 25, 2 (1993), 152–174.

Isaacman A., 'Historical Amnesia or the Logic of Capital Accumulation: Cotton Production in Colonial and Post-Colonial Mozambique', *Environment and Planning: Society and Space*, 15 (1997), 757–790.

Isaacman, A., 'Peasants, Social Protests and Africanists', *The Journal of African History, 22, 4* (1989), 745–765.

et al., 'Cotton is the Mother of Poverty': Peasant Resistance to Forced Cotton Production in Mozambique, 1938–1961', *The International Journal of African Historical Studies*, 13, 4 (1980), doi.org/10.2307/218197.

Jack W. R., 'Tobacco Pests of Southern Rhodesia', *Rhodesia Agricultural Journal*, 17.1 (February 1920), 28–33.

Jeater D., 'Imagining Africans: Scholarship, Fantasy, and Science in Colonial Administration, 1920s Southern Rhodesia', *The International Journal of African Historical Studies*, 38, 1 (2005), 1–26.

Johnson D., 'Settler Farmers and Coerced African Labour in Southern Rhodesia, 1936–46', *Journal of African History*, 33,1 (1992), doi.org/10.1017/S002185370003187X.

Johnson R. W., 'African Agricultural Development in Southern Rhodesia: 1945–1960', *Food Research Institute Studies*, 4:2 (1964), 165–223.

Kelsey H. E. A., 'Tobacco Experimental Station, Salisbury; Report of General Crop Experiments', *Rhodesia Agricultural Journal*, 28, 9 (September 1931), 919–926.

Keyter C. F., 'Maize Control in Southern Rhodesia, 1931–1941: The African Contribution to White Survival', 34, *Central Historical Association*, (1978).

Kramer R. A. and Batie S. S., 'Cross Compliance Concepts in Agricultural Programs: The New Deal to the Present', *Agricultural History*, 59, 2 (1985), 307–319.

Kroll G., 'The Silent Spring of Rachel Carson: Mass Media and the Origins of Modern Environmentalism', *Public Understanding of Science*, 10 (2001), 403–420.

Le Roux A. A., 'African Agriculture in Rhodesia', *Rhodesia Agricultural Journal*, 66, 2525 (July–August 1969), 84.

Lear L. J., 'Rachel Carson's Silent Spring', *Environmental History Review* 17, 2 (1993), 23–48.

Lecours N. et al., 'Environmental Health Impacts of Tobacco Farming: A Review of the Literature', *Tobacco Control*, 21, 2 (March 2012), 191–196.

Ling Q. et al., 'The Economic Geography of Kenyan Tobacco Farmers' Livelihood Decisions', *Nicotine and Tobacco Research* (2019), 1–4.

Lonsdale J., 'Agency in Tight Corners: Narrative and Initiative in African History', *Journal of African Cultural Studies*, 13:1 (2000), doi.org/10.1080/713674303.

Losman D. S., 'Rhodesia: A Decade Under Sanctions', *Il Politico*, 43, 2 (1978), 321–340.

Lown A. et al., 'Tobacco is Our Industry and We Will Support It: Exploring the Potential Implications of Zimbabwe's Accession to the Framework Convention on Tobacco Control', *Globalisation and Health*, 12, 2 (2016), 1–11.

Machingaidze V. E. M., 'Agrarian Change from Above: The Southern Rhodesia Native Land Husbandry Act and African Response', *The International Journal of African Historical Studies*, 24, 3 (1991), 557–588.

Mackenzie J. M., 'Colonial Labour Policy and Rhodesia', *Rhodesia Journal of Economics,* 8 (1974), 12–13.

Magadlela D., 'A Smoky Affair: Challenges Facing Some Small-Holder Burley Tobacco Producers in Zimbabwe,' *Zambezia*, XXIV.I, (1997), 13–30.

Maher N., 'Crazy Quilt Farming on Round Lands: The Great Plains: The Soil Conservation Scheme and the Politics of Landscape', *Western Historical Quarterly*, 31,3 (2000), 319–339.

Maier C., 'Consigning the Twentieth Century to History? Alternative Narratives for the Modern Era', *American Historical Review*, 105 (2000), 807–831.

Makana N. E., 'Peasant Response to Agricultural Innovations: Land Consolidation, Agrarian Diversification and Technical Change: The Case of Bungoma District in Western Kenya, 1954–1960', *Journal of Third World Studies*, 27, 1 (2010), doi.org/10.5070/F7351009560.

Malin J., 'Dust Storms: Part One,1850–1860', *Kansas Historical Quarterly*, 14 (May 1946), 129–140.

Masvongo J., Mutambara J. and Zvinavashe A., 'Viability in Tobacco Production Under the Smallholder Farming Sector in Mount Darwin District', *Journal of Development and Agriculture Economics,* 5, 8 (June 2013), 295–301.

Mbanda A. and Zaranyika M., 'DDT Residue in Terrestrial Environment in the Mount Darwin–Rushinga Area: Zimbabwe', *Journal of Applied Science in Southern Africa*, 7, 2 (2001), 83–96.

McCracken J., 'Planters, Peasants and the Colonial State: The Impact of the Native Tobacco Board in the Central Province of Malawi', *Journal of Southern African Studies*, 9, 2 (1983), 172–192.

McGregor J., 'Conservation Control and Ecological Change: The Politics and Ecology of Colonial Conservation in Shurugwi, Zimbabwe', *Environment and History*, 1, 3 (October 1995), 257–279.

McKinnell R., 'Sanctions and the Rhodesian Economy', *Journal of Modern African Studies*, 7, 4 (December 1969), 559–591.

Möllers N., 'Cur(at)ing the Planet: How to Exhibit the Anthropocene and Why?', *RCC Perspectives*, 3 (2013), 57–66.

Moroney S., 'The Development of the Compound as a Mechanism of Worker Control 1900–1912', *South African Labour Bulletin* 4, 3 (May 1978), 29–49.

Mosley P., 'Agricultural Development and Government Policy in Settler Economies: The Case of Kenya and Southern Rhodesia, 1900–60', *The Economic History Review*, 35, 3 (August 1982), 390–408.

Moyo S., 'Three Decades of Agrarian Reform in Zimbabwe', *The Journal of Peasant Studies*, 38, 3 (2011), 493–531.

Mpofu S. M., 'DDT and its Uses in Zimbabwe', *Zimbabwe Science News*, 21 (1987), 31–36.

Munangagwa C., 'The Economic Decline of Zimbabwe', *The Gettysburg Economic Review*, 3, 9 (2009), 110–129.

'Native Agriculture in Southern Rhodesia', *Rhodesia Agricultural Journal*, 27, 5 (May 1930), 466.

Ncube S., 'Beyond the State? Organised Settler Tobacco Interests and the Consolidation of Southern Rhodesia's Tobacco Industry in the Early Post-Second World War Years', *Journal of Southern African Studies*, DOI: 10.1080/03057070.2022.2049492.

'We Must Adapt to Survive: International Sanctions, Settler Politics, and White Tobacco Farmers' Struggles for Economic Survival in Rhodesia, 1966–1979', *African Economic History*, 48, 2 (2020), 67–91.

Nelson R., 'Environmental Colonialism: Saving Africa from Africans', *The Independent Review*, 8, 1 (Summer 2003), 65–86.

Nhapi T. G., 'Natural Resource Degradation through Tobacco Farming in Zimbabwe: CSR Implications and the Role of the Government', *South African Journal for Communication Theory and Research*, (April 2019), 1–15.

'Notes from the Irrigation Branch', *Rhodesia Agricultural Journal*, (April 1930), 308.

Nyambara P. S., 'Colonial Policy and Peasant Cotton Agriculture in Southern Rhodesia, 1904–1953', *The International Journal of African Historical Studies*, 33, 1 (2000), 81–111.

Nyambara P. S. and Nyandoro M., 'Tobacco Thrives, but the Environment Cries': The Sustainability of Livelihoods from Small-Scale Tobacco Growing in Zimbabwe, 2000–2017', *Global Environment*, 12, 2 (September 2019), 304–320.

Odlum G. M., 'Tobacco Notes', *Rhodesia Agricultural Journal*, 1 (1903–4), 185–187.

'Tobacco Notes', *Rhodesia Agricultural Journal*, 2, 1 (September 1904), 19–22.

'Tobacco Notes', *Rhodesia Agricultural Journal*, 4.1 (October 1906), 268–270.

O'Gorman E. and A. Gaynor., 'More-than-Human Histories', *Environmental History*, 25 (2020), 711–735.

Ohayo-Mitoko G. J. A et al., 'Acetylcholinesterase Inhibition as an Indicator of Organophosphate and Carbamate Poisoning in Kenyan Agricultural Workers, *International Journal of Occupational Environmental Health*, 3, 21 (1997),195–200.

Ortenez M. and Glantz S. A., 'Social Responsibility in Tobacco Production? Tobacco Companies Use of Green Supply Chains to Obscure the New

Costs of Tobacco Farming', *Tobacco Control*, 20, 6 (November 2011), 403–411.

Otañez M. G, Muggli M. E., Hurt R. D. and Glantz S. A., 'Eliminating Child Labour in Malawi: A British American Tobacco Corporate Responsibility Project to Sidestep Tobacco Labour Exploitation', *Tobacco Control*, 15, 3 (June 2006), 224–230.

Phelps R. J. and Billings T., 'Pesticide Levels from Animals in Southern Rhodesia', *Transactions of Rhodesia Science Association* 55 (1972), 6–9.

Philips J. E., 'African Smoking and Pipes', *Journal of African History*, 24 (1983), 303–319.

Phimister I., 'African Labour Conditions and Health in the Southern Rhodesia Mining Industry, 1893–1953, Part Three: Health', *The Central African Journal of Medicine*, 22, 9 (1976), 173–181.

'Peasant Production and Underdevelopment in Southern Rhodesia, 1890–1914', *African Affairs*, 73, 291 (April 1974), 217–228.

'Rethinking the Reserves: Southern Rhodesia's Land Husbandry Act Reviewed', *Journal of Southern African Studies*, 19, 2 (June 1993), 225–239.

Pilossof R., 'A Brief History of Tsetse Control Methods in Zimbabwe and Possible Effects of Climate Change on Their Distribution', *International Journal of African Development* 4, 1 (2016), 88–101.

Prowse M., 'A History of Tobacco Production and Marketing in Malawi, 1890–2010', *Journal of East African Studies*, 7, 4 (2013), 681–712.

Ramos A. K., 'Child Labour in Global Tobacco Production: A Human Rights Approach to an Enduring Dilemma', *Health and Human Rights Journal*, 20, 2 (2018), 235–248.

Results of Experiments, 1949–51, *Tobacco Research Bulletin* 1 (1952), 4.

Richter D., 'The Crisis of Environmental Narratives in the Anthropocene", in "Whose Anthropocene? Revisiting Dipesh Chakrabarty's 'Four Theses'", in Emmett R. and Lekan T. (eds.)., *RCC Perspectives: Transformations in Environment and Society,* 2 (2016), 97–100.

Roberts H. R., 'The Development of the Southern Rhodesian Tobacco Industry', *South African Journal of Economics,* 19, 2 (1951), 177–188.

Robertson W. R., 'Cotton Rotations on Sand Veld Farms', *Rhodesia Agricultural Journal*, 66 (1969), 2–6.

Rome A., 'Give Earth a Chance: The Environmental Movement and the Sixties', *The Journal of American History*, 90, 2 (September 2003), 525–554.

Salvi R. M et al., 'Neuro-psychiatric Evaluation in Subjects Chronically Exposed to Organophosphate Pesticides', *Toxicological Sciences*, 72, 2 (2003), 267–271.

Schlesinger A., 'The Future of Liberalism: The Challenge of Abundance', *Reporter*, (3 May 1956), 8–11.

Scoones I. et al, 'Tobacco, Contract Farming, and Agrarian Change in Zimbabwe', *Journal of Agrarian Change*, 28 (2018), 22–42.

Scott P. 'The Tobacco Industry of Southern Rhodesia', *Economic Geography*, 28, 3 (1952), 189–206.

Shonhe T., Scoones I. and Murimbarimba F., 'Agricultural Commercialization and Changing Labour Regimes in Zimbabwe', *Journal of Contemporary African Studies*, 10.1080/02589001.2021.1933397.

Shortis E., 'Lessons from the Last Continent: Science, Emotion, and the Relevance of History', in Katrin Kleeman and Jeroen Oomen (eds.), 'Communicating Climate Change: From Knowing Change to Changing Knowledge', *RCC Perspectives Transformations in Environment and Society*, 4 (2019), 53–60.

Showers K., 'Soil Erosion in the Kingdom of Lesotho: Origins and Colonial Responses, 1830s–1950s', *Journal of Southern African Studies*, 15, 2 (January 1989), 143–162.

Shutt A., 'Purchase Area Farmers and the Middle Class of Southern Rhodesia, c. 1931–1952',*The International Journal of African Historical Studies*, 30:3 (1997), doi.org/10.2307/220576.

'Squatters, Land Sales and Intensification in Marirangwe Purchase Area', *The Journal of African History*, 43, 3 (2002), 473–498.

Simms J., 'Report on Forestry in Southern Rhodesia', *Rhodesia Agricultural Journal*, 1, 3 (February 1911), 197–222.

Smith J. and Lee K., 'From Colonisation to Globalisation: A History of State Capture by the Tobacco Industry in Malawi', *Review of African Political Economy*, 45, 156 (May 2018), 186–202.

Smout M., 'Urbanization of the Rhodesian Population', *Zambezia*, 4:ii (1975), 79–91.

Steinberg T., 'Down, Down, Down, No More: Environmental History Moves beyond Declension', *Journal of the Early Republic*, 24, 2 (2004), 260–266.

Stephenson G. V., 'The Impact of International Economic Sanctions on the Internal Viability of Rhodesia', *Geographical Review*, 65, 3 (July 1975), 377–389.

Stinson F. A., 'Research and Sound Farming', *Rhodesia Tobacco*, 1 (June 1953), 4.

Storey H. H., 'Leaf Curl of Tobacco in Southern Rhodesia', *Rhodesia Agricultural Journal*, 29, 3 (March,1932), 186–192.

Stroud E., 'Does Nature Always Matter? Following Dirt through History,' *History and Theory* ,42 (December 2004), 75–81.

Taha A. and Ball K., 'Smoking in Africa: The Coming Epidemic', *World Smoking Health*, 7, 2 (1982), 25–30.

Tanser G. H., 'A History of the Tobacco Research Board: The First 25 Years', *The Zimbabwe Agricultural Journal Technical Handbook*, 7, (1991).

Tinley J. M., 'Control of Agriculture in South Africa', *South African Journal of Economics*, 8 (1940), 243–263.

'Tobacco Cultivation in France', *Rhodesia Agricultural Journal*, 27,4 (April 1930), 409–411.

'The Tobacco Quota Commission of Enquiry', *Rhodesia Agricultural Journal*, 32,2, (February 935), 78.

Tobin R. J and Knausenberger W., 'Dilemmas of Development: Burley Tobacco, the Environment and Economic Growth in Malawi', *Journal of Southern African Studies*, 24, 2 (1998), 405–424.

Twidle H., 'Rachel Carson and the Perils of Simplicity: Reading *Silent Spring* from the Global South', *Ariel: A Review of English Literature*, 44, 4 (2014), 49–88.

Uekotter F., 'Consigning Environmentalism to History? Remarks on the Place of the Environmental Movement in Modern History', *RCC Perspectives*, 7 (2011), 1–36.

Uledi P. and Hove G., 'A War of Man Against Locust'! Locust Invasions and Anti-locust Campaigns in Salisbury, Southern Rhodesia, 1918–1940s', *South African Historical Journal*, 70, 4 (2018), 689–707.

'The Umvukwesi Farmers and Tobacco Growers Association', *Rhodesia Agricultural Journal*, 27,8 (August 1930), 793.

Vail L., 'Ecology and History: The Example of Eastern Zambia', *Journal of Southern African Studies*, 3 (1977), 129–155.

Valenčius C. B., 'Mudslides Make Good History', *Journal of the Early Republic*, 24, 2 (Summer, 2004), 252–259.

Van den berg H. et al., 'Global Trends in the Production and Use of DDT for Control of Malaria and Other Vector-borne Diseases', *Malaria Journal* 16, 401 (2017), 1–8.

Van Sittert L., 'Reply', *The Journal of African History*, 46, 1 (2005), 135–137.

'The Nature of Power: Cape Environmental History, The History of Ideas and Neo-liberal Historiography', *Journal of African History*, 45 (2004), 305–313.

Veracini L., 'Settler Colonialism': Career of a Concept', *The Journal of Imperial and Commonwealth History*, 41, 2 (2013), 313–333.

Vinogradov A. and Petriashin S., 'Chemical Industry, the Environment and Russian Provincial Society: The Case of Kokshan Chemical Works, 1850–1925', *Ambix*, 1, 26 (April 2018), 1–26.

Watt W. M., 'The Dangers and Preservation of Soil Erosion', *Rhodesia Agricultural Journal*, 10, 5 (June 1913), 667–673.

Whitlow J. R., 'An Assessment of Cultivated Lands in Zimbabwe Rhodesia, 1972–1977', *Zimbabwe Rhodesia Science News*, 13, 10 (1979), 233–238.

'Land Use, Population Pressure and Rock Outcrops in the Tribal Areas of Zimbabwe-Rhodesia' *Rhodesia Agricultural Journal,* 77, 1 (January–February 1980), 173–181.

Wickens G. M, 'A New and Serious Disease of Tobacco in Southern Rhodesia', *Rhodesia Agricultural Journal*, 35, 3 (March,1938), 181–182.

Williams B. and M. Riley, 'The Challenge of Oral History to Environmental History', *Environment and History*, 26,2 (2020), 207–231.

Woelk G et al., 'Prospects for Tobacco Control in Zimbabwe: A Historical Perspective', *Health Policy*, 57, 3 (2001), 179–192.

Woods T., 'Why Not Persuade Them to Grow Tobacco? Planters, Tenants, and the Political Economy of Central Malawi, 1920–1940', *African Economic History,* 21 (1993), 131–150.

Worster D., 'The Dirty Thirties: A Study in Agricultural Capitalism', *Great Plains Quarterly,* 6, 2 (Spring 1986), 107–116.

'The Two Cultures Revisited: Environmental History and the Environmental Sciences', *Environment and History,* 2, 1 (February 1996), 3–14.

Zafereidou M., Hopkinson N. S. and Voulvoulis N., 'Cigarette Smoking: An Assessment of Tobacco's Global Environmental Footprint across Its Entire Supply Chain', *Environmental Science and Technology*, 52, 15 (2018), 8087–8094.

Index

AFRICAN STUDIES SERIES

1 *City Politics: A Study of Leopoldville, 1962–63*, J.S. La Fontaine
2 *Studies in Rural Capitalism in West Africa*, Polly Hill
3 *Land Policy in Buganda*, Henry W. West
4 *The Nigerian Military: A Sociological Analysis of Authority and Revolt, 1960–67*, Robin Luckham
5 *The Ghanaian Factory Worker: Industrial Man in Africa*, Margaret Peil
6 *Labour in the South African Gold Mines*, Francis Wilson
7 *The Price of Liberty: Personality and Politics in Colonial Nigeria*, Kenneth W. J. Post and George D. Jenkins
8 *Subsistence to Commercial Farming in Present-Day Buganda: An Economic and Anthropological Survey*, Audrey I. Richards, Fort Sturrock and Jean M. Fortt (eds)
9 *Dependence and Opportunity: Political Change in Ahafo*, John Dunn and A. F. Robertson
10 *African Railwaymen: Solidarity and Opposition in an East African Labour Force*, R. D. Grillo
11 *Islam and Tribal Art in West Africa*, Rene´ A. Bravmann
12 *Modern and Traditional Elites in the Politics of Lagos*, P. D. Cole
13 *Asante in the Nineteenth Century: The Structure and Evaluation of a Political Order*, Ivor Wilks
14 *Culture, Tradition and Society in the West African Novel*, Emmanuel Obiechina
15 *Saints and Politicians*, Donal B. Cruise O'Brien
16 *The Lions of Dagbon: Political Change in Northern Ghana*, Martin Staniland
17 *Politics of Decolonization: Kenya Europeans and the Land Issue 1960–1965*, Gary B. Wasserman
18 *Muslim Brotherhoods in the Nineteenth-Century Africa*, B. G. Martin
19 *Warfare in the Sokoto Caliphate: Historical and Sociological Perspectives*, Joseph P. Smaldone
20 *Liberia and Sierra Leone: An Essay in Comparative Politics*, Christopher Clapham
21 *Adam Kok's Griquas: A Study in the Development of Stratification in South Africa*, Robert Ross
22 *Class, Power and Ideology in Ghana: The Railwaymen of Sekondi*, Richard Jeffries
23 *West African States: Failure and Promise*, John Dunn (ed)
24 *Afrikaaners of the Kalahari: White Minority in a Black State*, Margo Russell and Martin Russell

25 *A Modern History of Tanganyika*, John Iliffe
26 *A History of African Christianity 1950–1975*, Adrian Hastings
27 *Slaves, Peasants and Capitalists in Southern Angola, 1840–1926*, W. G. Clarence-Smith
28 *The Hidden Hippopotamus: Reappraised in African History: The Early Colonial Experience in Western Zambia*, GywnPrins
29 *Families Divided: The Impact of Migrant Labour in Lesotho*, Colin Murray
30 *Slavery, Colonialism and Economic Growth in Dahomey, 1640–1960*, Patrick Manning
31 *Kings, Commoners and Concessionaries: The Evolution of Dissolution of the Nineteenth-Century Swazi State*, Philip Bonner
32 *Oral Poetry and Somali Nationalism: The Case of Sayid Mahammad 'Abdille Hasan*, Said S. Samatar
33 *The Political Economy of Pondoland 1860–1930*, William Beinart
34 *Volkskapitalisme: Class, Capitals and Ideology in the Development of Afrikaner Nationalism, 1934–1948*, Dan O'Meara
35 *The Settler Economies: Studies in the Economic History of Kenya and Rhodesia 1900–1963*, Paul Mosely
36 *Transformations in Slavery: A History of Slavery in Africa,1st edition*, Paul Lovejoy
37 *Amilcar Cabral: Revolutionary Leadership and People's War*, Patrick Chabal
38 *Essays on the Political Economy of Rural Africa*, Robert H. Bates
39 *Ijeshas and Nigerians: The Incorporation of a Yoruba Kingdom, 1890s-1970s*, J. D. Y. Peel
40 *Black People and the South African War, 1899–1902*, Peter Warwick
41 *A History of Niger 1850–1960*, Finn Fuglestad
42 *Industrialisation and Trade Union Organization in South Africa,1924–1955*, Stephen Ellis
43 *The Rising of the Red Shawls: A Revolt in Madagascar 1895–1899*, Stephen Ellis
44 *Slavery in Dutch South Africa*, Nigel Worden
45 *Law, Custom and Social Order: The Colonial Experience in Malawi and Zambia*, Martin Chanock
46 *Salt of the Desert Sun: A History of Salt Production and Trade in the Central Sudan*, Paul E. Lovejoy
47 *Marrying Well: Marriage, Status and Social Change among the Educated Elite in Colonial Lagos*, Kristin Mann
48 *Language and Colonial Power: The Appropriation of Swahili in the Former Belgian Congo, 1880–1938*, Johannes Fabian

49 *The Shell Money of the Slave Trade*, Jan Hogendorn and Marion Johnson
50 *Political Domination in Africa*, Patrick Chabal
51 *The Southern Marches of Imperial Ethiopia: Essays in History and Social Anthropology*, Donald Donham and Wendy James
52 *Islam and Urban Labor in Northern Nigeria: The Making of a Muslim Working Class*, Paul M. Lubeck
53 *Horn and Crescent: Cultural Change and Traditional Islam on the East African Coast, 800–1900*, Randall L. Pouwels
54 *Capital and Labour on the Kimberley Diamond Fields, 1871–1890*, Robert Vicat Turrell
55 *National and Class Conflict in the Horn of Africa*, John Markakis
56 *Democracy and Prebendal Politics in Nigeria: The Rise and Fall of the Second Republic*, Richard A. Joseph
57 *Entrepreneurs and Parasites: The Struggle for Indigenous Capitalism in Zaire*, Janet MacGaffey
58 *The African Poor: A History*, John Iliffe
59 *Palm Oil and Protest: An Economic History of the Ngwa Region, South-Eastern Nigeria, 1800–1980*, Susan M. Martin
60 *France and Islam in West Africa, 1860–1960*, Christopher Harrison
61 *Transformation and Continuity in Revolutionary Ethiopia*, Christopher Clapham
62 *Prelude to the Mahdiyya: Peasants and Traders in the Shendi Region, 1821–1885*, Anders Bjorkelo
63 *Wa and the Wala: Islam and Polity in Northwestern Ghana*, Ivor Wilks
64 *H.C. Bankole-Bright and Politics in Colonial Sierra Leone, 1919–1958*, Akintola Wyse
65 *Contemporary West African States, Donal Cruise O'Brien*, John Dunn and Richard Rathbone (eds)
66 *The Oromo of Ethiopia: A History, 1570–1860*, Mohammed Hassen
67 *Slavery and African Life: Occidental, Oriental, and African Slave Trades*, Patrick Manning
68 *Abraham Esau's War: A Black South African War in the Cape, 1899–1902*, Bill Nasson
69 *The Politics of Harmony: Land Dispute Strategies in Swaziland*, Laurel L. Rose
70 *Zimbabwe's Guerrilla War: Peasant Voices*, Norma J. Kriger
71 *Ethiopia: Power and Protest: Peasant Revolts in the Twentieth-Century*, Gebru Tareke
72 *White Supremacy and Black Resistance in Pre-Industrial South Africa: The Making of the Colonial Order in the Eastern Cape, 1770–1865*, Clifton C. Crais

73 *The Elusive Granary: Herder, Farmer, and State in Northern Kenya*, Peter D. Little
74 *The Kanyok of Zaire: An Institutional and Ideological History to 1895*, John C. Yoder
75 *Pragmatism in the Age of Jihad: The Precolonial State of Bundu*, Michael A. Gomez
76 *Slow Death for Slavery: The Course of Abolition in Northern Nigeria, 1897–1936*, Paul E. Lovejoy and Jan S. Hogendorn
77 *West African Slavery and Atlantic Commerce: The Senegal River Valley, 1700–1860*, James F. Searing
78 *A South African Kingdom: The Pursuit of Security in the Nineteenth-Century Lesotho*, Elizabeth A. Elredge
79 *State and Society in Pre-colonial Asante*, T. C. McCaskie
80 *Islamic Society and State Power in Senegal: Disciples and Citizens in Fatick*, Leonardo A. Villalon
81 *Ethnic Pride and Racial Prejudice in Victorian Cape Town: Group Identity and Social Practice*, Vivian Bickford-Smith
82 *The Eritrean Struggle for Independence: Domination, Resistance and Nationalism, 1941–1993*, Ruth Iyob
83 *Corruption and State Politics in Sierra Leone*, William Reno
84 *The Culture of Politics in Modern Kenya*, Angelique Haugerud
85 *Africans: The History of a Continent, 1st edition*, John Iliffe
86 *From Slave Trade to 'Legitimate' Commerce: The Commercial Transition in Nineteenth-Century West Africa*, Robin Law (ed)
87 *Leisure and Society in Colonial Brazzaville*, Phyllis Martin
88 *Kingship and State: The Buganda Dynasty*, Christopher Wrigley
89 *Decolonialization and African Life: The Labour Question in French and British Africa*, Frederick Cooper
90 *Misreading the African Landscape: Society and Ecology in an African Forest-Savannah Mosaic*, James Fairhead, and Melissa Leach
91 *Peasant Revolution in Ethiopia: The Tigray People's Liberation Front, 1975–1991*, John Young
92 *Senegambia and the Atlantic Slave Trade*, Boubacar Barry
93 *Commerce and Economic Change in West Africa: The Oil Trade in the Nineteenth Century*, Martin Lynn
94 *Slavery and French Colonial Rule in West Africa: Senegal, Guinea and Mali*, Martin A. Klein
95 *East African Doctors: A History of the Modern Profession*, John Iliffe
96 *Middlemen of the Cameroons Rivers: The Duala and Their Hinterland, c.1600–1960*, Ralph Derrick, Ralph A. Austen, and Jonathan Derrick
97 *Masters and Servants on the Cape Eastern Frontier, 1760–1803*, Susan Newton-King

98 *Status and Respectability in the Cape Colony, 1750–1870: A Tragedy of Manners*, Robert Ross
99 *Slaves, Freedmen and Indentured Laborers in Colonial Mauritius*, Richard B. Allen
100 *Transformations in Slavery: A History of Slavery in Africa, 2nd edition*, Paul E. Lovejoy
101 *The Peasant Cotton Revolution in West Africa: Cote d'Ivoire, 1880–1995*, Thomas J. Bassett
102 *Re-imagining Rwanda: Conflict, Survival and Disinformation in the Late Twentieth Century*, Johan Pottier
103 *The Politics of Evil: Magic, State Power and the Political Imagination in South Africa*, Clifton Crais
104 *Transforming Mozambique: The Politics of Privatization, 1975–2000*, M. Anne Pitcher
105 *Guerrilla Veterans in Post-War Zimbabwe: Symbolic and Violent Politics, 1980–1987*, Norma J. Kriger
106 *An Economic History of Imperial Madagascar, 1750–1895: The Rise and Fall of an Island Empire*, Gwyn Campbell
107 *Honour in African History*, John Iliffe
108 *Africans: A History of a Continent, 2nd edition*, John Iliffe
109 *Guns, Race, and Power in Colonial South Africa*, William Kelleher Storey
110 *Islam and Social Change in French West Africa: History of an Emancipatory Community*, Sean Hanretta
111 *Defeating Mau Mau, Creating Kenya: Counterinsurgency, Civil War and Decolonization*, Daniel Branch
112 *Christianity and Genocide in Rwanda*, Timothy Longman
113 *From Africa to Brazil: Culture, Identity, and an African Slave Trade, 1600–1830*, Walter Hawthorne
114 *Africa in the Time of Cholera: A History of Pandemics from 1817 to the Present*, Myron Echenberg
115 *A History of Race in Muslim West Africa, 1600–1960*, Bruce S. Hall
116 *Witchcraft and Colonial Rule in Kenya, 1900–1955*, Katherine Luongo
117 *Transformations in Slavery: A History of Slavery in Africa, 3rd edition*, Paul E. Lovejoy
118 *The Rise of the Trans-Atlantic Slave Trade in Western Africa, 1300–1589*, Toby Green
119 *Party Politics and Economic Reform in Africa's Democracies*, M. Anne Pitcher
120 *Smugglers and Saints of the Sahara: Regional Connectivity in the Twentieth Century*, Judith Scheele

121 *Cross-Cultural Exchange in the Atlantic World: Angola and Brazil during the Era of the Slave Trade*, Roquinaldo Ferreira
122 *Ethnic Patriotism and the East African Revival*, Derek Peterson
123 *Black Morocco: A History of Slavery and Islam*, Chouki El Hamel
124 *An African Slaving Port and the Atlantic World: Benguela and Its Hinterland*, Mariana Candido
125 *Making Citizens in Africa: Ethnicity, Gender, and National Identity in Ethiopia*, Lahra Smith
126 *Slavery and Emancipation in Islamic East Africa: From Honor to Respectability*, Elisabeth McMahon
127 *A History of African Motherhood: The Case of Uganda, 700–1900*, Rhiannon Stephens
128 *The Borders of Race in Colonial South Africa: The Kat River Settlement, 1829–1856*, Robert Ross
129 *From Empires to NGOs in the West African Sahel: The Road to Nongovernmentality*, Gregory Mann
130 *Dictators and Democracy in African Development: The Political Economy of Good Governance in Nigeria*, A. Carl LeVan
131 *Water, Civilization and Power in Sudan: The Political Economy of Military-Islamist State Building*, Harry Verhoeven
132 *The Fruits of Freedom in British Togoland: Literacy, Politics and Nationalism, 1914–2014*, Kate Skinner
133 *Political Thought and the Public Sphere in Tanzania: Freedom, Democracy and Citizenship in the Era of Decolonization*, Emma Hunter
134 *Political Identity and Conflict in Central Angola, 1975–2002*, Justin Pearce
135 *From Slavery to Aid: Politics, Labour, and Ecology in the Nigerian Sahel, 1800–2000*, Benedetta Rossi
136 *National Liberation in Postcolonial Southern Africa: A Historical Ethnography of SWAPO's Exile Camps*, Christian A. Williams
137 *Africans: A History of a Continent, 3rd edition*, John Iliffe
138 *Colonial Buganda and the End of Empire: Political Thought and Historical Imagination in Africa*, Jonathon L. Earle
139 *The Struggle over State Power in Zimbabwe: Law and Politics since 1950*, George Karekwaivanane
140 *Transforming Sudan: Decolonisation, Economic Development and State Formation*, Alden Young
141 *Colonizing Consent: Rape and Governance in South Africa's Eastern Cape*, Elizabeth Thornberry
142 *The Value of Disorder: Autonomy, Prosperity and Plunder in the Chadian Sahara*, Julien Brachet and Judith Scheele

143 *The Politics of Poverty: Policy-Making and Development in Rural Tanzania*, Felicitas Becker
144 *Boundaries, Communities, and State-Making in West Africa: The Centrality of the Margins*, Paul Nugent
145 *Politics and Violence in Burundi: The Language of Truth in an Emerging State*, Aidan Russel
146 *Power and the Presidency in Kenya: The Jomo Kenyatta Years*, Anaïs Angelo
147 *East Africa after Liberation: Conflict, Security and the State since the 1980s*, Jonathan Fisher
148 *Sultan, Caliph, and the Renewer of the Faith: Ahmad Lobbo, the Tārīkh al-fattāsh and the Making of an Islamic State in West Africa*, Mauro Nobili
149 *Shaping the African Savannah: From Capitalist Frontier to Arid Eden in Namibia*, Michael Bollig
150 *France's Wars in Chad: Military Intervention and Decolonization in Africa*, Nathaniel K. Powell
151 *Islam, Ethnicity, and Conflict in Ethiopia: The Bale Insurgency, 1963-1970*, Terje Østebø
152 *The Path to Genocide in Rwanda: Security, Opportunity, and Authority in an Ethnocratic State*, Omar Shahabudin McDoom
153 *Development, (Dual) Citizenship and Its Discontents in Africa: The Political Economy of Belonging to Liberia*, Robtel Neajai Pailey
154 *Salafism and Political Order in Africa*, Sebastian Elischer
155 *Performing Power in Zimbabwe: Politics, Law and the Courts since 2000*, Susanne Verheul
156 *Revolutionary State-Making in Dar es Salaam: African Liberation and the Global Cold War, 1961-1974*, George Roberts
157 *Race and Diplomacy in Zimbabwe: The Cold War and Decolonization, 1960-1984*, Timothy Lewis Scarnecchia
158 *Conflicts of Colonialism: The Rule of Law, French Soudan, and Faama Mademba Sèye*, Richard L. Roberts
159 *Invoking the Invisible in the Sahara: Islam, Spiritual Mediation, and Social Change*, Erin Pettigrew
160 *Wealth, Land and Property in Angola: A History of Dispossession, Slavery and Inequality*, Mariana P. Candido
161 *Trajectories of Authoritarianism in Rwanda: Elusive Control before the Genocide*, Marie-Eve Desrosiers
162 *Plunder for Profit: A Socio-environmental History of Tobacco Farming in Southern Rhodesia and Zimbabwe*, Elijah Doro

For EU product safety concerns, contact us at Calle de José Abascal, 56–1°, 28003 Madrid, Spain or eugpsr@cambridge.org.

www.ingramcontent.com/pod-product-compliance
Ingram Content Group UK Ltd.
Pitfield, Milton Keynes, MK11 3LW, UK
UKHW021638010625
458959UK00020B/667
9781009096256